THE Practical Stylist with Readings

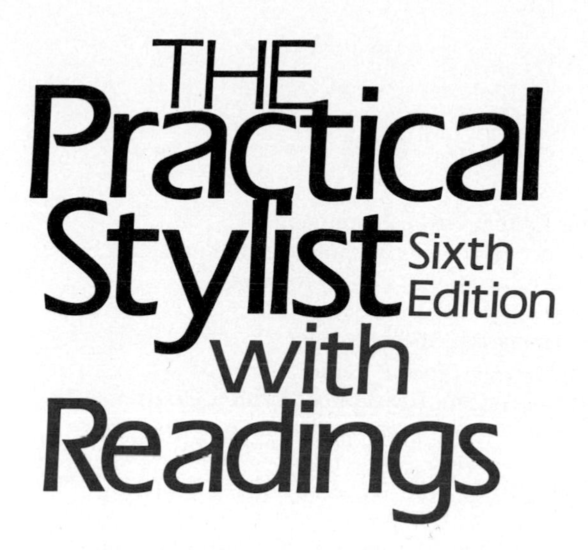

Sheridan Baker
The University of Michigan

Robert E. Yarber
San Diego Mesa College

1817

HARPER & ROW, PUBLISHERS, New York
Cambridge, Philadelphia, San Francisco,
London, Mexico City, São Paulo, Singapore, Sydney

Sponsoring Editor: Phillip Leininger
Project Editor: Nora Helfgott/Madelyn Elliott
Text Design Adaptation: Leon Bolognese
Cover Design: Jack Ribik
Text Art: Danmark & Michaels Inc.
Production Manager: Jeanie Berke
Compositor: ComCom Division of Haddon Craftsmen, Inc.
Printer and Binder: R. R. Donnelley & Sons Company

The Practical Stylist with Readings, Sixth Edition

Library of Congress Cataloging-in-Publication Data

Baker, Sheridan Warner, 1918–
The practical stylist with readings.

Bibliography: p.
Includes index.
1. English language—Rhetoric. 2. College readers.
I. Yarber, Robert E. II. Title.
PE1408.B283 1986 808′.0427 85-8714
ISBN 0-06-040444-2

87 88 9 8 7 6 5 4 3

Acknowledgments

Woody Allen, "My Speech to the Graduates." Copyright © 1980 by Woody Allen. Reprinted from *Side Effects,* by Woody Allen, by permission of Random House, Inc.

Roger Angell, "On the Ball." From *Five Seasons, A Baseball Companion.* Copyright © 1972, 1973, 1974, 1975 by Roger Angell. Reprinted by permission of Simon & Schuster, Inc.

Maya Angelou, "My First Valentine." From *I Know Why the Caged Bird Sings,* by Maya Angelou. Copyright © 1969 by Maya Angelou. Reprinted by permission of Random House, Inc.

Aristotle, [The Types of Human Character], in *Rhetoric,* II.ix.12–14, trans. by W. Rhys Roberts. From *The Oxford Translation of Aristotle,* ed. by W. D. Ross, Vol. II, 1925. Reprinted by permission of Oxford University Press.

Russell Baker, "From Song to Sound: Bing and Elvis." Copyright © 1977 by The New York Times Company. Reprinted by permission.

Wayne C. Booth, "What Is an Idea?" From *The Harper & Row Reader* by Wayne C. Booth and Marshall W. Gregory. Copyright © 1984 by Harper & Row, Publishers, Inc. Reprinted by permission of Harper & Row, Publishers, Inc.

Jacob Bronowski, "The Harvest of the Seasons." From *The Ascent of Man* by J. Bronowski. Copyright © 1973 by J. Bronowski. By permission of Little, Brown and Company.

William F. Buckley, Jr., "Capital Punishment." Copyright 1972–1975 by William F. Buckley, Jr. From *Execution Eve and Other Contemporary Ballads,* G. P. Putnam's Sons. Reprinted by permission of the author.

[Changing Horses in Mid-Dream], "Notes and Comments" in "The Talk of the Town," *The New Yorker,* November 10, 1980. Reprinted by permission; © 1980 The New Yorker Magazine, Inc.

Norman Cousins, "Pain Is Not the Ultimate Enemy" is reprinted from *Anatomy of an Illness* by Norman Cousins, by permission of W. W. Norton & Company, Inc. Copyright © 1979 by W. W. Norton & Company, Inc.

Annie Dillard, "Hidden Pennies." From *Pilgrim at Tinker Creek* by Annie Dillard. Copyright © 1974 by Annie Dillard. Reprinted by permission of Harper & Row, Publishers, Inc.

Barbara Ehrenreich, "A Feminist's View of the New Man." Copyright © 1984 by The New York Times Company. Reprinted by permission of the author.

Carl Sagan, "To Preserve a World Graced by Life." Copyright 1982 by Carl Sagan. Reprinted by permission of the author and the author's agents, Scott Meredith Literary Agency, Inc., 845 Third Avenue, New York, New York 10022.

Richard Selzer, "The Art of Surgery," from *Mortal Lessons* by Richard Selzer. Copyright © 1974, 1975, 1976 by Richard Selzer. Reprinted by permission of Simon & Schuster, Inc.

Wilfrid Sheed, "A Thought a Day Isn't Enough." Copyright © 1980 by The New York Times Company. Reprinted by permission.

Henry Villard, "Recollections of Lincoln," in *Jubilee: One Hundred Years of the Atlantic,* ed. Edward Weeks and Emily Flint. An Atlantic Monthly Press Book. © 1957 by Little, Brown and Company.

Stephen Weinberg, "The Creation: The First Three Minutes." From *The First Three Minutes* by Steven Weinberg. © 1977 by Steven Weinberg. Reprinted by permission of Basic Books, Inc., Publishers.

Eudora Welty, [Miss Duling]. Reprinted by permission of the publishers from *One Writer's Beginnings* by Eudora Welty, Cambridge Mass.: Harvard University Press, Copyright © 1983, 1984 by Eudora Welty.

E. B. White, "The Essayist." Specified excerpt of "Foreword" (pp. vii–viii) from *Essays of E. B. White.* Copyright © 1977 by E. B. White. Reprinted by permission of Harper & Row, Publishers, Inc.

George F. Will, "The Astrological Impulse." From *The Pursuit of Happiness, and Other Sobering Thoughts* by George F. Will. Copyright © 1978 by The Washington Post Company. Reprinted by permission of Harper & Row, Publishers, Inc.

Virginia Woolf, "The Death of the Moth." From *The Death of the Moth and Other Essays* by Virginia Woolf, copyright 1942 by Harcourt Brace Jovanovich, Inc.; renewed 1970 by Marjorie T. Parsons, Executrix. Reprinted by permission of the publishers.

William Zinsser, "Clutter." Copyright © 1976 by William K. Zinsser. Reprinted by permission of the author.

Contents

Preface

The process makes the product—the essay, the poem, the painting, the home, the achievement awarded, the effort satisfied. Teachers and students in thousands of classrooms, and many others who have faced a blank page and the problems of exposition, found the previous edition of *The Practical Stylist with Readings* useful in achieving the essentials of composition and the graces of good prose. But many faithful adherents have recently asked for more help with the process. Others have asked that the reading selections reflect more closely the rhetorical and stylistic concepts presented in the accompanying chapter. Hence, this new edition. Bob Yarber has joined me in this revision, and he has chosen readings that will generate discussion and stimulate writing, as well as illustrate the ideas introduced in each chapter.

The first chapter, on establishing a firm viewpoint and style of one's own, concludes with four readings, each distinguished by its author's clear argument and unique voice. The readings range from a meditation on one's strengths as a writer to an attack on noxious music, a plea for reading, and thoughts from Cicero on writing. Chapter 2 illustrates the movement from subject to thesis with observations on growing up in an alien society, on the death of a moth, on being a female in America, and on the threat of nuclear warfare. The readings in the rest of the book cover a variety of topics: the purchase of a horse, a cure for depression, the Equal Rights Amendment, capital punishment, computers, crooners and rock stars, a grade-school teacher and a prime minister, the building of a canoe and the creation of the universe, the wisdom of Lincoln, the art of surgery, and the foolishness of astrology. Names range from Aristotle to Angell to Angelou; from Swift, Orwell, and E. B. White to William Buckley, Russell Baker, and Woody Allen. The diversity of topics and authors is matched by the variety of points of view: conservatives, liberals, women, minorities, ancients, and moderns. In every case, instructors and students will notice that the suggestions for questions and writing, like the readings, are integrated with the corresponding chapters.

I have thoroughly revised and arranged the first three chapters into a smoother and more helpful progress through the process of writing—finding oneself and one's subject, making a thesis, the inner organizer, and managing the outer structure. In easy steps, we begin with the whole essay. Many books on writing begin with small steps and then lead the student cautiously to the ominous essay ahead. But students find early confidence in the opposite approach: "Why yes, even I can do it!" Once they see how easily one turns any familiar subject, from ping-pong to nuclear energy, into a thesis and then see the simple essentials of structure, they can proceed effectively to the smaller and more powerful elements—to paragraphs, to sentences, and to words, where the real dynamite of writing is.

I continue to emphasize argument because argument indeed subsumes all other expository principles and teaches easily the firmest organization of one's ideas. To the chapters on paragraphing, I have added the inductive and deductive structures, and what I call the "hybrid," the more open-ended arrangement of many seasoned essayists, but I also include the classic modes of description, narration, and exposition, with additional explanation of analogy, comparison and contrast, cause and effect, and process. A chapter on common-sense logic leads to the sentence and on to words.

Throughout, I have included exercises in thesis making, in paragraphing, in writing and punctuating various kinds of sentences, in using and spelling words, and in handling various figures of speech. I have encouraged the student to play with language, to write unusual and complicated sentences for exercise, to juggle with words, and especially to achieve clarity by learning to recognize and eliminate the various endemic kinds of wordiness, which everywhere befogs modern prose. The chapter on the research paper draws everything together, and includes for the first time the Modern Language Association's newly simplified system of citation, explained in simple steps and illustrated by a student's paper, "Can Animals Talk?"

The book concludes with a handbook of grammar, punctuation, spelling, capitalization, and usage—for supplementary teaching and permanent reference—with further exercises as needed. It also includes a surprise (Chapter 13)—a well-kept secret on how to answer an essay-question, how to improve one's grade on examinations—well worth a preliminary peek before midsemester. Inside the front cover is a "do's" list against which students may check their work; inside the back cover, a set of symbols for marking the "don'ts."

The teacher will find plenty of room here for any convenient approach, and ample opportunity for that almost necessary bonus of academic gratification, disagreeing with the book, out of which much of our best teaching comes. A great deal will certainly be familiar. Nothing here is really new. I am simply describing the natural linguistic facts discovered again and again by the heirs of Aristotle, in which lineage I seem inescapably to belong. For I have found that one practical need in all writing is to mediate gracefully between opposite possibilities—between simplicity and complexity, clarity and shade, economy and plentitude, the particular and the general.

I wish to acknowledge my great and unending debt to the teachers who, from the responses of more than two million students, have given me their encouragement and suggestions. I continue to be no less grateful to the individual students and private citizens who have written me from as far away as Kenya and as near home as Ann Arbor.

Sheridan Baker

THE Practical Stylist with Readings

1
Overview: The Point of It All

WRITE FOR YOUR SHARE

Writing is one of the most important things we do. It helps us catch our ideas, realize our thoughts, and stand out as fluent persuasive people both on paper and on our feet in front of the meeting or the boss. Reading and writing have already enlarged your education and your speech. Even television, in its news and advertising, and in most of its shows, pours into our thoughts the words and habits that literacy—and written scripts—has built into our speech and thinking.

This language we share is Standard English—sometimes called "edited Standard American English," unfortunately making it seem like some unnatural necessity for the business we would rather not do. But it is our living language, in speech as well as print. Actually, even our most local and private dialects partake of its forms and vocabulary, as do our silent thoughts, however fragmentary, our "inner speech," as several psychologists and linguists have recently called it.* In fact, we automatically "edit" all our fragmentary thoughts for even our most spontaneous expressions, intuitively selecting from our store of possibilities, filling in the grammar, expanding, rephrasing, just as if we were writing and rewriting: ". . . er . . . I mean . . . but really. . . ." So writing is an extension of the way we naturally handle language. Writing simply straightens out and clarifies our

---

*Lev Vygotsky, *Thought and Language* (Cambridge, Mass.: MIT Press, 1962), with "Comments" by Jean Piaget; James Moffett, "Writing, Inner Speech, and Meditation," *College English* 44 (1982): 231–246.

intuitive editing, and in turn makes the editing itself more fluent. Writing perfects thought and speech. Indeed, over the millions of years from our first emotive screams and gurgles of pleasure to the bright dawn of literacy, writing—thinking in full dress—seems to be where speech has been going all the time.

Your composition course prepares you for the challenges not only of college but of the business of life ahead, whether in the executive suite or the courtroom, the hospital or the consulate, the legislature or the press room. You must write in almost every course. You must write for admission to postgraduate studies. You must write proposals for grants and programs. You must write to persuade people of your worth—demonstrated in your literacy—and of the worth of your ideas. You must write to develop and advance them—and yourself. You must write for your share of life. Thinking and persuasion are your business, and the business of your course in composition. All communication is largely persuasion. Even your most factual survey as engineer or educator must persuade its audience to approval by its perception and clarity and organization—in short, by its writing.

ATTITUDE

Writing well is a matter of conviction. You learn in school by exercises, of course; and exercises are best when taken as such, as body-builders, flexions and extensions for the real contests ahead. But when you are convinced that what you write has meaning, that it has meaning for you—and not in a lukewarm, hypothetical way, but truly—then your writing will stretch its wings and have the whole wide world in range. For writing is simply a graceful and articulate extension of the best that is in you. Writing well is not easy. As it extends the natural way we express ourselves, it nevertheless takes unending practice. Each essay is a polished exercise for the next to come, each new trial, as T. S. Eliot says, a new "raid on the inarticulate."

In writing, you clarify your own thoughts, and strengthen your conviction. Indeed, you probably grasp your thoughts for the first time. Writing is a way of thinking. Writing actually creates thought, and generates your ability to think: you discover thoughts you hardly knew you had, and come to know what you know. You learn as you write. In the end, after you have rewritten and rearranged for your best rhetorical effectiveness, your words will carry your readers with you to see as you see, to believe as you believe, to understand your subject as you now understand it.

Don't Take Yourself Too Seriously

Take your subject seriously—if it is a serious subject—but take yourself with a grain of salt. Your attitude is the very center of your prose. If you take yourself too importantly, your tone will go hollow, your sentences will go moldy, your page will go fuzzy with *of*'s and *which*'s and nouns clustered in passive constructions. In your academic career, the worst dangers lie immediately ahead. Freshmen usually learn to write tolerably well, but from the sophomore to the senior year the academic mildew frequently sets in, and by graduate school you can cut it with a cheese knife.

You must constantly guard against acquiring the heavy, sober-sided attitude that makes for wordiness along with obscurity, dullness, and anonymity. Do not lose your personality and your voice in the monotone of official prose. You should work like a scholar and scientist, but you should write like a writer, one who cares about the economy and beauty of language, and has some individual personality. Your attitude, then, should form somewhere between a confidence in your own convictions and a humorous distrust of your own rhetoric, which can so easily carry you away. You should bear yourself as a member of humankind, knowing that we are all sinners, all redundant, and all too fond of big words. Here is an example from—I blush to admit—the pen of a professor:

> **The general problem is perhaps correctly stated as inadequacy of nursing personnel to meet demands for nursing care and services. Inadequacy, it should be noted, is both a quantitative and qualitative term and thus it can be assumed that the problem as stated could indicate insufficient numbers of nursing personnel to meet existing demands for their services; deficiencies in the competencies of those who engage in the various fields of nursing; or both.**

Too few good nurses, and a badly swollen author—that is the problem. "Nursing personnel" may mean nurses, but it also may mean "the nursing of employees," so that the author seems to say, for a wildly illogical moment, that someone is not properly pampering or suckling people. Notice the misfiring *it* (fourth line), which seems to refer to *term* but actually refers to nothing. And the ponderous jingle of "deficiencies in the competencies" would do for a musical comedy. The author has taken the wrong model, is taking herself too seriously, and taking her readers almost nowhere.

Consider Your Readers

If you are to take your subject with all the seriousness it deserves and yourself with as much skeptical humor as you can bear, how are you to take your readers? Who are they, anyway? Some teachers suggest using your classmates as your audience. This is a good beginning. But the problem remains with all those other classes, with those papers in history or social science, with the reports, the applications for jobs and grants, the letters to the editor. At some point, you must become a writer facing the invisible public.

To some extent, your audiences will vary. You imagine yourself addressing slightly different personalities when you write about snorkeling and when you write about nuclear reactors. Hypothetically, your vocabulary and your tone would vary all the way from Skid Row to Oxford as you turn from social work to Rhodes scholarship; and certainly the difference of audience would reflect itself somewhat in your language. Furthermore, you must indeed sense your audience's capacity, its susceptibilities and prejudices, if you are to win even a hearing. No doubt our language skids a bit when down on the Row, and we certainly speak different tongues with our friends, and with the friends of our parents.

But the notion of adjusting your writing to a whole scale of audiences, though attractive in theory, hardly works out in practice. You are *writing,* and the written word presupposes a literate norm that immediately eliminates all the lower ranges of mere talk. Even when you speak, you do not so lose your identity as to pass for a total illiterate. You stand on your own linguistic feet, in your own linguistic personality, and the only adjustment you should assiduously practice in writing and speaking is the upward one toward verbal adulthood, a slight grammatical tightening and rhetorical heightening to make your thoughts clear, emphatic, and attractive.

Consider your audience a mixed group of intelligent and reasonable adults. You want them to think of you as well informed and well educated. You wish to explain what you know and what you believe. You wish to persuade them pleasantly that what you know is important and what you believe is right. Try to imagine what they might ask you, what they might object to, what they might know already, what they might find interesting. Be simple and clear, amusing and profound, using plenty of illustration to show what you mean. *But do not talk down to them.* That is the great flaw in the slumming theory of communication. Bowing to your readers' supposed level, you insult them by assuming their inferiority. Thinking yourself humble, you are actually haughty. The best solution is simply to assume that your readers are as intelligent as you. Even if they are not, they will be flattered by the assumption. Your written language, in short, will be respectful toward your subject, considerate toward your readers, and somehow amiable toward human failings.

THE WRITTEN VOICE

Make Your Writing Talk

That the silent page should seem to speak with the writer's voice is remarkable. With all gestures gone, no eyes to twinkle, no notation at all for the rise and fall of utterance, and only a handful of punctuation marks, the level line of type can yet convey the writer's voice, the tone of his personality.

To achieve this tone, to find your own voice and style, simply try to write in the language of intelligent conversation, cleared of all the stumbles and weavings of talk. Indeed, our speech, like thought, is amazingly circular. We can hardly think in a straight line if we try. We think by questions and answers, repetitions and failures; and our speech, full of *you know's* and *I mean's,* follows the erratic ways of the mind, circling around and around as we stitch the simplest of logical sequences. Your writing will carry the stitches, not those editorial loopings and pauses and re-threadings. It should be literate. It should be broad enough of vocabulary and rich enough of sentence to show that you have read a book. It should not be altogether unworthy to place you in the company of those who have written well in your native tongue. But it should nevertheless retain the tone of intelligent and agreeable conversation. It should be alive with a human personality—yours—which is probably the most persuasive rhetorical force on earth. Good writing should have a voice, and the voice should be unmistakably your own.

Suppose your spoken voice sounded something like this (I reconstruct an actual response in one of my classes):

> **Well, I don't know, I like Shakespeare really, I guess—I mean, well, like when Lear divides up his kingdom like a fairy tale or something, I thought that was kind of silly, dividing his kingdom. Anyone could see that was silly if you wanted to keep your kingdom, why divide it? But then like, something begins to happen, like a real family, I mean. Cordelia really gets griped at her older sisters, I mean, like all older sisters, if you've ever had any. There's a kind of sibling rivalry, you know. Then she's kind of griped at her father, who she really loves, but she thinks, I mean, like saying it right out spoils it. You can't really speak right out, I mean, about love, well, except sometimes, I guess, without sounding corny.**

Your written voice might then emerge from this with something of the same tone, but with everything straightened out, filled in, and polished up:

> **The play begins like a fairy tale. It even seems at first a little abstract and silly. A king has three daughters. The two elder ones are bad; the youngest is good. The king wishes to keep his kingdom in peace, and keep his title as king, by dividing his kingdom in a senseless and almost empty ceremonial way. But very soon the play seems like real life. The family seems real, complete with sibling rivalry. The king, not the play, now seems foolish and senile. The older daughters are hypocrites. Cordelia, the youngest,**

is irritated at them, and at her father's foolishness. As a result, she remains silent, not only because she is irritated at the flattering words of her sisters, but because anything she could say about her real love for her father would now sound false.

You might wish to polish that some more. You might indeed have said it another way, one more truly your own. The point, however, is to write in a tidy, economical way that wipes up the lapses of talk and fills in the gaps of thought, and yet keeps the tone and movement of good conversation, in your own voice.

Establish a Firm Viewpoint

"In my opinion," the beginner will write repeatedly, until he seems to be saying "It is only *my* opinion, after all, so it can't be worth much." He has failed to realize that his whole essay represents his opinion—of what the truth of the matter is. Don't make your essay a personal letter to Diary, or to Mother, or to Teacher, a confidential report of what happened to you last night as you agonized upon a certain question. "*To me,* Robert Frost is a great poet"—this is really writing about yourself. You are only confessing private convictions. To find the public reasons often requires no more than a trick of grammar: a shift from "*To me,* Robert Frost is . . ." to "Robert Frost is . . . ," from "*I thought* the book was good" to "The book is good," from you and your room last night to your subject and what it *is. Generalize* your opinions and emotions. Change "I cried" to "The scene is very moving." The grammatical shift represents a whole change of viewpoint, a shift from self to subject. You become the informed adult, showing the reader around firmly, politely, and persuasively.

Once you have effaced yourself from your assertions, once you have erased *to me* and *in my opinion* and all such signs of amateur terror, you may later let yourself back into the essay for emphasis or graciousness: "Mr. Watson errs, I think, precisely at this point." You can thus ease your most tentative or violent assertions, and show that you are polite and sensible, reasonably sure of your position but aware of the possibility of error. Again: the reasonable adult.

You go easy on the *I,* in short, to keep your reader focused on your subject. But you can use the *I* as much as you like to *illustrate* your point, once established, using a personal experience among several other pieces of evidence, or even all by itself. Of course, your instructors will sometimes ask for a wholly autobiographical theme. Indeed, some courses focus altogether on the *I* of personal experience. And your autobiographical résumés in applying for medical and law school, for grants and jobs, will of course require the *I.* But for the usual essay, I repeat, use the personal anecdote and the *I* to illustrate a point or to interject a tactful remark.

Effacing the *I,* then letting it back in on occasion, fixes your point of view. But what about the other pronouns, *we, you, one? One* objectifies the personal *I,* properly generalizing the private into the public. But it can seem too formal, and get too thick:

> FAULTY: ***One* finds *one*'s opinion changing as *one* grows older.**
> REVISED: **Opinions change with age.**
> REVISED: ***Our* opinions change as *we* grow older.**

That *we* is sometimes a useful generalizer, a convenient haven between the isolating *I* and the impersonal *one. We* can seem pompous, but not if it honestly handles those experiences we know we share, or can share. Suppose we wrote:

> **As I watched program after program, I got bored and began to wonder what values, if any, they represented.**

We can easily transpose this to:

> **As *we* watch program after program, *we* are progressively bored, and *we* begin to wonder what values, if any, they represent.**

(Notice that shifting to the present tense is also part of the generalizing process.) Thus, *we* can generalize without going all the way to *one,* or to the fully objective:

> **Program after program, TV bores its audiences and leaves its sense of values questionable.**

We also quite naturally refers to earlier parts of your demonstration, through which you have led your reader: *as we have already seen.* But you will have noticed from the preceding examples that *we* tends slightly toward wordiness. Used sparingly, then, *we* can ease your formality and draw your reader in. Overused, it can seem too presumptuous or chummy. Try it out. See how it feels, and use it where it seems comfortable and right.

You raises two different problems. The first is the one we have been discussing: how to generalize that *I* effectively into something else, either *one* or *we* or full objectivity. The indefinite *you,* like the indefinite *they,* is usually too vague, and too adolescent.

> **FAULTY: You have your own opinion.**
> **FAULTY: They have their own opinion.**
> **REVISED: Everyone has his own opinion.**
> **REVISED: We all have our own opinions.**

You as direct address to the reader poses a different problem. I have consistently addressed this book to *you,* the reader. But this is a special case, the relationship of tutor to student projected onto the page. None of my essays, I think, contains any *you* at all. Our stance in an essay is a little more formal, a little more public. We are better holding our pronouns to *one* or *we,* an occasional *I,* or none at all, as we find a comfortable stance between our subject and audience, and find our written voice.

THE POINT: ARGUMENTATION

The point is persuasion. Your written voice, your personal style, remember, is a part of your persuasiveness. But having a point to make is the real center of persuasion, the likely goal of most of your writing and speaking in college and in contemporary life. Hence, the center of your composition course is indeed argumentation. Even explaining the Battle of Lexington or the Oedipus complex invites an argumentative thrust as you persuade your readers of the most significant causes and crucial events. Argumentation thus ranges through the coolest explanation, or exposition, up to the burning issues you support. Argument, as we will see as we move along, absorbs for its ends every kind of writing you can think of. Narration, dialogue, anecdotes, exposition, description, newspaper headlines, statistical tables, and chemical formulas may all illustrate the point you are making in that written personality of yours that gives it life.

Plan to Rewrite

As you write your weekly assignments and find your voice, you will also be learning to groom your thoughts, to present them clearly and fully, to make sure you have said what you thought you said. This is the process of composition, of putting your thoughts together, beginning with jotted questions and tentative ideas, all to be mulled over, selected, rejected, expanded as you discover your ideas and write them into full expression. Ultimately, good writing comes only from *re*writing. Even your happy thoughts will need resetting, as you join them to the frequently happier ones that a second look seems to call up. Even the letter-perfect paper will improve almost of itself if you simply sit down to type it through again. You will find, almost unbidden, sharper words, better phrases, new figures of speech, and new illustrations and ideas to replace the weedy patches not noticed before. Indeed, this process of rewriting is what strengthens that instinctive editing you do as you speak extemporaneously or write impromptu essays and exams when revision is out of the question. Rewriting improves your fluency, making each rewrite less demanding.

So allow time for revision. After you have settled on something to write about, have turned your ideas over on paper for a while, have found a central idea, and feel ready to write the whole thing out, plan for at least three drafts—and try to manage four. Thinking of things to say is the hardest part at first. Even a short assignment of 500 words seems to stretch ahead like a Sahara. You have asserted your central idea in a sentence, and that leaves 490 words to go. But if you step off boldly, one foot after the other, you will make progress, find an oasis or two, and perhaps end at a run in green pastures. With longer papers, you will want some kind of outline to keep you from straying, and probably some jotted notes even for short ones, but the principle is the same: step ahead and keep moving until you've arrived. That is the first draft.

The second draft is a penciled correction of the first. Here you refine and polish, checking your dubious spellings in the dictionary, sharpening your punctuation, clarifying your meaning, pruning away the deadwood, adding a thought here, extending an illustration there—running in a whole new paragraph on an inserted page. You will also be tuning your sentences, carefully adjusting your tone until it is clearly that of an intelligent, reasonable person at ease with his knowledge and his audience. Your third draft, a typing and smoothing of your penciled version, will generate further improvements.

Here is a passage from a student's paper that has gone the full course. First you see the student's initial draft, with his own corrections on it. Next you see the passage after a second typing (and some further changes), as it was returned by the instructor with his marks on it. Then you see the final revision, handed in again, as this particular assignment required:

First Draft

In a college education, students should be allowed to ~~make~~ choose their own course. ~~Too many~~ All the requirements ~~are discouraging to~~ they must take discourage people's creativity, and they cannot learn anything ~~which is~~ they are not motivated ~~for him~~ to learn. ~~With~~ ~~r~~R equirements restrict their freedom to choose ~~what he is interested in is taken away~~ and their eagerness to learn. They are only discouraged by having to study dull subjects like German, ~~which~~ in which ~~he is not interested in~~ they can see no relevance to their interests.

The Paper, with Instructor's Markings

can you get rid of the passive?
redundant?
relevant?
true?
activate

In a college education, students should be allowed to choose their own curricula and select their own courses. All the requirements they must take stifle their creativity. Moreover, they cannot learn anything they are not motivated to learn. Requirements restrict their freedom to choose and their eagerness to explore the subjects they are interested in. They are only discouraged by having to study dull subjects like German, in which they can see no relevance.

Revised Paper

Students should choose their own education, their own curricula, their own courses. Their education is really theirs alone. Every college requirement threatens to stifle the very enthusiasms upon which true education depends. Students learn best when motivated by their own interests, but, in the midst of a dozen complicated requirements, they can hardly find time for the courses they long to take. Requirements therefore not only restrict their freedom to choose but destroy their eagerness to explore. Dull subjects like German, in which they can see no relevance anyway, take all their time and discourage them completely.

AIMING FOR A STYLE OF YOUR OWN

By writing frequently, you will create a style of your own—and with it, a good bit of your future. But what is style? At its best, it is much like style in a car, a gown, a Greek temple—the ordinary materials of this world so poised and perfected as to stand out from the landscape and compel a second look, something that hangs in the reader's mind, like a vision. It is a writer's own voice, with the hems and haws chipped out, speaking the common language uncommonly well. It comes from a craftsman who has discovered the knots and potentials in his material, one who has learned to enjoy phrasing and syntax, and the very punctuation that keeps them straight. It is the labor of love, and like love it can bring pleasure and satisfaction.

But style is not for the gifted only. Quite the contrary. Indeed, as I have been suggesting, everyone already has a style, and a personality, and can develop both. The stylistic side of writing is, in fact, the only side that can be analyzed and learned. The stylistic approach is the practical approach: you learn some things to do and not to do, as you would learn strokes in tennis. Your ultimate game is up to you, but you can at least begin in good form. Naturally, it takes practice. You have to keep at it. Like the doctor and the lawyer and the golfer and the tennis player, you just keep practicing—even to write a nearly perfect letter. But if you like the game, you can probably learn to play it well. You will at least be able to write a respectable sentence, and to express your thoughts clearly, without puffing and flailing.

In the essay, as in business, trying to get started and getting off on the wrong foot account for most of our lost motion. So we will next consider how to find a thesis, which will virtually organize your essay for you. Then we will study the relatively simple structure of the essay, and the structure of the paragraph—the architecture of spatial styling. Then we will experiment with various styles of sentence, playing with length and complexity to help you find the right mix to convey your personal rhythm. And finally we will get down to words themselves. Here again you will experiment to find those personal ranges of vocabulary, those blends of the breezy and the formal, that will empower your personal style. Here, in the word, is where writing tells; and here, as in ancient times, you will be in touch with the mystery. But again, there are things to do and things not to do, and these can be learned. So, to begin.

Readings

Spanning two thousand years and a variety of topics, the readings in this section share two qualities of good writing: each projects a human personality, and each establishes a firm viewpoint. Theodore Roethke exhudes confidence as he assesses his strengths and weaknesses as a writer. Fran Lebowitz humorously but deftly attacks the kinds of music that interfere with her privacy. In a personal, conversational tone, Wilfrid Sheed pleads the case for staying intellectually alive after graduation from college. In the final selection, the ancient Roman philosopher Cicero argues genially but forcefully for the value of writing and its relationship to speaking.

THEODORE ROETHKE

I Can Write

1 I expect this course to open my eyes to story material, to unleash my too dormant imagination, to develop that quality utterly lacking in my nature—a sense of form. I do not expect to acquire much technique. I expect to be able to seize upon the significant, reject the trivial. I hope to acquire a greater love for humanity in all its forms.

2 I have long wondered just what my strength was as a writer. I am often filled with tremendous enthusiasm for a subject, yet my writing about it will seem a sorry attempt. Above all, I possess a driving sincerity,—that prime virtue of any creative worker. I write only what I believe to be the absolute truth,—even if I must

ruin the theme in so doing. In this respect I feel far superior to those glib people in my classes who often garner better grades than I do. They are so often pitiful frauds,—artificial—insincere. They have a line that works. They do not write from the depths of their hearts. Nothing of theirs was ever born of pain. Many an incoherent yet sincere piece of writing has outlived the polished product.

3 I write only about people and things that I know thoroughly. Perhaps I have become a mere reporter, not a writer. Yet I feel that this is all my present abilities permit. I will open my eyes in my youth and store this raw, living material. Age may bring the fire that molds experience into artistry.

4 I have a genuine love of nature. It is not the least bit affected, but an integral and powerful part of my life. I know that Cooper is a fraud—that he doesn't give a true sense of the sublimity of American scenery. I know that Muir and Thoreau and Burroughs speak the truth.

5 I can sense the moods of nature almost instinctively. Ever since I could walk, I have spent as much time as I could in the open. A perception of nature—no matter how delicate, how subtle, how evanescent,—remains with me forever.

6 I am influenced too much, perhaps, by natural objects. I seem bound by the very room I'm in. I've associated so long with prosaic people that I've dwarfed myself spiritually. When I get alone under an open sky where man isn't too evident—then I'm tremendously exalted and a thousand vivid ideas and sweet visions flood my consciousness.

7 I think that I possess story material in abundance. I have had an unusual upbringing. I was let alone, thank God! My mother insisted upon two things,—that I strive for perfection in whatever I did and that I always try to be a gentleman. I played with Italians, with Russians, Poles, and the "sissies" on Michigan Avenue. I was carefully watched, yet allowed to follow my own inclinations. I have seen a good deal of life that would never have been revealed to an older person. Up to the time I came to college then I had seen humanity in diverse forms. Now I'm cramped and unhappy. I don't feel that these idiotic adolescents are worth writing about. In the summer, I turn animal and work for a few weeks in a factory. Then I'm happy.

8 My literary achievements have been insignificant. At fourteen, I made a speech which was translated into twenty-six lan-

guages and used as Red Cross propaganda. When I was younger, it seemed that everything I wrote was eminently successful. I always won a prize when I entered an essay contest. In college, I've been able to get only one "A" in four rhetoric courses. I feel this keenly. If I can't write, what can I do? I wonder.

9 When I was a freshman, I told Carleton Wells that I knew I could write whether he thought so or not. On my next theme he wrote "You can Write!" How I have cherished that praise!

10 It is bad form to talk about grades, I know. If I don't get an "A" in this course, it wouldn't be because I haven't tried. I've made a slow start. I'm going to spend Christmas vacation writing. A "B" symbolizes defeat to me. I've been beaten too often.

11 I do wish that we were allowed to keep our stories until we felt that we had worked them into the best possible form.

12 I do not have the divine urge to write. There seems to be something surging within,—a profound undercurrent of emotion. Yet there is none of that fertility of creation which distinguishes the real writer.

13 Nevertheless, I have faith in myself. I'm either going to be a good writer or a poor fool.

Suggestions for Discussion and Writing

1. What does Roethke expect from his writing course? Do you think that he expects too much?
2. What does Roethke regard as his strengths as a writer? His weaknesses? On the basis of this selection, do you believe his assessment of his ability is correct?
3. Is Roethke arrogant, or only confident? What part does his tone play in conveying that attitude?
4. Roethke claims that a "driving sincerity" and "fertility of creation" distinguish the real writer. Can these qualities be learned? Is it possible to become an effective writer without them?
5. Richard Brinsley Sheridan, an Irish playwright of the eighteenth century, said that "easy writing's vile hard reading." Alexander Pope, an English poet from the same century, claimed that "True ease in writing comes from art, not chance." Would Roethke agree with either statement? Find the lines in this selection that support your answer.
6. Try writing an essay in which you describe your strengths and weaknesses as a writer. Consider such matters as having some-

thing to say, getting started, finding the right words, organizing your thoughts, and making your writing sound like *you.*

FRAN LEBOWITZ

The Sound of Music: Enough Already

1 First off, I want to say that as far as I am concerned, in instances where I have not personally and deliberately sought it out, the only difference between music and Muzak is the spelling. Pablo Casals practicing across the hall with the door open—being trapped in an elevator, the ceiling of which is broadcasting "Parsley, Sage, Rosemary, and Thyme"—it's all the same to me. Harsh words? Perhaps. But then again these are not gentle times we live in. And they are being made no more gentle by this incessant melody that was once real life.

2 There was a time when music knew its place. No longer. Possibly this is not music's fault. It may be that music fell in with a bad crowd and lost its sense of common decency. I am willing to consider this. I am willing even to try and help. I would like to do my bit to set music straight in order that it might shape up and leave the mainstream of society. The first thing that music must understand is that there are two kinds of music—good music and bad music. Good music is music that I want to hear. Bad music is music that I don't want to hear.

3 So that music might more clearly see the error of its ways I offer the following. If you are music and you recognize yourself on this list, you are bad music.

1. Music in Other People's Clock Radios

4 There are times when I find myself spending the night in the home of another. Frequently the other is in a more reasonable line of work than I and must arise at a specific hour. Ofttimes the

other, unbeknownst to me, manipulates an appliance in such a way that I am awakened by Stevie Wonder. On such occasions I announce that if I wished to be awakened by Stevie Wonder I would sleep with Stevie Wonder. I do not, however, wish to be awakened by Stevie Wonder and that is why God invented alarm clocks. Sometimes the other realizes that I am right. Sometimes the other does not. And that is why God invented *many* others.

2. Music Residing in the Hold Buttons of Other People's Business Telephones

5 I do not under any circumstances enjoy hold buttons. But I am a woman of reason. I can accept reality. I can face the facts. What I cannot face is the music. Just as there are two kinds of music—good and bad—so there are two kinds of hold buttons—good and bad. Good hold buttons are hold buttons that hold one silently. Bad hold buttons are hold buttons that hold one musically. When I hold I want to hold silently. That is the way it was meant to be, for that is what God was talking about when he said, "Forever hold your peace." He would have added, "and quiet," but he thought you were smarter.

3. Music in the Streets

6 The past few years have seen a steady increase in the number of people playing music in the streets. The past few years have also seen a steady increase in the number of malignant diseases. Are these two facts related? One wonders. But even if they are not—and, as I have pointed out, one cannot be sure—music in the streets has definitely taken its toll. For it is at the very least disorienting. When one is walking down Fifth Avenue, one does not expect to hear a string quartet playing a Strauss waltz. What one expects to hear while walking down Fifth Avenue is traffic. When one does indeed hear a string quartet playing a Strauss waltz while one is walking down Fifth Avenue, one is apt to become confused and imagine that one is not walking down Fifth Avenue at all but rather that one has somehow wound up in Old Vienna. Should one imagine that

one is in Old Vienna one is likely to become quite upset when one realizes that in Old Vienna there is no sale at Charles Jourdan. And that is why when I walk down Fifth Avenue I want to hear traffic.

4. Music in the Movies

7 I'm not talking about musicals. Musicals are movies that warn you by saying, "Lots of music here. Take it or leave it." I'm talking about regular movies that extend no such courtesy but allow unsuspecting people to come to see them and then assault them with a barrage of unasked-for tunes. There are two major offenders in this category: black movies and movies set in the fifties. Both types of movies are afflicted with the same misconception. They don't know that movies are supposed to be movies. They think that movies are supposed to be records with pictures. They have failed to understand that if God had wanted records to have pictures, he would not have invented television.

5. Music in Public Places Such as Restaurants, Supermarkets, Hotel Lobbies, Airports, Etc.

8 When I am in any of the above-mentioned places I am not there to hear music. I am there for whatever reason is appropriate to the respective place. I am no more interested in hearing "Mack the Knife" while waiting for the shuttle to Boston than someone sitting ringside at the Sands Hotel is interested in being forced to choose between sixteen varieties of cottage cheese. If God had meant for everything to happen at once, he would not have invented desk calendars.

Epilogue

9 Some people talk to themselves. Some people sing to themselves. Is one group better than the other? Did not God create all people equal? Yes, God created all people equal. Only to some he gave the ability to make up their own words.

Suggestions for Discussion and Writing

1. Underneath her acerbic wit, Lebowitz is expressing a firm conviction about music. What is it? Where does she state it?
2. What assumptions does she make about her audience? Consider, for example, her reference to Stevie Wonder (paragraph 4).
3. Describe the voice that the author projects in this essay. Does she write with tongue in cheek, or is her anger genuine?
4. Lebowitz divides music into "good music" and "bad music." Can you add other examples of "bad music" to her list? What examples would she probably include in her list of "good music"?
5. Write an essay about one of your own peeves. Likely topics could be junk mail, sales pitches on the telephone, or advertisements on television or radio.

WILFRID SHEED

A Thought a Day Isn't Enough

1 When I was, say, twenty, I thought I was a pretty bright and interesting fellow, although I was much too polite to show it. And I wondered why people of, say, forty were not twice as bright and interesting and so on up the line. A few, very few, of them were. Most of them seemed to get a little bit duller every year. They had fewer and fewer things to talk about—who are you going to vote for; how about those Yankees, etc. Their minds actually seemed to have shrunk, and they preferred the company of people in the same boat, fellow dentists or morticians, who would never bring up anything new. This meant that there was either some dreadful biological law at work whereby old age sets in on the very day you leave campus, or else there was a massive national act of laziness, of just giving up, performed every year at this time. Only later when I tried it myself did I come to realize how difficult it is to remain alive when nobody's watching and making you. Because we have this quaint custom of getting all our education over with early in life, we find ourselves fussed over excessively for sixteen

years and then just like that abandoned and left for dead. This process is known as graduation, and welcome to it.

2 Of course, only in extreme cases do graduates become dull immediately. I've seen some of them do it on the way out of the final examinations, but usually the first little gray hairs of the mind don't begin to show for ten years or so. At first, new jobs, marriages, relocations, etc., are stimulating enough. You don't need books or new ideas for a while. So you learn to live without them, and you learn all too well. The world of work actually encourages this narrowness if you let it. Outside interests only slow you down in the rat race anyway. So the professional world becomes a kind of Franz Kafka mansion where the rooms get spiritually smaller and grayer the further up the stairs you go, and this is known as promotion.

3 You start out in a large bright space with lots of friends and lots of windows to look out of, but the windows are removed one by one so you can concentrate better on your work until you reach top management where you live, to judge from the conversation, in almost total darkness. Since this is the exact opposite of the way it looks, because the offices actually seem to get bigger, many people sometimes go right to the top without knowing what's happening to them. I have met some quite prominent businessmen who had less to say for themselves than New York taxi drivers. Perhaps that's too high a standard, but these people hadn't read anything or heard of anybody outside their own tiny world in years and years. Even their politics were simple-minded. They would be ashamed to know so little about football. I don't read novels they say—clank, there's a window gone. I never get to the movies, theater, opera.

4 As my father used to say about people who don't read poetry—neither does a cow. I should add that I'm not just talking about business businessmen but about doctors, lawyers, the works. In every case, they claim that the pressure of work is walling them in. Yet in every field, you're likely to find that the very best people do miraculously make time for books and the arts and it's the second-raters who don't. So time isn't the real problem. The problem is character. Character, once upon a time, referred exclusively to work. It can also be applied to play. It requires will power to stay playful, to keep your mind open. It takes character to stay alive. And it is not only between nine and five that people age. There are plenty of unemployed bores who work at it around the clock. Whenever you find yourself repeating

the same thoughts in exactly the same words, you're jogging along with Father Time and gaining. Listen in on any barroom or even executive lunch and you will find people eagerly looking for ways to say the things they said a million times before. If you pull something new on them, they will look stunned and then drag it back somehow to their old turf. "As I always say" is their motto, and did you ever find yourself using this phrase yourself? You are in the club. And the next generation will be thinking, how did he get to be so dull?

5 The fact is that staying intellectually alive is very hard work. They made you do it in school, so you did it. But now that nobody's making you do it, you'll probably stop. Nobody marches you into the bookstore anymore, so you stop attending as with church. After all, what do books know anyway? You'll learn from life itself. But your particular life would fill no more than one slim volume in a library, and all around it there would be oceans of life in the other books. A book is just a stranger talking brilliantly; he's probably better company than you'll meet in a saloon. After all, he's usually sober and giving you the best hours of his day, and he's forcing you to look at things in a new way and face new experience. It's no use saying, "As I was saying," to a book; incidentally, the fact that I happen to be in the book business myself has nothing to do with all this, nor the fact that I'm counting on this generation to keep me in cigars and caviar. You can read other people's books if you insist. I'm sure equally impassioned cases can be made for music and painting, and there's no need to quarrel.

6 An educated European assumes, often to my own embarrassment, that a college man will at least know the names of the world's leading composers, painters, architects and what they've been up to lately. So, since a patriotic note is also appropriate to these occasions, I call on you simply as Americans to stop being the Mortimer Snerds of the Western world, the Fred Flintstones, and to pick up your hem of the Western tradition. It is not too late to recover from your rotten educations, not the one you got here in this excellent place, but from the tube and lesser schools. Simply read a book. If not today, well at least by the end of next year. And if you repeat the dose often enough, you will have done more to stay young than all the jogging and rolling put together. And not just stay young. You will have pulled that one-in-a-million trick—growing up. And you will be twice as good twenty years from now as you think you are today.

Suggestions for Discussion and Writing

1. According to Sheed, what is the secret to staying intellectually alive? Why is it difficult to avoid getting a little bit duller every year?
2. Why should business people read novels and poetry or attend concerts? Why don't they?
3. How do you account for the fact that most educated Europeans know more about the arts than their American counterparts do?
4. Point out evidence that this selection was originally delivered as a commencement address.
5. Sheed's tone is like that of a genial uncle giving advice to a young niece or nephew. Find several examples of specific words, phrases, or sentences that create this tone.
6. Look up the etymology of the word *sophomore.* Write an essay in which you demonstrate that the original meaning does (or does not) apply to your classmates.
7. Write an essay in which you discuss a book that changed or influenced you in a significant way. Avoid writing a mere summary of the book; instead, discuss its impact on you.

CICERO*

[How Writing Improves Speech]

The moving pen draws forth our thoughts.

1 But the main thing is what, to tell the truth, we do least—it is indeed hard work, which most of us flee—to write as much as

---

*Marcus Tullius Cicero (106–43 B.C.), Roman lawyer, consul, and philosopher. His orations in the law courts immediately became models in the schools, and his *De Oratore* (55 B.C.)—"Concerning the Orator"—had an enormous influence throughout the Western world well into modern times. His ideal of the eloquent orator, thoroughly in command of all branches of knowledge through constant study, became the ideal of the Renaissance man, equally capable in all things. He opposed the triumvirate of Marc Antony, Lepidus, and Octavius (Augustus), who had him murdered. This passage is from *De Oratore* (1.xxxiii.150–153); the translation is by Sheridan Baker.—Ed.

possible. The pen is rightly the supreme producer and teacher of speech. Just as a little meditation easily beats an offhand extemporaneous speech, so a diligent written speech will just as surely top the former. Indeed, all the ideas that immediately pertain to what we are writing, whether from others or from our own gifts and knowledge, rush forth as we ponder with the full sharpness of our gifts, and all thoughts and all words, the most sparkling, each in its way, must necessarily flow under and follow the point of the pen. Then, too, writing perfects the very arrangement and organization of words, but in the rhythm and measure of public speaking, not of poetry.

2 These perfected phrases, in a good orator, are what draw out the cheers and bursts of admiration, which no one will get unless he has written much and long, no matter how vehemently he exercises himself in offhand speeches. Moreover, he who comes from the habit of writing to speaking will bring his ability with him, so that, even if he speaks offhand, what he says will seem like writing. Furthermore, if in speaking he brings in something he has written, the rest of his oration will follow along the same when he departs from it. As when in a swiftly driven ship the rowers rest, the boat itself keeps moving on its course, even though the thrust and beat of the oars have stopped, so in a continuous oration, when what is written gives out, the rest of the oration nevertheless holds its course, driven by the similitude and force of writing.

Suggestions for Discussion and Writing

1. Why is it likely that the best orators and speakers are those who have "written much and long"?
2. Why do most of us avoid writing whenever possible? Does it have to do with our fear of making a mistake, or does it stem from some deeper fear of expressing ourselves exactly and specifically?
3. In what sense is the act of writing the act of self-discovery? What kinds of knowledge might be discovered?
4. Citing examples from history or from your own experience, write an essay demonstrating the truth of the adage, "The pen is mightier than the sword." Quote Cicero to support your argument.

5. The English essayist Francis Bacon said, "Reading maketh a full man, conference [conversation] a ready man, and writing an exact man." Write an essay giving examples that support Bacon's statement.

2
Making a Beginning: From Subject to Thesis

GETTING SET

Get set! Writing an essay isn't exactly a fifty-yard dash, but you do need to get ready and get set before you can go to it. Writing requires a time and place, an habitual environment to coax and support those inspired moments that seem to flow spontaneously into language. Your best scheme is to plan two or three sittings for each assignment. Your place should be fixed. It should be comfortable and convenient. Your times should be regular, varied in length from short to long, and set to fit your schedule and your personal rhythm, as morning person or night owl, sprinter or long-distance runner. Arrange your first period for a time as soon as possible after assignments, perhaps only half an hour for scribbling and thinking on paper. Your next two sessions should be longer, the last with expandable time to get the job done.

WHAT SHALL I WRITE?

First you need a subject, and then you need a thesis. Yes, but *what shall I write?* Here you are, an assignment before you and the paper as blank as your mind, especially if your instructor has left the subject up to you. Look for something that interests you, something you know about, some hobby—something that shook you up, left you perplexed, started you thinking.

Writing will help you discover that something. Don't stare at that blank page. Set yourself the task of writing for ten minutes, no matter what. Start your pencil moving and keep it going, even beginning with *Good grief, what shall I write? Write on anything, the big oaf said. OK, but what what what what what? Fishing? Baby-sitting? Skipping rope? Crime? Nuclear power? Oh no. Crime? Rape? How about the time I ripped off a candy bar and got caught? The shock of recognition. Everyone's done it at some time or other. Everyone's guilty. Everyone's tempted. Something for nothing. The universal temptation of crime. . . .* Keep it going until your watch tells you to stop. That's a good start. Take a break and let your thoughts sink in and accumulate.

Probe your own experiences and feelings for answers as to why people behave as they do, especially in times of crisis. Prestige? The admiration of peers? Fear of not going with the gang? Why is fishing (let us say) so appealing to you? Why more so than water skiing or swimming or sailing or tennis or painting? Why don't some people like it? What might they object to? Now have another bout on paper, perhaps just writing the questions down, perhaps discovering some answers as you go. You have found your subject—and indeed have already moved a good way toward a thesis. The more your subject matters to you, the more you can make it matter to your readers. It might be skiing. It might be dress. It might be roommates, the Peloponnesian War, a political protest, a personal discovery of racial tensions, an experience as a nurse's aide. But do not tackle a big philosophical abstraction, like Freedom, or a big subject, like the Supreme Court. They are too vast, your time and space and knowledge all too small. You would probably manage no more than a collection of platitudes. Start rather with something specific, like running, and let the ideas of freedom and justice and responsibility arise from there. An abstract idea is a poor beginning. To be sure, as you move ahead through your course in writing, you will work more directly with ideas, with problems posed by literature, with questions in the great civilizing debate about what we are doing in this strange world and universe. But again, look for something within your concern. The best subjects lie nearest at hand, and nearest the heart.

You can personalize almost any subject and cut it down to size, getting a manageable angle on it. On an assigned subject, particularly in courses like political science or anthropology or sociology, look for something that connects you with it. Suppose your instructor assigns a paper on Social Security. Think of a grandparent, a parent, a neighbor, a friend—or perhaps yourself as a student receiving benefits, and how reductions would or would not affect your life. You will have a vivid illustration as well as one corner of the huge problem to illuminate. Nuclear energy? Perhaps you have seen on television the appalling space suits and mechanical arms required to handle the radioactive stuff, along with something of its astounding problems. Perhaps you remember an article, or a sentence, that started you thinking. With subjects to find, keep an eye and an ear open as you read the newspaper or *Time,* or watch TV, and talk with your friends. Your classes and textbooks will inevitably turn up subjects for your composition course, if you watch for them, which you can bring into your personal range. Deregulating petroleum? You have probably seen the price of gas soar, your pocketbook shrink, and have taken to the bus, or your bike, or your heels. You need to find a personal interest in your subject to have something to say and to interest others.

FROM SUBJECT TO THESIS

Suppose, for the present, we start simply with "Drugs." Certainly, most of us have been tempted, or had to resist, or to go along, have experimented, or gotten hooked, or have known someone who has—especially if we include cigarettes and alcohol. "Drugs" is a subject easily personalized. Taking a subject like this will also show how to generalize from your own experience, and how to cut your subject down to manageable size. Your first impulse will probably be to write in the first person, but your experience may remain merely personal and may not point your subject into a thesis. As I have said, a personal anecdote makes a lively *illustration,* but first you need to generate your thesis and establish it for your reader. You need to move out of that bright, self-centered spotlight of consciousness in which we live before we really grow up, in which the child assumes that all his or her experiences are unique. If you shift from "me" to "the beginner" or "the young adult," however, you will be stepping into maturity: acknowledging that others have gone through exactly the same thing, that your experiences have illustrated once again the general dynamics of the individual and the group. So instead of writing "I was afraid to refuse," you write:

> **The *beginner* is afraid to refuse, and soon discovers the tremendous pressure of the group.**

By generalizing your private feelings, you change your subject into a thesis—your argumentative proposition. You simply assume you are normal and fairly representative, and you then generalize with confidence, transposing your particular experiences, your particular thoughts and reactions, into statements about the general ways of the world. Put your proposition, your thesis, into one sentence. This will get you focused. And now you are ready to begin.

WHERE ESSAYS FAIL

You can usually blame a bad essay on a bad beginning. If your essay falls apart, it probably has no primary idea, no thesis, to hold it together. "What's the big idea?" we used to ask. The phrase will serve as a reminder that you must find the "big idea" behind your several smaller thoughts and musings and drafts before you can start to shape your final essay. In the beginning was the *logos,* says the Bible—the idea, the plan, caught in a flash as if in a single word. Find your *logos,* and you are ready to round out your essay and set it spinning.

Suppose you had decided to write about a high-speed ride —another case of group dynamics. If you have not focused your big idea in a thesis, you might begin something like this:

> **Everyone thinks he is a good driver. There are more accidents caused by young drivers than any other group. Driver education is a good beginning, but further practice is very necessary. People who object to driver education do not realize that modern society, with its suburban pattern of growth, is built around the automobile. The car becomes a way of life and a status symbol. When teen-agers go too fast they are probably only copying their own parents.**

A little reconsideration, aimed at a good thesis-sentence, could turn this into a reasonably good opening paragraph, with your thesis, your big idea, asserted at the end to focus your reader's attention:

> **Modern society is built on the automobile. Children play with tiny cars; teen-agers long to take out the car alone. Soon they are testing their skills at higher and higher speeds, especially with a group of friends along. One final test at extreme speeds usually suffices. It is usually a sobering experience, if survived, and can open one's eyes to the deadly dynamics of the group.**

Thus your thesis is your essay's life and spirit. If it is sufficiently firm, it may tell you immediately how to organize your supporting material. But if you do not find a thesis, your essay will be a tour through the miscellaneous, replete with scaffolds and catwalks—"We have just seen this; now let us turn to this" —an essay with no vital idea. A purely expository essay, one simply on "Cats," for instance, will have to rely on outer scaffolding alone (some orderly progression from Persia to Siam), since it really has no idea at all. It is all subject, all cats, instead of being based on an idea *about* cats, with a thesis *about* cats.

THE ARGUMENTATIVE EDGE

Find Your Thesis

The *about*-ness puts an argumentative edge on the subject. When you have something to say *about* cats, you have found your underlying idea. You have something to defend, something to fight about: not just "Cats," but "The cat is really a person's best friend." Now the hackles on all dog people are rising, and you have an argument on your hands. You have something to prove. You have a thesis.

"What's the big idea, Mac?" Let the impudence in that time-honored demand remind you that the most dynamic thesis is a kind of affront to somebody. No one will be very much interested in listening to you deplete the thesis. "The dog is a person's best friend." Everyone knows that already. Even the dog lovers will be uninterested, convinced they know better than you. But the cat. . . .

So it is with any unpopular idea. The more unpopular the viewpoint and the stronger the push against convention, the stronger the thesis and the more energetic the essay. Compare the energy in "Democracy is good" with that in "Communism is good," for instance. The first is filled with platitudes, the second with plutonium. By the same token, if you can find the real energy in "Democracy is good," if you can get down through the sand to where the roots and water are, you will have a real essay, because the opposition against which you generate your energy is the heaviest in the world: boredom. Probably the most energetic thesis of all, the greatest inner organizer, is some tired old truth that you cause to spurt with new life, making the old ground green again.

To find a thesis and to put it into one sentence is to narrow and define your subject to workable size. Under "Cats" you must deal with all felinity from the jungle up, carefully partitioning the eons and areas, the tigers and tabbies. But proclaim the cat the friend of humanity, and you have pared away whole categories and chapters, and need only think up the arguments sufficient to overwhelm the opposition. So, put an argumentative edge on your subject—and you will have found your thesis.

Neutral exposition, to be sure, has its uses. You may want to tell someone how to build a doghouse, how to can asparagus, how to follow the outlines of relativity, or even how to write an essay. Performing a few exercises in simple exposition will no doubt sharpen your insight into the problems of finding orderly sequences, of considering how best to lead your readers through the hoops of writing clearly and accurately. It will also illustrate how much finer and surer an argument is.

You will see that picking an argument immediately simplifies the problems so troublesome in straight exposition: the defining, the partitioning, the narrowing of the subject. Not that you must be constantly pugnacious or aggressive. I have overstated my point to make it stick. Actually, you can put an argumentative edge on the flattest of expository subjects. "How to build a doghouse" might become "Building a doghouse is a thorough introduction to the building trades, including architecture and civil engineering." "Canning asparagus" might become "An asparagus patch is a course in economics." "Relativity" might become "Relativity is not so inscrutable as many suppose." Literary subjects take an argumentative edge almost by nature. You simply assert what the essential point of a poem or play seems to be: "*Hamlet* is essentially about a world that has lost its values." You assume that your readers are in search of clarity, that you have a loyal opposition consisting of the interested but uninformed. You have given your subject its edge; you have limited and organized it at a single stroke. Pick an *argument,* then, and you will automatically be defining and narrowing your subject, and all the partitions that you don't need will fold up. Instead of dealing with things, subjects, and pieces of subjects, you will be dealing with an idea and its consequences.

Sharpen Your Thesis

Come out with your subject pointed. You have chosen something that interests you, something you have thought about, read about, something preferably of which you have also had some experience—perhaps, let us say, seeing a friend loafing while cashing welfare checks. So take a stand. Make a judgment of value, make a *thesis.* Be reasonable, but don't be timid. It is helpful to think of your thesis, your main idea, as a debating question—"Resolved: Welfare payments must go"—taking out the "Resolved" when you actually write your thesis down. But your resolution will be even stronger, your essay clearer and tighter, if you can sharpen your thesis even further—"Resolved: Welfare payments must go because ______." Fill in that blank, and your worries are practically over. The main idea is to put your whole argument into one sentence.

Try, for instance: "Welfare payments must go because they are making people irresponsible." I don't know at all if that is true, and neither will you until you write your way into it, considering probabilities and alternatives and objections, and especially the underlying assumptions. In fact, no one, no master sociologist or future historian, can tell absolutely if it is true, so multiplex are the causes in human affairs, so endless and tangled the consequences. The basic assumption—that irresponsibility is growing—may be entirely false. No one, I repeat, can tell absolutely. But likewise, your guess may be as good as another's. At any rate, you are now ready to write. You have found your *logos.*

Now you can put your well-pointed thesis-sentence on a card on the wall in front of you to keep from drifting off target. But you will now want to dress it for the public, to burnish it and make it comely. Suppose you try:

> **Welfare payments, perhaps more than anything else, are eroding personal initiative.**

But is this fully true? Perhaps you had better try something like:

> **Despite their immediate benefits, welfare payments may actually be eroding personal initiative and depriving society of needed workers.**

This is your full thesis. You have acknowledged the opposition ("immediate benefits"); you have spelled out your *because* (erosion, deprivation). This is your opinion, stated as certainty. But how do you know, without all the facts? Well, no one knows everything. No one would write anything if he waited until he did. To a great extent, the writing of a thing is the learning of it—the discovery of truth. So make a desperate thesis and get into the arena. This is probably solution enough. If it becomes increasingly clear that your thesis is untrue, turn it around and use the other end. If your convictions have begun to falter with:

> **Despite their immediate benefits, welfare payments undermine initiative. . . .**

try it the other way around, with something like:

> **Although welfare payments may offend the rugged individualist, they relieve much want and anxiety, and they enable many a family to maintain its integrity.**

You will now have a beautiful command of the major objections to your new position. And you will have learned something about human fallibility and the nature of truth. You simply add enough evidence to persuade your reader that what you say is probably true, finding arguments that will stand up in the marketplace—public reasons for your private convictions.

Use Your Title

After your thesis, think of a title. A good title focuses your thinking even more sharply and catches your reader's thoughts on your finished paper. Your title is your opening opportunity. It is an integral part of your paper. Don't forget it.

Work up something from your thesis. It will be tentative, of course. Your thinking and your paper may change in the writing, and you will want to change your title to match. But a good title, like a good thesis, has a double advantage: (1) it helps you keep on track as you write; (2) it attracts and helps keep your reader on track as he reads. It is the first step in your persuasion. So try something attractive:

Welfare Not Warfare
Farewell to Welfare
Whom Does Welfare Benefit?

You can probably do better. You will do better when you finish your paper. But don't make it sound like a newspaper headline, and don't make it a complete statement. Don't forget your title as a starter, both for your writing and for your written paper. Capitalize all significant words (see 425–27 for details). Titles do not take periods, but do take question and exclamation marks if you need them. Your title and your opening sentence should be independent of each other. With a title like "Polluted Streams," for instance, don't begin with "*This* is a serious problem."

SAMPLE: FROM SUBJECT TO THESIS

Now with the concepts in hand, we need a framework, a structure, to put them in. This we will look at in the next chapter. But let us close with a student's paper to illustrate the points of this chapter as it looks ahead to the structural points of the next. In it, you can see the mechanics of typing, spacing, quoting, and so forth. The author has made a few small last-minute corrections in pencil, which are perfectly acceptable. Her writing is a little wordy and awkward. She is a little uncertain of her language. Her *one*'s, for instance, seem far too stiff and insistent. This is her first paper, and she has not yet fully discovered her own written voice. But it is an excellent beginning. It shows well how a personal experience produces a publicly valid thesis, then turns around to give that thesis its most lively and specific illustration. The assignment had asked for a paper of about five hundred words on some book (or movie, or TV program) that had proved personally meaningful. Even a memorable experience would do—fixing a car, or building a boat, or being arrested. The aim of the assignment was to generalize from a personally valuable experience and to explain to others how such an experience can be valuable to them.

On Finding Oneself in New Guinea

Opposing View

Reading for pleasure is not considered to be popular.* Young adults prefer the "boob tube," the television set with which they have spent so many childhood hours. Too many attractions beckon them away from the books which the teacher recommended to the class for summer reading. One's friends come by in their automobiles to drive down for a coke. The kids go to the moving pictures, or to the beach, and the book one had intended to read remains on the shelf, or probably the library, where one has not yet been able to find the time to go. Nevertheless, *a book can furnish real enjoyment.

Thesis

Generalized Support

***The reader enjoys the experience of being in another world.* While one reads, one forgets that one is in one's own room. The book has served as a magic carpet to take one to India, or Africa, or Sweden, or even to the cities and areas of one's own country where one has never been. It has also transported one into the lives of people with different experiences and problems, from which one can learn to solve one's own problems of the future. The young person, in particular, can learn by the experience of reading what it is like to be a complete adult.**

A book is able to help the young person to mature even

further, and change one's whole point of view. *Growing up in New Guinea* by Margaret Mead is a valuable experience for this reason. *I found the book on our shelf, after having seen Margaret Mead on TV.* I was interested in her because the teacher had referred to her book entitled *Coming of Age in Samoa.* I was surprised to find this one about New Guinea. I thought it was a mistake. I opened it and read the first sentence:

Personal Experience

> The way in which each human infant is transformed into the finished adult, into the complicated individual version of his city and his century, is one of the most fascinating studies open to the curious minded.

Quotation

The idea that the individual is a version of his city and his century was fascinating. I started reading and was surprised when I was called to dinner to learn that two hours had passed. I could hardly eat my dinner fast enough so that I could get back to New Guinea.

From this book I learned that different cultures have very different conceptions about what is right and wrong, in particular about the sex relations and the marriage ceremony, but that people have the same problems all over the world, namely the problem of finding one's place in society. *I also learned that books can be more enjoyable than any other form of pleasure.* Books fascinate the reader because while one is learning about other people and their problems, particularly about the problem of becoming a full member of society, one is also learning about one's own problems.

Thesis Restated

EXERCISES

1. *Put down quickly the first four or five subjects that come to mind—golf, cars, architecture, lipstick, tomatoes. These must have interested you sometime, somewhere. Now make each into an established one-sentence argumentative thesis on the pattern* Although ______, golf accomplishes more because ______.
2. *Supply a thesis-statement and a title for each of the following subjects:*

   1. Nuclear armament
   2. The appearance of our campus
   3. Jogging

4. A book you have read
5. Opportunities for blacks and whites

3. *Now expand one of your thesis-statements from the preceding exercises into a paper about the length of the preceding example. First, introduce your thesis with a few remarks to get your reader acquainted with your subject, then write your paper straight through to illustrate your thesis as fully as you can. Then go back over this draft and make it publicly presentable, revising until you know you have done your best.*

4. *Making a thesis can also help your reading, and in all your courses. Therefore, at the end of each chapter, or other reading, try to put down in one sentence (and right in your textbook) that chapter's point: not* This chapter discusses racial discrimination, *but* Racial discrimination arises from powerful biological drives to seek one's own kind and to shun aliens. *This practice strengthens your knowledge, aids your analysis—has your author said it anywhere as well as you have?—and develops your ability to generate theses for your own thoughts. It works equally well for poems, stories, and plays.*

Readings

The following selections transpose particular experiences, thoughts, and reactions into statements about the general ways of the world. Richard Rodriguez presents the moving story of his growth to maturity in a society alien to his ethnic background. Virginia Woolf observes a moth flying about a window, and then watches it struggle and die. Nora Ephron reacts with irritation to a conversation and a book, both on the subject of "being female in America." And Carl Sagan, speaking from his perspective as one of this nation's leading astronomers, describes human life in cosmic terms.

From these private feelings and observations, each author distills a thesis. Rodriguez learns something about himself, his family, and American society. From the struggles of the moth, Woolf extracts a meditation on human life and death. Ephron derides the notion that beauty is the subject most important to women in all the world. Finally, Sagan asserts that no cause is more urgent than the elimination of the threat of nuclear war.

RICHARD RODRIGUEZ

Los Pobres

1 I went to college at Stanford, attracted partly by its academic reputation, partly because it was the school rich people went to. I found myself on a campus with golden children of western America's upper middle class. Many were students both ambitious for academic success *and* accustomed to leisured life in the

sun. In the afternoon, they lay spread out, sunbathing in front of the library, reading Swift or Engels or Beckett. Others went by in convertibles, off to play tennis or ride horses or sail. Beach boys dressed in tank-tops and shorts were my classmates in undergraduate seminars. Tall tan girls wearing white strapless dresses sat directly in front of me in lecture rooms. I'd study them, their physical confidence. I was still recognizably kin to the boy I had been. Less tortured perhaps. But still kin. At Stanford, it's true, I began to have something like a conventional sexual life. I don't think, however, that I really believed that the women I knew found me physically appealing. I continued to stay out of the sun. I didn't linger in mirrors. And I was the student at Stanford who remembered to notice the Mexican-American janitors and gardeners working on campus.

2 It was at Stanford, one day near the end of my senior year, that a friend told me about a summer construction job he knew was available. I was quickly alert. Desire uncoiled within me. My friend said that he knew I had been looking for summer employment. He knew I needed some money. Almost apologetically he explained: It was something I probably wouldn't be interested in, but a friend of his, a contractor, needed someone for the summer to do menial jobs. There would be lots of shoveling and raking and sweeping. Nothing too hard. But nothing more interesting either. Still, the pay would be good. Did I want it? Or did I know someone who did?

3 I did. Yes, I said, surprised to hear myself say it.

4 In the weeks following, friends cautioned that I had no idea how hard physical labor really is. ("You only *think* you know what it is like to shovel for eight hours straight.") Their objections seemed to me challenges. They resolved the issue. I became happy with my plan. I decided, however, not to tell my parents. I wouldn't tell my mother because I could guess her worried reaction. I would tell my father only after the summer was over, when I could announce that, after all, I did know what "real work" is like.

5 The day I met the contractor (a Princeton graduate, it turned out), he asked me whether I had done any physical labor before. "In high school, during the summer," I lied. And although he seemed to regard me with skepticism, he decided to give me a try. Several days later, expectant, I arrived at my first construction site. I would take off my shirt to the sun. And at last grasp desired sensation. No longer afraid. At last become like a *bracero.* "We

need those tree stumps out of here by tomorrow," the contractor said. I started to work.

6 I labored with excitement that first morning—and all the days after. The work was harder than I could have expected. But it was never as tedious as my friends had warned me it would be. There was too much physical pleasure in the labor. Especially early in the day, I would be most alert to the sensations of movement and straining. Beginning around seven each morning (when the air was still damp but the scent of weeds and dry earth anticipated the heat of the sun), I would feel my body resist the first thrusts of the shovel. My arms, tightened by sleep, would gradually loosen; after only several minutes, sweat would gather in beads on my forehead and then—a short while later—I would feel my chest silky with sweat in the breeze. I would return to my work. A nervous spark of pain would fly up my arm and settle to burn like an ember in the thick of my shoulder. An hour, two passed. Three. My whole body would assume regular movements; my shoveling would be described by identical, even movements. Even later in the day, my enthusiasm for primitive sensation would survive the heat and the dust and the insects pricking my back. I would strain wildly for sensation as the day came to a close. At three-thirty, quitting time, I would stand upright and slowly let my head fall back, luxuriating in the feeling of tightness relieved.

7 Some of the men working nearby would watch me and laugh. Two or three of the older men took the trouble to teach me the right way to use a pick, the correct way to shovel. "You're doing it wrong, too fucking hard," one man scolded. Then proceeded to show me—what persons who work with their bodies all their lives quickly learn—the most economical way to use one's body in labor.

8 "Don't make your back do so much work," he instructed. I stood impatiently listening, half listening, vaguely watching, then noticed his work-thickened fingers clutching the shovel. I was annoyed. I wanted to tell him that I enjoyed shoveling the wrong way. And I didn't want to learn the right way. I wasn't afraid of back pain. I liked the way my body felt sore at the end of the day.

9 I was about to, but, as it turned out, I didn't say a thing. Rather it was at that moment I realized that I was fooling myself if I expected a few weeks of labor to gain me admission to the world of the laborer. I would not learn in three months what my father had meant by "real work." I was not bound to this job; I

could imagine its rapid conclusion. For me the sensations of exertion and fatigue could be savored. For my father or uncle, working at comparable jobs when they were my age, such sensations were to be feared. Fatigue took a different toll on their bodies—and minds.

10 It was, I know, a simple insight. But it was with this realization that I took my first step that summer toward realizing something even more important about the "worker." In the company of carpenters, electricians, plumbers, and painters at lunch, I would often sit quietly, observant. I was not shy in such company. I felt easy, pleased by the knowledge that I was casually accepted, my presence taken for granted by men (exotics) who worked with their hands. Some days the younger men would talk and talk about sex, and they would howl at women who drove by in cars. Other days the talk at lunchtime was subdued; men gathered in separate groups. It depended on who was around. There were rough, good-natured workers. Others were quiet. The more I remember that summer, the more I realize that there was no single *type* of worker. I am embarrassed to say I had not expected such diversity. I certainly had not expected to meet, for example, a plumber who was an abstract painter in his off hours and admired the work of Mark Rothko. Nor did I expect to meet so many workers with college diplomas. (They were the ones who were not surprised that I intended to enter graduate school in the fall.) I suppose what I really want to say here is painfully obvious, but I must say it nevertheless: The men of that summer were middle-class Americans. They certainly didn't constitute an oppressed society. Carefully completing their work sheets; talking about the fortunes of local football teams; planning Las Vegas vacations; comparing the gas mileage of various makes of campers—they were not *los pobres* my mother had spoken about.

11 On two occasions, the contractor hired a group of Mexican aliens. They were employed to cut down some trees and haul off debris. In all, there were six men of varying age. The youngest in his twenties; the oldest (his father?) perhaps sixty years old. They came and they left in a single old truck. Anonymous men. They were never introduced to the other men at the site. Immediately upon their arrival, they would follow the contractor's directions, start working—rarely resting—seemingly driven by a fatalistic sense that work which had to be done was best done as quickly as possible.

12 I watched them sometimes. Perhaps they watched me. The

only time I saw them pay me much notice was one day at lunchtime when I was laughing with the other men. The Mexicans sat apart when they ate, just as they worked by themselves. Quiet. I rarely heard them say much to each other. All I could hear were their voices calling out sharply to one another, giving directions. Otherwise, when they stood briefly resting, they talked among themselves in voices too hard to overhear.

13 The contractor knew enough Spanish, and the Mexicans—or at least the oldest of them, their spokesman—seemed to know enough English to communicate. But because I was around, the contractor decided one day to make me his translator. (He assumed I could speak Spanish.) I did what I was told. Shyly I went over to tell the Mexicans that the *patrón* wanted them to do something else before they left for the day. As I started to speak, I was afraid with my old fear that I would be unable to pronounce the Spanish words. But it was a simple instruction I had to convey. I could say it in phrases.

14 The dark sweating faces turned toward me as I spoke. They stopped their work to hear me. Each nodded in response. I stood there. I wanted to say something more. But what could I say in Spanish, even if I could have pronounced the words right? Perhaps I just wanted to engage them in small talk, to be assured of their confidence, our familiarity. I thought for a moment to ask them where in Mexico they were from. Something like that. And maybe I wanted to tell them (a lie, if need be) that my parents were from the same part of Mexico.

15 I stood there.

16 Their faces watched me. The eyes of the man directly in front of me moved slowly over my shoulder, and I turned to follow his glance toward *el patrón* some distance away. For a moment I felt swept up by that glance into the Mexicans' company. But then I heard one of them returning to work. And then the others went back to work. I left them without saying anything more.

17 When they had finished, the contractor went over to pay them in cash. (He later told me that he paid them collectively—"for the job," though he wouldn't tell me their wages. He said something quickly about the good rate of exchange "in their own country.") I can still hear the loudly confident voice he used with the Mexicans. It was the sound of the *gringo* I had heard as a very young boy. And I can still hear the quiet, indistinct sounds of the Mexican, the oldest, who replied. At hearing that voice I was sad for the Mexicans. Depressed by their vulnerability. Angry at my-

self. The adventure of the summer seemed suddenly ludicrous. I would not shorten the distance I felt from *los pobres* with a few weeks of physical labor. I would not become like them. They were different from me.

18 After that summer, a great deal—and not very much really—changed in my life. The curse of physical shame was broken by the sun; I was no longer ashamed of my body. No longer would I deny myself the pleasing sensations of my maleness. During those years when middle-class black Americans began to assert with pride, "Black is beautiful," I was able to regard my complexion without shame. I am today darker than I ever was as a boy. I have taken up the middle-class sport of long-distance running. Nearly every day now I run ten or fifteen miles, barely clothed, my skin exposed to the California winter rain and wind or the summer sun of late afternoon. The torso, the soccer player's calves and thighs, the arms of the twenty-year-old I never was, I possess now in my thirties. I study the youthful parody shape in the mirror: the stomach lipped tight by muscle; the shoulders rounded by chin-ups; the arms veined strong. This man. A man. I meet him. He laughs to see me, what I have become.

19 The dandy. I wear double-breasted Italian suits and custom-made English shoes. I resemble no one so much as my father—the man pictured in those honeymoon photos. At that point in life when he abandoned the dandy's posture, I assume it. At the point when my parents would not consider going on vacation, I register at the Hotel Carlyle in New York and the Plaza Athenée in Paris. I am as taken by the symbols of leisure and wealth as they were. For my parents, however, those symbols became taunts, reminders of all they could not achieve in one lifetime. For me those same symbols are reassuring reminders of public success. I tempt vulgarity to be reassured. I am filled with the gaudy delight, the monstrous grace of the nouveau riche.

20 In recent years I have had occasion to lecture in ghetto high schools. There I see students of remarkable style and physical grace. (One can see more dandies in such schools than one ever will find in middle-class high schools.) There is not the look of casual assurance I saw students at Stanford display. Ghetto girls mimic high-fashion models. Their dresses are of bold, forceful color; their figures elegant, long; the stance theatrical. Boys wear shirts that grip at their overdeveloped muscular bodies. (Against a powerless future, they engage images of strength.) Bad nutrition does not yet tell. Great disappointment, fatal to youth, awaits

them still. For the moment, movements in school hallways are dancelike, a procession of postures in a sexual masque. Watching them, I feel a kind of envy. I wonder how different my adolescence would have been had I been free. . . . But no, it is my parents I see—their optimism during those years when they were entertained by Italian grand opera.

21 The registration clerk in London wonders if I have just been to Switzerland. And the man who carries my luggage in New York guesses the Caribbean. My complexion becomes a mark of my leisure. Yet no one would regard my complexion the same way if I entered such hotels through the service entrance. That is only to say that my complexion assumes its significance from the context of my life. My skin, in itself, means nothing. I stress the point because I know there are people who would label me "disadvantaged" because of my color. They make the same mistake I made as a boy, when I thought a disadvantaged life was circumscribed by particular occupations. That summer I worked in the sun may have made me physically indistinguishable from the Mexicans working nearby. (My skin was actually darker because, unlike them, I worked without wearing a shirt. By late August my hands were probably as tough as theirs.) But I was not one of *los pobres.* What made me different from them was an attitude of *mind,* my imagination of myself.

22 I do not blame my mother for warning me away from the sun when I was young. In a world where her brother had become an old man in his twenties because he was dark, my complexion was something to worry about. "Don't run in the sun," she warns me today. I run. In the end, my father was right—though perhaps he did not know how right or why—to say that I would never know what real work is. I will never know what he felt at his last factory job. If tomorrow I worked at some kind of factory, it would go differently for me. My long education would favor me. I could act as a public person—able to defend my interests, to unionize, to petition, to speak up—to challenge and demand. (I will never know what real work is.) I will never know what the Mexicans knew, gathering their shovels and ladders and saws.

23 Their silence stays with me now. The wages those Mexicans received for their labor were only a measure of their disadvantaged condition. Their silence is more telling. They lack a public identity. They remain profoundly alien. Persons apart. People lacking a union obviously, people without grounds. They depend upon the relative good will or fairness of their employers each

day. For such people, lacking a better alternative, it is not such an unreasonable risk.

24 Their silence stays with me. I have taken these many words to describe its impact. Only: the quiet. Something uncanny about it. Its compliance. Vulnerability. Pathos. As I heard their truck rumbling away, I shuddered, my face mirrored with sweat. I had finally come face to face with *los pobres.*

Suggestions for Discussion and Writing

1. Rodriguez narrates a series of experiences he had while working one summer between semesters in college. How are those experiences generalized into a thesis statement? Where is the statement presented?
2. What is the author's attitude toward his family? Toward the Mexicans he works with? Is he, for example, condescending, sympathetic, or snobbish?
3. Rodriguez's experiences in college and on the job led him to several self-discoveries. What were the most important of those discoveries?
4. If you have a cultural background different from that of most of your friends or fellow students, write an essay presenting insights you have gained as an *outsider.* Remember that your essay should have a *point*: a thesis based on your personal experience.
5. If you have worked while attending college, try your hand at writing an essay describing your reactions to your job. Consider such matters as the physical aspects of the job and your relationship to your fellow workers. Be sure to offer your readers a generalization or conclusion based on your experiences.

VIRGINIA WOOLF

The Death of the Moth

1 Moths that fly by day are not properly to be called moths; they do not excite that pleasant sense of dark autumn nights and ivy-blossom which the commonest yellow-underwing asleep in the shadow of the curtain never fails to rouse in us. They are hybrid creatures, neither gay like butterflies nor sombre like their

own species. Nevertheless the present specimen, with his narrow hay-coloured wings, fringed with a tassel of the same colour, seemed to be content with life. It was a pleasant morning, mid-September, mild, benignant, yet with a keener breath than that of the summer months. The plough was already scoring the field opposite the window, and where the share had been, the earth was pressed flat and gleamed with moisture. Such vigour came rolling in from the fields and then down beyond that it was difficult to keep the eyes strictly turned upon the book. The rooks too were keeping one of their annual festivities; soaring round the tree tops until it looked as if a vast net with thousands of black knots in it had been cast up into the air; which, after a few moments sank slowly down upon the trees until every twig seemed to have a knot at the end of it. Then, suddenly, the net would be thrown into the air again in a wider circle this time, with the utmost clamour and vociferation, as though to be thrown into the air and settle slowly down upon the tree tops were a tremendously exciting experience.

2 The same energy which inspired the rooks, the ploughmen, the horses, and even, it seemed, the lean bare-backed downs, sent the moth fluttering from side to side of his square of the window pane. One could not help watching him. One was, indeed, conscious of a queer feeling of pity for him. The possibilities of pleasure seemed that morning so enormous and so various that to have only a moth's part in life, and a day moth's at that, appeared a hard fate, and his zest in enjoying his meagre opportunities to the full, pathetic. He flew vigorously to one corner of his compartment, and, after waiting there a second, flew across to the other. What remained for him but to fly to a third corner and then to a fourth? That was all he could do, in spite of the size of the downs, the width of the sky, the far-off smoke of houses, and the romantic voice, now and then, of a steamer out at sea. What he could do he did. Watching him, it seemed as if a fibre, very thin but pure, of the enormous energy of the world had been thrust into his frail and diminutive body. As often as he crossed the pane, I could fancy that a thread of vital light became visible. He was little or nothing but life.

3 Yet, because he was so small, and so simple a form of the energy that was rolling in at the open window and driving its way through so many narrow and intricate corridors in my own brain and in those of other human beings, there was something marvelous as well as pathetic about him. It was as if someone had taken

a tiny bead of pure life and decking it as lightly as possible with down and feathers, had set it dancing and zigzagging to show us the true nature of life. Thus displayed one could not get over the strangeness of it. One is apt to forget all about life, seeing it humped and bossed and garnished and cumbered so that it has to move with the greatest circumspection and dignity. Again, the thought of all that life might have been had he been born in any other shape caused one to view his simple activities with a kind of pity.

4 After a time, tired by his dancing apparently, he settled on the window ledge in the sun, and, the queer spectacle being at an end, I forgot about him. Then, looking up, my eye was caught by him. He was trying to resume his dancing, but seemed either so stiff or so awkward that he could only flutter to the bottom of the windowpane; and when he tried to fly across it he failed. Being intent on other matters, I watched these futile attempts for a time without thinking, unconsciously waiting for him to resume his flight, as one waits for a machine, that has stopped momentarily, to start again without considering the reason of its failure. After perhaps a seventh attempt he slipped from the wooden ledge and fell, fluttering his wings, on to his back on the window sill. The helplessness of his attitude roused me. It flashed upon me that he was in difficulties; he could no longer raise himself; his legs struggled vainly. But, as I stretched out a pencil, meaning to help him to right himself, it came over me that the failure and awkwardness were the approach of death. I laid the pencil down again.

5 The legs agitated themselves once more. I looked as if for the enemy against which he struggled. I looked out of doors. What had happened there? Presumably it was midday, and work in the fields had stopped. Stillness and quiet had replaced the previous animation. The birds had taken themselves off to feed in the brooks. The horses stood still. Yet the power was there all the same, massed outside indifferent, impersonal, not attending to anything in particular. Somehow it was opposed to the little hay-coloured moth. It was useless to try to do anything. One could only watch the extraordinary efforts made by those tiny legs against an oncoming doom which could, had it chosen, have submerged an entire city, not merely a city, but masses of human beings; nothing, I knew, had any chance against death. Nevertheless after a pause of exhaustion the legs fluttered again. It was superb this last protest, and so frantic that he succeeded at last

in righting himself. One's sympathies, of course, were all on the side of life. Also, when there was nobody to care or to know, this gigantic effort on the part of an insignificant little moth, against a power of such magnitude, to retain what no one else valued or desired to keep, moved one strangely. Again, somehow, one saw life, a pure bead. I lifted the pencil again, useless though I knew it to be. But even as I did so, the unmistakable tokens of death showed themselves. The body relaxed, and instantly grew stiff. The struggle was over. The insignificant little creature now knew death. As I looked at the dead moth, this minute wayside triumph of so great a force over so mean an antagonist filled me with wonder. Just as life had been strange a few minutes before, so death was now as strange. The moth having righted himself now lay most decently and uncomplainingly composed. O yes, he seemed to say, death is stronger than I am.

Suggestions for Discussion and Writing

1. This essay falls into two sections, each corresponding to the behavior of the moth. What paragraphs comprise the first section? What links these paragraphs? Where does the second part begin? What is its topic?
2. How does Woolf's attitude toward the moth change in the two sections? Notice, for example, the words she uses to describe it in the first part: a "fibre, very thin but pure, of the enormous energy of the world," "a thread of vital light," and "little or nothing but life." Find the descriptive phrases in the second section that suggest a change of attitude toward the moth.
3. Woolf carefully relates the behavior of the moth to the activities outside the window. Point out examples of these parallels. Why are they important to the essay?
4. On one level, this essay is merely about the death of a moth. On another level, it is an analogy of life and death. When read this way, what do the moth's actions symbolize?
5. Woolf's meditation on life and death was prompted by a common occurrence: the death of a moth. Write an essay in which you present your response to a seemingly unimportant or trivial event in nature that you have observed.
6. Write an essay in which you describe an animal (it doesn't have to be as small or insignificant as an insect) from two different points of view—one objective, as a zoologist or other scientist might describe it, and one subjective, as a fiction writer or animal lover might describe it.

NORA EPHRON

On Never Having Been a Prom Queen

1 The other night, a friend of mine sat down at the table and informed me that if I was going to write a column about women, I ought to deal straight off with the subject most important to women in all the world. "What is that?" I asked. "Beauty," she said. I must have looked somewhat puzzled—as indeed I was—because she then went into a long and painful opening monologue about how she was losing her looks and I had no idea how terrible it was and that just recently an insensitive gentleman friend had said to her, "Michelle, you used to be such a beauty." I have no idea if this woman is really losing her looks—I have known her only a couple of years, and she looks pretty much the same to me—but she is certainly right in saying that I have no idea of what it is like. One of the few advantages to not being beautiful is that one usually gets better-looking as one gets older; I am, in fact, at this very moment gaining my looks. But what interested me about my response to my friend was that rather than feeling empathy for her—and I like to think I am fairly good at feeling empathy—I felt nothing. I like her very much, respect her, even believe she believes she is losing her looks, recognize her pain, but I just couldn't get into it.

2 Only a few days later, a book called *Memoirs of an Ex-Prom Queen,* by Alix Kates Shulman (Knopf), arrived in the mail. Shulman, according to the jacket flap, had written a "bitterly funny" book about "being female in America." I would like to read such a book. I would like to write such a book. As it turns out, however, Alix Shulman hasn't. What she has written is a book about the anguish and difficulty of being beautiful. And I realized, midway through the novel, that if there is anything more boring to me than the problems of big-busted women, it is the problems of beautiful women.

3 "They say it's worse to be ugly," Shulman writes. "I think it must only be different. If you're pretty, you are subject to one set

of assaults; if you're plain you are subject to another. Pretty, you may have more men to choose from, but you have more anxiety too, knowing your looks, which really have nothing to do with you, will disappear. Pretty girls have few friends. Kicked out of mankind in elementary school, and then kicked out of womankind in junior high, pretty girls have a lower birthrate and a higher mortality. It is the beauties like Marilyn Monroe who swallow twenty-five Nembutals on a Saturday night and kill themselves in their thirties."

4 Now I could take that paragraph one sentence at a time and pick nits (What about the pretty girls who *have* friends? What has Marilyn Monroe's death to do with all this? What does it mean to say that pretty girls have a lower birthrate—that they have fewer children or that there are less of them than there are of us?), but I prefer to say simply that it won't wash. There isn't an ugly girl in America who wouldn't exchange her problems for the problems of being beautiful; I don't believe there's a beautiful girl anywhere who would honestly prefer not to be. "They say it's worse to be ugly," Alix Shulman writes. Yes, they do say that. And they're right. It's also worse to be poor, worse to be orphaned, worse to be fat. Not just *different* from rich, families, and thin—actually worse. (I am a little puzzled as to why Ms. Shulman uses the words "plain" and "ugly" interchangeably; the difference between plain and ugly is as vast as the one between plain and pretty. As William Raspberry pointed out in a recent Washington *Post* column, ugly women are the most overlooked victims of discrimination in America.)

5 The point of all this is not about beauty—I hope I have made it clear that I don't know enough about beauty to make a point—but about divisions. I am separated from Alix Shulman and am in fact almost unable to judge her work because she is obsessed with being beautiful and I am obsessed with not being beautiful. We might as well be on separate sides altogether. And what makes me sad about the women's movement in general is my own inability, and that of so many other women, to get across such gulfs, to join hands, to unite on anything.

6 The women's liberation movement at this point in history makes the American Communist Party of the 1930s look like a monolith. I have been to meetings where the animosity between the gay and straight women was so strong and so unpleasant that I could not bear to be in the room. That is the most dramatic division in the movement, and one that has considerably

slowed its forward momentum; but there are so many others. There is acrimony between the single and married women, working women and housewives, childless women and mothers. I have even heard a woman defend her affection for cooking to an incredulous group who believed that to cook at all—much less to like it—was to swallow the worst sort of cultural conditioning. Once I tried to explain to a fellow feminist why I liked wearing makeup; she replied by explaining why she does not. Neither of us understood a word the other said.

7 Every so often, I turn on the television and see one of the movement leaders being asked some idiot question like, "Isn't the women's movement in favor of all women abandoning their children and going off to work?" (I can hear David Susskind asking it now.) The leader usually replies that the movement isn't in favor of all women doing anything; what the movement is about, she says, is options. She is right, of course. At its best, that is exactly what the movement is about. But it just doesn't work out that way. Because the hardest thing for us to accept is the right to those options. I hear myself saying those words: *What this movement is about is options.* I say it to friends who are frustrated, or housebound, or guilty, or child-laden, and what I am really thinking is, If you really got it together, the option you would choose is mine.

8 I would like to be able to leap across the gulf that divides me from Alix Shulman. After all, her experience is not totally foreign to me: once I had a date with someone who thought I was beautiful. He talked all night, while I—who spent years developing my conversational ability to compensate for my looks (my life has been spent in compensation)—said nothing. At the end of the evening, he made a pass at me, and I was insulted. So I understand. I recognize that people who are beautiful have problems. But so do people who get upset stomachs from raw onions, and men with blue-orange color blindness, and left-handed persons everywhere. I just can't get into it; what interests me these days tends to have more to do with the problems of women who were not prom queens in high school. I'm sorry about this—my point of view is not fair to Alix Shulman, or to my friend who thinks she is losing her looks, or to me, or to the movement. But that's where it is. I'm working on it. Like all things about liberation, sisterhood is difficult.

August 1972

Suggestions for Discussion and Writing

1. Ephron's thesis is generated as a result of a conversation with a friend and her reactions to a book, as well as by her own experiences. What is that thesis? Where is it stated?
2. This essay is divided into two main sections: paragraphs 1–4 and 5–8. What is the subject of the first section? Notice, for example, the first sentence of paragraph 5. What is the subject of the last section?
3. Ephron wrote this essay in 1972. If she were revising it today, can you think of any significant changes she might make that would reflect events of the last decade or so?
4. What is Ephron's real attitude (underneath her humor) toward the women's liberation movement? How do you know?
5. Ephron refers to a newspaper columnist in paragraph 4 who claims that ugly women are the most overlooked victims of discrimination in America. Can you think of other groups that are discriminated against but do not receive widespread support or recognition?
6. Ephron claims (paragraph 5) that it is difficult for women "to join hands, to unite on anything." Can you think of other movements and organizations to whom this might apply?
7. Adopting Ephron's humorous but sincere tone, write an essay in defense of being fat (or ugly). Male students may want to try an essay on never having been a football star.
8. If you are not comfortable with the preceding topics, write an essay titled, "On Being Female [*or* Male] in America."

CARL SAGAN

To Preserve a World Graced by Life

1 There is no issue more important than the avoidance of nuclear war. Whatever your interests, passions, or goals, they and you are threatened fundamentally by the prospect of nuclear war. We have achieved the capability for the certain destruction of our civilization and perhaps of our species as well. I find it incredible that any thinking person would not be concerned in the deepest way about this issue.

2 In the last twenty years, the United States and the Soviet

Union have accomplished something stunning and historic—the close-up examination of all those points of light, from Mercury to Saturn, that moved our ancestors to wonder and to science. Every one of these worlds is lovely and instructive, and there are premonitions and stirrings of life on Titan and Iapetus and some other worlds. But apparently life does not exist on these worlds. Something has gone wrong. Some critical step was lacking. Or perhaps life arose once and subsequently died out. The lesson we have learned is that life is a comparative rarity, that you can have twenty or thirty or forty worlds and on only one of them does life appear and sustain itself.

3 What has evolved on our planet is not just life, not just grass or mice or beetles or microbes, but beings with a great intelligence, with a capacity to anticipate the future consequences of present actions, with the ability even to leave their home world and seek out life elsewhere. What a waste it would be if, after four billion years of tortuous biological evolution, the dominant organism on the planet contrived its own annihilation. No species is guaranteed its tenure on this planet. And we've been here for only about a million years, we, the first species that has devised the means for its self-destruction. I look at those other worlds, cratered, airless, cold, here and there coated with a hopeful stain of organic matter, and I remind myself what an astonishing thing has happened here. How privileged we are to live, to influence and control our future. I believe we have an obligation to fight for that life, to struggle not just for ourselves, but for all those creatures who came before us, and to whom we are beholden, and for all those who, if we are wise enough, will come after us. There is no cause more urgent, no dedication more fitting for us than to strive to eliminate the threat of nuclear war. No social convention, no political system, no economic hypothesis, no religious dogma is more important.

4 The dangers of nuclear war are, in a way, well-known. But in a way they are not well-known, because there is a psychological factor—psychiatrists call it denial—that makes us feel it's so horrible that we might as well not think about it. That element of denial is, I believe, one of the most serious problems we face. If everyone had a profound and immediate sense of the actual consequences of nuclear war, we would be much more willing to confront and challenge national leaders of all nations when they present narrow and self-serving arguments for the continuation of mutual nuclear terror.

5 Denial, however, is remarkably strong and there are many cases in human history where, faced with the clearest signs of extreme danger, people refuse to take simple corrective measures. Some twenty-five years ago, a tsunami, a tidal wave in the Pacific, was approaching the Hawaiian Islands. The people there were given many hours warning to flee the lowlands and run to safety. But the idea of a great, crashing wave of water thirty feet high surging inland, inundating and washing your house out to sea was so unbelievable, so unpleasant, that many people simply ignored the warning and were killed. In fact, one schoolteacher thought the report to be so interesting that she gathered up her children and took them down to the water's edge to watch. I believe that one of the most important jobs that scientists have in this dialogue on the dangers of nuclear war is to state very clearly what the dangers are.

6 The evidence is compelling that weapons proliferation leads to a substantial, indeed to an exponential growth of nuclear weapons worldwide. The situation is like that of two or more coupled linear differential equations; each nation's rate of growth of nuclear weapons is proportional to some other nation's stockpile of nuclear weapons. No nation is ever satisfied that it has enough weapons. Any "improvements" by the other side force us to "improve" our weapons systems. Exponentials not only go up, they also go down, suggesting that a concerted effort to increase the nuclear weapons systems stockpiled by one nation will result in a corresponding increase by other nations. But likewise, a concerted effort by any one nuclear power to decrease its stockpile might very well have as a consequence a decline in the stockpiles of other nations, and, at least up to a point, the process can be self-sustaining. I therefore raise the question of whether the nation that first developed and used nuclear weapons on human populations has some special obligation to decelerate the nuclear arms race. There is a wide range of possible options, including small and safe unilateral steps to test the responses of other nations, and major bilateral and multilateral efforts to negotiate substantial, verifiable force reductions.

7 Disarmament, done in such a way as to preserve deterrence against a nuclear attack, is in everybody's interest. It's only a matter of getting started. Of course there's some risk. It takes courage. But as Einstein asked, in precisely this context, "What is the alternative?"

8 An extraterrestrial being coming upon the Earth might note

that a few nations, one of them being the United States, actually have organizations devoted to peace as well as to war. The United States has something called the Arms Control and Disarmament Agency. But its budget is less than one hundred thousandth of the budget of the Department of Defense. This is a numerical measure of the relative importance that we place on finding ways to make war and finding ways to make peace. Is it possible that the intelligence, compassion, and even self-interest of the American people have been thoroughly exhausted in the pursuit of solutions to the threat of nuclear war? Or is it more likely that so little attention is given to it, so little encouragement is provided to bright young people to consider this issue, that we have not even begun to find innovative and imaginative solutions?

9 Through the courageous examination of these deep painful issues, and through the political process, I am convinced we can make an important contribution toward preserving and enhancing the life that has graced our small world.

Suggestions for Discussion and Writing

1. According to Sagan, how can we avoid nuclear war? If his solution is so obvious, why aren't we disarming? Are there any risks or fallacies in his reasoning?
2. As paragraph 3 suggests, the author is an astronomer. How does he use his background to support his argument?
3. Where is the thesis-statement in this essay? Why does Sagan place it there?
4. What is the purpose of the references to the tsunami (paragraph 5) and the comparison of the budgets of the Arms Control and Disarmament Agency and the Department of Defense (paragraph 8)? How do they bolster his thesis-statement?
5. If you disagree with Sagan's stand on nuclear weapons, write a rebuttal. Your thesis-statement might follow the pattern "Although Carl Sagan's arguments for disarmament at first glance appear logical and informed, his ideas are unworkable because ________."
6. If you have strong opinions about another threat to humanity, such as the "greenhouse effect" or over-population, present your views in an essay. To get a manageable angle on your topic, be sure that your essay contains a well-pointed thesis-statement.

3
Your Paper's Basic Structure

BEGINNING, MIDDLE, END

As Aristotle long ago pointed out, works that spin their way through time need a beginning, a middle, and an end to be complete. You need a clear beginning to give your essay character and direction so the reader can tell where he is going and can look forward with expectation. Your beginning, of course, will set forth your thesis. You need a middle to amplify and fulfill. This will be the body of your argument, the bulk of your essay. You need an end to let readers know that they have arrived. This will be your final paragraph, a summation and reassertion of your theme. So give your essay the three-part *feel* of completion, of beginning, middle, and end. Many a freshman's essay has no structure and leaves no impression. It is all chaotic middle. It has no beginning, it just starts; it has no end, it just stops, burned out at two in the morning.

The beginning must feel like a beginning, not just like an accident. It should be at least a full paragraph that leads your reader into the subject and culminates with your thesis. The end, likewise, should be a full paragraph, one that drives the point home, pushes the implications wide, and brings the reader to rest, back on the fundamental thesis with a sense of completion. When we consider paragraphing in the next chapter, we will look more closely at beginning paragraphs and end paragraphs. The "middle" of your essay, which constitutes its bulk, needs further structural consideration now.

MIDDLE TACTICS

Arrange Your Points in Order of Increasing Interest

Once your thesis has sounded the challenge, your reader's interest is probably at its highest pitch. He wants to see how you can prove so outrageous a thing, or to see what the arguments are for this thing he has always believed but never tested. Each step of the way into your demonstration, he is learning more of what you have to say. But, unfortunately, his interest may be relaxing as it becomes satisfied: the reader's normal line of attention is a progressive decline, arching down like a wintry graph. Against this decline you must oppose your forces, making each successive point more interesting. And save your best till last. It is as simple as that.

Here, for example, is the middle of a short, three-paragraph essay on the thesis that "Working your way through college is valuable." The student's three points ascend in interest:

> **The student who works finds that the experience is worth more than the money. First, he learns to budget his time. He now supports himself by using time he would otherwise waste, and he studies harder in the time he has left because he knows it is limited. Second, he makes real and lasting friends on the job, as compared to the other casual acquaintances around the campus. He has shared rush hours, and nighttime cleanups with the dishes piled high, and conversation and jokes when business is slow. Finally, he gains confidence in his ability to get along with all kinds of people, and to make his own way. He sees how businesses operate, and how waitresses, for instance, can work cheerfully at a really tiring job without much hope for the future. He gains an insight into the real world, which is a good contrast to the more intellectual and idealistic world of the college student.**

Again, each successive item should be more interesting than the last, or you will suddenly seem anticlimactic. Actually, minor regressions of interest make no difference so long as the whole tendency is uphill and your last item clearly the best. Suppose, for example, you were to try a thesis about cats. You decide that four points would make up the case, and that you might arrange them in the following order of increasing interest: (1) cats are affectionate but make few demands; (2) cats actually look out for themselves; (3) cats have, in fact, proved extremely useful to society throughout history in controlling mice and other plaguy rodents; (4) cats satisfy some human need for a touch of the jungle, savagery in repose, ferocity in silk, and have been worshiped for the exotic power they still seem to represent. It may be, as you write, that you will find Number 1 developing attractive or amusing instances, and perhaps even virtually usurping the whole essay. Numbers 2, 3, and 4 should then be moved ahead as interesting but brief preliminaries.

Interests vary, of course. This is the point. And various subjects will suggest different kinds of importance: from small physical details to large, from incidental thought to basic principles. Sometimes chronology will supply a naturally ascending order of interest: as a tennis match or hockey game reaches its climax; or as in any contest against natural hazards and time itself, like crossing a glacier with supplies and endurance dwindling. Space, too, may offer natural progressions of interest, as you move from portico to inner shrine. But usually interest ascends in ideas, and these quite naturally ascend from your own interest in your subject, in which, with a little thought, you can tell which points to handle first and which to arrange for more and more importance, saving best till last. In short, your middle structure should range from least important to most important, from simple to complex, from narrow to broad, from pleasant to hilarious, from mundane to metaphysical—whatever "leasts" and "mosts" your subject suggests.

ACKNOWLEDGING AND DISPOSING OF THE OPPOSITION

Your cat essay, because it is moderately playful, can proceed rather directly, throwing only an occasional bone of concession to the dogs, and perhaps most of your essays, as you discuss the

Constitutional Convention or explain a poem, will have no opposition to worry about. But a serious controversial argument demands one organizational consideration beyond the simple structure of ascending interest. Although you have taken your stand firmly as a *pro,* you will have to allow scope to the *cons,* or you will seem not to have thought much about your subject. The more opposition you can manage as you carry your point, the more triumphant you will seem, like a high-wire artist daring the impossible.

This balancing of *pros* against *cons* is one of the most fundamental orders of thought: the dialectic order, which is the order of argument, one side pitted against the other. Our minds naturally swing from side to side as we think. In dialectics, we simply give one side an argumentative edge, producing a thesis that cuts a clear line through any subject: "This is better than that." The basic organizing principle here is to get rid of the opposition first, and to end on your own side. Probably you will have already organized your thesis-sentence in a perfect pattern for your *con-pro* argument:

> **Despite their many advantages, welfare payments. . . . Although dogs are fine pets, cats. . . .**

The subordinate clause (see 250–52) states the subordinate part of your argument, which is your concession to the *con* viewpoint; your main clause states your main argument. As the subordinate clause comes first in your thesis sentence, so does the subordinate argument in your essay. Sentence and essay both reflect a natural psychological principle. You want, and the reader wants, to get the opposition out of the way. And you want to end on your best foot. (You might try putting the opposition last, just to see how peculiarly the last word insists on seeming best, and how, when stated last by you, the opposition's case seems to be your own.)

Your opposition, of course, will vary. Some of your audience will agree with you but for different reasons. Others may disagree hotly. You need, then, to imagine what these varying objections might be, as if you were before a meeting in open discussion, giving the hottest as fair a hearing as possible. You probably would not persuade them, but you would ease the pressure and probably persuade the undecided by your reasonable stance. Asking what objections might arise will give you the opposing points that your essay must meet—and overcome.

GET RID OF THE OPPOSITION FIRST. This is the essential tactic of argumentation. You have introduced and stated your thesis in your beginning paragraph. Now start the middle with a paragraph of concession to the *cons:*

> **Dog-lovers, of course, have tradition on their side. Dogs are indeed affectionate and faithful. . . .**

And with that paragraph out of the way, go to bat for the cats, showing their superiority to dogs in every point. In a very brief essay, you can use the opposition itself to introduce your thesis in the first paragraph, and dispose of your opponents at the same time:

> **Shakespeare begins *Romeo and Juliet* with ominous warnings about fate. His lovers are "star-crossed," he says: they are doomed from the first by their contrary stars, by the universe itself. They have sprung from "fatal loins." Fate has already determined their tragic end. The play then unfolds a succession of unlucky and presumably fated accidents. Nevertheless, we soon discover that Shakespeare really blames the tragedy not on fate but on human stupidity and error.**

But usually your beginning paragraph will lead down to your thesis somewhat neutrally, and you will attack your opposition head-on in paragraph two, as you launch into the middle.

If the opposing arguments seem relatively slight and brief, you can get rid of them neatly all together in one paragraph before you get down to your case. Immediately after your beginning, which has stated your thesis, you write a paragraph of concession: "Of course, security is a good thing. No one wants people begging." And so on to the end of the paragraph, deflating every conceivable objection. Then back to the main line: "But the price in moral decay is too great." The structure of the essay, paragraph by paragraph, might be diagrammed something like the scheme shown in Diagram I:

Diagram I

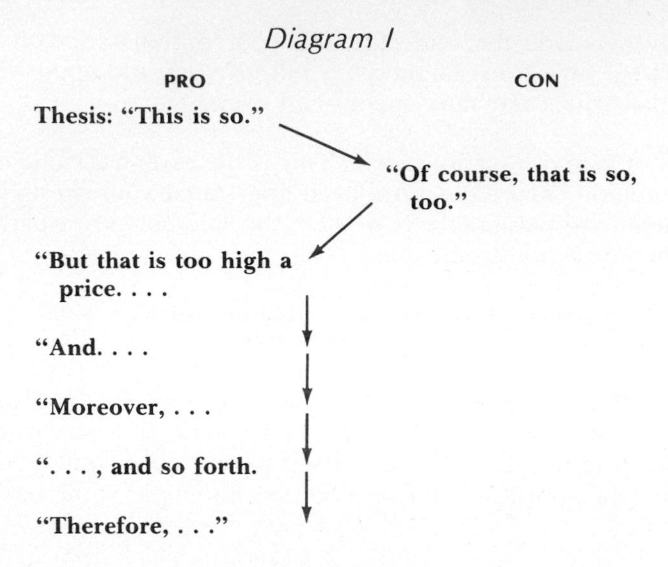

If the opposition is more considerable, demolish it point by point, using a series of *cons* and *pros,* in two or three paragraphs, before you steady down to your own side. Each paragraph can be a small argument that presents the opposition, then knocks it flat —a kind of Punch-and-Judy show: "We must admit that. . . . But. . . ." And down goes the poor old opposition again. Or you can swing your argument through a number of alternating paragraphs: first your beginning, the thesis, then a paragraph to the opposition *(con),* then one for your side *(pro),* then another paragraph of *con,* and so on. The main point, again, is this: *get rid of the opposition first.* One paragraph of concession right after your thesis will probably handle most of your adversaries, and the more complicated argumentative swingers, like the ones shown in Diagram II, will develop naturally as you need them.

You will notice that *But* and *however* are always guides for the *pros,* serving as switches back to the main line. Indeed, *But, however,* and *Nevertheless* are the basic *pros. But* always heads its turning sentence (not followed by a comma); *nevertheless* usually does (followed by a comma). I am sure, however, that *however* is always better buried in the sentence between commas. "However, . . ." at a sentence's beginning is the habit of heavy prose. *But* is for the quick turn; the inlaid *however* for the more elegant sweep.

The structural line of your arguments, then, might look like Diagram II:

Diagram II. Controlling Handguns—Pro and Con

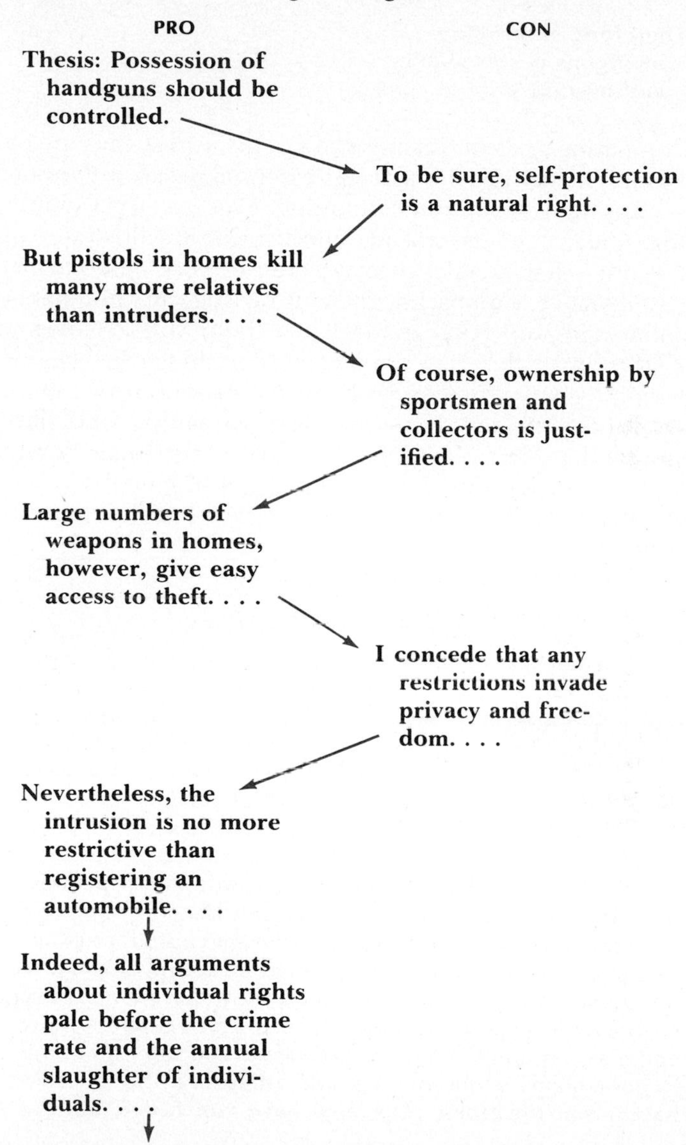

↓

Besides, handguns kill thousands more in the United States than in any other country.

↓

Therefore, controlling handguns is reasonable and necessary.

Comparing and contrasting two poems, two stories, two ball players, are further instances of this essential process of thought, of this important way to understanding. You may wish simply to set two similars, or dissimilars, side by side to illustrate some larger point—that excellence may come in very different packages, for instance. Comparing and contrasting can illuminate the unfamiliar with the familiar, or it can help you discover and convey to your readers new perspectives on things well known—two popular singers, two of Shakespeare's sonnets, two nursery rhymes. But, whether or not you are presenting one side as superior to the other, the structural tactic is the same: compare point for point, so long as the comparison illuminates.

Here is a short *pro-con* essay that gets rid of the opposition early and in one paragraph.

Woman and Human Superiority

Woman has kept the home fire burning for eons, probably since the discovery of fire. Her place has been in the home, and men have been all too happy to keep her in her place. Men are usually taller, stronger, and more aggressive, as war paths through forest and battlefield and stock market have demonstrated. Women themselves tend to give men the edge of superiority, if the men haven't already grabbed it for themselves. But although the weaker sex has been outshone and outshown in many ways, women are actually superior in the most fundamental qualities.

Of course, men are more muscular, but both the actuarial statistics and accounts of extended hardship, like that of the Donner Party in the last century, show that women have more physical endurance. Pictures of women runners at the end of marathons like the annual Boston run show them still in good shape while the men are collapsing, though both have given their best. The men have run faster, but the

women have outlasted just as they will in the race of life. Women are also immune to a number of sex-linked diseases, which, like hemophilia, they carry while the men succumb. Women have achieved less in the arts and sciences, but actually their brains are bigger in proportion to their weight. Clearly, they have had less time and motivation to compete.

Their achievement and motivation lie where their true superiority is: in the compassion that nurtures and holds together the human race that men seem bent on tearing apart. Compassion distinguishes humanity from inhumanity. Jane Goodall, who, *In the Shadow of Man* (1971), found chimpanzees so very human in many ways, saw their indifference toward their suffering fellows as the crucial distinction. Woman has nurtured the young and the aged from long before that first fire put her in her place. If, as some anthropologists believe, man learned to walk by carrying food back to the wife and kids, he learned this consideration from the mother who cared for him during the human infant's extended dependency. Woman's superiority lies in her instinctive sympathy, her caring, her loving. As Ashley Montagu says, "*It is the function of woman to teach men how to be human.*"* Women may well catch up in the arts and sciences, in business and government, but if we ever achieve a peace on earth in which humanity can fulfill itself, we will do so because men have at last caught up to woman's true superiority.

THE INDUCTIVE STRUCTURE

The natural dialectical swing of the way we think gives us the basic *pro-con* structure. Our two essential directions of thinking —induction and deduction—provide structures for organizing an essay. In fact, we have been talking about deductive structure all along: setting your Big Idea, your thesis, then demonstrating, illustrating, and arguing its validity in detail, showing the parts that support the whole. This is the essay's most useful structure.

---

*"The Natural Superiority of Women," *Saturday Review* (1 March 1952):35—to which I am indebted for the main point and several details.

But the inductive structure, though more infrequent, can give your essays variety. Inductive reasoning starts with details and, considering *pros* and *cons,* works up to their significance. An inductive essay follows this same pattern. The writer knows where he is going, but he leads the reader from detail to significant detail upward to his thesis, simulating an inductive search and taking the reader along. Both inductive and deductive structures thus follow an ascending order of interest, considering *pros* and *cons* along the way. The inductive saves the opening thesis, however, for the end. You lead your reader in—by successive questions and their dismissal, or partial answers—to your main and conclusive point. "Is it this? Well, no." "Then may it be this? No, not exactly this either." "Then how about this? Ah, yes, this is it." The deductive order, beginning with your thesis and then explaining it, is clearer. But the inductive order has suspense, an intellectual excitement, if you can keep your answer from slipping out.

Inductive order works best for short essays, since you must keep the cat in the bag, and you can't keep him in too long. You use a question for your thesis-sentence and then simulate your speculation. Here is an inductive paragraph from an interview with George Harris, a man reminiscing about the Depression:

Topical Question

***What was the worst thing about the Depression?* Well, I don't know. I guess**

Answer 1

***for some folks it was losing their savings.* For us that wasn't so bad. I only had about $400 in the McLain County Bank when it closed and I got some of that back later, about ten cents on the dollar. Then too,**

Answer 2

***being out of work was rough for a lot of people.* But even that wasn't so bad for me. I lost my job with the coal company in 1931, but we lived on a farm. And with that and some odd jobs I picked up, I managed to keep pretty busy until I got a steady job again. Of course, I know**

Answer 3

***a lot of people didn't have enough to eat or enough to wear during the Depression.* For us that wasn't too bad. We grew most of our own food, and my wife is pretty handy at sewing, so we got by. Nothing very fancy, you understand, but we managed. No, I guess for us**

Main Answer (Thesis)

***the worst thing about the Depression was we got to feeling after a while that times just weren't ever going to get better.* It just went on too long. For us, things got a little rough in 1931 and they stayed pretty rough until I got a job with the Highway Commission in 1938. Seven years is a long time to keep hoping. It just went on so long.**

This will give you an idea of inductive order. You may well use a short inductive section in a longer essay, especially for dismissing the opposition's arguments by putting them as questions ("Do we want unlimited freedom?") and then reducing them to absurdities. But a wholly inductive essay is usually short, and you won't find many of these, because your answer, your thesis, keeps slipping out of the bag and spoiling your surprise.

THE DEDUCTIVE STRUCTURE

Hang Your Essay from Your Big Idea

The deductive structure is basic, much more widely used, and useful, than the inductive one, because it sustains itself page after page, even through chapters in a whole book. You set down your thesis, your general proposition, then *explain* it in detail and at length, presenting *pros* and *cons* as needed. The mode of induction is question and partial answer; the mode of deduction is assertion and explanation. As we have seen, however, the usual deductive order does not simply begin with your Big Idea and then dwindle down to nothing. You match some of the inductive's suspense by saving your best for last. You can even include a short inductive paragraph or two for more suspense and variety. You start with your thesis, then jump down to your smallest small and work progressively uphill until you again reach your thesis, which is now restated as your conclusion and rounded off in a concluding paragraph. Again, the deductive order is the normal one we have been talking about all along.

To change Mr. Harris's inductive rumination about the Depression into a deductive structure, we make his opening question a thesis to be demonstrated: not "What was the worst thing about the Depression?" but "The worst thing about the Depression was its hopeless duration." In the following example, notice how deduction expands the inductive structure in detail, thought, and explanation. Notice how it uses first-person statement, which fell into an inductive pattern, as a piece of evidence in the more ample deductive structure, still giving the facts as Harris stated them.

Topic *For most Americans, the stock market crash was not the worst thing about the Depression.* True, it carried away billions of dollars of investors' money, but relatively few of us felt directly affected. Few of us owned stock, and for most of us the market collapse was something that happened to other people, not to us. Of course, as we found out, the stock-market collapse was only the trigger, and soon more and more Americans found their lives directly affected. By 1932, twenty-five percent of the workers had no jobs. Yet, for many Americans, the worst thing about the Depression was not the bank closures, or being out of work, or even short-

Thesis ages of food and clothing. For many of us, *the worst thing about the Depression was that it lasted so long we almost gave up hoping that times would ever get better.* George Harris of Wellsburg, West Virginia, is a good example of how the Depression hit most of us.

Demon-stration *In 1931, Mr. Harris had a job with the Green Coal Company as a tender on a boat that pushed coal barges up and down the Ohio River.* His income was generally good, and Mr. Harris had managed to buy a small farm just outside town. *But cutbacks in industrial production,* particularly in the production of steel, soon *forced cutbacks in coal mining as well.* And in August of 1931, *Mr. Harris was laid off.* The next year, in 1932, *the McLain County Bank closed, and with it went the only savings the Harrises had,* $400, although later he did manage to collect ten percent of his lost savings. And so *for the next seven years, Mr. Harris bounced from job to job,* whatever he could get: a few days here, a few days there. *He was thus able to hold onto his small farm,* and on it he raised most of the food for the Harris family for the next seven years. *Mrs. Harris, too, helped to cut corners* by making most of the family's clothes, and by repairing things when they wore out. In this way, taking it one day at a time, and living as simply and as frugally as possible, *the Harrises managed to get by until, in 1938, Mr. Harris once again got a secure and well-paying job* with the County Road Commission.

Restatement *So the Harrises are a good example of how the Depression hit many Americans.* They lost some savings, they lost their jobs, they had to tighten their belts, but they managed to get by. *For them, the worst thing about the Depression was not the deprivation; it was simply that the Depression went on year after year.* As Mr. Harris says, "Seven years is a long time to keep hoping. It just went on so long."

THE HYBRID STRUCTURE

Halfway between, many essayists blend deduction with induction. They trim a fully assertive thesis about welfare to "We need some system to help those in need." They ask, "How should one plan a vacation?" They have the answers, as we know, and they feed them to us in successive steps of significance: "First, decide where you want to go." But the essential mode is deductive. The essayist knows, or discovers, what he believes, and persuades with successively convincing points. His thesis is open-ended, merely implied by a leading question, or suggested indirectly in the first paragraph or so, as in the opening of E. B. White's "Farewell, My Lovely":

> **I see by the new Sears Roebuck catalogue that it is still possible to buy an axle for a 1909 Model T Ford, but I am not deceived. The great days have faded, the end is in sight. Only one page in the current catalogue is devoted to parts and accessories for the Model T; yet everyone remembers springtimes when the Ford gadget section was larger than men's clothing, almost as large as household furnishings. The last Model T was built in 1927, and the car is fading from what scholars call the American scene—which is an understatement, because to a few million people who grew up with it, the old Ford practically *was* the American scene.**
>
> **It was a miracle God had wrought. And it was patently the sort of thing that could only happen once. Mechanically uncanny, it was like nothing that had ever come to the world before. Flourishing industries rose and fell with it. As a vehicle, it was hard-working, commonplace, heroic; and it often seemed to transmit those qualities to the persons who rode in it. My own generation identifies it with Youth, with its gaudy, irretrievable excitements; before it fades into the mist, I would like to pay it the tribute of the sigh that is not a sob, and set down random entries in a shape somewhat less cumbersome than a Sears Roebuck catalogue.***

---

*© 1936, 1964, The New Yorker Magazine, Inc. From *Essays of E. B. White* (New York: Harper & Row, 1977): 162, originally published in *The New Yorker* in 1936 over the pseudonym "Lee Strout White." Richard L. Strout had submitted a manuscript on the Ford, and White, with his collaboration, rewrote it.

A fully inductive essay might have posed the question "Why did the Model T dominate the American scene?" A deductive thesis might have been "The Model T caught the American heart and mind because it was unique, exciting, and heroically serviceable." We get White's point indirectly, but it is clearly there, by the end of the second paragraph, setting the deductive frame for his not-so-random entries.

EXERCISES

1. *Write three con-and-pro thesis-sentences beginning "Although. . . ."*

2. *For the following assertions, write one argument against and one argument for. Now combine your statements into one thesis-sentence:*

EXAMPLE *Assertion: Movies should not be censored.*

Con: *Children should not be exposed to obscene and explicitly sexual images on the screen.*

Pro: *Obscenity is far too subjective a thing for any person to define for anyone else.*

Thesis-Statement: *Although young people probably should not be exposed to explicit sex in films, movies still should not be censored because obscenity is so subjective that no one can legitimately serve as censor for the rest of us.*

1. Assertion: Discussion classes are superior to lectures.
2. Assertion: Rapid and convenient transit systems must be built in our cities.
3. Assertion: The federal government should subsidize large companies forced near bankruptcy.
4. Assertion: Medical schools should reduce the time required for a degree in general medicine from four years to two.
5. Assertion: States should prohibit the sale of beverages in nonreturnable containers.

3. *Trim three of these into open-ended "hybrid" theses, like "We need some system to help those in need" or the question "How should one plan a vacation?"*

4. *Write a dialectical swinger, an essay following Diagrams I or II (62–64).*

Readings

Each of these four pieces handles the basic pro-and-con dialectics of thought differently. An anonymous horsewoman sets up her dialectics in a neat opening paragraph and a thesis so clear that half of her contrast, the cat, can then vanish—only to reappear and make her point at the end. Walker Percy sets forth the traditional diagnosis of depression and its various treatments, then proceeds, in a series of pro-and-con paragraphs, to replace them with his own unconventional cure. William Buckley knocks down his opposition with a barrage of jabs that counters each argument raised by his opponents. Jonathan Swift's classic essay is in fact a dialogue in which his shocking, literal arguments pose the dark side of the argument against his unspoken but real intention. All of these selections illustrate how essential the dialectical swing is to any question we can raise, or to any idea we can assert.

[Changing Horses in Mid-Dream]

1 Sometimes I make scientific discoveries that I would like to share with the world, but because I don't have the sort of proof scientific journals require, my findings, I know, would not be accepted. Nevertheless, I write them down just to see how they look on paper. A recent discovery has to do with an important difference between the minds of cats (predators) and horses (herbivores). Herbivores live in the present. For predators, the future is all.

2 I have two horses. One of them, Sunny, is a pinto pony about fourteen hands high. I got him fifteen years ago, when my son went away to school and I was lonely. The pony is very pretty, with flashy chestnut-and-white markings and a neck that can arch like those of the horses in Greek marbles. But he is small and has faults—a balky disposition and a jolting trot, owing to his short stride. After I'd had Sunny a few years, I was invited to ride a friend's mare, Maisie, and fell in love with her. She was considerably bigger—a nice-looking, eighteen-year-old chestnut with smooth gaits and a responsiveness that made riding her an easy thing, like dancing with a good dancer. I bought Maisie and retired Sunny. They have spent a peaceful decade grazing in my pasture. They look beautiful together. The chestnut patches on Sunny's sleek hide match Maisie's coat perfectly, and Sunny's white mane and tail heighten the whiteness of the daisies in June and the Queen Anne's lace later in the summer.

3 However, ten years passed, and Maisie was twenty-eight. She still looked fine, but the summer before last, when I rode her, I found that though she still had plenty of life—at a light touch, she would, as always, break into her airy trot—there were also unexpected little near-mishaps along the trail that had never happened before. A root would trip her. She would lurch, and I would lurch. We always recovered together, but it was a little scary all the same. The vet came and looked her over. She was remarkably sound, he said, but twenty-eight years is a lot of years.

4 I like this vet. He is a tall, casual young man, friendly and kind. He doesn't scorn to make calls on what they call in the trade "a backyard horse," whereas a lot of vets won't come unless you have a string of valuable show horses. I stood holding Maisie in the bright stable yard and chatted with the vet. He pointed out that riding a horse that stumbles has its dangers. Sooner or later, she might go down. "You can ride her very slow, on level ground," he said. "Or else"—and here I was aware of a faintly quizzical smile as he gazed at the two of us—"you might look for another horse."

5 The summer of 1979 was a difficult summer for me. I had little time for anything except a long, grueling piece of work that kept me grinding away at the typewriter day after day. I seldom rode.

The work was so filled with tension that at night it took a long time to go to sleep. To pass the time and try to relax, I revived a childhood habit of deliberately turning my thoughts to something beautiful, something wonderful to contemplate, something I wanted very much. Now my choice was a horse. Next summer, when my work was finished and I was free again, I would buy a new horse. I feel about beautiful animals the way some people feel about art—enraptured and covetous. I decided I would buy a very beautiful horse. This must, after all, be my last horse. A horse aged eight or ten (when horses begin to be sensible) would last the rest of my riding days. Therefore, I would get the most beautiful horse I could find. Money wouldn't matter. I began to picture what I would like most. The image that became fixed in my mind was a white mare—possibly an Arab. She would have a delicate head, small, perfect feet, a lovely conformation, smooth gaits. She must be small, so that mounting wouldn't be difficult. I was able to picture her completely—a white horse grazing in a green pasture—and feel her under me as I imagined riding her through the fields and into the woods. Night after night, these thoughts put me to sleep.

6 This spring, I made a phone call to a man who breeds horses and asked him what he had to sell. I didn't mention my fantasy horse, because in the light of day it sounded absurd to shop for something so specific. He described a number of unsuitable horses and then said, "I do have a brood mare I'm thinking of selling. She may be a bit high-priced for you, but she's a real beauty." I asked what sort of horse she was, and he said she was an Arab, with elegant conformation and gaits. "How big?" I asked. "On the small side," he replied. "About fourteen two." I had an almost eerie feeling as I asked what color the mare was. He answered, "White." I made an appointment to see her the next day.

7 When I got to the farm, the owner took me into the stable where the mare, named Rassi, was. She was in a box stall. At the sight of us, she was on her toes—ears forward, nostrils quivering. She was lovely. The man snapped a shank to her halter and brought her out. She snorted and danced a little in the aisle. When I patted her neck, she shied nervously. "That doesn't mean anything," the man said. "She's really gentle, but she hasn't been handled much lately. Wait until you see her

move. This mare has wings on her feet." Rassi's owner picked up a lunge line, and we walked out to the meadow. She arched her neck like a horse in a Grecian marble—she was the color of marble, too—and her small black hooves, neat and perfect, danced on the green turf. She tossed her head, looking at everything, and the owner—a strong man—took a tight grip on the shank. I could see his muscles strain as he held her. In the center of the meadow, at the crest of a little hill, he let out the line and Rassi took off, trotting in a wide circle at the end of the tether. She had been lovely before. Now she was breathtaking. Just as the owner had said, she had wings on her feet. As she extended her trot, she seemed hardly to touch the ground. Her head high, ears pricked, she fixed her gaze on the horizon as though if released she would simply soar across the meadow and into the woods. She cantered, then galloped. Her mane and tail had the grace of flowing water: the enchanted horse.

8 Rassi's owner slowed her down and pulled her in. "What do you think?" he asked. "Did you ever see such power? When you're on her, it's just like floating." Then he explained that though he would like me to ride her, he had no bridle or saddle—all his tack had been sent off to a horse show. He suggested I come back. I said I would telephone him and make a date. He led Rassi to a pasture, where other horses were grazing. The moment he unsnapped the lead, she was off like an arrow. She galloped around once and then, with the quick change of mood characteristic of horses, settled down to graze. A horse's thoughts center on the present: a mouthful of grass, then another; sudden alarm at something unexpected, such as a rabbit starting up; then quietness again when the danger is over. It makes sense for herbivores to think that way. They have no need to scheme or to plan. They have only one need—to evade the predator as long as possible. For them, each moment is sufficient unto itself.

9 I said goodbye and drove home, thinking, of course, about Rassi. She remained as clear in my mind's eye as the white mare of my fantasy with which this quest had begun. But there was now an added element in the picture: her hot, nervous temperament and the man's arm muscles straining as he held her. By the time I got home, I had made my decision. I knew that I wanted her even more now that she was real, but I was afraid of

her. Ten years ago, I could have handled her, but not now. With all that power and spirit, anything might happen, and I wouldn't be strong enough, quick enough, brave enough to cope. Rassi was ideal for someone young, but not for me.

10 It was late afternoon, and I made a drink and took it out on the porch and tried to read the paper. The air was soft and calm, and the sun slanted beautifully through the leaves of overhanging trees, but the birds were noisy and distracting. I couldn't read. I thought, It is very foolish to get a new horse and risk your neck. Any new horse could give you trouble. And, face it, you don't ride that much anymore. Stick with Maisie and just go out for long, slow walks. If you only walk her, she'll be good for some years yet. While I was thinking these things, my black cat was in my lap. Like Maisie, she has slowed down lately. She used to hunt far out in the meadow, but now she knows her limitations and sticks pretty close to the shelter of the house. I was a little surprised when she jumped off my lap and went out on the lawn. As I watched, she walked purposefully over to the well, where a rambler rose makes a weedy thicket. At the edge of it, she arranged herself in a comfortable crouch and settled down to stare with steadfast patience into the leafy depths, whence, she no doubt had good reason to hope, some incautious mouse might at any moment emerge.

11 I turned back to the newspaper, in spite of the distracting birds and the distracting beauty of the trees and grass and sunshine. At the same time, wordless thoughts flowed through the back of my mind. After a while, I was aware that, without conscious thought, I had made a new decision. I would buy a horse after all. I would look for an older horse—maybe ten or fifteen—well-schooled and with a placid disposition; a horse that I could ride quietly and effortlessly. She would be a white mare, perhaps an Arab, with a flowing mane and tail. I saw her grazing in the pasture—Grecian marble in the green grass. It might take a long time to find her, but I would keep looking. I would find her.

12 I glanced out at the rosebush and saw my cat, still motionless after all that time, her lemon-yellow gaze unwaveringly fixed on the motionless leaves, and I thought, She is enjoying herself because she is thinking of the moment when the mouse will emerge. She is a predator, and predators wait, anticipate. Her-

bivores live in the present. For predators, the future is all. My cat and I, we live in our dreams.

Suggestions for Discussion and Writing

1. How does the author of this selection set up her pro-and-con structure in the opening paragraph? Where does she place her thesis-statement?
2. The author devotes eight paragraphs (2–9) to one side of her contrast but only three (10–12) to the other side. What topic unifies each section? How does she keep the imbalance from making her contrast vanish?
3. Several contrasts are presented in this essay: between horses and cats, between horses, between the young vet who called on her and other vets, between the author and horses, and even between her young self and her older self. What is the purpose of these contrasts? How are they related to her thesis-statement?
4. The author alludes to horses in Greek marbles in paragraphs 2, 7, and 11. Why?
5. Explain the significance of the color of Rassi and the color of her cat.
6. What analogies does the author establish between herself and the cat? How is she more like her cat than like Rassi? In a broader sense, what does the cat symbolize? What does Rassi symbolize?
7. Write an essay in which you contrast pets you have known, men and women tennis players, country singers, roommates, or other pairs of objects. Be sure that your thesis-statement sets up a pro-and-con dialectic of thought. You may want to review pages 64–68 before organizing your essay.

WALKER PERCY

The Depressed Self

1 The only cure for depression is suicide.

2 This is not meant as a bad joke but as the serious proposal

of suicide as a valid option. Unless the option is entertained seriously, its therapeutic value is lost. No threat is credible unless the threatener means it.

3 This treatment of depression requires a reversal of the usual therapeutic rationale. The therapeutic rationale, which has never been questioned, is that depression is a symptom. A symptom implies an illness; there is something wrong with you. An illness should be treated.

4 Suppose you are depressed. You may be mildly or seriously depressed, clinically depressed, or suicidal. What do you usually do? Or what does one do with you? Do nothing or something. If something, what is done is always based on the premise that something is wrong with you and therefore it should be remedied. You are treated. You apply to friend, counselor, physician, minister, group. You take a trip, take anti-depressant drugs, change jobs, change wife or husband or "sexual partner."

5 Now, call into question the unspoken assumption: something is wrong with you. Like Copernicus and Einstein, turn the universe upside down and begin with a new assumption.

6 Assume that you are quite right. You are depressed because you have every reason to be depressed. No member of the other two million species which inhabit the earth and who are luckily exempt from depression—would fail to be depressed if it lived the life you lead. You live in a deranged age—more deranged than usual, because despite great scientific and technological advances, man has not the faintest idea of who he is or what he is doing.

7 Begin with the reverse hypothesis, like Copernicus and Einstein. You are depressed because you should be. You are entitled to your depression. In fact, you'd be deranged if you were not depressed. Consider the only adults who are never depressed: chuckleheads, California surfers, and fundamentalist Christians who believe they have had a personal encounter with Jesus and are saved for once and all. Would you trade your depression to become any of these?

8 Now consider, not the usual therapeutic approach, but a more ancient and honorable alternative, the Roman option. I do not care for life in this deranged world, it is not an honorable way to live; therefore, like Cato, I take my leave. Or, as Ivan said to

God in *The Brothers Karamazov:* If you exist, I respectfully return my ticket.

9 Now notice that as soon as suicide is taken as a serious alternative, a curious thing happens. *To be or not to be* becomes a true choice, where before you were stuck with *to be.* Your only choice was how *to be* least painfully, either by counseling, narcotizing, boozing, groupizing, womanizing, man-hopping, or changing your sexual preference.

10 If you are serious about the choice, certain consequences follow. Consider the alternatives. Suppose you elect suicide. Very well. You exit. Then what? What happens after you exit? Nothing much. Very little, indeed. After a ripple or two, the water closes over your head as if you had never existed. You are not indispensable, after all. You are not even a black hole in the Cosmos. All that stress and anxiety was for nothing. Your fellow townsmen will have something to talk about for a few days. Your neighbors will profess shock and enjoy it. One or two might miss you, perhaps your family, who will also resent the disgrace. Your creditors will resent the inconvenience. Your lawyers will be pleased. Your psychiatrist will be displeased. The priest or minister or rabbi will say a few words over you and down you will go on the green tapes and that's the end of you. In a surprisingly short time, everyone is back in the rut of his own self as if you had never existed.

11 Now, in the light of this alternative, consider the other alternative. You can elect suicide, but you decide not to. What happens? All at once, you are dispensed. Why not live, instead of dying? You are free to do so. You are like a prisoner released from the cell of his life. You notice that the door to the cell is ajar and that the sun is shining outside. Why not take a walk down the street? Where you might have been dead, you are alive. The sun is shining.

12 Suddenly you feel like a castaway on an island. You can't believe your good fortune. You feel for broken bones. You are in one piece, sole survivor of a foundered ship whose captain and crew had worried themselves into a fatal funk. And here you are, cast up on a beach and taken in by islanders who, it turns out, are themselves worried sick—over what? Over status, saving face, self-esteem, national rivalries, boredom, anxiety, depression from which they seek relief mainly in wars

and the natural catastrophes which regularly overtake their neighbors.

13 And you, an ex-suicide, lying on the beach? In what way have you been freed by the serious entertainment of your hypothetical suicide? Are you not free for the first time in your life to consider the folly of man, the most absurd of all the species, and to contemplate the comic mystery of your own existence? And even to consider which is the more absurd state of affairs, the manifest absurdity of your predicament: lost in the Cosmos and no news of how you got into such a fix or how to get out—or the even more preposterous eventuality that news did come from the God of the Cosmos, who took pity on your ridiculous plight and entered the space and time of your insignificant planet to tell you something.

14 The consequences of entertainable suicide? Lying on the beach, you are free for the first time in your life to pick up a coquina and look at it. You are even free to go home and, like the man from Chicago, dance with your wife.

15 The difference between a non-suicide and an ex-suicide leaving the house for work, at eight o'clock on an ordinary morning:

16 The non-suicide is a little traveling suck of care, sucking care with him from the past and being sucked toward care in the future. His breath is high in his chest.

17 The ex-suicide opens his front door, sits down on the steps, and laughs. Since he has the option of being dead, he has nothing to lose by being alive. It is good to be alive. He goes to work because he doesn't have to.

Suggestions for Discussion and Writing

1. Arrange the pros and cons of this essay—the dialectic order—in a diagram similar to the model on page 63(Diagram II).
2. What was your initial reaction to Percy's opening paragraph? What point is he trying to make by his startling statement?
3. Percy states (paragraph 3) that suicide is usually regarded as a symptom of an illness that should be treated. Does he agree with this analysis? How do you know?
4. Is the author serious when he says that the only adults who are never depressed are "chuckleheads, California surfers, and fun-

damental Christians who believe they have had a personal encounter with Jesus and are saved for once and all"? Do you agree with his statement?

5. For whom is Percy writing this essay? Would it be helpful to someone seriously considering suicide?
6. Why do so many teenagers and younger people in our society attempt suicide?
7. Write a letter to a friend in which you present alternative solutions to a problem he or she is facing. Like Percy's essay, your letter should clearly advocate the superiority of one of the alternatives.

WILLIAM F. BUCKLEY, JR.

Capital Punishment

1 There is national suspense over whether capital punishment is about to be abolished, and the assumption is that when it comes it will come from the Supreme Court. Meanwhile, (a) the prestigious State Supreme Court of California has interrupted executions, giving constitutional reasons for doing so; (b) the death wings are overflowing with convicted prisoners; (c) executions are a remote memory; and—for the first time in years—(d) the opinion polls show that there is sentiment for what amounts to the restoration of capital punishment.

2 The case for abolition is popularly known. The other case less so, and (without wholeheartedly endorsing it) I give it as it was given recently to the Committee of the Judiciary of the House of Representatives by Professor Ernest van den Haag, under whose thinking cap groweth no moss. Mr. van den Haag, a professor of social philosophy at New York University, ambushed the most popular arguments of the abolitionists, taking no prisoners.

3 (1) The business about the poor and the black suffering excessively from capital punishment is no argument against capital punishment. It is an argument against the *administration* of justice, not against the penalty. Any punishment can be unfairly

or unjustly applied. Go ahead and reform the processes by which capital punishment is inflicted, if you wish; but don't confuse maladministration with the merits of capital punishment.

4 (2) The argument that the death penalty is "unusual" is circular. Capital punishment continues on the books of a majority of states, the people continue to sanction the concept of capital punishment, and indeed capital sentences are routinely handed down. What has made capital punishment "unusual" is that the courts and, primarily, governors have intervened in the process so as to collaborate in the frustration of the execution of the law. To argue that capital punishment is unusual, when in fact it has been made unusual by extra-legislative authority, is an argument to expedite, not eliminate, executions.

5 (3) Capital punishment is cruel. That is a historical judgment. But the Constitution suggests that what must be proscribed as cruel is (a) a particularly painful way of inflicting death, or (b) a particularly undeserved death; and the death penalty, as such, offends neither of these criteria and cannot therefore be regarded as objectively "cruel."

6 Viewed the other way, the question is whether capital punishment can be regarded as useful, and the question of deterrence arises.

7 (4) Those who believe that the death penalty does not intensify the disinclination to commit certain crimes need to wrestle with statistics that, in fact, it can't be proved that *any* punishment does that to any particular crime. One would rationally suppose that two years in jail would cut the commission of a crime if not exactly by one hundred percent more than a penalty of one year in jail, at least that it would further discourage crime to a certain extent. The proof is unavailing. On the other hand, the statistics, although ambiguous, do not show either (a) that capital punishment net discourages; or (b) that capital punishment fails net to discourage. "The absence of proof for the additional deterrent effect of the death penalty must not be confused with the presence of proof for the absence of this effect."

8 The argument that most capital crimes are crimes of passion committed by irrational persons is no argument against the death penalty, because it does not reveal how many crimes might, but for the death penalty, have been committed by rational persons who are now deterred.

9 And the clincher. (5) Since we do not know for certain whether or not the death penalty adds deterrence, we have in effect the choice of two risks.

10 Risk One: If we execute convicted murderers without thereby deterring prospective murderers beyond the deterrence that could have been achieved by life imprisonment, we may have vainly sacrificed the life of the convicted murderer.

11 Risk Two: If we fail to execute a convicted murderer whose execution might have deterred an indefinite number of prospective murderers, our failure sacrifices an indefinite number of victims of future murderers.

12 "If we had certainty, we would not have risks. We do not have certainty. If we have risks—and we do—better to risk the life of the convicted man than risk the life of an indefinite number of innocent victims who might survive if he were executed."

Suggestions for Discussion and Writing

1. Like the other readings in this section, Buckley's essay is a dialectical swinger, presenting a series of counterarguments to the opponents of capital punishment. Which of the three structures presented in this chapter—inductive, deductive, or hybrid—does his essay follow? Explain your answer.
2. Buckley occasionally introduces a bit of humor into his discussion. Is such a device appropriate for a serious topic like the death penalty? Does it strengthen or weaken his argument?
3. Which of Buckley's arguments for capital punishment are most convincing? Which are least convincing? Explain your answers.
4. Reread paragraph 9 of Buckley's essay. How does he arrange his points? Would another arrangement have been more effective? Explain.
5. The author uses words and expressions that serve as guides for his readers; for example, "On the other hand . . ." (paragraph 7). Find other examples and explain how they indicate shifts in the movement of thought in the essay.
6. If you disagree with Buckley on this subject, write an essay in which you refute his arguments. Your essay should follow the pro-and-con pattern discussed in this chapter.
7. Write an essay presenting your views on a controversial subject. Acknowledge the opposition in the subordinate part of your

thesis-sentence, and arrange your points in order of increasing interest.

JONATHAN SWIFT

A Modest Proposal

For Preventing the Children of Poor People in Ireland from Being a Burden to Their Parents or Country, and for Making Them Beneficial to the Public

1 It is a melancholy object to those who walk through this great town or travel in the country, when they see the streets, the roads, and cabin doors, crowded with beggars of the female sex, followed by three, four, or six children, all in rags and importuning every passenger for an alms. These mothers, instead of being able to work for their honest livelihood, are forced to employ all their time in strolling to beg sustenance for their helpless infants: who as they grow up either turn thieves for want of work, or leave their dear native country to fight for the pretender in Spain, or sell themselves to the Barbadoes.

2 I think it is agreed by all parties that this prodigious number of children in the arms, or on the backs, or at the heels of their mothers, and frequently of their fathers, is in the present deplorable state of the kingdom a very great additional grievance; and, therefore, whoever could find out a fair, cheap, and easy method of making these children sound, useful members of the commonwealth, would deserve so well of the public as to have his statue set up for a preserver of the nation.

3 But my intention is very far from being confined to provide only for the children of professed beggars; it is of a much greater extent, and shall take in the whole number of infants at a certain age who are born of parents in effect as little able to support them as those who demand our charity in the streets.

4 As to my own part, having turned my thoughts for many

years upon this important subject, and maturely weighed the several schemes of our projectors, I have always found them grossly mistaken in their computation. It is true, a child just dropped from its dam may be supported by her milk for a solar year, with little other nourishment; at most not above the value of two shillings, which the mother may certainly get, or the value in scraps, by her lawful occupation of begging; and it is exactly at one year old that I propose to provide for them in such a manner as instead of being a charge upon their parents or the parish, or wanting food and raiment for the rest of their lives, they shall on the contrary contribute to the feeding, and partly to the clothing, of many thousands.

5 There is likewise another great advantage in my scheme, that it will prevent those voluntary abortions, and that horrid practice of women murdering their bastard children, alas! too frequent among us! sacrificing the poor innocent babes I doubt more to avoid the expense than the shame, which would move tears and pity in the most savage and inhuman breast.

6 The number of souls in this kingdom being usually reckoned one million and a half, of these I calculate there may be about 200,000 couple whose wives are breeders; from which number I subtract thirty thousand couple who are able to maintain their own children (although I apprehend there cannot be so many, under the present distress of the kingdom); but this being granted, there will remain 170,000 breeders. I again subtract fifty thousand for those women who miscarry, or whose children die by accident or disease within the year. There only remain 120,000 children of poor parents annually born. The question therefore is, how this number shall be reared and provided for? which, as I have already said, under the present situation of affairs, is utterly impossible by all the methods hitherto proposed. For we can neither employ them in handicraft or agriculture; we neither build houses (I mean in the country) nor cultivate land; they can very seldom pick up a livelihood by stealing, till they arrive at six years old, except where they are of towardly parts; although I confess they learn the rudiments much earlier; during which time they can, however, be properly looked upon only as probationers; as I have been informed by a principal gentleman in the county of Cavan, who protested to me that he never knew above one or two instances under the age of six, even in a part of the kingdom so renowned for the quickest proficiency in that art.

7 I am assured by our merchants, that a boy or a girl before twelve years old is no saleable commodity; and even when they come to this age they will not yield above 3l. or 3l. 2s. 6d. at most on the exchange; which cannot turn to account either to the parents or kingdom, the charge of nutriment and rags having been at least four times that value.

8 I shall now therefore humbly propose my own thoughts, which I hope will not be liable to the least objection.

9 I have been assured by a very knowing American of my acquaintance in London, that a young healthy child well nursed is at a year old a most delicious, nourishing, and wholesome food, whether stewed, roasted, baked, or broiled; and I make no doubt that it will equally serve in a fricassee or a ragout.

10 I do therefore humbly offer it to public consideration that of the 120,000 children already computed, twenty thousand may be reserved for breed, whereof only one-fourth part to be males; which is more than we allow to sheep, black cattle, or swine; and my reason is, that these children are seldom the fruits of marriage, a circumstance not much regarded by our savages; therefore one male will be sufficient to serve four females. That the remaining 100,000 may, at a year old, be offered in sale to the persons of quality and fortune through the kingdom; always advising the mother to let them suck plentifully in the last month, so as to render them plump and fat for a good table. A child will make two dishes at an entertainment for friends; and when the family dines alone, the fore or hind quarter will make a reasonable dish, and seasoned with a little pepper or salt will be very good boiled on the fourth day, especially in winter.

11 I have reckoned upon a medium that a child just born will weigh twelve pounds, and in a solar year, if tolerably nursed, will increase to twenty-eight pounds.

12 I grant this food will be somewhat dear, and therefore very proper for landlords, who, as they have already devoured most of the parents, seem to have the best title to the children.

13 Infant's flesh will be in season throughout the year, but more plentiful in March, and a little before and after: for we are told by a grave author, an eminent French physician, that fish being a prolific diet, there are more children born in Roman Catholic countries about nine months after Lent than at any other season; therefore, reckoning a year after Lent, the markets will be more glutted than usual, because the number of popish infants is at

least three to one in this kingdom: and therefore it will have one other collateral advantage, by lessening the number of papists among us.

14 I have already computed the charge of nursing a beggar's child (in which list I reckon all cottagers, laborers, and four-fifths of the farmers) to be about two shillings per annum, rags included; and I believe no gentleman would repine to give ten shillings for the carcass of a good fat child, which, as I have said, will make four dishes of excellent nutritive meat, when he has only some particular friend or his own family to dine with him. Thus the squire will learn to be a good landlord, and grow popular among the tenants; the mother will have eight shillings net profit, and be fit for work till she produces another child.

15 Those who are more thrifty (as I must confess the times require) may flay the carcass; the skin of which artificially dressed will make admirable gloves for ladies, and summer boots for fine gentlemen.

16 As to our city of Dublin, shambles may be appointed for this purpose in the most convenient parts of it, and butchers we may be assured will not be wanting: although I rather recommend buying the children alive, and dressing them hot from the knife as we do roasting pigs.

17 A very worthy person, a true lover of his country, and whose virtues I highly esteem, was lately pleased in discoursing on this matter to offer a refinement upon my scheme. He said that many gentlemen of this kingdom, having of late destroyed their deer, he conceived that the want of venison might be well supplied by the bodies of young lads and maidens, not exceeding fourteen years of age nor under twelve; so great a number of both sexes in every country being now ready to starve for want of work and service; and these to be disposed of by their parents, if alive, or otherwise by their nearest relations. But with due deference to so excellent a friend and so deserving a patriot, I cannot be altogether in his sentiments; for as to the males, my American acquaintance assured me from frequent experience that their flesh was generally tough and lean, like that of our schoolboys by continual exercise, and their taste disagreeable; and to fatten them would not answer the charge. Then as to the females, it would, I think, with humble submission be a loss to the public, because they soon would become breeders themselves: and besides, it is not improbable that some scrupulous people might be

apt to censure such a practice (although indeed very unjustly), as a little bordering upon cruelty; which, I confess, has always been with me the strongest objection against any project, how well soever intended.

18 But in order to justify my friend, he confessed that this expedient was put into his head by the famous Psalmanazar, a native of the island Formosa, who came from thence to London about twenty years ago: and in conversation told my friend, that in his country when any young person happened to be put to death, the executioner sold the carcass to persons of quality as a prime dainty; and that in his time the body of a plump girl of fifteen, who was crucified for an attempt to poison the emperor, was sold to his imperial majesty's prime minister of state, and other great mandarins of the court, in joints from the gibbet, at four hundred crowns. Neither indeed can I deny, that if the same use were made of several plump young girls in this town, who without one single groat to their fortunes cannot stir abroad without a chair, and appear at the playhouse and assemblies in foreign fineries which they never will pay for, the kingdom would not be the worse.

19 Some persons of a desponding spirit are in great concern about that vast number of poor people, who are aged, diseased, or maimed, and I have been desired to employ my thought what course may be taken to ease the nation of so grievous an encumbrance. But I am not in the least pain upon that matter, because it is very well known that they are every day dying and rotting by cold and famine, and filth and vermin, as fast as can be reasonably expected. And as to the young laborers, they are now in as hopeful a condition: they cannot get work, and consequently pine away for want of nourishment, to a degree that if at any time they are accidentally hired to common labor, they have not strength to perform it; and thus the country and themselves are happily delivered from the evils to come.

20 I have too long digressed, and therefore shall return to my subject. I think the advantages by the proposal which I have made are obvious and many, as well as of the highest importance.

21 For first, as I have already observed, it would greatly lessen the number of papists, with whom we are yearly overrun, being the principal breeders of the nation as well as our most dangerous enemies; and who stay at home on purpose to deliver the kingdom to the Pretender, hoping to take their advantage by the

absence of so many good Protestants, who have chosen rather to leave their country than stay at home and pay tithes against their conscience to an Episcopal curate.

22 Secondly, The poor tenants will have something valuable of their own, which by law may be made liable to distress and help to pay their landlord's rent, their corn and cattle being already seized, and money a thing unknown.

23 Thirdly, Whereas the maintenance of 100,000 children from two years old and upward, cannot be computed at less than ten shillings a-piece per annum, the nation's stock will be thereby increased fifty thousand pounds per annum, beside the profit of a new dish introduced to the tables of all gentlemen of fortune in the kingdom who have any refinement in taste. And the money will circulate among ourselves, the goods being entirely of our own growth and manufacture.

24 Fourthly, The constant breeders beside the gain of eight shillings sterling per annum by the sale of their children, will be rid of the charge of maintaining them after the first year.

25 Fifthly, This food would likewise bring great custom to taverns, where the vintners will certainly be so prudent as to procure the best receipts for dressing it to perfection, and consequently have their houses frequented by all the fine gentlemen, who justly value themselves upon their knowledge in good eating; and a skilful cook who understands how to oblige his guests, will contrive to make it as expensive as they please.

26 Sixthly, This would be a great inducement to marriage, which all wise nations have either encouraged by rewards or enforced by laws and penalties. It would increase the care and tenderness of mothers toward their children, when they were sure of a settlement for life to the poor babes, provided in some sort by the public, to their annual profit instead of expense. We should see an honest emulation among the married women, which of them would bring the fattest child to the market. Men would become as fond of their wives during the time of their pregnancy as they are now of their mares in foal, their cows in calf, their sows when they are ready to farrow; nor offer to beat or kick them (as is too frequent a practice) for fear of a miscarriage.

27 Many other advantages might be enumerated. For instance, the addition of some thousand carcasses in our exportation of barreled beef, the propagation of swine's flesh, and improvement

in the art of making good bacon, so much wanted among us by the great destruction of pigs, too frequent at our table; which are no way comparable in taste or magnificence to a well-grown, fat, yearling child, which roasted whole will make a considerable figure at a lord mayor's feast or any other public entertainment. But this and many others I omit, being studious of brevity.

28 Supposing that one thousand families in this city would be constant customers for infants' flesh, besides others who might have it at merry-meetings, particularly at weddings and christenings, I compute that Dublin would take off annually about twenty thousand carcasses; and the rest of the kingdom (where probably they will be sold somewhat cheaper) the remaining eighty thousand.

29 I can think of no one objection that will possibly be raised against this proposal, unless it should be urged that the number of people will be thereby much lessened in the kingdom. This I freely own, and it was indeed one principal design in offering it to the world. I desire the reader will observe, that I calculate my remedy for this one individual kingdom of Ireland and for no other that ever was, is, or I think ever can be upon earth. Therefore let no man talk to me of other expedients: of taxing our absentees at five shillings a pound: of using neither clothes nor household furniture except what is of our own growth and manufacture: of utterly rejecting the materials and instruments that promote foreign luxury: of curing the expensiveness of pride, vanity, idleness, and gaming in our women: of introducing a vein of parsimony, prudence, and temperance: of learning to love our country, in the want of which we differ even from Laplanders and the inhabitants of Topinamboo: of quitting our animosities and factions, nor acting any longer like the Jews, who were murdering one another at the very moment their city was taken: of being a little cautious not to sell our country and conscience for nothing: of teaching landlords to have at least one degree of mercy toward their tenants: lastly, of putting a spirit of honesty, industry, and skill into our shopkeepers; who, if a resolution could now be taken to buy only our native goods, would immediately unite to cheat and exact upon us in the price, the measure, and the goodness, nor could ever yet be brought to make one fair proposal of just dealing, though often and earnestly invited to it.

30 Therefore I repeat, let no man talk to me of these and the like expedients, till he has at least some glimpse of hope that

there will be ever some hearty and sincere attempt to put them in practice.

31 But as to myself, having been wearied out for many years with offering vain, idle, visionary thoughts, and at length utterly despairing of success, I fortunately fell upon this proposal; which, as it is wholly new, so it has something solid and real, of no expense and little trouble, full in our own power, and whereby we can incur no danger in disobliging England. For this kind of commodity will not bear exportation, the flesh being of too tender a consistence to admit a long continuance in salt, although perhaps I could name a country which would be glad to eat up our whole nation without it.

32 After all, I am not so violently bent upon my own opinion as to reject any offer proposed by wise men, which shall be found equally innocent, cheap, easy, and effectual. But before something of that kind shall be advanced in contradiction to my scheme, and offering a better, I desire the author or authors will be pleased maturely to consider two points. First, as things now stand, how they will be able to find food and raiment for 100,000 useless mouths and backs. And secondly, there being a round million of creatures in human figure throughout this kingdom, whose subsistence put into a common stock would leave them in debt two million pound sterling, adding those who are beggars by profession to the bulk of farmers, cottagers, and laborers, with the wives and children who are beggars in effect; I desire those politicians who dislike my overture, and may perhaps be so bold as to attempt an answer, that they will first ask the parents of these mortals, whether they would not at this day think it a great happiness to have been sold for food at a year old in the manner I prescribe, and thereby have avoided such a perpetual scene of misfortunes as they have since gone through by the oppression of landlords, the impossibility of paying rent without money or trade, the want of common sustenance, with neither house nor clothes to cover them from the inclemencies of the weather, and the most inevitable prospect of entailing the life or greater miseries upon their breed for ever.

33 I profess, in the sincerity of my heart, that I have not the least personal interest in endeavoring to promote this necessary work, having no other motive than the public good of my country, by advancing our trade, providing for infants, relieving the poor, and giving some pleasure to the rich. I have no children by which

I can propose to get a single penny; the youngest being nine years old, and my wife past child-bearing.

Some background information is in order. When Jonathan Swift wrote this essay in 1729, Ireland was impoverished because of taxes and harsh legislation enacted by England. Born in Ireland of English parents, Swift was outraged at the indignities suffered by the Irish people. In "A Modest Proposal," he expresses that outrage through the use of *irony,* a literary device for expressing ideas which are the *opposite* of the writer's literal meaning.

In the eighteenth century, a "proposal" was usually an impractical idea (often a get-rich-quick scheme or far-fetched solution to a social or economic problem) offered by a "projector." Hence, Swift's contemporaries (or most of them, at any rate) readily understood that in offering this "solution" he was satirizing the visionary proposals of his day, as well as criticizing the treatment of the Irish by their English overlords.

Suggestions for Discussion and Writing

1. Although Swift intends to shock his reader, he leads up to his "modest" proposal calmly and matter-of-factly. At what point in the essay did you realize that he is being ironic rather than literal in his presentation?
2. What is the effect of describing people with words like "breeder," "dam," "carcass," and "yearling child"?
3. How does the "projector" or narrator disarm possible objections to his proposal?
4. Describe the projector in this essay. How does he differ from Swift? How do you know that his opinions are not shared by Swift?
5. At what point in this essay does the projector's mask fall off, revealing the real attitudes of Swift?
6. What is the projector trying to persuade his readers to do? What, by contrast, is Swift trying to propose?
7. In what ways is Swift parodying the usual techniques of argumentation?
8. The purpose of satire is to criticize people and their habits in order to expose some defect and consequently encourage improvement. It can range from gentle encouragement to stringent attacks. How would you describe Swift's satire?
9. Examine the final sentence of Swift's essay. In what way does it embody his view of human nature?

10. If you, like Swift, are indignant at what you perceive as an injustice or inequitable situation in our society, write a "modest proposal" in which you clothe your ideas in Swiftian irony. You might consider such topics and groups as the aged, the handicapped, the Social Security system, the nuclear arms race, or various forms of discrimination.

4
Paragraphs: Beginning, Middle, End

THE STANDARD PARAGRAPH

A paragraph is a structural convenience—a building block to get firmly in mind. I mean the standard, central paragraph, setting aside for the moment the peculiarly shaped beginning paragraph and ending paragraph. You build the bulk of your essay with standard paragraphs, with blocks of concrete ideas, and they must fit smoothly. But they must also remain as perceptible parts, to rest your reader's eye and mind. Indeed, the paragraph originated, among the Greeks, as a resting place and place-finder, being first a mere mark *(graphos)* in the margin alongside *(para)* an unbroken sheet of handwriting—the proofreader's familiar ¶. You have heard that a paragraph is a single idea, and this is true. But so is a word, usually; and so is a sentence, sometimes. It seems best, after all, to think of a paragraph as something you use for your reader's convenience, rather than as some granitic form laid down by molten logic.

The medium determines the size of the paragraph. Your average longhand paragraph may look the same size as a typewritten one, much like a paragraph in a book. But the printed page would show your handwritten paragraph a short embarrassment, and your typewritten one barely long enough for decency. The beginner's insecurity produces inadequate paragraphs, often only a sentence each. Journalists, of course, are one-sentence paragraphers. The narrow newspaper column makes a sentence look like a paragraph, and narrow columns and short paragraphs serve the newspaper's rapid transit. A paragraph from a book might fill a whole newspaper column with solid lead. It would have to be broken—paragraphed—for the reader's convenience. A news story on the page of a book would look like a gap-toothed comb, and would have to be consolidated for the reader's comfort. So make your paragraphs ample.

Plan for the Big Paragraph

Imagine yourself writing for a book. Force yourself to four or five sentences at least, visualizing your paragraphs as identical rectangular frames to be filled. This will allow you to build with orderly blocks, to strengthen your feel for structure. Since the beginner's problem is usually one of thinking of things to say rather than of trimming the overgrowth, you can do your filling out a unit at a time, always thinking up one or two sentences more to fill the customary space. You will probably be repetitive and wordy at first—this is our universal failing—but you will soon learn to fill your paragraph with interesting details. You will develop a constructional rhythm, coming to rest at the end of each paragraphic frame.

Once accustomed to a five-sentence frame, say, you can then begin to vary the length for emphasis, letting a good idea swell out beyond the norm, or bringing a particular point home in a paragraph short and sharp—even in one sentence, like this.

The paragraph's structure, then, has its own rhetorical message. It tells the reader visually whether or not you are in charge of your subject. Tiny, ragged paragraphs display your hidden uncertainty, unless clearly placed among big ones for emphasis. Brief opening and closing paragraphs sometimes can emphasize your thesis effectively, but usually they make your beginning seem hasty and your ending perfunctory. So aim for the big paragraph all the way, and vary it only occasionally and knowingly, for rhetorical emphasis.

Find a Topic Sentence

Looked at as a convenient structural frame, the paragraph reveals a further advantage. Like the essay itself, it has a beginning, a middle, and an end. The beginning and the end are usually each one sentence long, and the middle gets you smoothly from one to the other. Since, like the essay, the paragraph flows through time, its last sentence is the most emphatic. This is your home punch. The first sentence holds the next most emphatic place. It will normally be your *topic sentence,* stating the paragraph's point, like a small thesis of a miniature essay, something like this:

> ***Jefferson believed in democracy because he firmly believed in reason.*** **He knew that reason was far from perfect, but he also knew that it was the best faculty we have. He knew that it was better than all the frightened and angry intolerances with which we fence off our own back yards at the cost of injustice. Thought must be free. Discussion must be free. Reason must be free to range among the widest possibilities. Even the opinion we hate, and have reasons for believing wrong, we must leave free so that reason can operate on it, so that we advertise our belief in reason and demonstrate a faith unafraid of the consequences—because we know that the consequences will be right. Freedom is really not the aim and end of Jeffersonian democracy: freedom is the means by which democracy can rationally choose justice for all.**

If your topic sentence covers everything within your paragraph, your paragraph is coherent, and you are using your paragraphs with maximum effect, leading your reader into your community block by block. If your end sentences bring him briefly to rest, he will know where he is and appreciate it.

This is the basic frame. As you write, you will discover your own variations, a paragraph that illustrates its topic sentence with parallel items and no home punch at the end at all, or one beginning with a hint and ending with its topical idea in the most emphatic place, like the best beginning paragraphs.

BEGINNING PARAGRAPHS: THE FUNNEL

State Your Thesis at the END of Your Beginning Paragraph

Your beginning paragraph should contain your main idea, and present it to best advantage. Its topic sentence is also the *thesis sentence* of your entire essay. The clearest and most emphatic place for your thesis sentence is at the *end*—not at the beginning—of the beginning paragraph. Of course, many an essay begins with a subject-statement, a kind of open topic sentence for the whole essay, and unfolds amiably from there. But these are usually the more personal meditations of seasoned writers and established authorities. Bacon, for instance, usually steps off from a topical first sentence: "Studies serve for delight, for ornament, and for ability." Similarly, A. A. Milne begins with "Of the fruits of the earth, I give my vote to the orange"—and just keeps going.

But for the less assured and the more structurally minded, the funnel is the reliable form, as the thesis-sentence brings the reader to rest for a moment at the end of the opening paragraph, with his bearings established. If you put your thesis-sentence first, you may have to repeat some version of it as you bring your beginning paragraph to a close. If you put it in the middle, the reader will very likely take something else as your main point, probably whatever the last sentence contains. The inevitable psychology of interest, as you move your reader through your first paragraph and into your essay, urges you to put your thesis last—in the last sentence of your beginning paragraph.

Think of your beginning paragraph, then, not as the middle paragraph's frame to be filled, but as a funnel. Start wide and end narrow:

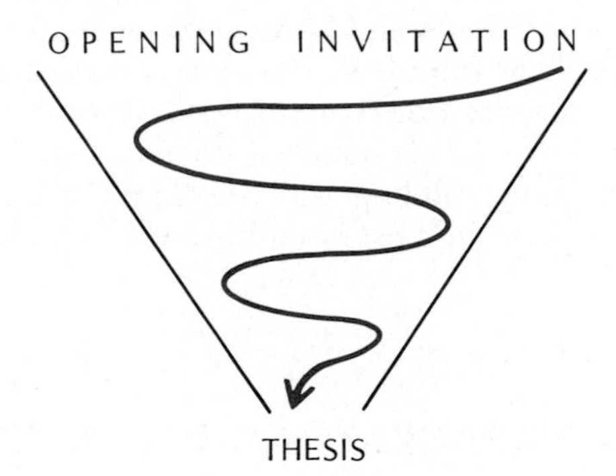

If, for instance, you wished to show that "Learning to play the guitar pays off in friendship"—your thesis—you would start somewhere back from that thesis-idea with something more general—about music, about learning, about the pleasures of achievement, about guitars: "Playing the guitar looks easy,"

"Music can speak more directly than words," "Learning anything is a course in frustration." You can even open with something quite specific, *as long as it is more general than your thesis:* "Pick up a guitar, and you bump into people." A handy way to find an opener is to take one word from your thesis—*learning, play,* or *guitar,* for instance—and make a sentence out of it. Say something about it, and you are well on your way to your thesis, three or four sentences later.* Your opening line, in other words, should look forward to your thesis, should be something to engage interest easily, something to which most readers would assent without a rise in blood pressure. (Antagonize and startle if you wish, but beware of having the door slammed before you have a chance and of making your thesis an anticlimax.) Therefore: broad and genial. From your opening geniality, you move progressively down to smaller particulars. You narrow down: from learning the guitar, to its musical and social complications, to its rewards in friendship (your thesis). Your paragraph might run, from broad to narrow, like this:

> **Learning anything has unexpected rocks in its path, but the guitar seems particularly rocky. Playing it looks so simple. A few chords, you think, and you are on your way. Then you discover not only the musical and technical difficulties, but a whole unexpected crowd of human complications. Your friends think you are showing off; the people you meet think you are a fake. Then the frustrations drive you to achievement. You learn to face the music and the people honestly. You finally learn to play a little, but you also discover something better. You have learned to make and keep some real friends, because you have discovered a kind of ultimate friendship with yourself.**

Now, that paragraph turned out a little different from what I anticipated. I used the informal *you,* and it seemed to suit the subject. I also overshot my original thesis, discovering, as I wrote, a thesis one step farther—an underlying cause—about coming to friendly terms with oneself. But it illustrates the funnel, from the broad and general to the one particular point that will be your essay's main idea, your thesis. Here is another example:

---

*I am grateful to James C. Raymond, of the University of Alabama, for this helpful idea.

The environment is the world around us, and everyone agrees it needs a cleaning. Big corporations gobble up the countryside and disgorge what's left into the breeze and streams. Big trucks rumble by, trailing their fumes. A jet roars into the air, and its soot drifts over the trees. Everyone calls for massive action, and then tosses away his cigarette butt or gum wrapper. The world around us is also a sidewalk, a lawn, a lounge, a hallway, a room right here. Cleaning the environment can begin by reaching for the scrap of paper at your feet.

In a more argumentative paper, you can sometimes set up your thesis effectively by opening with the opposition, as we have already noted (59):

Science is the twentieth century's answer to everything. We want the facts. We conduct statistical polls to measure the President's monthly popularity. We send space ships to bring back pieces of the moon and send back data from the planets. We make babies in test tubes. We believe that eventually we will discover the chemical formula for life itself, creating a human being from the basic elements. Nevertheless, one basic element, what has been called the soul, or spirit, may be beyond science and all human planning, as Gore Vidal's recent novel *Kalki* suggests.

MIDDLE PARAGRAPHS

Make Your Middle Paragraphs Full, with Transitions

The middle paragraph is the standard paragraph, the little essay in itself, with its own little beginning and little end. But it must also declare its allegiance to the paragraphs immediately before and after it. Each topic sentence must somehow hook onto the paragraph above it, must include some word or phrase to ease the reader's path: a transition. (1) You may simply repeat a word from the sentence that ended the paragraph just above. (2) You may bring down a thought generally developed or left slightly hanging in air: "Smith's idea is different" might be a tremendously economical topic sentence with automatic transition. (3) Or you may get from one paragraph to the next by the usual steppingstones, like *But, however* (within the sentence), *Nevertheless, Therefore, Indeed, Of course.* One brief transitional touch in your topic sentence, or opening sentence, is usually sufficient.

The topic sentences in each of the following three paragraphs by James Baldwin contain neat transitions. I have just used an old standby myself: repeating the words *topic sentence* from the close of my preceding paragraph. Baldwin has just described the young people of Harlem who have given up, escaping into day-long TV, or the local bar, or drugs. He now begins his next paragraph with *And the others,* a strong and natural transition, referring back, reinforced with the further transitional reference *all of these deaths.* In the next paragraph, *them* does the trick; in the last, *other* again makes the transition and sets the contrast. The paragraphs are nearly the same length, all cogent, clear, and full. No one-sentence paragraphing here, no gaps, but all a vivid, orderly progression:

> **_And the others,_ who have avoided _all of these deaths,_ get up in the morning and go downtown to meet "the man." They work in the white man's world all day and come home in the evening to this fetid block. They struggle to instill in their children some private sense of honor or dignity which will help the child to survive. This means, of course, that they must struggle, stolidly, incessantly, to keep this sense alive in themselves, in spite of the insults, the indifference, and the cruelty they are certain to encounter in their working day. They patiently browbeat the landlord into fixing the heat, the plaster, the plumbing; this demands prodigious patience; nor is patience usually enough. In trying to make their hovels habitable, they are perpetually throwing good money after bad. _Such frustration, so long endured, is driving many strong, admirable men and women whose only crime is color to the very gates of paranoia._**

Topic Sentence with Transition

End Sentence: The Point

> **_One remembers them from another time_—playing handball in the playground, going to church, wondering if they were going to be promoted at school. One remembers them going off to war—gladly, to escape this block. One remembers their return. Perhaps one remembers their wedding day. _And one sees where the girl is now—vainly looking for salvation from some other embittered, trussed, and struggling boy—and sees the all-but-abandoned children in the streets._**

Topic Sentence with Transition

End Sentence: The Point

Topic Sentence with Transition

Now I am perfectly aware that there are other slums in which white men are fighting for their lives, and mainly losing. **I know that blood is also flowing through those streets and that the human damage there is incalculable. People are continually pointing out to me the wretchedness of white people in order to console me for the wretchedness of blacks. But an itemized account of the American failure does not console me and it should not console anyone else. That hundreds of thousands of white people are living, in effect, no better than the "niggers" is not a fact to be regarded with complacency.** ***The social and moral bankruptcy suggested by this fact is of the bitterest, most terrifying kind.*** *

End Sentence: The Point

Check Your Paragraphs for Clarity and Coherence

Baldwin's paragraphs run smoothly from first sentence to last. They are coherent. The *topic sentence* is the key. It assures that the subsequent sentences will fall into line, and it is the first point to check when you look back to see if they really do. Many a jumbled paragraph can be unifed by writing a broader topic sentence. Consider this disjointed specimen:

> **Swimming is healthful. The first dive into the pool is always cold. Tennis takes a great deal of energy, especially under a hot sun. Team sports, like basketball, baseball, and volleyball, always make the awkward player miserable. Character and health go hand in hand.**

What is all that about? From the last sentence, we can surmise what the writer intended. But the first sentence about swimming in no way covers the paragraph, which treats several sports not in the least like swimming, and seems to be driving at something other than health. The primary remedy is to find the paragraph's thesis and to devise a topic sentence that will state it, thus covering everything in the paragraph. Think of your topic sentence as a roof—covering your paragraph and pulling its contents together.

---

*Excerpt from "Fifth Avenue Uptown: A Letter from Harlem," from *Nobody Knows My Name* by James Baldwin. Copyright © 1960 by James Baldwin. A Dial Press book, reprinted by permission of Doubleday & Company, Inc.

POOR COVERAGE

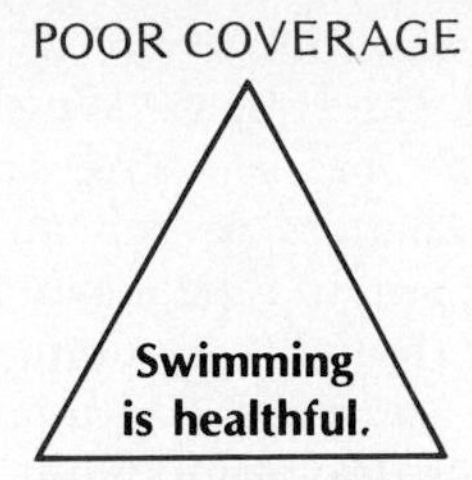

The first dive. Tennis. Basketball, baseball, volleyball. Character and health.

GOOD COVERAGE

Sports build health and character.

Swimming. The first dive. Tennis. Basketball, baseball, volleyball. Character and health.

Suppose we add only a topic sentence, suggested by our right-hand diagram. It will indeed pull things together:

> ***Sports demand an effort of will and muscle that is healthful for the soul as well as the body.*** **Swimming is healthful. The first dive into the pool is always cold. Tennis takes a great deal of energy, especially under a hot sun. Team sports, like basketball, baseball, and volleyball, always make the awkward player miserable. Character and health go hand in hand.**

Topic Sentence

But the paragraph is still far from an agreeable coherence. The islands of thought still need some bridges. Gaining coherence is primarily a filling in, or a spelling out, of submerged connections. You may fill in with (1) thought and (2) specific illustrative detail; you may spell out by tying your sentences together with (3) transitional tags and (4) repeated words or syntactical patterns. Let us see what we can do with our sample paragraph.

From the first, you probably noticed that the writer was thinking in pairs: the pleasure of sports is balanced off against their difficulty; the difficulty is physical as well as moral; character and health go hand in hand. We have already indicated this doubleness of idea in our topic sentence. Now to fill out the thought, we need merely expand each sentence so as to give each half of the double idea its due expression. We need also to qualify the thought here and there with *perhaps, often, some, sometimes, frequently, all in all,* and the like. As we work through the possibilities, more specific detail will come to mind. We have already made the general ideas of *character* and *health* more specific with *will, muscle, soul,* and *body* in our topic sentence, and we shall add a touch or two more of illustration, almost automatically, as our imagination becomes more stimulated by the subject. We shall add a number of transitional ties like *but, and, of course, nevertheless,* and *similarly.* We shall look for chances to repeat key words, like *will,* if we can do so gracefully; and to repeat syntactical patterns, if we can emphasize similar thoughts by doing so, as with *no matter how patient his teammates . . . no matter how heavy his heart,* toward the end of our revision below (the original phrases are in italics):

Topic Sentence

Illustrative Sentences with Transitions

End Sentence: The Point

Sports demand an effort of will and muscle that is healthful for the soul as well as the body. Swimming is **physically** ***healthful,*** **of course, although it may seem undemanding and highly conducive to lying for hours inert on a deck chair in the sun. But** ***the first dive into the pool is always cold:*** **taking the plunge always requires some effort of will. And the swimmer soon summons his will to compete, against himself or others, for greater distances and greater speed, doing twenty laps where he used to do one. Similarly,** ***tennis takes*** **quantities** ***of energy,*** **physical and moral,** ***especially*** **when the competition stiffens** ***under a hot sun. Team sports, like basketball, baseball, and volleyball,*** **perhaps demand even more of the amateur.** ***The awkward player*** **is** ***miserable*** **when he strikes out, or misses an easy fly, or an easy basket, no matter how patient his teammates. He must drive himself to keep on trying, no matter how heavy his heart. Whatever the sport, a little determination can eventually conquer one's awkwardness and timidity, and the reward will be more than physical.** ***Character and health frequently go hand in hand.***

Here we can see the essence of coherence: REPETITION, (1) repeating parallel examples, like *swimming, tennis, team sports,* as if stacking them up to support your topic sentence; or (2) stringing them along by idea and word, sentence by sentence, as in *sports, swimming, dive, tennis, team sports,* and so forth, as one thought suggests the next. Finally, transitions *within* a paragraph contribute importantly to its coherence. Since beginners usually do not think of transitions, try to include a helpful *of course, but, and, similarly, perhaps, consequently, still,* and the like.

Here are the five points to remember about middle paragraphs. First, think of the middle paragraph as a miniature essay, with a beginning, a middle, and an end. Its beginning will normally be its topic sentence, the thesis of this miniature essay. Its middle will develop, explain, and illustrate your topic sentence. Its last sentence will drive home the idea. Second, remember that this kind of paragraph is the norm, which you may instinctively vary when your topic sentence requires only a series of parallel illustrations *(swimming, tennis, golf, basketball, hockey),* or when you open your paragraph with some hint to be fulfilled in a topical conclusive sentence *(Sports build body and soul).* Third, see that your paragraph is coherent, not only flowing smoothly but with nothing in it not covered by the topic sentence. Fourth, make your paragraphs full and well developed, with plenty of details, examples, and full explanations, or you will end up with a skeletal paper with very little meat on its bones. Fifth, remember transitions. Though each paragraph is a kind of miniature essay, it is also a part of a larger essay. Therefore, hook each paragraph smoothly to the paragraph preceding it, with some transitional touch in each opening sentence.

END PARAGRAPHS: THE INVERTED FUNNEL

Reassert Your Thesis

If the beginning paragraph is a funnel, the end paragraph is a funnel upside down: the thought starts moderately narrow—it is more or less the thesis you have had all the time—and then pours out broader and broader implications and finer emphases. The end paragraph reiterates, summarizes, and emphasizes with decorous fervor. This is your last chance. This is what your reader will carry away—and if you can carry *him* away, so much the better. All within decent intellectual bounds, of course. You are the person of reason still, but the person of reason supercharged with conviction, sure of your idea and sure of its importance.

If your essay is anecdotal, however, largely narrative and descriptive, your ending may be no more than a sentence, or it may be a ruminative paragraph generalizing upward and outward from the particulars to mirror your beginning paragraph, as in a more argumentative essay. The dramatic curve of your illustrative incident will tell you what to do. An essay illustrating how folly may lead to catastrophe—a friend dead from an overdose, or drowned by daring too far on thin ice—might end when the story has told itself out and made its point starkly: "The three of us walked numbly up the street toward home."

But the usual final paragraph conveys a sense of assurance and repose, of business completed. Its topic sentence is usually some version of the original thesis sentence, since the end paragraph is the exact structural opposite and complement of the beginning one. Its transitional word or phrase is often one of finality or summary—*then, finally, thus,* and *so:*

> **So, the guitar is a means to a finer end.**
> **The environment, then, is in our lungs and at our fingertips.**

The paragraph would then proceed to expand and elaborate this revived thesis. We would get a confident assertion that both the music and the friendships are really by-products of an inner alliance; we would get an urgent plea to clean up our personal environs and strengthen our convictions. One rule of thumb: the longer the paper, the more specific the summary of the points you have made. A short paper will need no specific summary of your points at all; the renewed thesis and its widening of implications are sufficient.

Here is an end paragraph by Sir James Jeans. His transitional phrase is *for a similar reason.* His thesis was that previous concepts of physical reality had mistaken surfaces for depths:

> **The purely mechanical picture of visible nature fails for a similar reason. It proclaims that the ripples themselves direct the workings of the universe instead of being mere symptoms of occurrences below; in brief, it makes the mistake of thinking that the weather-vane determines the direction from which the wind shall blow, or that the thermometer keeps the room hot.***

Here is an end paragraph of Professor Richard Hofstadter's. His transitional word is *intellectuals,* carried over from the preceding paragraphs. His thesis was that intellectuals should not abandon their defense of intellectual and spiritual freedom, as they have tended to do, under pressure to conform:

**The New Background of Science* (Cambridge: Cambridge University Press, 1933): 261.

> **This world will never be governed by intellectuals—it may rest assured. But *we* must be assured, too, that intellectuals will not be altogether governed by this world, that they maintain their piety, their longstanding allegiance to the world of spiritual values to which they should belong. Otherwise there will be no intellectuals, at least not above ground. And societies in which the intellectuals have been driven underground, as we have had occasion to see in our own time, are societies in which even the anti-intellectuals are unhappy.***

Remember a conclusion when you have used up all your points and had your say. You and your argument are both exhausted. You will be tempted to stop, but don't stop. You need an end, or the whole thing will unravel in your reader's mind. You need to buttonhole him in a final paragraph, to imply "I told you so" without saying it, to hint at the whole round experience he has just had, and to leave him convinced, satisfied, and admiring. One more paragraph will do it: beginning, middle, *and* end.

THE WHOLE ESSAY

You have now discovered the main ingredients of a good essay. You have learned to find and to sharpen your thesis in one sentence, to give your essay that all-important argumentative edge. You have learned to arrange your points in order of increasing interest, and you have practiced disposing of the opposition in a *pro-con* structure. You have seen that your beginning paragraph should seem like a funnel, working from broad generalization to thesis. You have tried your hand at middle paragraphs, which are almost like little essays with their own beginnings and ends. And finally, you have learned that your last paragraph should work like an inverted funnel, broadening and embellishing your thesis.

Some students have pictured the essay as a Greek column, with a narrowing beginning paragraph as its top, or capital, and a broadening end paragraph as its base. Others have seen it as

---

*"Democracy and Anti-intellectualism in America," *Michigan Alumnus Quarterly Reivew,* 59 (1953): 295.

a keyhole (see the keyhole diagram).* Picturing your structure like this is very handy. This is the basic pattern. Keeping it in mind helps as you write. Checking your drafts against it will show you where you might amplify, or rearrange. As you write more and more, you will discover new variations as each new subject pushes its way to fulfillment, like a tree growing toward full light. But every tree is a tree. Each follows the general pattern, as if fulfilling some heavenly arboreal keyhole. Similarly, this essayistic one works out in convenient detail the inevitability of Aristotle's Beginning, Middle, and End.

The student's essay that follows illustrates this basic structure fairly well. He has clearly thought about, and talked about, his subject, picking up facts from the daily news, and evidently, as he sat down to put his thoughts on paper, has looked to see what *The Encyclopaedia Britannica* had to say about "Conscription."

The Need for a Democratic Draft

Broad Subject, Illustration

Armies make wars. **The bigger the army, the greater the threat, as we saw twice in 1982, when Argentinian generals with a large army of conscripts thought invading the Falkland Islands would establish their regime, and when Israel's tanks rumbled into southern Lebanon and just kept going to Beirut.**

Narrowing

Now, America faces the question of expanding its army by conscription, and against considerable resistance both from a distrust of militarism and from a championship of democratic rights.

Thesis

Nevertheless, this country needs conscription, including, for effectiveness and fairness, the conscription of women.

Topic Sentence, Opposition 1

Of course, ***the draft creates military and philosophical problems.*** **Militarily,** ***it forces men into a trade, or an apprenticeship, they do not choose, and forces them to fight and die. Ideally, a volunteer army is the best army,*** **fired by patriotism, resentment, or even despair, to defend home and country, like the Athenians at Marathon or the Spartans at Thermopylae.**

Middle: Specific Evidence

In times of war, when patriotism rises, a drafted army approaches the spirit of a voluntary one, as farm boys, like Henry Fleming in Stephan Crane's ***The Red Badge of Courage,*** **rush off to enlist in the Civil War, or a fraternity class,**

---

*Mrs. Fran Measley of Santa Barbara, California, has devised for her students a mimeographed sheet to accompany my discussion of structure and paragraphing —to help them to visualize my points, through a keyhole, as it were. I am grateful to Mrs. Measley to be able to include it here.

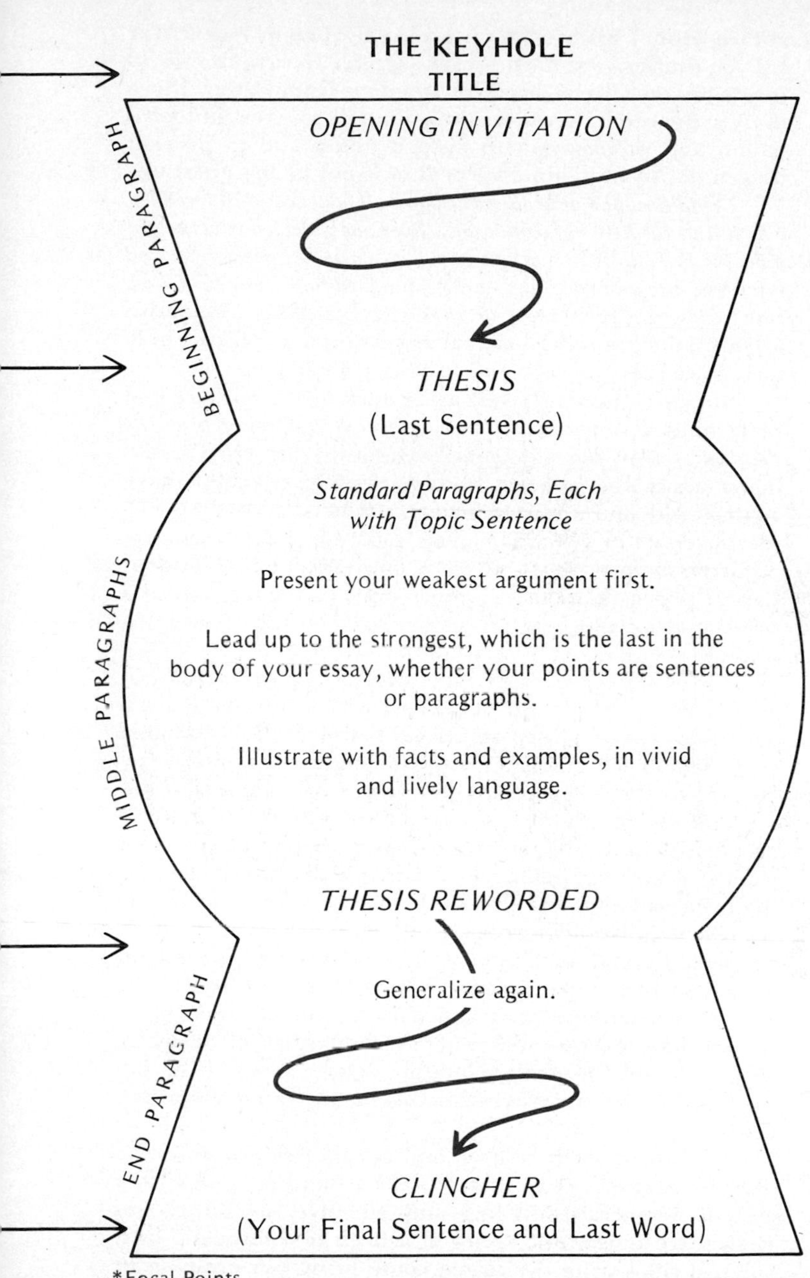
THE KEYHOLE
TITLE
OPENING INVITATION
BEGINNING PARAGRAPH
THESIS
(Last Sentence)
Standard Paragraphs, Each with Topic Sentence
Present your weakest argument first.
Lead up to the strongest, which is the last in the body of your essay, whether your points are sentences or paragraphs.
Illustrate with facts and examples, in vivid and lively language.
MIDDLE PARAGRAPHS
THESIS REWORDED
Generalize again.
END PARAGRAPH
CLINCHER
(Your Final Sentence and Last Word)
*Focal Points

at Princeton, I believe, volunteers as a group in World War I. Even draftees are fired up for sacrifice to save the world for democracy, or at least for freedom from Hitler. But a draft in peacetime requires the military's severest indoctrination and punishment to keep it going and to prevent desertion. An individual's freedom is out of the question.

Topic Sentence, Opposition 2

The philosophical problem of the draft concerns that freedom, which is at the heart of democracy. Does one's elected government have the right to take him out of college or off his chosen job and force him into an endurance contest designed for killing his fellow man? Those who resist the draft say an emphatic "No." They also argue on the grounds of sexual discrimination, picking only men from their careers and leaving women free.

Topic Sentence, *Pro*

But harsh necessity sets aside most of the military and philosophical objections. *The volunteer system, set up after the Vietnamese War, has not worked.* The army has tried it and failed. Only the poorest and marginally educated have volunteered, and not in sufficient numbers, according to a recent report in *Time.* The army's call for a draft, and the registration enacted for it by Congress under President Carter, prove that the volunteer army is inadequate in a world blazing with wars from *Cambodia* to the *Falkland Islands.*

Middle: Authoritative Evidence

Specific Allusions

Topic Sentence

The idea of a peacetime draft, which the protesters resist, is unreal. The world is not at peace, and has not been for a single day since Hitler invaded Poland in 1939. Almost every nation maintains an army through conscription, according to *The Encyclopaedia Brittanica,* with required training and service varying from several months to several years. Both *Israel* and *China* require service of both men and women, on the old democratic principle of everyone's sharing responsibility, and this evidently contributes to reducing resentment and increasing willingness to serve. Japan is a notable exception, with no army at all. But we are pledged to defend her, as we are our NATO allies, confronted by Russia's tremendous conscripted army. We must wake up to the war-like realities and generate some spirit of necessity to counteract the draft's built-in defect: the lack of the professionalism and patriotism that makes a good voluntary army.

Middle: Authoritative Evidence

Contemporary Examples

Thesis Restated

In short, America needs a draft of both men and women to face the necessities of an armed world around us, and with a system democratically fair and effective, as Israel has shown. No one would think of a draft if volunteers, with squirrel rifles from the cabin, could bring our army up to

strength in numbers and intelligence. But the volunteer system has failed. ***A draft, or at least a registration of both sexes to be ready for a draft when dire reality hits us, is necessary now.*** The Clincher

EXERCISES

1. *Below is a list of thesis-sentences. Choose one (or its opposite), or make one of your own on the same pattern. Then back off from it at least four or five sentences, and write a funnel-like beginning paragraph leading your reader down to it: your thesis, the last sentence of your beginning funnel.*

EXAMPLE *with thesis italicized as follows:*

The coal operators will tell you that stripping is cheaper and more efficient than conventional mining. Their 250-cubic-yard drag-lines, their 200-cubic-yard shovels, their 50-ton trucks, can rip the top off a mountain and expose a whole seam of coal in a fraction of the time it takes to sink a shaft. "It is cheaper," they will say, "to bring the surface to the coal than to bring the coal to the surface." And of course they are right; in a sense it is cheaper. But visit Eastern Kentucky and look at the real price we pay for stripped coal. Visit a stripped area and you will see that, no matter how low the price for a truckload of stripped coal, *the real price for strip-mining has to be reckoned in terms of blighted land, poisoned streams, and stunted human lives.*

1. Although motivated by proper concern for the public welfare, the FCC's ban of cigarette advertising on television is ineffective and discriminatory.
2. The computer has contributed to the modern sense of alienation.
3. If the filibuster is supposed to guarantee respect for minority opinion, it usually turns out to be a flagrant waste of time.
4. The new sense of black pride is our increasing awareness of black accomplishments in the past.
5. If women are discriminated against in schools and in industry, they are far more discriminated against in politics.

2. *Now try the inverted funnel, in which your topic sentence is some version of the thesis with which you began and your final paragraph broadens its implications outward to leave the reader fully convinced and satisfied. Using the thesis-sentences in Exercise 1, write two ending paragraphs for imaginary papers.*

EXAMPLE *with the rephrased thesis (its topic sentence) italicized, and some of the evidence from the paper's middle summarized for emphasis:*

> *So, at last, we should add up the real costs of strip-mining; we should admit that the ultimate price of coal is far too high if we must rape the land, poison the streams, and wreck human lives to mine it.* For after the drag-lines have gone, even after the coal itself has been burned, the bills for strip-mining will keep coming in. So far, following the expedient path, we have laid bare more than 2,600 square miles of our land, and we show no signs of stopping. Every year we strip an additional 50,000 acres. Just as we cut down our forests in the nineteenth century and fouled our air in the twentieth, we still blunder along toward ecological and social disaster. Isn't it time to stop?

3. *Staying with the same topic sentence, develop a full middle paragraph, remembering the four points: (1) the miniature essay, with beginning, middle, and end; (2) coherence; (3) fullness; (4) transition.*

EXAMPLE *with transitional touches italicized:*

> The streams tell the story *as drearily as* the *eroded land.* In winter, *they* are red with running silt, and sometimes black with *coal* dust. *In summer, many* are no *streams* at all, merely gullies through which the *winter* rains have rushed. Before *the drag-lines stripped* the earth of its skin, the massed roots of grasses, shrubs, and trees held the soil in place and soaked up the *water,* easing it into the *streams* for a full year's run. Fish fed in pools below *grassy* banks and among the weeds that slowed the *water* to a leisurely pace. Now the *water* is soon gone, if not *poisoned* with *industrial waste,* and the *land* is *gone* with it.

Now you will have a three-paragraph essay that should convey a thorough sense of beginning, middle, end.

4. *Now, to make an even richer, fuller essay, add two or more middle paragraphs, with good transitions, to give a stronger impetus to the implications of your end paragraph. If you had developed the sample paragraphs in these exercises, for example, you could develop separate paragraphs, each with several illustrations, on ruined land, streams, and lives.*

Readings

The three writers in this section—a journalist, a professor of political science, and an astronomer—demonstrate their mastery of paragraphing. Norman Cousins examines some of the causes and varieties of pain and the effects of pain-killers. Andrew Hacker offers the theory that it was women, not men, who defeated the amendment for equal rights. Robert Jastrow explains the similarities and differences between computers and human brains. Each writer begins with a funnel paragraph that leads the reader to the thesis statement. Remember, however, that the funnel is a model—not a mold. After you become more confident as a writer, you may occasionally want to put your thesis-statement first and step right into the body of your essay.

As you read these selections, notice that they contain full, developed paragraphs that begin with topic sentences, and that each paragraph is hooked to the paragraphs immediately before and after it through the use of transitions.

NORMAN COUSINS

Pain Is Not the Ultimate Enemy

1 Americans are probably the most pain-conscious people on the face of the earth. For years we have had it drummed into us—in print, on radio, over television, in everyday conversation—that any hint of pain is to be banished as though it were the ultimate evil. As a result, we are becoming a nation of pill-grab-

bers and hypochondriacs, escalating the slightest ache into a searing ordeal.

2 We know very little about pain and what we don't know makes it hurt all the more. Indeed, no form of illiteracy in the United States is so widespread or costly as ignorance about pain—what it is, what causes it, how to deal with it without panic. Almost everyone can rattle off the names of at least a dozen drugs that can deaden pain from every conceivable cause—all the way from headaches to hemorrhoids. There is far less knowledge about the fact that about ninety percent of pain is self-limiting, that it is not always an indication of poor health, and that, most frequently, it is the result of tension, stress, worry, idleness, boredom, frustration, suppressed rage, insufficient sleep, overeating, poorly balanced diet, smoking, excessive drinking, inadequate exercise, stale air, or any of the other abuses encountered by the human body in modern society.

3 The most ignored fact of all about pain is that the best way to eliminate it is to eliminate the abuse. Instead, many people reach almost instinctively for the painkillers—aspirins, barbiturates, codeines, tranquilizers, sleeping pills, and dozens of other analgesics or desensitizing drugs.

4 Most doctors are profoundly troubled over the extent to which the medical profession today is taking on the trappings of a pain-killing industry. Their offices are overloaded with people who are morbidly but mistakenly convinced that something dreadful is about to happen to them. It is all too evident that the campaign to get people to run to a doctor at the first sign of pain has boomeranged. Physicians find it difficult to give adequate attention to patients genuinely in need of expert diagnosis and treatment because their time is soaked up by people who have nothing wrong with them except a temporary indisposition or a psychogenic ache.

5 Patients tend to feel indignant and insulted if the physician tells them he can find no organic cause for the pain. They tend to interpret the term "psychogenic" to mean that they are complaining of nonexistent symptoms. They need to be educated about the fact that many forms of pain have no underlying physical cause but are the result, as mentioned earlier, of tension, stress, or hostile factors in the general environment. Sometimes a pain may be a manifestation of "conversion hysteria," as men-

tioned earlier, the name given by Jean Charcot to physical symptoms that have their origins in emotional disturbances.

6 Obviously, it is folly for an individual to ignore symptoms that could be a warning of a potentially serious illness. Some people are so terrified of getting bad news from a doctor that they allow their malaise to worsen, sometimes past the point of no return. Total neglect is not the answer to hypochondria. The only answer has to be increased education about the way the human body works, so that more people will be able to steer an intelligent course between promiscuous pill-popping and irresponsible disregard of genuine symptoms.

7 Of all forms of pain, none is more important for the individual to understand than the "threshold" variety. Almost everyone has a telltale ache that is triggered whenever tension or fatigue reaches a certain point. It can take the form of a migraine-type headache or a squeezing pain deep in the abdomen or cramps or a pain in the lower back or even pain in the joints. The individual who has learned how to make the correlation between such threshold pains and their cause doesn't panic when they occur; he or she does something about relieving the stress and tension. Then, if the pain persists despite the absence of apparent cause, the individual will telephone the doctor.

8 If ignorance about the nature of pain is widespread, ignorance about the way pain-killing drugs work is even more so. What is not generally understood is that many of the vaunted pain-killing drugs conceal the pain without correcting the underlying condition. They deaden the mechanism in the body that alerts the brain to the fact that something may be wrong. The body can pay a high price for suppression of pain without regard to its basic cause.

9 Professional athletes are sometimes severely disadvantaged by trainers whose job it is to keep them in action. The more famous the athlete, the greater the risk that he or she may be subjected to extreme medical measures when injury strikes. The star baseball pitcher whose arm is sore because of a torn muscle or tissue damage may need sustained rest more than anything else. But his team is battling for a place in the World Series; so the trainer or team doctor, called upon to work his magic, reaches for a strong dose of butazolidine or other powerful pain suppressants. Presto, the pain disappears! The pitcher takes his place on

the mound and does superbly. That could be the last game, however, in which he is able to throw a ball with full strength. The drugs didn't repair the torn muscle or cause the damaged tissue to heal. What they did was to mask the pain, enabling the pitcher to throw hard, further damaging the torn muscle. Little wonder that so many star athletes are cut down in their prime, more the victims of overzealous treatment of their injuries than of the injuries themselves.

10 The king of all painkillers, of course, is aspirin. The U.S. Food and Drug Administration permits aspirin to be sold without prescription, but the drug, contrary to popular belief, can be dangerous and, in sustained doses, potentially lethal. Aspirin is self-administered by more people than any other drug in the world. Some people are aspirin-poppers, taking ten or more a day. What they don't know is that the smallest dose can cause internal bleeding. Even more serious perhaps is the fact that aspirin is antagonistic to collagen, which has a key role in the formation of connective tissue. Since many forms of arthritis involve disintegration of the connective tissue, the steady use of aspirin can actually intensify the underlying arthritic condition. . . .

11 Aspirin is not the only pain-killing drug, of course, that is known to have dangerous side effects. Dr. Daphne A. Roe, of Cornell University, at a medical meeting in New York City in 1974, presented startling evidence of a wide range of hazards associated with sedatives and other pain suppressants. Some of these drugs seriously interfere with the ability of the body to metabolize food properly, producing malnutrition. In some instances, there is also the danger of bone-marrow depression, interfering with the ability of the body to replenish its blood supply.

12 Pain-killing drugs are among the greatest advances in the history of medicine. Properly used, they can be a boon in alleviating suffering and in treating disease. But their indiscriminate and promiscuous use is making psychological cripples and chronic ailers out of millions of people. The unremitting barrage of advertising for pain-killing drugs, especially over television, has set the stage for a mass anxiety neurosis. Almost from the moment children are old enough to sit upright in front of a television screen, they are being indoctrinated into the hypochondriac's

clamorous and morbid world. Little wonder so many people fear pain more than death itself.

13 It might be a good idea if concerned physicians and educators could get together to make knowledge about pain an important part of the regular school curriculum. As for the populace at large, perhaps some of the same techniques used by public-service agencies to make people cancer-conscious can be used to counteract the growing terror of pain and illness in general. People ought to know that nothing is more remarkable about the human body than its recuperative drive, given a modicum of respect. If our broadcasting stations cannot provide equal time for responses to the pain-killing advertisements, they might at least set aside a few minutes each day for common-sense remarks on the subject of pain. As for the Food and Drug Administration, it might be interesting to know why an agency that has so energetically warned the American people against taking vitamins without prescriptions is doing so little to control over-the-counter sales each year of billions of pain-killing pills, some of which can do more harm than the pain they are supposed to suppress.

Suggestions for Discussion and Writing

1. According to Cousins, what are the dangers of taking drugs to relieve pain? Does he denounce all kinds of painkillers?
2. Who is to blame, according to the author, for the fact that "we are becoming a nation of pill-grabbers and hypochondriacs"? What evidence can you cite to support his charge?
3. If *pain* is not the ultimate enemy, as the title of this selection suggests, what is?
4. Do you agree with Cousins's contention (paragraph 2) that "no form of illiteracy in the United States is so widespread or costly as ignorance about pain"? What about the inability to read or write?
5. How do stories about "blood doping" and the use of steroids among Olympic athletes support Cousins's claims in paragraph 9?
6. Should advertisements for pain-killers be banned from television, just as they were for cigarettes and whiskey?
7. How practical is Cousins's suggestion (paragraph 13) that

knowledge about pain become an important part of the school curriculum? Aren't the schools already burdened with too many nonacademic responsibilities like driver training and sex education?

8. Reread the last sentence of the selection. Why isn't the Food and Drug Administration doing more to control the sale of over-the-counter painkilling pills?
9. Does the opening paragraph contain the thesis sentence of this essay? Does it follow the "funnel" structure described on pages 95–98? Explain your answer. Where is the thesis statement?
10. This selection contains a series of well-developed paragraphs that derive their coherence, in part, from the use of transitional words and expressions. Examples include "as a result" (paragraph 1), "indeed" (paragraph 2), and "instead" (paragraph 3). Find several other instances of this technique, and explain how they help the reader follow the curvature of Cousins's thought.
11. Nearly every paragraph in this selection begins with a topic sentence that states the paragraph's point. Select one of Cousins's paragraphs and demonstrate how each sentence supports or illustrates its topic sentence.
12. If you are familiar with the claims of holistic medicine, write an essay in which you present its benefits or weaknesses. Try to follow the funnel structure in your opening paragraph by beginning with a generalization and ending with your thesis statement.
13. If you have experienced "conversion hysteria" (paragraph 5), write an essay in which you describe the experience.
14. Write an essay in which you explore the reason medical doctors are regarded as virtual divinities or members of a priestly caste in our society.

ANDREW HACKER

E.R.A.—R.I.P.

1 The Equal Rights Amendment expired in the final stretch, three states short of the finish line. And before the postmortems begin, it would be well to scotch one myth. The Equal Rights Amendment was never a battle between the sexes, with men

having the final say. Ronald Reagan notwithstanding, few men cared much either way. On the contrary, a crucial reason for the ERA's defeat was opposition from women.

2 Legislators who voted against it could point to their negative mail, which came mainly from women. For them that was excuse enough. Even the polls were deceptive, for they failed to show the depth of feeling on the against side. It would be well to understand why so many women ended up opposing a measure intended for their benefit.

3 As originally proposed, the Equal Rights Amendment seemed altogether innocuous. Its two dozen words ("Equality of rights under the law shall not be denied or abridged by the United States or by any state on account of sex") simply summarized a principle accepted by the courts and embodied in legislation. The amendment cleared Congress in March of 1972, with only eight dissents in the Senate and twenty-four in the House. Before the year was over, no fewer than twenty-two state legislatures had ratified the ERA. The sixteen others needed for its adoption were expected to follow suit in 1973.

4 As everyone now knows, however, it did not turn out that way. Over the ensuing five years, only thirteen more states added their approval, with Indiana the last, in 1977. Not only that, five of the ratifying states moved to rescind their passage—an unusual step now facing legal challenge. And if only five went on record as changing their minds, soundings show that at least as many more would not repeat their ratifications were they to vote today. In 1978 an embarrassed Congress—this time with 225 dissenting votes—gave the amendment thirty-nine more months to muster three more states. But when, this June, Illinois's moderately liberal legislature failed to act favorably, it became clear that the amendment had reached the end of its road.* Principle apart, the Republicans' repudiation of the ERA can be seen as a refusal to align with a lost cause.

5 What happened is that early in its course, the ERA lost its innocent status. In fact, this change occurred during the nine months after the amendment had left Congress and while it was

* Anyone inclined to believe that ratification is still possible is invited to identify three candidates for conversion among the fifteen holdouts: Alabama, Arkansas, Arizona, Florida, Georgia, Illinois, Louisiana, Mississippi, Missouri, Nevada, North Carolina, Oklahoma, South Carolina, Utah, and Virginia.

winning quick approval from half the necessary states. Stirred by this success, women who had worked for the ERA began to talk as if, quite literally, it signaled a new era. What began as a request for equal rights merged into the more militant cause of women's liberation. Guarantees purposely left vague in the wording of the amendment were now being discussed in concrete terms.

6 One such guarantee was that women, no less than men, should be free to choose what to do with whatever might happen to grow within the confines of their bodies. Needless to say, such an interpretation had serious implications. It was not as if women were demanding the right to decide about having their adenoids removed. In addition, much began to be said about what property rights women should be able to claim, either at the breakup of a marriage or even prior to the wedding. Here the hidden message seemed to be that divorce was an eventuality every woman could expect. There was also the whole "Ms." phenomenon—the magazine bearing that name started at just that time—which was part of a more generalized attack on all the disabilities inhering in the double standard. (And at the same time it was easy to imply that the title "Mrs." showed passive acquiescence to a subordinate condition.) Thus the passage of the ERA would be a sign that women were gaining not only legal rights but the power and the sanction to lead lives of their own choosing. Nor could its supporters imagine how any rational woman could object to these goals.

7 Still, the main impetus for the amendment arose from inequities in the area of employment—in particular, the obstacles women encountered in entering certain fields, obtaining equal pay, and getting merited promotions. At its simplest, equal rights would mean that fire departments could not refuse to consider a certain application because of the candidate's sex. But those in the vanguard of the ERA appeared also to be saying that for real emancipation to come about, women must begin filling the positions hitherto held by men. While there were polite murmurings about how other avenues were acceptable, the word was that you had better get out of the house and into something serious. Nor was it legitimate to settle for being a secretary or stewardess; little girls were reprimanded for playing at being nurses. Given this expanded outlook, the last letter in the ERA came to stand for more than the amendment. It signified an atmosphere and an

attitude that could cut across class lines. Women could be miners or state troopers as well as executives or attorneys. To the aim of equality was joined the spirit of independence.

8 It was at this point that Phyllis Schlafly gave form to a following that in fact was waiting for her. It is too easy to say that those for whom she spoke misunderstood the amendment. Allusions to unisex toilets and front-line combat duty were good for getting attention, but they weren't the central concern. The women who responded to Mrs. Schlafly were under no illusions about the impetus for the ERA. More than that, they were aware of how they would be affected, and, at the same time, were hesitant to air their underlying anxieties, at least in a public forum. So instead they spoke as if their chief concern were to preserve the family. But in so doing they were talking about themselves. For the women who felt most threatened by the ERA were housewives—and their number should not be underestimated, even in 1980.

9 There has been a great deal of talk about how housewives are a disappearing species. Betty Friedan, for example, likes to cite the statistic that among American households only seventeen percent remain with a father as the wage earner, the mother a full-time homemaker, and one or more resident children. In fact, the figures tell a different story. But before examining them, it would be well to realize that this country still has many millions of women for whom caring for a home has been their lifetime calling. Moreover, most of them remember when the vocation of housewife was an honored estate. Some are old enough to recall when on radio or television a woman was asked her occupation, if she answered "housewife" the rafters rang with applause.

10 It does little good to tell these women that remaining at home is still a respectable option. They know the esteem is no longer there. Now, when asked what they do, they find themselves saying "just a housewife" in apologetic tones. And from this grows an edge of anger over being made to feel outmoded. Nor do they feel better after reading articles about women who are going back to school and starting over at forty. For better or for worse, not all women have a taste for the competition that such a course entails. Indeed, the ERA is quintessentially American in that what it offers women is the legal right to vie with men for professions and promotions. Quite clearly, there are many

women who feel that with a fair chance they will end up among the winners. Other women, however, would rather not be tested. But the issue is not whether they are afraid of competing with men alone, as the working world already contains many ambitious women.

11 Nor for that matter should it be assumed that all younger women are committed to careers. Students at my college tell me that many women in high school set having a home and a husband as their overriding aim. Even today most marriages take place before the bride is twenty-two, and children are born soon thereafter. Younger women are liberated in many ways, and most ritually answer that they favor equal rights. But how far how many of them want to carve out identities of their own is more difficult to say. It may be replied that they need some consciousness-raising. If that is so, supporters of the ERA might do well to work on that before reviving the amendment.

12 What of reports that more married women are employed than ever before, and thus have a stake in a better deal at work? Here it would be well to see just what the figures say. To begin with, the Labor Department regards as having a job anyone who works ("for pay or profit") one hour or more during a given week. Under this generous interpretation, it is not surprising that so many women are classed as being in the labor force. The school crossing guard who goes on duty for ten hours a week gets the same statistical weight as an advertising executive who puts in a ten-hour day.

13 The Census Bureau also has tables showing that of all married women currently living with their husbands, fewer than a third have full-time jobs. Among mothers with children under six, three-quarters do not work at all or take only part-time jobs. And with wives whose children are all over eighteen, two-thirds either have not chosen employment or have limited themselves to part-time work. In fact, the majority of married women choose not to go to work once their children have left home.

14 Thus, in the typical two-income marriage, the wife contributes less than twenty-two percent of the family's total earnings, a fraction owing less to discrimination than to her supplemental schedule. Even for those who can say that they are more than "just a housewife," their obligations at home still take priority. At every class level the full-time working wife remains relatively

rare. Cases where one spouse is an urban planner and the other a financial analyst, with their two-year-old at a super day-care center, are not yet common enough to weight the statistical columns.

15 One of the more compelling arguments for the ERA addressed itself to women who find they must support themselves because of divorce or desertion or early widowhood. When circumstances require women to make it on their own, they discover just how limited their rights and opportunities are. Even now no one is entirely sure what claims a wife can make after twenty years of marriage. While alimony is less and less granted to a spouse, it has yet to be settled whether a husband must pay the bills while his former wife tries to equip herself for a gainful occupation. As was indicated earlier, these are rights any number of women may someday wish to assert.

16 Yet therein lies the rub. It is not that women who have stayed at home see themselves as second-class creatures deserving a lesser set of rights. Rather they look on themselves as having entered into a complementary contract. In return for caring for a husband and raising their children, what the wife expects in return is love and companionship, of course, but also a status of some honor and a measure of protection. To put the matter even more bluntly, she does not want to be divorced; nor does she even wish to contemplate how she would survive were that situation ever to come about. This may be a foolish attitude, but to label it as such is not the way to win converts to the ERA.

17 For the typical wife is shrewd enough to realize that the more women assert their rights, the more controls loosen over men. Until recently, men acquiesced to the moral and cultural pressures that kept marriages intact. Men may have stayed married out of duty; but at least they stayed. It is in this sense that the ERA atmosphere threatens family life. Moral obligations that once bound partners cannot be replaced by provisos and demands.

18 Germaine Greer once offered a two-word solution to a wife unhappy with her husband: "Leave him." Yet it would be well to acknowledge that as the middle years approach there are not that many marriages where the woman wants to pack her bags. Her situation may seem pathetic, especially if he wants out and she still wants to keep him. Or so it may appear to liberated women on whom years have yet to take a toll. At this point there is still

one unfairness even the ERA will not remedy: In our society women depreciate faster than men. Divorce can spell opportunities for a husband. For a wife it often means the end of the road she chose.

19 At this point we come to a phase of the ERA no one really wants to discuss. The divorce rate is not only rising, but is now hitting marriages once believed immune. Increasingly husbands in their forties are deciding they want another time around and are seeking this rejuvenation with a younger second wife. Of course, this situation is not entirely new. In the past, however, the other woman tended to be a manicurist or a chorus girl, a plot line more for the movies than for actual life. But now husbands are increasingly apt to have as colleagues high-powered younger women who understand their professional problems in ways a wife never can. These affinities can emerge as easily in a patrol car as in planning a marketing campaign. Shared work, particularly under pressure, has aphrodisiac effects.

20 For wives who mainly stay at home, the ERA stands for new relationships at work that can lead to losing a husband. Even if the wife at home has never seen the statistics, she knows that if she finds herself divorced at the age of forty her own chances of remarriage are less than one in three. This realization is hardly one to align her with women who seem ready to give their husbands a second stab at life. It is difficult to support an amendment that consigns you to the shelf.

21 With Phyllis Schlafly always in the limelight, many people concluded that opposition to the ERA was a one-woman operation. In fact, the rank and file were always there, but their support never took the form of a coherent movement. Women anxious about the ERA were not the sort to go on marches or bare their souls in public. Yet in countless informal ways they got their feelings across: in coffee hours, at country clubs, even over dinner at home. This was especially apparent at July's Republican convention, where close to a quarter of the delegates were women.

22 When a party aspiring to the presidency takes a stand against an amendment thought to have strong support, it should not be dismissed as an impulsive act. It could just be that the Republicans have been studying the political statistics over the past few years. They know that the people who count in politics are those

who actually go to the polls. And as it turns out, among married women close to two-thirds vote in most elections, whereas fewer than half of single women do. In addition, the median age of the American electorate is fast approaching fifty. Of persons between the ages of forty-five and sixty-four about 60 percent usually vote, while for those from twenty-five to thirty-four the figure is less than 40 percent. Ronald Reagan may hope to reap rewards by showing that he cares about citizens most likely to cast ballots.

23 The ERA was definitely a "woman's issue," with women dominating both sides of the struggle. If the amendment's supporters erred, it was in ignoring the sensibilities of women not avid for careers or for whom that option appears to come too late. Women opposed the ERA because it jeopardized a way of life they had entered in good faith. And their legislators listened.

Suggestions for Discussion and Writing

1. According to Hacker, what was the chief cause for the defeat of the Equal Rights Amendment? What were some of the mistaken notions or misinterpretations of the ERA that many people believed? Did you share any of these ideas? Did you change your mind after reading this article?
2. Is Hacker suggesting that most state legislators voted against the ERA because they were intimidated by its women opponents, or because they were against it in principle?
3. The author claims (paragraph 5) that early in its course, "the ERA lost its innocent status." What did the proposed amendment become, in the eyes of its opponents? What (*or* who) was responsible for that change?
4. Is it wrong to want to be a secretary, nurse, or flight attendant? Why have young women aspiring to these jobs often been made to feel they have "sold out"?
5. Is it true, as Hacker claims, that the women most threatened by the ERA were housewives? If he is correct, what image do most housewives have of themselves? Why do many women identify themselves as "just a housewife"?
6. Do you agree with Hacker's assessment of the "typical wife" (paragraph 17)? Is Germaine Greer's advice (paragraph 18) practical?
7. Explain why you agree or disagree with Hacker's claim (paragraph 19) that, "Increasingly husbands in their forties are de-

ciding they want another time around. . . ." If he is correct, what does this say about the permanence of marriage in our society?

8. How do the first and last paragraphs of this selection follow the funnel structure recommended in this chapter?
9. What paragraphs comprise the body or middle section of this essay? What pattern or strategy does Hacker use to arrange his ideas?
10. As explained in this chapter, the last sentence of a paragraph is the most emphatic, and the first sentence (normally the topic sentence) holds the next most emphatic place. Select two or three paragraphs from this selection to illustrate this idea.
11. Is Hacker neutral and objective in his discussion of the ERA, or does he reveal his biases and attitudes? Explain your answer by citing specific passages.
12. Write an essay in which you explain why you are for (or against) the Equal Rights Amendment. Follow the funnel structure in your introductory and concluding paragraphs, and try to begin all of your middle paragraphs with topic sentences.
13. Hacker claims (paragraph 18) that, "In our society women depreciate faster than men." If you agree with his observation, write an essay probing the causes of this disparity. If you believe that the opposite is true—that men depreciate faster than women—explain why it is true. In either case, follow the directions in question 12.
14. Is it true that "Younger women are liberated in many ways" (paragraph 11)? If you agree with this statement, write an essay demonstrating its truth. Follow the directions in question 13.

ROBERT JASTROW

Brains and Computers

1 Circuits, wires, and computing are strange terms to use for a biological organ like the brain, made largely of water, and without electronic parts. Nonetheless, they are accurate terms because brains work in very much the same way as computers. Brains think; computers add and subtract; but both devices seem

to work on the basis of the same fundamental steps in logical reasoning.

2 All arithmetic and mathematics can be broken down into these fundamental steps. Most kinds of thinking can also be broken down into such steps. Only the highest realms of creative activity seem to defy this analysis, but it is possible that even creative thinking could be broken down in this way, if the subconscious mind could be penetrated to examine the processes that appear at the conscious level as the flash of insight, or the stroke of genius.

3 The basic logical steps that underlie all mathematics and all reasoning are surprisingly simple. The most important ones are called AND and OR. AND is a code name for the reasoning that says, "If 'a' is true *and* 'b' is true, then 'c' is true." OR is a code name for the reasoning that says, "IF 'a' is true *or* 'b' is true, then 'c' is true." These lines of reasoning are converted into electrical circuits by means of devices called "gates." In a computer, the gates are made out of electronic parts—diodes or transistors. In the brain of an animal or a human, the gates are neurons or nerve cells. A gate—in a computer or in a brain—is an electrical pathway that opens up and allows electricity to pass through when certain conditions are satisfied. Normally, two wires go into one side of the gate, and another wire emerges from the other side of the gate. The two wires coming into the gate on one side represent the two ideas "a" *and* "b." The wire going out the other side of the gate represents the conclusion "c" based on these ideas. When a gate is wired up to be an AND gate, it works in such a way that if electrical signals flow into it from both the "a" and "b" wires, an electrical signal then flows out the other side through the "c" wire. From an electrical point of view, this is the same as saying, "If 'a' *and* 'b' are true, then 'c' is true."

4 When the gate is wired as an OR gate, on the other hand, it permits electricity to pass through the outgoing, or "c," wire if an electrical signal comes into the other side through either the "a" wire *or* the "b" wire. Electrically, this is the same as saying, "If 'a' *or* 'b' is true, then 'c' is true."

5 How do these two kinds of gates do arithmetic? How do they carry on a line of reasoning? Suppose a computer is about to add "1" and "1" to make "2"; this means that inside the computer a gate has two wires coming into it on one side, representing "1"

and "1," and a wire coming out on the other side, representing "2." If the gate is wired as an AND gate, then, when electrical signals come into it through both of the "1" wires, it sends a signal out the other side through the "2" wire. This gate has added "1" and "1" electrically to make "2."

6 Slightly different kinds of gates, but based on the same idea, can subtract, multiply, and divide. Thousands of such gates, wired together in different combinations, can do income tax returns, algebra problems, and higher mathematics. They can also be connected together to do the kinds of thinking and reasoning that enter into everyday life. Suppose, for example, that a company distributes several different lines of goods, and its management assigns a computer the task of keeping a continuous check on the inventories in these various product lines. Inside that computer, certain gates will be wired as AND gates to work in the following way: two wires coming into one side of the gate carry signals that indicate "stock depleted" and "sales volume heavy." If the stock is depleted *and* the sales are brisk, the gate opens, and a decision comes through: Order more goods!

7 OR gates are just as important in reasoning. Suppose that the same company also relies on its computer for guidance in setting prices. That means that a certain gate inside the computer is wired as an OR gate; coming into one side of this gate is a wire that indicates cash flow, another wire that indicates prices charged by a competitor for similar products, and a third wire that indicates the inventory in this particular product. If the company needs cash, *or* it is being undersold by its competitors, *or* it has an excess inventory, then the decision gate opens and a command comes through: Cut prices!

8 In a simple computer, the gates are wired together permanently, so that the computer can only do the same tasks over and over again. This kind of computer comes into the world wired to do one set of things, and can never depart from its fixed repertoire. A computer that solves the same problems in the same way, over and over again, is like a frog that can only snap at dark, moving spots; if either kind of brain is presented with a novel situation, it will react stupidly, or not react at all, because it lacks the wiring necessary for a new response to a new challenge. Such brains are unintelligent.

9 Larger, more complex computers have greater flexibility. In

these computers, the connections between the gates can be changed, and they can be wired up to do different kinds of things at different times; their repertoire is variable. The instructions for connecting the gates to do each particular kind of problem are stored in the computer's memory banks. These instructions are called the computer's "program." When a computer expert wants his machine to stop one kind of task and start another, he inserts a new program into the computer's memory. The new program automatically erases the old one, takes command of the machine, and sets about doing its appointed task.

10 However, this computer is still not intelligent; it has no innate flexibility. The flexibility and intelligence reside in its programmer. But if the memory banks of the computer are extremely large, a great advance in computer design becomes possible, that marks a highlight in the evolution of computers comparable to the first appearance of the mammals on the earth. A computer with a very large memory can store a set of instructions lengthy enough to permit it to learn by experience, just like an intelligent animal. Learning by experience requires a large memory and a very long set of instructions, i.e., a complicated program, because it is a much more elaborate way of solving problems than a stereotyped response would be. When a brain—electronic or animal—learns by experience, it goes through the following steps: first, it tries an approach; then it compares its result with the desired result, i.e., the goal; then, if it succeeds in achieving its goal, it sends an instruction to its memory to use the same approach next time; in the case of failure, it searches through its reasoning or computations to pinpoint the main source of error; finally, the brain adjusts the faulty part of its program to bring the result into line with its desires. Every time the same problem arises, the brain repeats the sequence and makes new adjustments to its program. A large computer has programs that work in just that fashion. Like a brain, it modifies its reasoning as its experience develops. In this way, the computer gradually improves its performance. It is learning.

11 A brain that can learn possesses the beginnings of intelligence. The requirements for this invaluable trait are, first, a good-sized memory, and, second, a wiring inside the brain that permits the circuits connecting the gates to be changed by the

experience of life. In fact, in the best brains—judging brain quality entirely by intelligence—many circuits are unwired initially; that is, the animal is born with a large number of the gates in its brain more or less unconnected with one another. The gates become connected gradually, as the animal learns the best strategies for its survival. In man, the part of the brain filled with blank circuits at birth is greater than in any other animal; that is what is meant by the plasticity of human behavior.

12 Large computers have some essential attributes of an intelligent brain: they have large memories, and they have gates whose connections can be modified by experience. However, the thinking of these computers tends to be narrow. The richness of human thought depends to a considerable degree on the enormous number of wires, or nerve fibers coming into each gate in the human brain. A gate in a computer has two, or three, or at most four wires entering on one side, and one wire coming out the other side. In the brain of an animal, the gates may have thousands of wires entering one side, instead of two or three. In the human brain, a gate may have as many as 100,000 wires entering it. Each wire comes from another gate or nerve cell. This means that every gate in the human brain is connected to as many as 100,000 other gates in other parts of the brain. During the process of thinking innumerable gates open and close throughout the brain. When one of these gates "decides" to open, the decision is the result of a complicated assessment involving inputs from thousands of other gates. This circumstance explains much of the difference between human thinking and computer thinking.

13 Furthermore, the gates in the brains of an animal or a human do not work on an "all-or-nothing" basis. The AND gate in a computer, for example, will only open if *all* the wires coming into it carry electrical signals. If one wire entering a computer gate fails to carry a signal, the gate remains shut. If every one of the 100,000 pathways into a gate in a human brain had to transmit an electrical signal before that gate could open, the brain would be paralyzed. Instead, most gates in the brain work on the principle of ALMOST, rather than AND or OR. The ALMOST gate makes human thought so imprecise, but so powerful. Suppose that 50,000 wires enter one side of a gate in a human brain; if this were an AND gate in a computer, all 50,000 things would have

to be true simultaneously before that gate opened and let a signal through. In real life, 50,000 things are rarely true at the same time, and any brain that waited for such a high degree of assurance before it acted would be an exceedingly slow brain. It would hardly ever reach a decision, and the possessor of a brain like that would not be likely to pass its genes on to the next generation.

14 Real brains work very differently. Wired largely out of ALMOST gates, they only require that, say, 10,000 or 15,000 things out of 50,000 shall be true about a situation before they act, or perhaps an even smaller number than that. As a consequence, they are inaccurate; they make mistakes sometimes; but they are very fast. In the struggle for survival, the value to the individual of the speed of such a brain more than offsets the disadvantages in its imprecision.

Suggestions for Discussion and Writing

1. As presented in this essay, what are the similarities between computers and brains? What are the most important differences?
2. Did Jastrow write his essay for those people already familiar with computers and their related terminology, or for laypeople? How do you know?
3. Using your own words, define an AND gate, an OR gate, and an ALMOST gate. How do these concepts relate to the ways humans think?
4. How does Jastrow keep his complicated subject readable and interesting—or does he?
5. Does Jastrow believe that computers are more intelligent than humans? Explain your answer.
6. How does the opening paragraph of this selection serve to organize the discussion that follows? What are the major sections of the essay?
7. Where is the thesis of this selection stated? Could it have been placed in another location?
8. If you believe that computers have had, on the whole, a harmful effect on our society, present your views in an essay. Be sure to write full, developed paragraphs with topic sentences.
9. Write an essay in which you speculate on the effect that computers will have on our society in the future. To avoid being general and vague, narrow the topic to a specific area: the

possible application of computers to farming, to music or another art, or to your own intended profession, for example.

10. Should students in grade school or secondary school be required to take courses in computers? Present your views in an essay that begins with a funnel paragraph.

5
Middle Tactics: Description, Narration, Exposition

With the whole essay in mind, we will now look more closely at the possibilities in arranging those middle points, the descriptive, narrative, and expository orders that illustrate your argument and carry your ideas. Description talks about what we see; narration, about what we do. Exposition, which may include both, essentially follows modes of thought, the ancient *topoi* of comparison and contrast, cause and effect, classification, definition. All are tactics for arrangement and persuasion.

DESCRIPTION

Description is essentially *spatial.* Arranging details in some kind of tour through space is as natural as walking. When your subject dwells in and upon physical space—the layout of a campus, for instance—you literally take your reader with you. You organize your paragraphs virtually as units of space, one for the gate, one for the first building, conducting your reader in an orderly progress down the mall or around the quadrangle. Or you show him a rooming house floor by floor, from the apartment by the entry to the garret four flights up, where the graduate student lives on books and cheese. Within the paragraph, you similarly take your reader from one detail to the next in spatial order. Your topic sentence summarizes the total effect: "The Whistler Building was once elegant, three classic stories of brick with carved stone pediments." Then your paragraph proceeds with noteworthy details in any convenient spatial order: first the sagging front door, then the windows to the left, then those to the right, then the second-floor windows, with their suggestion of dingy apartments, then those of the third, which suggest only emptiness.

A city's slum or its crowded parking, a river's pollution, a mountain's trees from valley to timberline—any spatial subject will offer a convenient route, from bottom to top, or top to bottom, left to right, east to west, center to periphery. You will instinctively use a series of spatial signals: *on the right, above, next, across, down the slope.* Your concern is to keep your progress orderly, to help your reader see what you are talking about. This is exactly the way Oliver Statler, in his *Japanese Inn,* takes us to the place he loves:

> **On this day, I have already progressed along the old Tokaido Road to the village of Yui. A new highway has been built a few hundred yards inland to avoid the congested main street of the village, but leaving Yui it swings back to the shore and runs between the sea wall on my left and the sheer face of Satta Mountain on my right.**
>
> **It is here, as I drive almost into the sea, that my spirits always quicken, for only Satta Mountain divides Yui from Okitsu, the next village, where my inn lies. . . . I notice men and women diving around the off-shore rocks, sharp knives in hand, hunting for abalone. Beyond them, fishing boats dot Suruga Bay. . . .**
>
> **At the highest point of the pass, where the path breaks out of the pines and into the open, there is a breath-taking view, and anyone who finds himself there must turn to drink it in. He faces the great sweep of Suruga Bay and the open Pacific beyond, while waves break into flowers on the rocks far beneath his feet. Yui lies on the shore to his left and Okitsu at his right. Beyond Yui, bathed in mist far off on the left, looms the mountainous coast of Izu. Beyond Okitsu, on the right, is one of the loveliest sights in Japan, for the harbor that lies there is protected by a long arm of curving black sand, covered with ancient and twisted pines. This is the fabled beach of Miho. . . .***

---

*Oliver Statler, *Japanese Inn* (New York: Pyramid Books, Random House, 1962): 14–16. Copyright © 1961, Oliver Statler.

As you can *see,* literally, the best spatial description follows the perceptions of a person looking at or entering the space described, reporting the impressions, the colors, textures, sights, or sounds as they come, as again with the imaginary visitor in this description by R. Prawer Jhabvala of a modern house in India:

> **Our foreign visitor stands agape at the wonderful residence his second host has built for himself. No expense has been spared here, no decoration suggested by a vivid taste omitted. There are little Moorish balconies and Indian domes and squiggly lattice work and an air-conditioner in every window. Inside, all is marble flooring, and in the entrance hall there is a fountain lit up with green, yellow, and red bulbs. The curtains on the windows and in the doorways are of silk, the vast sofa-suites are upholstered in velvet, the telephone is red, and huge vases are filled with plastic flowers.***

Some novels proceed like this paragraph after paragraph, as in the beginning of Thomas Hardy's *The Return of the Native,* for instance, in which we are moved into the setting from a great distance, as if, years before moving pictures, we are riding a cameraman's dolly.

Description frequently blends time and space, picking out striking features then moving along. This is the usual way of describing people, as in this paragraph about an actual Englishman whose odd occupation is mending the broken eggs brought to him by bird's-egg collectors:

> **Colonel Prynne, who is sixty-seven, lives and carries on his singular pursuit in a rambling, thatch-roofed, five-hundred-year-old cottage in the tiny village of Spaxton, Somerset, and there, on a recent sunny afternoon, he received us. A man of medium build who retains a military carriage, he was sprucely turned out in a brown suit, a tan jersey vest, a green shirt and tie, and tan oxfords. He has a bald, distinctly egg-shaped head, wears a close-cropped mustache and black shell-rimmed glasses, and seems always to have his nose tilted slightly upward and the nostrils faintly distended, as if he were sniffing the air. After taking us on a**

**Encounter* 22 (1964): 42–43.

rather cursory tour of his garden, which is as neat and well tended as its owner, he remarked crisply that it was time to get cracking, and we followed him indoors, past an enormous fireplace, which burns five-foot logs, and up a flight of stairs to a room that he calls his studio.*

NARRATION

In contrast with description, narration is essentially *temporal.* Like space, time is a natural organizer. Hour follows hour, day follows day, year follows year, life follows life. Again, you simply take your reader along the natural sequence of what happens—to us, or to nations, or to any items in experience or experiment. We understand processes most clearly by tracking the way they move through time, even processes complicated by other, simultaneous events:

And when this wheel turns, that lever tips the food into the trough.
While this conveyor moves into the oven, the other one is bringing the chassis to point B.
And all the time he talked, his hands were moving the shells and flicking the invisible pea.

Any event, whether a football game or the inauguration of a president, can be best perceived as you have perceived it—through time—and you can bring your reader to perceive it by following the sequence of things as they happened, stepping aside as necessary to explain background and simultaneous events, guiding your reader along with temporal signposts: *at the same time, now, when, while, then, before, after, next, all the time.*

As Audubon, the nineteenth-century naturalist, describes in his *Ornithological Biography* the passenger pigeon and its astounding flights in masses a mile wide and 180 long, he naturally gives us his observations through the order of time. I have italicized the temporal words in one of his paragraphs:

---

*"Talk of the Town," *The New Yorker* (23 May 1964): 37. © 1964, The New Yorker Magazine, Inc. Reprinted by permission.

As soon as the pigeons discover a sufficiency of food to entice them to alight, they fly round in circles, reviewing the country below. *During* their evolutions, *on such occasions,* the dense mass which they form exhibits a beautiful appearance, *as* it changes direction, *now* displaying a glistening sheet of azure, *when* the backs of the birds come *simultaneously* into view, *and anon, suddenly* presenting a mass of rich deep purple. They *then* pass lower, over the woods, and *for a moment* are lost among the foliage, *but again* emerge, and are seen gliding aloft. They *now* alight, but *the next moment,* as if *suddenly* alarmed, they take to wing, producing by the flappings of their wings a noise like the roar of distant thunder, and sweep through the forests to see if danger is near. Hunger, however, *soon* brings them to the ground. *When* alighted, they are seen industriously throwing up the withered leaves. . . .

You can most clearly explain any kind of development or decline—the civil rights movement, the decay of a neighborhood—by taking your reader up or down the path of time. But you will do your reader a favor by keeping to your order, whether forward or backward, and not reversing it inadvertently somewhere along the way. Any event invites chronological narration, and such narration naturally includes a rich infusion of description, often alive with pictorial metaphors to convey the writer's impressions. Frank A. Worsley does this surpassingly well as he describes his sailing journey, with Sir Ernest Shackleton and four others, in a small boat through grotesquely melting Antarctic icebergs:

They rose and fell on the heaving sea, drawing deceptively apart, then closing with a thud that would have smashed our boat like a gas-mantle between thumb and finger. Castles, towers, and churches swayed unsteadily around us. Small pieces gathered and rattled against the boat. Swans of weird shape pecked at our planks; a gondola steered by a giraffe ran foul of us, which much amused a duck sitting on a crocodile's head. Just then a bear, leaning over the top of a mosque, nearly clawed our sail. An elephant, about to spring from a Swiss chalet on to a battleship's deck, took no notice at all; but a hyena, pulling a lion's teeth, laughed so much that he fell into the sea, whereupon a sea-boot and three real penguins sailed lazily through a lovely archway to see what was to do, by the

> **shores of a floe littered with the ruins of a beautiful white city and surrounded by huge mushrooms with thick stalks. All the strange, fantastic shapes rose and fell in stately cadence, with a rustling, whispering sound and hollow echoes to the thudding seas, clear green at the water-line, shading to a deep blue far below, all snowy purity and cool blue shadows above.***

Sometimes an argumentative essay will give over its entire middle to a narrative of some event that illustrates its thesis. Of this kind is George Orwell's great "Shooting an Elephant." Orwell's thesis is that imperialism tyrannizes over the rulers as well as the ruled. To illustrate it, he tells of an incident during his career as a young police officer in Burma, when he was compelled, by the expectations of the crowd, to shoot a renegade elephant. Here is a narrative paragraph in which Orwell reports a crucial moment; notice how he mixes external events and snippets of conversation with his inner thoughts, pegging all perfectly with a topic sentence:

> **But I did not want to shoot the elephant. I watched him beating his bunch of grass against his knees, with that preoccupied grandmotherly air that elephants have. It seemed to me that it would be murder to shoot him. At that age I was not squeamish about killing animals, but I had never shot an elephant and never wanted to. (Somehow it always seems worse to kill a *large* animal.) Besides, there was the beast's owner to be considered. Alive, the elephant was worth at least a hundred pounds; dead, he would only be worth the value of his tusks, five pounds, possibly. But I had got to act quickly. I turned to some experienced-looking Burmans who had been there when we arrived, and asked them how the elephant had been behaving. They all said the same thing: he took no notice of you if you left him alone, but he might charge if you went too close to him.†**

---

*Commander F. A. Worsley, *Shackleton's Boat Journey,* Introduction and Notes by Duncan Carse (London: The Folio Society, 1974): 66–67.

Orwell is simply recounting events, and his thoughts, as they happened, one after the other. Almost any kind of essay could use a similar paragraph of narrative to illustrate a point.

EXPOSITION

Exposition is a setting forth, an explaining, which naturally may include both description and narration. But it also includes some essential modes of thought: comparison and contrast, cause and effect, classification, and definition. Good exposition depends on specific details to illustrate its general point.

Loren Eisley, for instance, illustrates his generalization "these apes are not similar" not only with comparative contrasts but with particularized specifics. He has been writing about Alfred Russel Wallace's and Charles Darwin's conflicting views as to the evolution of man's brain from that of the humanoid ape:

> **These apes are not all similar in type or appearance. They are men and yet not men. Some are frailer-bodied, some have great, bone-cracking jaws and massive gorilloid crests atop their skulls. This fact leads us to another of Wallace's remarkable perceptions of long ago. With the rise of the truly human brain, Wallace saw that man had transferred to his machines and tools many of the alterations of parts that in animals take place through evolution of the body. Unwittingly, man had assigned to his machines the selective evolution which in the animal changes the nature of its bodily structure through the ages. Man of today, the atomic manipulator, the aeronaut who flies faster than sound, has precisely the same brain and body as his ancestors of twenty thousand years ago who painted the last Ice Age mammoths on the walls of caves in France.***

Notice how he spells out the specifics of bodies, jaws, and skulls. He does not say *aeronauts,* plural, but *the* single and specific *aeronaut,* adding the further specific *who flies faster than sound,*

---

*"The Real Secret of Piltdown," in *The Immense Journey* (New York: Random House, Inc., 1955). © Copyright 1955 by Loren C. Eiseley.

letting that single specific person illustrate the whole general range of what man can do with machines. He does not say merely "ancestors," but ancestors of specifically *twenty thousand years ago;* not merely "lived," but *who painted,* and not merely "pictures," but *the last Ice Age mammoths,* and specifically on *walls* in specific *caves* in one specific country, *France.* The point is to try to extend each of your generalizations by adding some specific detail to illustrate it. Don't stop with *awkward player:* go on to *when he strikes out, or misses an easy fly, or an easy basket.*

Your illustration may also be hypothetical, as it frequently is in scientific explanation. "Suppose you are riding along in a car," the scientist will say, as he tries to convey the idea of relative motion. "You drop a baseball straight down from your hand to the floor between your feet." And he continues by explaining that this vertical drop describes a long line slanting downward in relation to the line of the rapidly receding highway beneath the car, illustrating each new aspect of relativity, by the same dropped ball in its relation to curves in the road, the earth itself, the sun, and to whatever hypothetical platforms he may wish to put into orbit.

Comparison and Contrast: Run Contrasts Side by Side

Comparison and contrast is a natural mode of thought, a natural organizer of exposition, making two specifics vivid by bringing them side by side. It may be the very basis of thought itself. All knowledge involves comparing things for their similarities and noticing their contrasting differences. We group all people as people, and then tell them apart as individuals.

We instinctively know our friends in this way, for instance. Two of them drift side by side in our thoughts. We are comparing them. They are both boys; they are the same age and stature; we like them both. But one bubbles up like a mountain spring, and the other runs deep. Their appearances, mannerisms, and tastes match their contrasting personalities. One's room is messy; the other's is neat. One races his car; the other collects stamps. We compare the similar categories—looks, habits, hobbies, goals—and contrast the differences.

Your topic sentence sets the comparison and makes the contrast:

Contrast

Opposites seem to attract. ***My father is tall, blond, and outgoing. My mother is small, and even her dark brown hair, which is naturally wavy, has a certain quiet repose about it. My dad does everything at a cheerful run,*** **whether he is off to a sales conference or off to the golf course with his foursome on Saturday mornings.** ***My mother never seems to hurry.*** **She hums at her work, and the house seems to slip into order without effort. She plays bridge with a few friends, and belongs to a number of organizations, but she is just as happy with a book. When dad bursts in at the end of the day, her face lights up. They grin at each other. They obviously still find each other attractive.**

Comparison and Contrast: Illustrate by Analogy

An analogy points up similarities between things otherwise dissimilar. With an analogy, you help your reader grasp your subject by showing how it is like something familiar. Your topic sentence asserts the comparison, and then your paragraph unfolds the comparison in detail:

School spirit is like patriotism. Students take their school's fortunes as their own, defending and promoting them against those of another school, as citizens champion their country, right or wrong. Their school is not only their alma mater but their fatherland as well. Like soldiers, they will give their utmost strength in field games and intellectual contests for both personal glory and the greater glory of the domain they represent. And, in defeat, they will mourn as if dragged in chains through the streets of Rome.

Here is E. B. White describing Thoreau's *Walden.* His comparison shows that analogy is really a form of extended metaphor:

Topic Sentence with Analogy

Thoreau's assault on the Concord society of the mid-nineteenth century has the quality of a modern Western: he rides into the subject at top speed, shooting in all direc-

Analogy Extended Analogy Extended

tions. Many of his shots ricochet and nick him on the rebound, and throughout the melee there is a horrendous cloud of inconsistencies and contradictions, and when the shooting dies down and the air clears, one is impressed chiefly by the courage of the rider and by how splendid it was that somebody should have ridden in there and raised all that ruckus.*

That is probably as long as an analogy can effectively run. One paragraph is about the limit. Beyond that, the reader may tire of it.

Comparison and Contrast: Develop Differences Point by Point

Your *comparisons* present helpful illustrations of your subject by emphasizing similarities. Contrasts, on the other hand, compare similar things to emphasize their differences—West Germany as against East Germany, for example—usually to persuade your reader that one is in some or most ways better than the other.

The danger lies in losing your contrastive advantage, writing about one side of your contrast and forgetting the other. Make your comparisons point for point. Don't write all about sheep for three pages, for instance, then all about goats. Every time you say something about a sheep, say something comparable about a goat, pelt for pelt, horn for horn, beard for beard. Otherwise your essay will fall in two, your reader will be surprised when the goats come along, and you will need to repeat all your sheep points when you at last begin the comparison. So keep your contrasts vivid, point for point.

Keep both sides before the reader. You may do this in one of two ways: (1) by making a topic sentence to cover one point —agriculture, let us say—and then continuing your paragraph in paired sentences, one for the West, one for the East, another for the West, another for the East, and so on; or (2) by writing your

---

*From "A Slight Sound at Evening," *The Essays of E. B. White* (New York: Harper & Row, 1982): 235–36.

paragraphs in pairs, one paragraph for the West, one for the East, using the topic sentence of the first paragraph to govern the second, something like this:

> *West Germany's agriculture is far ahead of the East's.* **Everywhere about the countryside, one sees signs of prosperity. Trucks and tractors are shiny. Fences are mended and in order. Buildings all seem newly painted, as if on exhibit for a fair. New Volkswagens buzz along the country roads. The annual statistics spell out the prosperous details. . . .**
>
> *East Germany, on the other hand, seems to be dropping progressively behind.* **The countryside is drab and empty. On one huge commune, everything from buildings to equipment seems to be creaking from rusty hinges. . . . The annual statistics are equally depressing. . . .**

Topic Sentence West

Contrast

In an extended contrast, you will probably want to contrast some things sentence against sentence, within single paragraphs, and to contrast others by giving a paragraph to each. Remember only to keep your reader sufficiently in touch with both sides.

Here are two paragraphs from a student's paper neatly contrasted without losing touch:

> **In fact,** *in some respects the commercials are really better than the shows they sponsor.* **The** *commericals are carefully rehearsed, expertly photographed, highly edited and polished.* **They are made with absolute attention to detail and to the clock. One split-second over time, one bad note, one slightly wrinkled dress, and they are done over again. Weeks, even months, go into the production of a single sixty-second commerical.**
>
> *The shows, on the other hand, are slapped together hastily by writers and performers who have less than a week to put together an hour show.* **Actors have little time to rehearse, and often the pieces of a show are put together for the first time in front of the camera. Lighting, sound reproduction, and editing are workmanlike, but unpolished; a shadow from an overhead microphone on an actor's face causes no real concern in the control room. A blown line or a muffed cue is "just one of those things that happen." In all, it often takes less time and money to do an hour show than to do the four sixty-second commercials that sponsor it.**

Topic Sentence First Subject

The Contrast

Contrasts done sentence by sentence, or by clauses hinged on a semicolon, are also effective:

> **The most essential distinction between athletics and education lies in the institution's own interest in the athlete as distinguished from its interest in its other students. Universities attract students in order to teach them what they do not already know; they recruit athletes only when they are already proficient. Students are educated for something which will be useful to them and to society after graduation; athletes are required to spend their time on activities the usefulness of which disappears upon graduation or soon thereafter. Universities exist to do what they can for students; athletes are recruited for what they can do for the universities. This makes the operation of the athletic program in which recruited players are used basically different from any educational interest of colleges and universities.***

Cause and Effect: Trace Back or Look Ahead

Because is the impulse here: "Such and such is so *because. . . .*" You think back through a train of causes, each one the effect of something prior; or you think your way into the future, speculating about the possible effects of some present cause. In other words, you organize your paragraph in one of two ways:

1. You state a general effect, then deal with its several causes.
2. You state a general cause, then deal with its possible effects.

In Arrangement 1, you know the effect (a lost football game, or the solar system, let us say), and you speculate as to causes. In Arrangement 2, you know the cause (a new restriction, or abolishing nuclear weapons, let us say), and you speculate as to the effects.

---

*Harold W. Stoke, "College Athletics: Education or Show Business?" *Atlantic Monthly* (March 1954): 46–50. Copyright © 1954 by Harold W. Stoke. Reprinted by permission.

Arrangement 1: Effect Followed by Causes

An unusual cluster of bad luck lost the game. Many blamed Fraser's failure to block the tackler who caused the fumble that produced the winning touchdown. But even here, bad weather and bad luck shared the blame. Both teams faced a slippery field, of course. But Fraser was standing in a virtual bog when he lunged for the block and slipped. Moreover, the storm had delayed the bus for hours, tiring and frustrating the team, leaving them short of sleep and with no chance to practice. Furthermore, Hunter's throwing arm was still not back in shape from his early injury. Finally, one must admit, the Acorns were simply heavier and stronger, which is the real luck of the game.

You will probably notice, as you try to explain causes and effects, that they do not always run in a simple linear sequence, one thing following another, like a row of falling dominoes. Indeed, mere sequence is so famously untrustworthy in tracing causes that one of the classical errors of thought is named *post hoc, ergo propter hoc* ("after this, therefore because of this"). In other words, we cannot reasonably suppose that *A* caused *B* simply because *A* preceded *B*. The two may have been entirely unrelated. But the greatest danger in identifying causes is to fasten upon a single cause while ignoring others of equal significance. Both your paragraph and your persuasiveness will be better if you do not insist, as some did, that only Fraser's failure to block the tackler lost the game.

In the lost ball game, you were interested in explaining causes, but sometimes your interest will lie with effects. When describing a slum problem, for instance, your topic sentence might be *The downtown slum is a screaming disgrace* (the effect), and you might then in a single sentence set aside the causes as irrelevant, as water over the dam, as so much spilt milk: "perhaps caused by inefficiency, perhaps by avarice, perhaps by the indifference of Mayor Richman." Your interests will dictate your proportions of cause and effect. You might well write an entire essay that balances the slum's causes and effects in equal proportions: a paragraph each on inefficiency, avarice, and the mayor's indifference, then a paragraph each on ill health, poor education, and hopelessness.

Here is how a brief essay, in three paragraphs, can deal with cause and effect alone. I have begun and ended with the *effect* (the peculiar layout of a town). First, I located the *immediate cause* (cattle) as my thesis, and then, in the middle paragraph, I moved through the cause and its *conditions* up to the *effect* again—the town as it stands today:

North of the Tracks

Effect — **If you drive out west from Chicago, you will notice something happening to the towns.** ***After the country levels into Nebraska, the smaller towns are built only on one side of the road.*** **When you stop for a rest, and look south across the broad main street, you will see the railroad immediately beyond.** ***All of these towns spread northward from the tracks. Why?*** **As you munch your hamburger and look at the restaurant's murals,** ***you will realize that the answer is cattle.***

Effect

Thesis

Cause

Conditions — ***These towns were the destinations of the great cattle drives from Texas.*** **They probably had begun at the scattered watering places in the dry land. Then** ***the wagon trails and,*** **finally,** ***the transcontinental railroad had strung them together.*** **Once the railroad came, the whole Southwest could raise cattle for the slaughter-houses of Chicago. The droves of cattle came up from the south, and** ***all of these towns reflect the traffic:*** **corrals beside the tracks to the south, the road for passengers and wagons paralleling the tracks on the northern side, then, along the road, the row of hotels, saloons, and businesses, with the town spreading northward behind the businesses.**

Causes

Effect

Cause — ***The cattle-business itself shaped these one-sided Nebraska towns.*** **The conditions in which this immediate cause took root were the growing population in the East and the railroad that connected the plains of the West, and Southwest, with the tables of New York. The towns took their hopeful being north of the rails, on the leeward side of the vast cattle drives from the south. The trade in cattle has now changed, all the way from Miami to Sacramento. But** ***the great herds of the old Southwest, together with the transcontinental railroad and man's need to make a living, plotted these Western towns north of the tracks.***

Effect

Arrangement 2: Cause Followed by Probable Effects

Arrangement 2 is the staple of deliberative rhetoric, of all political and economic forecasting, for instance. Your order of presenting cause and effect is reversed. You are looking to the future. You state a known cause (a new restriction on dormitory hours) or a hypothetical cause ("If this restriction is passed"), and then you speculate about the possible, or probable, effects. Your procedure will then be much the same as before. But for maximum persuasiveness, try to keep your supposed effects, which no one can really foresee, as nearly probable as you can. Occasionally, of course, you may put an improbable hypothetical cause to good use in a satiric essay, reducing some proposal to absurdity: "If all restrictions were abolished. . . ." "If no one wore clothes. . . ." Or the improbable *if* may even help clarify a straightforward explanation of real relationships, as in the following excerpt from *Time* magazines's report on Fred Hoyle, the British astronomer and mathematician who has been modifying Newton's gravity and Einstein's relativity. The paragraph states the general condition, proposes its hypothetical cause with an *if,* then moves to the effects, first in temporal order and then in order of human interest:

> **The masses, and therefore the gravity, of the sun and the earth are partly due to each other, partly to more distant objects such as the stars and galaxies. According to Hoyle, if the universe were to be cut in half, local solar-system gravitation would double, drawing the earth closer to the sun. The pressure in the sun's center would increase, thus raising its temperature, its generation of energy, and its brightness. Before being seared into a lump of charcoal, a man on earth would find his weight increasing from 150 to 300 lbs.**

Classification: Use the Natural Divisions

Many subjects fall into natural or customary classifications, as if they were blandly jointed, like a good roast of pork ready for carving, contrasting one joint with the next: freshman, sophomore, junior, senior; Republicans, Democrats; right, middle, left; legislative, executive, judicial. You can easily follow these divisions in organizing a paragraph, or you can write one paragraph for each division, and attain a nicely coherent essay. Similarly, any manufacturing process, or any machine, will already have distinct steps and parts. These customary divisions will help your reader, since he knows something of them already. Describe the Democratic position on inflation, and he will naturally expect your description of the Republican position to follow. If no other divisions suggest themselves, you can often organize your paragraph—or your essay—into a consistent series of parallel answers, or "reasons for," or "reasons against," something like this:

> **A broad liberal education is best:**
> **1. It prepares you for a world of changing employment.**
> **2. It enables you to function well as a citizen.**
> **3. It enables you to make the most of your life.**

Many problems present natural classifying joints. Take the Panama Canal, for instance. Its construction divides into three nicely jointed problems, political, geological, and biological, each with its solutions, as the following paragraph shows:

Problem 1
Solution 1
Problem(s) 2
Solution to 2
Problem 3
Solution to 3

> **Building the Panama Canal posed problems of politics, geology, and human survival from the beginning.** ***A French company, organized in 1880 to dig the canal, repeatedly had to extend its treaties at higher and higher prices as the work dragged on.*** **Uneasy about the French,** ***the United States made treaties with Nicaragua and Costa Rica*** **to dig along the other most feasible route.** ***This political threat,*** **together with the failure of the French and the revolt of Panama from Colombia,** ***finally enabled the United States to buy the French rights and negotiate new treaties,*** **which, nevertheless, continue to cause political trouble to this day.** ***Geology also posed its ancient problems:*** **how to manage torrential rivers and inland lakes; whether to build a longer but more enduring canal at sea level, or** ***a shorter, cheaper, and safer canal with locks.*** **Economy eventually won, but the problem of** ***yellow fever and malaria,*** **which had plagued the French, remained.** ***By detecting and combating the fever-carrying mosquito, William Gorgas solved these ancient tropical problems.*** **Without him, the political and geological solutions would have come to nothing.**

You could easily organize this into three paragraphs of problem and solution, with topic sentences like these:

> **The Panama Canal posed three major problems, the first of which was political.**
> **The second problem was geological, a massive problem of engineering.**
> **The third problem, that of human survival, proved the most stubborn of all.**

Any problem and its solution can produce a neatly ordered paragraph—or essay, for that matter: choosing a college, or something to wear (if you want to be light-hearted), making an apartment or a commune work, building the Eiffel Tower or the pyramids. You can often similarly classify sets of comparisons and contrasts, causes and effects, combining your tactics with magnified force.

Describing Processes: Follow the Natural Steps

Describing a process combines description and narration with classification. This is probably exposition at its most basic intent: explaining how to assemble the Christmas toy, the new hibachi or deck chair, how to build a sun dial or plant a vegetable garden or write an essay. Your subject will again offer natural sequences in space and time and natural divisions in classification. As always, you will find a topic sentence to govern the job. Then you proceed through those steps that will most clearly help your reader to do the job:

> **Growing the iris, the poor man's orchid, is easy. Irises grow almost like weeds in well drained soil, but a little care pays glorious dividends. Plant your rhizomes—the iris root—in early fall. First, enrich your soil with an organic fertilizer low in nitrogen, at about one ounce to the square foot, three weeks before planting. Then plant the rhizomes almost even with the surface. Spruce up each plant in the spring with a quarter of a cup of superphosphate. In the fourth or fifth year, dig them up in late July or early September. Cut off the old tubers with a sharp knife. Let the hardy tubers harden in the sun for a day. Then replant them. They bloom long in the spring, and their attractive fans of leaves stand green until fall.**

In the following paper, a student has nicely amalgamated description, narration, and the classification implied in a problem and its solution to analyze a fascinating process.

Nothing Primitive About It

Thesis
Problem 1
Description and Narration
Problem 2

Stonehenge, the gigantic prehistoric construction on Salisbury Plain in England, cannot fail to fascinate us with a number of nearly unanswerable questions. How long has it been there? Who built it? Why? But of all the questions Stonehenge raises, none is more intriguing than *"How was it built?" How did these primitive people,* whose only tools were rock, bone, or crudely fashioned sticks, who had not yet even discovered the wheel, *manage to transport* the *huge rocks,* most of them more than twenty feet in length and weighing over thirty tons, *more than twenty miles overland? And by what ingenuity did they manage,* having transported the rocks, *to stand them on end and support them so that now,* thousands of years later, *most* of them *still stand?* What primitive engineering geniuses were these?

Narrating the Process
Solutions to 1
First Classification
Second Classification
Narrating and Describing the Process
Third Classification

Transporting the stones from their original site at Marlborough Downs, some twenty miles to the north of Stonehenge, must have been, by any of the possible means, a very slow process. One possibility is that *hundreds of men,* some pulling on the rock, some cutting down trees and filling in holes as they went, *simply dragged the stones over the bare ground. Or perhaps they used snow or mud to "grease" the path.* Foot by foot, and day by day, they may have dragged the rocks all the way from Marlborough Downs to Stonehenge. *Another guess is that these primitive men,* even though they had not yet invented the wheel, *knew about using logs as rollers.* If so, perhaps they mounted each stone on a sledge, and rolled the sledge slowly forward, workmen placing logs in its path as it moved. Such a method, while a good deal easier than dragging the rock along the ground, would still have required as many as seven or eight hundred men, and perhaps as much as a decade to move all the stones. *A third possibility is that the stones were moved along riverbeds,* the shallow water helping to buoy the weight, and the muddy banks helping to slide the weight along. Though much less direct than the overland route, the riverbed route would have provided these primitive men with a relatively clear path that ran approximately halfway from the stones' point of origin to their final location. Of course, the point is that any of these three means of transporting the stones must have been an

incredibly laborious task, occupying as many as a thousand men, year after year after year.

Lifting the stones into an upright position, **once they had been transported,** *was another triumph of ingenuity and brute strength.* **Apparently, the workmen dug closely fitted holes where they wanted the stones eventually to stand. Probably they cut away one side of the hole, the side nearest the stone, to form a ramp. Perhaps they also lined the hole with wooden skids. Then gradually they eased the stone down the ramp until it rested in a tilted position at the bottom of the hole. Next, they used brute strength, some men pushing, some pulling on primitive ropes, to raise the rock into a vertical position. If we suppose each man lifted only his own weight, say 150 pounds, it might have taken as many as 400 men to stand the stones upright. Finally, while some workers held the rock in position, others quickly filled in the excavation left by the ramp. For many months afterward they probably refilled and pounded the dirt until it was completely firm. They probably placed the huge transverse pieces across the tops of columns by similarly dragging them up long earthern ramps. The fact that most of the rocks are still standing after thousands of years is testimony of their planning and workmanship.**

Solutions to 2 Describing and Narrating the Process

We may never know quite why these primitive men chose to build Stonehenge, or who the men were. We may never know where they came from, or where they went. *In Stonehenge, however, they have left a testament to their perserverance and their ingenuity. Clearly, they rivaled any of the builders of the ancient world.*

Thesis Restated

Definition: Clear Up Your Terms

Definition is another mode of classification, in which we clear away hidden assumptions along with unwanted categories. What the Russians and Chinese call a People's Democracy is the very opposite of what the Americans and British call democracy, assumed also to be of and for and by the people. Ideally, your running prose should make your terms clear to your reader, avoiding those definitions that seem too stiff and stuffy, and especially avoid quoting the dictionary: "As *Webster's* says. . . ." Nevertheless, what we mean by *egotism, superiority, education,* or *character* may need laying on the table.

Richard Hofstadter, for instance, found it necessary in his essay "Democracy and Anti-Intellectualism in America" to devote a number of paragraphs to defining both *democracy* and *intellectual,* each paragraph examining the evidence and clarifying one aspect of his term. Coming early in his essay, after he has set his thesis and surveyed his subject, his section of definition begins with the following paragraph:

Topic Sentence as Question

What It Is *Not*

What It *Is*

Con: Examples

Pro: Examples

Con: Detailed Opposition

But what is an intellectual, really? This is a problem of definition that I found, when I came to it, far more elusive than I had anticipated. *A great deal of what might be called the journeyman's work of our culture*—the work of engineers, physicians, newspapermen, and indeed of most professors—*does not strike me as distinctively intellectual,* although it is certainly work based in an important sense on ideas. *The distinction that we must recognize,* then, *is one* originally made by Max Weber *between living* for *ideas and living* off *ideas. The intellectual lives for ideas;* the journeyman lives off them. *The engineer or the physician*—I don't mean here to be invidious—*needs to have a pretty considerable capital stock in frozen ideas* to do his work; but they *serve for him a purely instrumental purpose: he lives off them, not for them.* Of course *he may also be, in his private role and his personal ways of thought, an intellectual,* but it is not necessary for him to be in order to work at his profession. There is in fact no profession which demands that one be an intellectual. *There do seem to be vocations, however, which almost demand that one be an anti-intellectual,* in which those who live off ideas seem to have implacable hatred for those who live for them. The marginal intellectual workers and the unfrocked intellectuals who work in journalism, advertising, and mass communication are the bitterest and most powerful among those who work at such vocations.*

Your subject will prompt you in one of two ways, toward inclusiveness or toward exclusiveness. Hofstadter found that he needed to be inclusive about the several essentials in *democracy* and *intellectual*—terms used commonly, and often loosely. Inclusiveness is the usual need, as you will find in trying to define *love* or *loyalty* or *education.* But you may sometimes need to move

---

* *The Michigan Alumnus Quarterly Review* 59 (1953): 282. Copyright © 1953 by the University of Michigan.

in the opposite direction, toward exclusiveness, as in sociological, philosophical, or scientific discussion, when you need to nail your terms firmly to single meanings: "By *reality,* I mean only that which exists in the physical world excluding our ideas about it."

Such exclusive defining is called *stipulative,* since you stipulate the precise meaning you want. But you should avoid the danger of trying to exclude more than the word will allow. If you try to limit the meaning of the term *course* to "three hours a week a semester," your discussion will soon encounter courses with different hours; or you may find yourself inadvertently drifting to another meaning, as you mention something about graduating from an "engineering course." At any rate, if you can avoid the sound of dogmatism in your stipulation, so much the better. You may well practice some disguise, as with *properly speaking* and *only* in the following stipulative definition: "Properly speaking, the *structure* of any literary work is only that framelike quality we can picture in two, or three, dimensions."

Definitions frequently seem to develop into paragraphs, almost by second nature. A sentence of definition is usually short and crisp, seeming to demand some explanation, some illustration and sociability. The definition, in other words, is a natural topic sentence. Here are three classic single-sentence kinds of definition that will serve well as topics for your paragraphs:

1. DEFINITION BY SYNONYM. A quick way to stipulate the single meaning you want: "Virtue means moral rectitude."
2. DEFINITION BY FUNCTION. "A barometer measures atmospheric pressure"—"A social barometer measures human pressures"—"A good quarterback calls the signals and sparks the whole team's spirits."
3. DEFINITION BY SYNTHESIS. A placing of your term in striking (and not necessarily logical) relationship to its whole class, usually for the purposes of wit: "The fox is the craftiest of beasts"—"A sheep is a friendlier form of goat"—"A lexicographer is a harmless drudge"—"A sophomore is a sophisticated moron."

Three more of the classic kinds of definition follow, of broader dimensions than the single-sentence kinds above, but also ready-made for a paragraph apiece, or for several. Actually, in making paragraphs from your single-sentence definitions, you have undoubtedly used at least one of these three kinds, or a mixture of them all. They are no more than the natural ways we define our meanings.

4. DEFINITION BY EXAMPLE. The opposite of *definition by synthesis.* You start with the class ("crafty beasts") and then name a member or two ("fox"—plus monkey and raccoon). But of course you would go on to give further examples or illustrations—accounts of how the bacon was snitched through the screen—that broaden your definition beyond the mere naming of class and members.
5. DEFINITION BY COMPARISON. You just use a paragraph of comparison to expand and explain your definition. Begin with a topic sentence something like: "Love is like the sun." Then extend your comparison on to the end of the paragraph (or even separate it, if your cup runneth over, into several paragraphs), as you develop the idea: love is like the sun because it too gives out warmth, makes everything bright, shines even when it is not seen, and is indeed the center of our lives.
6. DEFINITION BY ANALYSIS. This is Hofstader's way, a searching out and explaining of the essentials in terms used generally, loosely, and often in ways that emphasize incidentals for biased reasons, as when it is said that an *intellectual* is a manipulator of ideas.

Here are four good steps to take in reaching a thorough definition of something, assuring that you have covered all the angles. Consider:

1. What it *is not like*
2. What it *is like.*
3. What it *is not.*
4. What it *is.*

This program can produce a good paragraph of definition:

Love may be many things to many people, but, all in all,
1 **we agree on its essentials.** ***Love is not like a rummage sale,*** **in**
2 **which everyone tries to grab what he wants.** ***It is more like a Christmas,*** **in which gifts and thoughtfulness come just a little unexpectedly, even from routine directions.** ***Love, in***

> ***short, is not a matter of seeking self-satisfaction; it is first a matter of giving and then discovering,* as an unexpected gift, *the deepest satisfaction one can know.*** 3 4

The four steps above can also furnish four effective paragraphs, which you would present in the same order of ascending interest and climax. The same tactics also work well in reverse order:

> ***Black Power means, for example, that in Lowndes County, Alabama, a black sheriff can end police brutality.* A black tax assessor and tax collector and county board of revenue can lay, collect, and channel tax monies for the building of better roads and schools serving black people. In such areas as Lowndes, where black people have a majority, they will attempt to use power to exercise control. This is what they seek: control. When black people lack a majority, Black Power means proper representation and sharing of control. It means the creation of power bases, of strength, from which black people can press to change local or nation-wide patterns of oppression—instead of from weakness.**
>
> **It does not mean *merely* putting black faces into office. *Black visibility is not Black Power.* Most of the black politicians around the country today are not examples of Black Power. *The power must be that of a community, and emanate from there.* The black politicians must start from there. The black politicians must stop being representatives of "downtown" machines, whatever the cost might be in terms of patronage and holiday handouts.***

What It *Is*
Definition by Example

Definition by Analysis

What It *Is Not*

What It *Is*

Avoid the Pitfalls

1. Avoid echoing the term you are defining. Do not write "Courtesy is being courteous" or "Freedom is feeling free." Look around for synonyms: "Courtesy is being polite, being attentive to others' needs, making them feel at ease, using what society accepts as good manners." You can go against this rule to great advantage, however, if you repeat the *root* of the word meaningfully: "Courtesy is treating your girl like a princess in her *court.*"

---

*Stokely Carmichael and Charles V. Hamilton, *Black Power, the Politics of Liberation in America* (New York: Random House, 1967): 15.

2. Don't make your definitions too narrow—except for humor ("Professors are only disappointed students"). Do not write: "Communism is subversive totalitarianism." Obviously, your definition needs more breadth, something about sharing property, and so forth.
3. Don't make your definition too broad. Do not go uphill in your terms, as in "Vanity is pride" or "Affection is love." Bring the definers down to the same level: "Vanity is a kind of frivolous personal pride"—"Affection is a mild and chronic case of love."

EXERCISES

1. *Write a paragraph describing a unit of space, taking your reader from the outside to the inside of your own home, for instance, or dealing with some interesting spatial unit as in the following paragraph from a student's paper.*

The courtyard of the hotel at Uxmal was a wonderfully cool and welcome surprise after the sweaty bus trip out from Mérida. Surrounding the whole yard was a large *galería,* its ceiling blocking out the few rays of the sun that managed to filter through the heavy plantings that filled the yard. Overhead, along the *galería,* ceiling fans quietly turned, and underfoot the glazed tile floors felt smooth and delightfully cool even though the temperature on the road had pushed up past 100 degrees. Airy wicker chairs lined the railing, and just a few feet away, flowering jungle plants rose almost to the top of the stone arches on the second floor. Under the branches of a tall tree in the middle of the courtyard, out beyond the rail and the thick plantings, raised tile walkways crisscrossed the yard, bordered all along by neatly cultivated jungle flowers. And right in the middle of the yard, at the base of the big tree, a small waterfall splashed down over mossy rocks into a tiny bathing pool. The splashing water, the shade, the cool tile, all made the road outside seem very far off indeed.

2. *Write a narrative paragraph in which you blend the incidents and thoughts of a crucial moment, as in Orwell's paragraph on 136.*

3. *Write a paragraph comparing two people—like the one on 139.*

4. **(a)** *Write a paragraph developed by contrasts, running them point by point, as in the paragraph contrasting "students" and "athletes" on 142.*

(b) *Write two paragraphs contrasting something like high school and college, small town and city, football and baseball, men and women —the first paragraph describing one, the second the other, and the two using parallel contrasting terms, as in the example contrasting the two Germanys or the television commercials and shows on 141.*

5. *Write a paragraph of* effect *followed by* causes *like that on 143, Arrangement 1.*

6. *Write a paragraph about some* cause *followed by its probable* effects, *Arrangement 2. See 144–45. Work in a hypothetical effect if you can.*

7. *Here are some topics that fall conveniently into natural divisions. For each topic, list the divisions that occur to you.*

1. Causes affecting the rate at which a population grows.
2. Levels of government.
3. Undersea exploration.
4. Geological eras.
5. Mathematics in public schools.

8. *Write a paragraph using one of the topics and the divisions you have worked out in Exercise 7.*

9. *Write a paragraph describing a process you know well—how to make a bracelet, a belt, a cake, how an internal combustion engine works.*

10. *Now find a thesis that will change this described process into an argument making some statement about the subject: making a cake is no child's play; what's under the hood is really no mystery. Rewrite your descriptive-narrative paragraph into a brief three-paragraph essay, using everything you said before and expanding your points with comments rising from your thesis, and with further descriptive and narrative details. Hand in your original paragraph with your essay.*

11. *Using the classifications of problem and solution, write a three- or four-paragraph paper in which you describe the process behind some particularly interesting architectural or engineering accomplishment. Choose any topic you wish. For example, how did architects design the high-rise buildings in San Francisco so that they would withstand the shock of the severe earthquakes of 1971? Or how did medieval man make a suit of armor? Or how do you plan to convert your VW bus into a camper that will sleep four people? In the first paragraph, state the problem as your thesis sentence. Then go on to describe how the problem could be, or was, solved.*

12. *Work out a paragraph defining some term like barometer, computer, class, humanities, intelligence. Avoid the scent of the dictionary. Consider, and use if possible: (1) what it is not like, (2) what it is like, (3) what it is not, and, finally, (4) what it is. See 152–53.*

Readings

Description, narration, and exposition: these orders illustrate your argument and carry your ideas, as the following selections demonstrate. The first three essays describe a teacher, a president, and a baseball in vivid detail; the fourth recounts the embarrassment and giggles of first love. The eight remaining readings show a variety of expository tactics and modes of thought. A crooner and a rock-and-roll singer compare and contrast; an analogy between hidden pennies and "free gifts" emerges. We learn the genesis and far-reaching effects of one of the world's great religions, and classify the ages of men and the ways of reading. We follow the process of building a boat and creating the universe, and define an elusive term. As you read, look for the details that make each author's point.

EUDORA WELTY

Miss Duling

1 Miss Duling, a lifelong subscriber to perfection, was a figure of authority, the most whole-souled I have ever come to know. She was a dedicated schoolteacher who denied herself all she might have done or whatever other way she might have lived (this possibility was the last that could have occurred to us, her subjects in school). I believe she came of well-off people, well-educated, in Kentucky, and certainly old photographs show she was a beautiful, high-spirited-looking young lady—and came down to Jackson to its new grammar school that was going beg-

ging for a principal. She must have earned next to nothing; Mississippi then as now was the nation's lowest-ranking state economically, and our legislature has always shown a painfully loud reluctance to give money to public education. That challenge *brought* her.

2 In the long run she came into touch, as teacher or principal, with three generations of Jacksonians. My parents had not, but everybody else's parents had gone to school to her. She'd taught most of our leaders somewhere along the line. When she wanted something done—some civic oversight corrected, some injustice made right overnight, or even a tree spared that the fool telephone people were about to cut down—she telephoned the mayor, or the chief of police, or the president of the power company, or the head doctor at the hospital, or the judge in charge of a case, or whoever, and calling them by their first names, *told* them. It is impossible to imagine her meeting with anything less than compliance. The ringing of her brass bell from their days at Davis School would still be in their ears. She also proposed a spelling match between the fourth grade at Davis School and the Mississippi Legislature, who went through with it; and that told the Legislature.

3 Her standards were very high and of course inflexible, her authority was total; why *wouldn't* this carry with it a brass bell that could be heard ringing for a block in all directions? That bell belonged to the figure of Miss Duling as though it grew directly out of her right arm, as wings grew out of an angel or a tail out of the devil. When we entered, marching, into her school, by strictest teaching, surveillance, and order, we learned grammar, arithmetic, spelling, reading, writing, and geography; and she, not the teachers, I believe, wrote out the examinations: need I tell you, they were "hard."

4 She's not the only teacher who has influenced me, but Miss Duling, in some fictional shape or form, has stridden into a larger part of my work than I'd realized until now. She emerges in my perhaps inordinate number of schoolteacher characters. I loved those characters in the writing. But I did not, in life, love Miss Duling. I was afraid of her high-arched bony nose, her eyebrows lifted in half-circles above her hooded, brilliant eyes, and of the Kentucky R's in her speech, and the long steps she took in her hightop shoes. I did nothing but fear her bearing-down authority, and did not connect this (as of course we were meant to) with our

own need or desire to learn, perhaps because I already had this wish, and did not need to be driven.

5 She was impervious to lies or foolish excuses or the insufferable plea of not knowing any better. She wasn't going to have any frills, either, at Davis School. When a new governor moved into the mansion, he sent his daughter to Davis School; her name was Lady Rachel Conner. Miss Duling at once called the governor to the telephone and told him, "She'll be plain Rachel here."

6 Miss Duling dressed as plainly as a Pilgrim on a Thanksgiving poster we made in the schoolroom, in a longish black-and-white checked gingham dress, a bright thick wool sweater the red of a railroad lantern—she'd knitted it herself—black stockings and her narrow elegant feet in black hightop shoes with heels you could hear coming, rhythmical as a parade drum down the hall. Her silky black curly hair was drawn back out of curl, fastened by high combs, and knotted behind. She carried her spectacles on a gold chain hung around her neck. Her gaze was in general sweeping, then suddenly at the point of concentration upon you. With a swing of her bell that took her whole right arm and shoulder, she rang it, militant and impartial, from the head of the front steps of Davis School when it was time for us all to line up, girls on one side, boys on the other. We were to march past her into the school building, while the fourth-grader she nabbed played time on the piano, mostly to a tune we could have skipped to, but we didn't skip into Davis School.

Suggestions for Discussion and Writing

1. Welty's description of Miss Duling is that of a stern, austere figure of authority. Is the portrait relieved by any touches of warmth or humanity? If so, how?
2. In what sense was Miss Duling "whole-souled" (paragraph 1)?
3. Explain the significance of the brass bell mentioned in paragraphs 2, 3, and 6.
4. In paragraphs 4 and 6, the author piles up a series of physical details that flesh out her picture of Miss Duling. Comment on several of those details, and explain how they add to the overall sketch.
5. Most of us encountered a Miss (or Mister) Duling in our early school years. If your memories are vivid, try your hand at a character sketch. Before writing, determine the dominant im-

pression that you want to convey to your reader and select those details that support that impression.

HENRY VILLARD*

Recollections of Lincoln

1 The first joint debate between Douglas and Lincoln which I attended (the second in the series of seven) took place on the afternoon of August 27, 1858, at Freeport, Illinois. It was the great event of the day, and attracted an immense concourse of people from all parts of the state. Douglas spoke first for an hour, followed by Lincoln for an hour and a half; upon which the former closed in another half hour. The Democratic spokesman commanded a strong, sonorous voice, a rapid, vigorous utterance, a telling play of countenance, impressive gestures, and all the other arts of the practiced speaker. As far as all external conditions were concerned, there was nothing in favor of Lincoln. He had a lean, lank, indescribably gawky figure, an odd-featured, wrinkled, inexpressive, and altogether uncomely face. He used singularly awkward, almost absurd, up-and-down and sidewise movements of his body to give emphasis to his arguments. His voice was naturally good, but he frequently raised it to an unnatural pitch. Yet the unprejudiced mind felt at once that, while there was on the one side a skillful dialectician and debater arguing a wrong and weak cause, there was on the other a thoroughly earnest and truthful man, inspired by sound convictions in consonance with the true spirit of American institutions. There was nothing in all Douglas's powerful effort that appealed

---

*Henry Villard was a twenty-three-year-old German immigrant, well educated and fluent in English, when a German newspaper in New York City, the *Staats-Zeiting,* sent him to cover the Lincoln-Douglas debates in Illinois in 1858. The Republican party had recently formed in opposition to Democratic Senator Stephen Douglas's bill to open the western territory to slavery. Lincoln joined the new party, challenged Douglas for his seat in the Senate, and lost. But Lincoln attracted sufficient attention for the New York papers to send sophisticated reporters like young Villard way out west to Illinois. Villard wrote this rare view of Lincoln forty-six years later, in 1904.—Ed.

to the higher instincts of human nature, while Lincoln always touched sympathetic chords. Lincoln's speech excited and sustained the enthusiasm of his audience to the end. When he had finished, two stalwart young farmers rushed on the platform, and, in spite of his remonstrances, seized and put him on their shoulders and carried him in that uncomfortable posture for a considerable distance. It was really a ludicrous sight to see the grotesque figure holding frantically to the heads of his supporters, with his legs dangling from their shoulders and his pantaloons pulled up so as to expose his underwear almost to his knees. Douglas made dexterous use of this incident in his next speech, expressing sincere regret that, against his wish, he had used up his old friend Lincoln so completely that he had to be carried off the stage. Lincoln retaliated by saying at the first opportunity that he had known Judge Douglas long and well, but there was nevertheless one thing he could not say of him, and that was that the Judge always told the truth.

2 I was introduced to Lincoln at Freeport, and met him frequently afterwards in the course of the campaign. I must say frankly that, although I found him most approachable, good-natured, and full of wit and humor, I could not take a real personal liking to the man, owing to an inborn weakness for which he was even then notorious and so remained during his great public career. He was inordinately fond of jokes, anecdotes, and stories. He loved to hear them, and still more to tell them himself out of the inexhaustible supply provided by his good memory and his fertile fancy. There would have been no harm in this but for the fact that, the coarser the joke, the lower the anecdote, and the more risky the story, the more he enjoyed them, especially when they were of his own invention. He possessed, moreover, a singular ingenuity in bringing about occasions in conversation for indulgences of this kind. I have to confess, too, that, aside from the prejudice against him which I felt on this account, I shared the belief of a good many independent thinkers at the time, including prominent leaders of the Republican party, that, with regard to separating more effectively the antislavery Northern from the proslavery Southern wing of the Democracy* it would have been better if the re-election of Douglas had not been opposed.

---

*The Democratic party.

3 The party warfare was hotly continued in all parts of the state from early summer till election day in November. Besides the seven joint debates, both Douglas and Lincoln spoke scores of times separately, and numerous other speakers from Illinois and other states contributed incessantly to the agitation. The two leaders visited almost every county in the state. I heard four of the joint debates, and six other speeches by Lincoln and eight by his competitor. Of course, the later efforts became substantial repetitions of the preceding ones, and to listen to them grew more and more tiresome to me. As I had seen something of political campaigns before, this one did not exercise the full charm of novelty upon me. Still, even if I had been a far more callous observer, I could not have helped being struck with the efficient party organizations, the skillful tactics of the managers, the remarkable feats of popular oratory, and the earnestness and enthusiasm of the audiences I witnessed. It was a most instructive object lesson in practical party politics, and filled me with admiration for the Anglo-American method of working out popular destiny.

4 I firmly believe that if Stephen A. Douglas had lived, he would have had a brilliant national career.* Freed by the Southern rebellion from all identification with proslavery interests, the road would have been open to the highest fame and position for which his unusual talents qualified him. As I took final leave of him and Lincoln, doubtless neither of them had any idea that within two years they would be rivals again in the presidential race. I had it from Lincoln's own lips that the United States senatorship was the greatest political height he at the time expected to climb.

5 He and I met accidentally, about nine o'clock on a hot, sultry evening, at a flag railroad station about twenty miles west of Springfield, on my return from a great meeting at Petersburg in Menard County. He had been driven to the station in a buggy and left there alone. I was already there. The train that we intended to take for Springfield was about due. After we waited vainly half an hour for its arrival, a thunderstorm compelled us to take refuge in an empty freight car standing on a side track, there being no buildings of any sort at the station. We squatted down on the floor of the car and fell to talking on all sorts of subjects.

---

*Douglas died of typhoid fever on June 3, 1861, just after war had begun.—Ed.

It was then and there he told me that, when he was clerking in a country store, his highest political ambition was to be a member of the state legislature. "Since then, of course," he said laughingly, "I have grown some, but my friends got me into *this* business [meaning the canvass]. I did not consider myself qualified for the United States Senate, and it took me a long time to persuade myself that I was. Now, to be sure," he continued, with another of his peculiar laughs, "I am convinced that I am good enough for it; but, in spite of it all, I am saying to myself every day: 'It is too big a thing for you; you will never get it.' Mary [his wife] insists, however, that I am going to be Senator and President of the United States, too." These last words he followed with a roar of laughter, with his arms around his knees, and shaking all over with mirth at his wife's ambition. "Just think," he exclaimed, "of such a sucker as me as President!"

6 He then fell to asking questions regarding my antecedents, and expressed some surprise at my fluent use of English after so short a residence in the United States.* Next he wanted to know whether it was true that most of the educated people in Germany were "infidels." I answered that they were not openly professed infidels, but such a conclusion might be drawn from the fact that most of them were not churchgoers. "I do not wonder at that," he rejoined, "my own inclination is that way." I ventured to give expression to my own disbelief in the doctrine of the Christian Church relative to the existence of God, the divinity of Christ, and immortality. This led him to put other questions to me to draw me out. He did not commit himself, but I received the impression that he was of my own way of thinking.

[In the last days of November 1860, the Associated Press sent Villard to Springfield, Illinois, to report current events by telegraph, until the departure of Lincoln for Washington. This duty brought Villard into daily relations with the President-elect, who gave him a most friendly welcome and told him to ask for information any time he wished.]

7 Mr. Lincoln soon found, after his election, that his modest two-story frame dwelling was altogether inadequate for the

*Five years.—Ed.

throng of local callers and of visitors from a distance, and, accordingly, he gladly availed himself of the offer of the use of the governor's room in the Capitol building. On my arrival, he had already commenced spending a good part of each day in it. He appeared daily, except Sundays, between nine and ten o'clock, and held a reception till noon, to which all comers were admitted without even the formality of first sending in cards. Whoever chose to call received the same hearty greeting. At noon, he went home to dinner and reappeared at about two. Then his correspondence was given proper attention, and visitors of distinction were seen by special appointment at either the State House or the hotel. Occasionally, but very rarely, he passed some time in his law office. In the evening, old friends called at his home for the exchange of news and political views. At times, when important news was expected, he would go to the telegraph or newspaper offices after supper, and stay there till late. Altogether, probably no other President-elect was so approachable to everybody, at least during the first weeks of my stay. But he found in the end, as was to be expected, that this popular practice involved a good deal of fatigue, and that he needed more time for himself; and the hours he gave up to the public were gradually restricted.

0 I was present almost daily for more or less time during his morning receptions. I generally remained a silent listener, as I could get at him at other hours when I was in need of information. It was a most interesting study to watch the manner of his intercourse with callers. As a rule, he showed remarkable tact in dealing with each of them, whether they were rough-looking Sangamon County farmers still addressing him familiarly as "Abe," sleek and pert commercial travelers, staid merchants, sharp politicians, or preachers, lawyers, or other professional men. He showed a very quick and shrewd perception of and adaptation to individual characteristics and peculiarities. He never evaded a proper question, or failed to give a fit answer.

9 None of his hearers enjoyed the wit—and wit was an unfailing ingredient—of his stories half as much as he did himself. It was a joy indeed to see the effect upon him. A high-pitched laughter lighted up his otherwise melancholy countenance with thorough merriment. His body shook all over with gleeful emotion, and when he felt particularly good over his performance, he

followed his habit of drawing his knees, with his arms around them, up to his very face, as I had seen him do in 1858. I am sorry to state that he often allowed himself altogether too much license in the concoction of the stories.

10 I often availed myself of his authorization to come to him at any time for information. There were two questions in which the public, of course, felt the deepest interest, and upon which I was expected to supply light, namely, the composition of his cabinet and his views upon the secession movement that was daily growing in extent and strength. As to the former, he gave me to understand early, by indirection, that, as everybody expected, William H. Seward and S. P. Chase, his competitors for the presidential nomination, would be among his constitutional advisers. It was hardly possible for him not to recognize them, and he steadily turned a deaf ear to the remonstrances that were made against them as "extreme men" by leading politicians from the Border States, particularly from Kentucky and Missouri. As to the remaining members of his cabinet, they were definitely selected much later, and after a protracted and wearisome tussle with the delegations of various states that came to Springfield to urge the claims of their "favorite sons."

11 No one who heard him talk upon the other question could fail to discover his "other side," and to be impressed with his deep earnestness, his anxious contemplation of public affairs, and his thorough sense of the extraordinary responsibilities that were coming upon him. He did not hesitate to say that the Union ought to, and in his opinion would, be preserved, and to go into long arguments in support of the proposition. But he could not be got to say what he would do in the face of Southern secession, except that as President he should be sworn to maintain the Constitution of the United States, and that he was therefore bound to fulfill that duty. I think I interpret his views up to the time of his departure for Washington correctly in saying that he had not lost faith in the preservation of peace between the North and the South, and he certainly did not dream that his principal duty would be to raise great armies and fleets, and the means to maintain them, for the suppression of the most determined and sanguinary rebellion in defense of slavery that our planet ever witnessed.

Suggestions for Discussion and Writing

1. What would you guess Villard means in saying that Lincoln was "inspired by sound convictions in consonance with the true spirit of American institutions"?
2. Villard's description of Lincoln also reveals something about himself. How were the two men different?
3. Comment on Villard's inability to "take a real personal liking" to Lincoln. Why does he like Douglas better?
4. Although Douglas kept his seat in the U.S. Senate, defeating Lincoln, Villard thinks that "it would have been better," presumably for the Republicans and the country, if Lincoln had not run against Douglas. Why?
5. What does Lincoln mean by "infidels"? What does his asking suggest?
6. Comment on Villard's description of Lincoln's receiving "all comers . . . without even the formality of first sending in cards."
7. Villard says that it "was a joy indeed to see" Lincoln's pleasure at his own jokes. Does his description bear this out?
8. Find a portrait of Lincoln and write an essay comparing it descriptively with Villard's description.

ROGER ANGELL

On the Ball

1 It weighs just over five ounces and measures between 2.86 and 2.94 inches in diameter. It is made of a composition-cork nucleus encased in two thin layers of rubber, one black and one red, surrounded by 121 yards of tightly wrapped blue-gray wool yarn, 45 yards of white wool yarn, 53 more yards of blue-gray wool yarn, 150 yards of fine cotton yarn, a coat of rubber cement, and a cowhide (formerly horsehide) exterior, which is held together with 216 slightly raised red cotton stitches. Printed certifications, endorsements, and outdoor advertising spherically attest to its authenticity. Like most institutions, it is considered inferior in its present form to its ancient archetypes, and in this case the complaint is probably justified; on occasion in recent years it has

actually been known to come apart under the demands of its brief but rigorous active career. Baseballs are assembled and hand-stitched in Taiwan (before this year the work was done in Haiti, and before 1973 in Chicopee, Massachusetts), and contemporary pitchers claim that there is a tangible variation in the size and feel of the balls that now come into play in a single game; a true peewee is treasured by hurlers, and its departure from the premises, by fair means or foul, is secretly mourned. But never mind: any baseball is beautiful. No other small package comes as close to the ideal in design and utility. It is a perfect object for a man's hand. Pick it up and it instantly suggests its purpose; it is meant to be thrown a considerable distance—thrown hard and with precision. Its feel and heft are the beginning of the sport's critical dimensions; if it were a fraction of an inch larger or smaller, a few centigrams heavier or lighter, the game of baseball would be utterly different. Hold a baseball in your hand. As it happens, this one is not brand-new. Here, just to one side of the curved surgical welt of stitches, there is a pale-green grass smudge, darkening on one edge almost to black—the mark of an old infield play, a tough grounder now lost in memory. Feel the ball, turn it over in your hand; hold it across the seam or the other way, with the seam just to the side of your middle finger. Speculation stirs. You want to get outdoors and throw this spare and sensual object to somebody or, at the very least, watch somebody else throw it. The game has begun.

Suggestions for Discussion and Writing

1. Angell moves from a matter-of-fact objective description of a baseball to a subjective description of the feelings it evokes about the ball and game. Where does he make the transition? How does he do it?
2. Why doesn't Angell tell his reader he's describing a baseball until the fifth sentence?
3. Why is a baseball "a perfect object for a man's hand"? Why is it a "sensual object"?
4. Would this essay make any sense to someone who has never seen a baseball? Explain.
5. To Angell, a baseball is more than an object to be thrown. What else does it represent?
6. Select another ball or an object used in sports—a football, tennis

ball, a boxing glove, a soccer ball, for example—and write a description of two paragraphs. In the first paragraph describe the subject objectively, and in the second paragraph describe the feelings or emotions it evokes.

MAYA ANGELOU

My First Valentine

1 In school one day, a girl whom I barely knew and had scarcely spoken to brought me a note. The intricate fold indicated that it was a love note. I was sure she had the wrong person, but she insisted. Picking the paper loose, I confessed to myself that I was frightened. Suppose it was somebody being funny? Suppose the paper would show a hideous beast and the word YOU written over it. Children did that sometimes just because they claimed I was stuck-up. Fortunately I had got permission to go to the toilet—an outside job—and in the reeking gloom I read:

> Dear Friend, M. J.
>
> Times are hard and friends are few
> I take great pleasure in writing you
> Will you be my Valentine?
>
> *Tommy Valdon*

2 I pulled my mind apart. Who? Who was Tommy Valdon? Finally a face dragged itself from my memory. He was the nice-looking brown-skinned boy who lived across the pond. As soon as I had pinned him down, I began to wonder, Why? Why me? Was it a joke? But if Tommy was the boy I remembered, he was a very sober person and a good student. Well, then, it wasn't a joke. All right, what evil dirty things did he have in mind? My questions fell over themselves, an army in retreat. Haste, dig for

cover. Protect your flanks. Don't let the enemy close the gap between you. What did a Valentine do, anyway?

3 Starting to throw the paper in the foul-smelling hole, I thought of Louise. I could show it to her. I folded the paper back in the original creases, and went back to class. There was no time during the lunch period, since I had to run to the Store and wait on customers. The note was in my sock, and every time Momma looked at me, I feared that her church gaze might have turned into X-ray vision and she could not only see the note and read its message but would interpret it as well. I felt myself slipping down a sheer cliff of guilt, and a second time I nearly destroyed the note, but there was no opportunity. The take-up bell rang, and Bailey raced me to school, so the note was forgotten. But serious business is serious, and it had to be attended to. After classes, I waited for Louise. She was talking to a group of girls, laughing. But when I gave her our signal (two waves of the left hand), she said goodbye to them and joined me in the road. I didn't give her the chance to ask what was on my mind (her favorite question); I simply gave her the note. Recognizing the fold, she stopped smiling. We were in deep waters. She opened the letter and read it aloud twice. "Well, what do you think?"

4 I said, "What do I think? That's what I'm asking you? What is there to think?"

5 "Looks like he wants you to be his valentine."

6 "Louise, I can read. But what does it mean?"

7 "Oh, you know. His valentine. His love."

8 There was that hateful word again. That treacherous word that yawned up at you like a volcano.

9 "Well, I won't. Most decidedly I won't. Not ever again."

10 "Have you been his valentine before? What do you mean never again?"

11 I couldn't lie to my friend, and I wasn't about to freshen old ghosts.

12 "Well, don't answer him then, and that's the end of it." I was a little relieved that she thought it could be gotten rid of so quickly. I tore the note in half and gave her a part. Walking down the hill, we minced the paper in a thousand shreds and gave it to the wind.

13 Two days later a monitor came into my classroom. She spoke quietly to Miss Williams, our teacher. Miss Williams said, "Class, I believe you remember that tomorrow is Valentine's

Day, so named for St. Valentine, the martyr, who died around A.D. 270 in Rome. The day is observed by exchanging tokens of affection, and cards. The eighth-grade children have completed theirs, and the monitor is acting as mailman. You will be given cardboard, ribbon and red tissue paper during the last period today so that you may make your gifts. Glue and scissors are here at the work table. Now, stand when your name is called."

14 She had been shuffling the colored envelopes and calling names for some time before I noticed. I had been thinking of yesterday's plain invitation and the expeditious way Louise and I took care of it.

15 We who were being called to receive valentines were only slightly more embarrassed than those who sat and watched as Miss Williams opened each envelope. "Helen Gray." Helen Gray, a tall, dull girl from Louisville, flinched. "Dear Valentine"—Miss Williams began reading the badly rhymed childish drivel. I seethed with shame and anticipation and yet had time to be offended at the silly poetry that I could have bettered in my sleep.

16 "Margue-you-reete Anne Johnson. My goodness, this looks more like a letter than a valentine. 'Dear Friend, I wrote you a letter and saw you tear it up with your friend Miss L. I don't believe you meant to hurt my feelings so whether you answer or not you will always be my valentine. T. V.' "

17 "Class"—Miss Williams smirked and continued lazily without giving us permission to sit down—"although you are only in the seventh grade, I'm sure you wouldn't be so presumptuous as to sign a letter with an initial. But here is a boy in the eighth grade, about to graduate—blah, blah, blooey, blah. You may collect your valentines and these letters on your way out."

18 It was a nice letter and Tommy had beautiful penmanship. I was sorry I tore up the first. His statement that whether I answered him or not would not influence his affection reassured me. He couldn't be after you-know-what if he talked like that. I told Louise that the next time he came to the Store I was going to say something extra nice to him. Unfortunately, the situation was so wonderful to me that each time I saw Tommy I melted in delicious giggles and was unable to form a coherent sentence. After a while he stopped including me in his general glances.

Suggestions for Discussion and Writing

1. Good narration makes a point—it is not merely a series of incidents strung together. What point is Angelou making in this selection? How does she blend description with her narrative?
2. Comment on paragraph 11. What might some of those "old ghosts" be? Should she have told us?
3. How does Angelou establish the contrast between Miss Williams and the students?
4. What accounts for the sudden shift in Angelou's attitude toward Tommy in the last paragraph?
5. How does Angelou establish a kind of distance between herself as an adult and as a grade school student?
6. If you had an attack of puppy love (and most of us have known its dizzying effects), write an essay recounting the experience.

RUSSELL BAKER

From Song to Sound: Bing and Elvis

1 The grieving for Elvis Presley and the commercial exploitation of his death were still not ended when we heard of Bing Crosby's death the other day. Here is a generational puzzle. Those of an age to mourn Elvis must marvel that their elders could really have cared about Bing, just as the Crosby generation a few weeks ago wondered what all the to-do was about when Elvis died.

2 Each man was a mass culture hero to his generation, but it tells us something of the difference between generations that each man's admirers would be hard-pressed to understand why the other could mean very much to his devotees.

3 There were similarities that ought to tell us something. Both came from obscurity to national recognition while quite young and became very rich. Both lacked formal music education and went on to movie careers despite lack of acting skills. Both developed distinctive musical styles which were originally scorned by critics and subsequently studied as pioneer developments in the art of popular song.

4 In short, each man's career followed the mythic rags-to-triumph pattern in which adversity is conquered, detractors are given their comeuppance and estates, fancy cars, and world tours become the reward of perseverance. Traditionally this was supposed to be the history of the American business striver, but in our era of committee capitalism it occurs most often in the mass entertainment field, and so we look less and less to the board room for our heroes and more and more to the microphone.

5 Both Crosby and Presley were creations of the microphone. It made it possible for people with frail voices not only to be heard beyond the third row but also to caress millions. Crosby was among the first to understand that the microphone made it possible to sing to multitudes by singing to a single person in a small room.

6 Presley cuddled his microphone like a lover. With Crosby the microphone was usually concealed, but Presley brought it out on stage, detached it from its fitting, stroked it, pressed it to his mouth. It was a surrogate for his listener, and he made love to it unashamedly.

7 The difference between Presley and Crosby, however, reflected generational differences which spoke of changing values in American life. Crosby's music was soothing; Presley's was disturbing. It is too easy to be glib about this, to say that Crosby was singing to, first, Depression America, and, then, to wartime America, and that his audiences had all the disturbance they could handle in their daily lives without buying more at the record shop and movie theater.

8 Crosby's fans talk about how "relaxed" he was, how "natural," how "casual and easy going." By the time Presley began causing sensations, the entire country had become relaxed, casual, and easy going, and its younger people seemed to be tired of it, for Elvis's act was anything but soothing and scarcely what a parent of that placid age would have called "natural" for a young man.

9 Elvis was unseemly, loud, gaudy, sexual—that gyrating pelvis!—in short, disturbing. He not only disturbed parents who thought music by Crosby was soothing but also reminded their young that they were full of the turmoil of youth and an appetite for excitement. At a time when the country had a population coming of age with no memory of troubled times, Presley spoke to a yearning for disturbance.

10 It probably helped that Elvis's music made Mom and Dad

climb the wall. In any case, people who admired Elvis never talk about how relaxed and easy going he made them feel. They are more likely to tell you he introduced them to something new and exciting.

11 To explain each man in terms of changes in economic and political life probably oversimplifies the matter. Something in the culture was also changing. Crosby's music, for example, paid great attention to the importance of lyrics. The "message" of the song was as essential to the audience as the tune. The words were usually inane and witless, but Crosby—like Sinatra a little later—made them vital. People remembered them, sang them. Words still had meaning.

12 Although many of Presley's songs were highly lyrical, in most it wasn't the words that moved audiences; it was the "sound." Rock 'n' roll, of which he was the great popularizer, was a "sound" event. Song stopped being song and turned into "sound," at least until the Beatles came along and solved the problem of making words sing to the new beat.

13 Thus a group like the Rolling Stones, whose lyrics are often elaborate, seems to the Crosby-tuned ear to be shouting only gibberish, a sort of accompanying background noise in a "sound" experience. The Crosby generation has trouble hearing rock because it makes the mistake of trying to understand the words. The Presley generation has trouble with Crosby because it finds the sound unstimulating and cannot be touched by the inanity of the words. The mutual deafness may be a measure of how far we have come from really troubled times and of how deeply we have come to mistrust the value of words.

Suggestions for Discussion and Writing

1. Russell Baker points out some similarities between Crosby and Presley before devoting the bulk of his essay to their differences. Why does he begin with the similarities?
2. Locate the sentence that serves as a transition when the author moves from similarities to differences.
3. What is the thesis sentence in this selection? How does it set the comparison and make the contrast?
4. This selection is an extended contrast (see page 141, in which the author contrasts some things sentence against sentence and

other things paragraph against paragraph. Find examples of each strategy in this essay; you might begin by examining paragraph 6.

5. How is the microphone (paragraphs 5 and 6) a symbol of the similarities *and* the differences between Crosby and Presley?
6. Does Baker lose the contrastive advantage and write chiefly about one singer, forgetting the other? Is he impartial in his comments, or does he betray a preference?
7. The conclusion of this essay is an inverted funnel paragraph, similar to the models on pages 104 and 105. Explain.
8. Following the suggestions in this chapter, select one of the topics below and write an extended contrast.
   a. community colleges and four-year universities
   b. two cities you are familiar with
   c. two actors or musicians
   d. two cultures you are familiar with (for example, Hispanic and Anglo, or black and white)
   e. dormitory life and living at home
   f. commercial television and public television
   g. two authors or novels
   h. traveling by car or plane versus hitchhiking

ANNIE DILLARD

Hidden Pennies

1 When I was six or seven years old, growing up in Pittsburgh, I used to take a precious penny of my own and hide it for someone else to find. It was a curious compulsion; sadly, I've never been seized by it since. For some reason I always "hid" the penny along the same stretch of sidewalk up the street. I'd cradle it at the roots of a maple, say, or in a hole left by a chipped-off piece of sidewalk. Then I'd take a piece of chalk and, starting at either end of the block, draw huge arrows leading up to the penny from both directions. After I learned to write I labeled the arrows "SURPRISE AHEAD" or "MONEY THIS WAY." I was greatly excited, during all this arrow-drawing, at the thought of the first lucky passerby who would receive in this way, regardless of merit, a free gift from the universe. But I never lurked about. I'd go straight

home and not give the matter another thought, until, some months later, I would be gripped by the impulse to hide another penny.

2 There are lots of things to see, unwrapped gifts and free surprises. The world is fairly studded and strewn with pennies cast broadside from a generous hand. But—and this is the point—who gets excited by a mere penny? If you follow one arrow, if you crouch motionless on a bank to watch a tremulous ripple thrill on the water, and are rewarded by the sight of a muskrat kit paddling from its den, will you count that sight a chip of copper only, and go your rueful way? It is very dire poverty indeed for a man to be so malnourished and fatigued that he won't stoop to pick up a penny. But if you cultivate a healthy poverty and simplicity, so that finding a penny will make your day, then, since the world is in fact planted in pennies, you have with your poverty bought a lifetime of days. What you see is what you get.

3 Unfortunately, nature is very much a now-you-see-it, now-you-don't affair. A fish flashes, then dissolves in the water before my eyes like so much salt. Deer apparently ascend bodily into heaven; the brightest oriole fades into leaves. These disappearances stun me into stillness and concentration; they say of nature that it conceals with a grand nonchalance, and they say of vision that it is a deliberate gift, the revelation of a dancer who for my eyes only flings away her seven veils.

4 For nature does reveal as well as conceal: now-you-don't-see-it, now-you-do. For a week this September, migrating red-winged black-birds were feeding heavily down by Tinker Creek at the back of the house. One day I went out to investigate the racket; I walked up to a tree, an Osage orange, and a hundred birds flew away. They simply materialized out of the tree. I saw a tree, then a whisk of color, then a tree again. I walked closer and another hundred blackbirds took flight. Not a branch, not a twig budged: the birds were apparently weightless as well as invisible. Or, it was as if the leaves of the Osage orange had been freed from a spell in the form of red-winged blackbirds; they flew from the tree, caught my eye in the sky, and vanished. When I looked again at the tree, the leaves had reassembled as if nothing had happened. Finally I walked directly to the trunk of the tree and a final hundred, the real diehards, appeared, spread, and vanished. How could so many hide in the tree without my seeing

them? The Osage orange, unruffled, looked just as it had looked from the house, when three hundred red-winged blackbirds cried from its crown. I looked upstream where they flew, and they were gone. Searching, I couldn't spot one. I wandered upstream to force them to play their hand, but they'd crossed the creek and scattered. One show to a customer. These appearances catch at my throat; they are the free gifts, the bright coppers at the roots of trees.

Suggestions for Discussion and Writing

1. Dillard says that the world is strewn "with pennies cast broadside from a generous hand" (paragraph 1). What are some of those "pennies"? Who has cast them?
2. At what point in the essay did you realize that the hidden pennies are used to set up an analogy? What is the second subject of her analogy?
3. Underline the transitions in paragraph 4 that help to move the anecdote along.
4. How does the last sentence of the essay emphasize Dillard's analogy?
5. Dillard occasionally shifts the level of her diction, incorporating a bit of slang or an old familiar phrase into her essay. Do these shifts detract from the overall effect of this selection, or do they add to it? Explain.
6. Write an essay in which you clarify or explain an object or concept by using a homey analogy. You might want to compare something as familiar as a large city with a beehive, or an idea as complex as religious faith with a compass or map. In either case, you will probably find that you have to supplement your analogy with other expository modes.

MAURICIO OBREGÓN

The Rise of Islam

1 In A.D. 682, an Arab general rode his charger across a Moroccan beach and into the Atlantic surf. "God is my witness," he

proclaimed, "that only the ocean has put a limit on what I have conquered in His name!"

2 Fifty years after the death of Muhammad, the followers of the prophet had wrested the north coast of Africa from the shrinking Byzantine Empire. They had already conquered the Byzantine provinces of Syria and Palestine, had engulfed the empire of Persia, and were still on the move. In another fifty years, the domains of Islam would reach from Spain to the frontiers of China.

3 No great empire could have kept a looser hold on its conquered territories, or bound conquered peoples with a stronger religious faith. None has shown a greater capacity to assimilate the best of the cultures it overran, while adding its own abundant creativity.

4 As the great empires of the Mediterranean world weakened, the horsemen of Islam led a charge that aroused three continents. Its architects glorified God in structures as magnificent as the Alhambra and the Taj Mahal. To painting, weaving, poetry, and song, its artists brought fresh visions and idioms. Its scholars preserved the learning of the ancient world, and extended the frontiers of knowledge. Their stewardship helped lay the foundations of the European Renaissance.

5 What produced this explosion of military might, artistic vigor, and scholarly attainment? The answer may lie in the word *Islam* itself. Its literal meaning is "submission to God." Thus it closely parallels the archaic sense of our word *enthusiasm,* "possession by God" (from the Greek *en theos*). Enthusiasm, perhaps more than any other attribute, identifies the Renaissance with Western antiquity, and distinguishes both from the Oriental inclination to seek God in withdrawal.

6 The enthusiasm of Islam consumed the known world as if driven by the four winds; its religious message spoke to the spiritual and social needs of peoples as diverse as Egyptians, Black Africans, Central Asians, and inhabitants of the Malay archipelago. And this message was the word of Allah, spoken by the prophet Muhammand.

7 Muhammad was born about A.D. 570, in the city of Mecca. England's conversion to Christianity had barely begun. The Visigoths were still conquering Spain. Buddhism had just been brought to Japan. Aya Sophia, the most impressive church in all of

Christendom, had but recently been consecrated in Constantinople.

8 In his middle twenties, Muhammad entered the service of Khadijah, a wealthy widow. At the age of forty, he received his first revelation while meditating on Mount Hira, near Mecca. Khadijah, by this time his wife, believed from the first in his One God, "who created man and teaches him everything through the scriptures." She became Muhammad's first disciple.

9 Muhammad, and his preachings of monotheism and social justice, did not please the idolatrous merchants of Mecca. Their persecution drove him out of the city in 622. With his few disciples, he took sanctuary in Yathrib—today Madinat al-Nabi, or "City of the Prophet"—two hundred miles to the north. From this exodus, or Hegira (*Hijrah*), the lunar calendar of Islam numbers its years.

10 The archangel Gabriel, as God's messenger, had ordered the prophet to convert the unfaithful. Successfully attacking a caravan from Damascus, Muhammad and his followers began to draw tribes of Bedouins to their cause. In 629, the prophet returned to Mecca at the head of ten thousand men. Having taken the city with relative ease, they destroyed the idols in the Ka'bah, Mecca's most sacred shrine, which has become the focal point of the pilgrimage (*Hajj*) that all able Muslims are asked to make at least once in a lifetime.*

11 Muhammad himself was probably illiterate, but his followers memorized or transcribed his revelations, collecting them after his death as the *Korun* ("recitation"). Its basic precepts are five: faith, prayer, charity, fasting, and pilgrimage. In A.D. 632, Muhammad proclaimed his last revelation to the faithful on the plain of Arafat, and died in the arms of his favorite wife, A'ishah. He was buried in Medina.

12 Muhammad was succeeded as caliph by A'ishah's father, Abut Bakr, who had been a wealthy businessman before becom-

*The Ka'bah's holy of holies is a black stone, sacred to the memory of the patriarch Abraham and his son Ishmael (Isma'il), from whom Arabs trace their descent. Muslim tradition holds that the original shrine was built after Abraham, submitting to God, had prepared to sacrifice Ishmael. Judaic tradition identifies Isaac, Ishmael's half-brother, as the intended sacrifice, and makes Isaac the progenitor of the twelve tribes of Israel. Thus Arabs and Jews, despite intermittent enmity, are, in a sense, blood brothers.

ing the prophet's foremost disciple. The new caliph's first task was to subdue two rebellious tribes. Then, to the cry of *Allahu akbar* ("God is great"), Islam began its eastward expansion. Within a decade it had defeated its two great neighbors, Byzantium and Persia—taking from the Byzantine emperor Heraclius first Damascus and then Jerusalem, and from Persia the fertile crescent between the Tigris and Euphrates rivers.

13 Three factors aided the Muslims in building their empire: the mobility of their mounted warriors; the keen blade of their "holy war" (*Jihad*), to which the constant invocation of God gave a sharpened sense of destiny; and their equally godly clemency, commanded by the Koran, toward the vanquished.

14 Many Christians and Jews converted to Islam, but those who refused were allowed to live in peace if they paid the *jizyah,* an annual tax that sometimes comprised no more than a measure of wheat. Conversely, some segments of a divided Christianity found it possible to tolerate a prophet who acknowledged the teachings of the Old and New Testaments. "We believe in God," says the Koran, "and in what He revealed to Abraham, Ishmael, Isaac, Jacob, Moses, Jesus, and the Prophets: make no distinction between them, and submit only to Him." Adds the Hadith, which with the Koran completes Muslim written tradition: "When you die, your neighbors will ask what goods you have left; but the Angel will ask what good you have done."

15 Islam expanded in every direction. Turning west, the second caliph, Umar, invaded Egypt and occupied Alexandria.

16 In 682, the Muslim general Uqbah ibn Nafi overran the south coast of the Mediterranean and occupied Tripoli, Carthage, and Tangiers, the last of the Byzantine bases in Africa. With the annihilation of Byzantium's imperial fleet in Cilicia, the Muslims were masters of the southern Mediterranean.* On reaching West Africa, Uqbah rode his charger into the surf at Agadir, proclaiming that only the ocean could limit his conquests in God's name.

17 In the east, the seventeen-year-old general Abu Qasim al-Thaqafi led an army that occupied Samarkand and Tashkent. Crossing the Indus and Oxus (today's Amu Darya, which flows from Afghanistan into the Aral Sea), the Muslim forces estab-

---

*In the north, Constantinople resisted for almost eight centuries. It finally fell in 1453, when the Turks reduced it.

lished Islam first in India, then on the frontiers of Cathay. "Always seek knowledge, even in China," advises the Hadith. And from Central Asia the Muslims brought back the Chinese art of papermaking.

18 Six centuries later, Tamerlane ruled the Muslim East from Samarkand. His tomb there is still preserved by the Soviet authorities, for atheistic Marxism has not been able to eradicate Islam; nine percent of the U.S.S.R.'s population is still Muslim (and watches the Ayatollah). The Muslim *madrasa,* or mosque-college, whose minaret once served as a lighthouse for caravans, is still open to students in Soviet Bukhara, and there are active mosques even in Alma-Ata, on the frontier of China. At the end of the thirteenth century Marco Polo found Muslims in Sumatra, and in the fifteenth, Portuguese traders met them in the Spice Islands.

19 Turning south, Muslim armies reached East African lands that are now Tanzania; in West Africa, they went as far as Cape Verde—where, in his map of 1500, Juan de la Cosa placed the crescent moon. When Vasco da Gama rounded the Cape of Good Hope, the pilot who led him to India was the seventy-year-old Ahmad ibn Majid. In Africa today, there are twice as many Muslims as Christians; I have hunted in Nigeria with ebony-skinned Hausa Muslims who ride like Arabs of yore, turbaned and brandishing scimitars.

20 While Islam was becoming master of half of Africa, it was also turning north. In 711, Tariq ibn Ziyad landed on Gibraltar (from *Jabal Tariq,* or Mount Tariq). His Moors went on to defeat Roderick and his Visigoths near Cádiz, corner the Christians in the mountains of northern Spain, and penetrate France. At Tours, in 732, they were finally stopped by Charles Martel, Charlemagne's grandfather.

21 But Islamic culture flourished for almost eight centuries in Spain—embroidering the language with more than four thousand Arabic words, adorning the austere peninsula with jewels like Córdoba and Granada, and producing heroes like El Cid, who, in the eleventh century, took the field as often for the Moors as against them. When the Catholic sovereigns completed the reconquest of Granada in 1492, the defeated Moorish king, Boabdil, was not the only one to weep. Andalusian song and poetry still cry for the heyday of Islam, as do the fountains of the

Alhambra. If Columbus had not met Ferdinand and Isabella in Granada, and if Portugal had not given him caravels derived from Arab designs, the future of reconquered Spain would have been hard. She might well have forgotten how to inlay steel with gold, how to sing to the guitar, how to embellish love with Arab poetry: *Weep not for your robe, daughter of Bakili, or the river will also carry away your youth. Come into the shade, and I will weave for you a robe more precious than the one you have lost, a robe made of caresses.*

22 Driven over the known world as they were, the enthusiasts of Islam were nonetheless daunted by the ocean, which they called the "sea of darkness." And so they confined themselves to the coastal navigation they had learned from the Greeks (and vastly refined).

23 With their lateen sails, they could have tacked from island to island into the Pacific. With ease, they could have sailed into the Atlantic from Cape Verde, where the trade winds blow westward. But in the East they were content to coast from the Bay of Bengal to the Isles of Spice, and in the West to turn southward across the Sahara's sea of sand. (Their knowledge of stars was as useful to them there as at sea; the most important stars in the south, and half of the brightest in the north, have Arab names.)

24 So Uqbah was right. It was the ocean that set Islam's limits. The Muslims never ventured beyond Eurasia, not even reaching the Canary Islands. And at the other end of the known world, they never sailed farther than the Philippines—where, in the sixteenth century, Magellan's fleet found Spanish-speaking Moors.

25 Inevitably, the expansion of Islam to the ends of the Eurasian continent was a factor in a long series of wars of succession. The first was provoked by Ali, husband of Muhammad's favorite daughter, Fatimah, after the assassination of Uthman, the third caliph. There were also many sectarian movements, like that of the *Hashshashin* (Assassins), who drugged themselves with hashish and spread terror in the eleventh and twelfth centuries.

26 With the Umayyad dynasty, the Muslim capital passed from Mecca to Damascus (661–750). With the Abbasid dynasty, it passed to Baghdad, where, at the end of the eighth century, Harun al-Rashid presided over an opulent court later immortalized in *The Thousand and One Nights.* With the Fatimid dynasty, the capital passed to Cairo (969–1171), today the intellectual center of Islam.

27 In one form or another, Muslim empires endured for a millennium. Islam gave rise to the last of the great ancient empires,

and the newest of the great world religions. By the time of Columbus, it was also the largest of the world's religions. Today its precepts guide the lives of more than 600 million people from Indonesia to Guinea, from the Soviet Union to Madagascar. Only Christianity, claiming more than a billion, numbers more adherents.

28 As it found the leisure to absorb the cultures it conquered, Islam became a bridge over which the West could reclaim its classical heritage. The combination of Islamic enthusiasm with the cultures of Egypt, Greece, Persia, India, and Byzantium produced artists and scientists who resowed the wisdom of the ancient world, cultivated it in the Middle Ages, and passed it on to the European Renaissance.

29 In the seventh century, a few years after the death of Muhammad, Arabs began to make contact with classical learning through their libraries. In the eighth century, before the time of Charlemagne, Jabir ibn Hayyan developed new theories of the geologic formation of metals, magnetism, and the astrolabe. In the ninth, while the mosque at Córdoba was being built and Ptolemy's *Geographia* was being translated into Arabic, al-Khawarizmi wrote the first book in Arabic on algebra. In the tenth, while the university at Córdoba was being founded, al-Hasan (Alhazen) codified the laws of physics; and al-Sufi, in his "book of stars," mentioned nebulae, which the seventeenth century had to rediscover.

30 In the eleventh century, while the crypt of Chartres was being built, Ibn Sina (Avicenna) wrote the canon that dominated Western medicine for centuries. In the eleventh and twelfth centuries—before the troubadours sang their first love songs in France—the mathematician and philosopher Umar Khayyam, who lived to be almost a hundred, composed *The Ruba'iyyat*; and Ibn Rushd (Averroës) wrote commentaries on Plato and Aristotle. In the thirteenth, while Genghis Khan led the Mongols westward, while Saint Francis preached in Assisi, and while the Alcazar was being built in Seville, Yaqut wrote his geographic encyclopedia, and Ibn al-Baytar his work on pharmacology. In the fourteenth, while the Alhambra was being built in Granada, the Swiss Confederation was being formed, and the Black Death was ravaging Europe, Ibn Battutah's description of his travels earned him the title of "the Muslim Marco Polo," and Ibn Khaldun wrote a history not unworthy of Herodotus.

31 "The most sublime homage that can be offered to God is to know His work," wrote Averroës. And it was Islam, seldom thought of as Western, that gave the West the first complete map of the Eurasian continent—drawn at the dawn of the twelfth century by Muhammad al-Idrisi for King Roger II of Sicily. (The Muslims, who measured the circumference of the globe far better than Columbus did, had no chronometer with which to measure longitude. The Eurasian continent, as they mapped it, was too broad to leave room for America in the single ocean that washed the continent at its extremes.)

32 With the reconquest of Iberia, Spain and Portugal tried to reject their Muslim and Judaic heritages. But Islam's enthusiasm to know God's work would not be extinguished. Quite the contrary: it ignited Columbus's faith in the ocean. And from the Iberian Peninsula—where Islamic culture had reached perhaps its highest expression—the conquest of the oceans completed the Renaissance's knowledge of the globe.

Suggestions for Discussion and Writing

1. How do you explain the rapid growth of Islam, particularly when contrasted with the relatively slow development of Buddhism and other Eastern religions?
2. In light of the origins of Islam, why is the intermittent enmity between Arabs and Jews particularly ironic?
3. Does Obregón ignore any aspects of Islam and its beliefs that might show another side of its culture or teachings?
4. This essay moves back and forth from cause to effect as its author traces the rise of Islam. The first four paragraphs, for example, set forth some of its early accomplishments, and paragraphs 5–17 trace their causes. Find other examples of cause and effect in the rest of the essay.
5. Write an essay in which you trace the causes or effects of an historical or religious event or a scientific invention. Likely subjects might include the Great Depression of the 1930's, the Vietnam War, the growth of the Church of the Latter-Day Saints (Mormons) or the Protestant Reformation, and the invention of television, the automobile, or the telephone. Follow either Arrangement 1 (page 143), in which you state a general effect and then deal with its several causes, or Arrangement 2 (144), stating a general cause and then dealing with its possible effects.

ARISTOTLE*

[The Types of Human Character]

1 Let us now consider the various types of human character, in relation to the emotions and moral qualities, showing how they correspond to our various ages and fortunes. By emotions, I mean anger, desire, and the like. . . . By moral qualities, I mean virtues and vices . . . as well as the various things that various types of men tend to will and to do. By ages, I mean youth, the prime of life, and old age. By fortune, I mean birth, wealth, power, and their opposites—in fact, good fortune and ill fortune.

2 To begin with the Youthful type of character. Young men have strong passions, and tend to gratify them indiscriminately. Of the bodily desires, it is the sexual by which they are most swayed and in which they show absence of self-control. They are changeable and fickle in their desires, which are violent while they last, but quickly over: their impulses are keen but not deep-rooted, and are like sick people's attacks of hunger and thirst. They are hot-tempered and quick-tempered, and apt to give way to their anger; bad temper often gets the better of them, for owing to their love of honour they cannot bear being slighted, and are indignant if they imagine themselves unfairly treated. While they love honour, they love victory still more; for youth is eager for superiority over others, and victory is one form of this. They love both more than they love money, which indeed they love very little, not having yet learnt what it means to be without it—this is the point of Pittacus's remark about Amphiaraus.† They look at the good side rather than the bad, not having yet witnessed many instances of wickedness. They trust others readily, because they have not yet often been cheated. They are sanguine; nature warms their blood as though with excess of wine;

*Aristotle (384–322 B.C.), Plato's greatest pupil, set out to define and classify the things of this world, which his master had ignored as mere shadows of the Ideal. He almost filled the gap, with works on logic, philosophy, natural history, ethics, politics, poetics (epic poetry, tragedy, comedy), and rhetoric, from which this excerpt comes.—Ed.

†The remark is unknown.

and besides that, they have as yet met with few disappointments. Their lives are mainly spent not in memory but in expectation; for expectation refers to the future, memory to the past, and youth has a long future before it and a short past behind it: on the first day of one's life one has nothing at all to remember, and can only look forward. They are easily cheated, owing to the sanguine disposition just mentioned. Their hot tempers and hopeful dispositions make them more courageous than older men are; the hot temper prevents fear, and the hopeful disposition creates confidence; we cannot feel fear so long as we are feeling angry, and any expectation of good makes us confident. They are shy, accepting the rules of society in which they have been trained, and not yet believing in any other standard of honour. They have exalted notions, because they have not yet been humbled by life or learnt its necessary limitations; moreover, their hopeful disposition makes them think themselves equal to great things—and that means having exalted notions. They would always rather do noble deeds than useful ones: their lives are regulated more by moral feeling than by reasoning; and whereas reasoning leads us to choose what is useful, moral goodness leads us to choose what is noble. They are fonder of their friends, intimates, and companions than older men are, because they like spending their days in the company of others, and have not yet come to value either their friends or anything else by their usefulness to themselves. All their mistakes are in the direction of doing things excessively and vehemently. They disobey Chilon's* precept by overdoing everything; they love too much and hate too much, and the same with everything, and are always quite sure about it; this, in fact, is why they overdo everything. If they do wrong to others, it is because they mean to insult them, not to do them actual harm. They are ready to pity others, because they think every one an honest man, or anyhow better than he is: they judge their neighbour by their own harmless natures, and so cannot think he deserves to be treated in that way. They are fond of fun and therefore witty, wit being well-bred insolence.

3 Such, then, is the character of the Young. The character of Elderly Men—men who are past their prime—may be said to be formed for the most part of elements that are the contrary of all these. They have lived many years; they have often been taken in,

---

*One of the Seven Sages of ancient Greece. The precept is "Nothing in excess."

and often made mistakes; and life on the whole is a bad business. The result is that they are sure about nothing and *under-do* everything. They "think," but they never "know"; and because of their hesitation they always add a "possibly" or a "perhaps," putting everything this way and nothing positively. They are cynical; that is, they tend to put the worse construction on everything. Further, their experience makes them distrustful and therefore suspicious of evil. Consequently, they neither love warmly nor hate bitterly, but following the hint of Bias* they love as though they will some day hate and hate as though they will some day love. They are small-minded, because they have been humbled by life: their desires are set upon nothing more exalted or unusual than what will help them to keep alive. They are not generous, because money is one of the things they must have, and at the same time their experience has taught them how hard it is to get and how easy to lose. They are cowardly, and are always anticipating danger; unlike that of the young, who are warm-blooded, their temperament is chilly; old age has paved the way for cowardice; fear is, in fact, a form of chill. They love life; and all the more when their last day has come, because the object of all desire is something we have not got, and also because we desire most strongly that which we need most urgently. They are too fond of themselves; this is one form that small-mindedness takes. Because of this, they guide their lives too much by considerations of what is useful and too little by what is noble—for the useful is what is good for oneself, and the noble what is good absolutely. They are not shy, but shameless rather; caring less for what is noble than for what is useful, they feel contempt for what people may think of them. They lack confidence in the future; partly through experience—for most things go wrong, or anyhow turn out worse than one expects; and partly because of their cowardice. They live by memory rather than by hope; for what is left to them of life is but little as compared with the long past; and hope is of the future, memory of the past. This, again, is the cause of their loquacity; they are continually talking of the past, because they enjoy remembering it. Their fits of anger are sudden but feeble. Their sensual passions have either altogether gone or have lost their vigour: consequently, they do not feel their passions much, and their actions are inspired less by what they do feel than by the

*Bias of Pirene, the last of the Seven Sages.

love of gain. Hence men at this time of life are often supposed to have a self-controlled character; the fact is that their passions have slackened, and they are slaves to the love of gain. They guide their lives by reasoning more than by moral feeling; reasoning being directed to utility and moral feeling to moral goodness. If they wrong others, they mean to injure them, not to insult them. Old men may feel pity, as well as young men, but not for the same reason. Young men feel it out of kindness; old men out of weakness, imagining that anything that befalls any one else might easily happen to them, which . . . is a thought that excites pity. Hence they are querulous, and not disposed to jesting or laughter—the love of laughter being the very opposite of querulousness.

4 Such are the characters of Young Men and Elderly Men. People always think well of speeches adapted to, and reflecting, their own character: and we can now see how to compose our speeches so as to adapt both them and ourselves to our audiences.

5 As for Men in their Prime, clearly we shall find that they have a character between that of the young and that of the old, free from the extremes of either. They have neither that excess of confidence which amounts to rashness, nor too much timidity, but the right amount of each. They neither trust everybody nor distrust everybody, but judge people correctly. Their lives will be guided not by the sole consideration either of what is noble or of what is useful, but by both; neither by parsimony nor by prodigality, but by what is fit and proper. So, too, in regard to anger and desire; they will be brave as well as temperate, and temperate as well as brave; these virtues are divided between the young and the old; the young are brave but intemperate, the old temperate but cowardly. To put it generally, all the valuable qualities that youth and age divide between them are united in the prime of life, while their excesses or defects are replaced by moderation and fitness. The body is in its prime from thirty to five-and-thirty; the mind about forty-nine.

Suggestions for Discussion and Writing

1. Aristotle wrote his essay over two thousand years ago. Has human nature as he represents it changed in any significant way?

For example, does his idea that youth accepts the rules of society apply today?
2. Why doesn't Aristotle present the three types of men chronologically rather than move from youth to old men to those in their prime?
3. Are his descriptions exaggerated or excessive? Does he reveal a bias in favor of one particular type or age?
4. Are Aristotle's categories exclusive? Do they overlap?
5. In what way do comparison and contrast seem necessary to classification?
6. Write an essay applying Aristotle's description of youth, age, or the prime to your own observations, illustrating from people you know, including yourself.
7. Using classification as your basic method of development, write an essay in which you sort out one of the following topics into categories: methods of relaxation, instructors, part-time jobs, heroes, hobbies, actors.

DONALD HALL

Four Ways of Reading

1 Everywhere one meets the idea that reading is an activity desirable in itself. It is understandable that publishers and librarians—and even writers—should promote this assumption, but it is strange that the idea should have general currency. People surround the idea of reading with piety, and do not take into account the purpose of reading or the value of what is being read. Teachers and parents praise the child who reads, and praise themselves, whether the text be *The Reader's Digest* or *Moby Dick.* The advent of TV has increased the false values ascribed to reading, since TV provides a vulgar alternative. But this piety is silly; and most reading is no more cultural nor intellectual nor imaginative than shooting pool or watching *What's My Line.*

2 It is worth asking how the act of reading became something to value in itself, as opposed for instance to the act of conversation or the act of taking a walk. Mass literacy is a recent phenomenon, and I suggest that the aura which decorates reading is a relic

of the importance of reading to our great-great-grandparents. Literacy used to be a mark of social distinction, separating a small portion of humanity from the rest. The farm laborer who was ambitious for his children did not daydream that they would become schoolteachers or doctors; he daydreamed that they would learn to read, and that a world would therefore open up to them in which they did not have to labor in the fields fourteen hours a day for six days a week in order to buy salt and cotton. On the next rank of society, ample time for reading meant that the reader was free from the necessity to spend most of his waking hours making a living of any kind. . . . Reading is an inactivity, and therefore a badge of social class. Of course, these reasons for the piety attached to reading are never acknowledged. They show themselves in the shape of our attitudes toward books; reading gives off an air of gentility.

3 It seems to me possible to name four kinds of reading, each with a characteristic manner and purpose. The first is reading for information—reading to learn about a trade, or politics, or how to accomplish something. We read a newspaper this way, or most textbooks, or directions on how to assemble a bicycle. With most of this sort of material, the reader can learn to scan the page quickly, coming up with what he needs and ignoring what is irrelevant to him, like the rhythm of the sentence, or the play of metaphor. Courses in speed reading can help us read for this purpose, training the eye to jump quickly across the page. If we read *The New York Times* with the attention we should give a novel or a poem, we will have time for nothing else, and our mind will be cluttered with clichés and dead metaphor. Quick eye-reading is a necessity to anyone who wants to keep up with what's happening, or learn much of what has happened in the past. The amount of reflection, which interrupts and slows down the reading, depends on the material.

4 But it is not the same activity as reading literature. There ought to be another word. If we read a work of literature properly, we read slowly, and we hear all the words. If our lips do not actually move, it's only laziness. The muscles in our throats move, and come together when we see the word "squeeze." We hear the sounds so accurately that if a syllable is missing in a line of poetry we hear the lack, though we may not know what we are lacking. In prose we accept the rhythms, and hear the adjacent sounds. We also register a track of feeling through the meta-

phors and associations of words. Careless writing prevents this sort of attention, and becomes offensive. But the great writers reward this attention. Only by the full exercise of our powers to receive language can we absorb their intelligence and their imagination. This kind of reading goes through the ear—though the eye takes in the print, and decodes it into sound—to the throat and the understanding, and it can never be quick. It is slow and sensual, a deep pleasure that begins with touch and ends with the sort of comprehension that we associate with dream.

5 Too many intellectuals read in order to reduce images to abstractions. With a philosopher one reads slowly, as if it were literature, but much time must be spent with the eyes turned away from the pages, reflecting on the text. To read literature this way is to turn it into something it is not—to concepts clothed in character, or philosophy sugar-coated. I think that most literary intellectuals read this way, including the brighter Professors of English, with the result that they miss literature completely, and concern themselves with a minor discipline called the history of ideas. I remember a course in Chaucer at my University in which the final exam largely required the identification of a hundred or more fragments of Chaucer, none as long as a line. If you liked poetry, and read Chaucer through a couple of times slowly, you found yourself knowing them all. If you were a literary intellectual, well-informed about the great chain of being, chances are you had a difficult time. To read literature is to be intimately involved with the words on the page, and never to think of them as the embodiments of ideas which can be expressed in other terms. On the other hand, intellectual writing—closer to mathematics on a continuum that has at its opposite pole lyric poetry—requires intellectual reading, which is slow because it is reflective and because the reader must pause to evaluate concepts.

6 But most of the reading which is praised for itself is neither literary nor intellectual. It is narcotic. Novels, stories, and biographies—historical sagas, monthly regurgitations of book clubs, four- and five-thousand word daydreams of the magazines—these are the opium of the suburbs. The drug is not harmful except to the addict himself, and is no more injurious to him than Johnny Carson or a bridge club, but it is nothing to be proud of. This reading is the automated daydream, the mild trip of the housewife and the tired businessman, interested not in experience and feeling but in turning off the possibilities of experience

and feeling. Great literature, if we read it well, opens us up to the world, and makes us more sensitive to it, as if we acquired eyes that could see through things and ears that could hear smaller sounds. But by narcotic reading, one can reduce great literature to the level of *The Valley of the Dolls.* One can read *Anna Karenina* passively and inattentively, and float down the river of lethargy as if one were reading a confession magazine: "I Spurned My Husband for a Count."

7 I think that everyone reads for narcosis occasionally, and perhaps most consistently in late adolescence, when great readers are born. I remember reading to shut the world out, away at a school where I did not want to be; I invented a word to name my disease: "bibliolepsy," on the analogy of narcolepsy. But after a while the books became a window on the world, and not a screen against it. This change doesn't always happen. I think that late adolescent narcotic reading accounts for some of the badness of English departments. As a college student, the boy loves reading and majors in English because he would be reading anyway. Deciding on a career, he takes up English teaching for the same reason. Then in graduate school he is trained to be a scholar, which is painful and irrelevant, and finds he must write papers and publish them to be a Professor—and at about this time he no longer requires reading for narcosis, and he is left with nothing but a Ph.D. and the prospect of fifty years of teaching literature; and he does not even like literature.

8 Narcotic reading survives the impact of television, because this type of reading has even less reality than melodrama; that is, the reader is in control: once the characters reach into the reader's feelings, he is able to stop reading, or glance away, or superimpose his own daydream. The trouble with television is that it writes its own script. Literature is often valued precisely because of its distance from the tangible. Some readers prefer looking into the text of a play to seeing it performed. Reading a play, it is possible to stage it oneself by an imaginative act; but it is also possible to remove it from real people. Here is Virginia Woolf, who was lavish in her praise of the act of reading, talking about reading a play rather than seeing it: "Certainly there is a good deal to be said for reading *Twelfth Night* in the book if the book can be read in a garden, with no sound but the thud of an apple falling to the earth, or of the wind ruffling the branches of the trees." She sets her own stage; the play is called *Virginia Woolf*

Reads Twelfth Night in a Garden. Piety moves into narcissism, and the high metaphors of Shakespeare's lines dwindle into the flowers of an English garden; actors in ruffles wither, while the wind ruffles branches.

Suggestions for Discussion and Writing

1. What are some of the "false values" ascribed to reading that Hall wants to correct?
2. What are the four types of reading? Does Hall discuss them in random order, or does he introduce them logically? Explain.
3. Which of the four types mentioned by Hall does he write about in greatest detail? Why?
4. What is the chief difference between reading for information and reading literature? What are the demands of each?
5. What are some of the benefits of narcotic reading? Some of the negative aspects?
6. Explain Hall's comments about the way some English professors read.
7. What is Hall's attitude toward the quotation by Virginia Woolf in paragraph 8? Why does he use it to end his essay? Does his essay bear out his assertion that our conventional piety toward reading is silly? How might Sheed respond?
8. Using Hall's essay as a model, classify the television programs you watch or the music you listen to into categories. Then write an essay in which you evaluate the relative merits of each kind of program or music and its importance to you.

JOHN McPHEE

Building a Bark Canoe

1 In the middle of one morning, Vaillancourt left the shop, got into his car, drove two or three miles down the road, and went into woods to cut a birch. The weather was sharp, and he was wearing a heavy red Hudson's Bay coat. His sandy-brown hair, curling out in back, rested on the collar. He carried a sheathed Hudson's Bay axe and a long wooden wedge and a wooden club

(he called it a mallet) of the type seen in cartoons about cave societies. His eyes—they were pale blue, around an aquiline nose over a trapper's mustache—searched the woodlot for a proper tree. It need not be a giant. There were no giants around Greenville anyway. He wanted it for its sapwood, not its bark—for thwarts (also called crosspieces and crossbars) in a future canoe. After walking several hundred feet in from the road, he found a birch about eight inches in diameter, and with the axe he notched it in the direction of a free fall. He removed his coat and carefully set it aside. Beneath it was a blue oxford-cloth button-down shirt, tucked into his blue-jeans. He chopped the tree, and it fell into a young beech. "Jesus Christ!" he said. "It is so frustrating when Nature has you beat." The birch was hung up in the beech. He heaved at it and hauled it until it at last came free.

2 What he wanted of the tree was about six feet of its trunk, which he cut away from the rest. Then he sank the axe into one end of the piece, removed the axe, placed the wedge in the cut, and tapped the wedge with the mallet. He tapped twice more, and the entire log fell apart in two even halves. He said, "You get some birch, it's a bastard to split out, I'll tell you. But, Christ, this is nice. That's good and straight grain. Very often you get them twisted." Satisfied, he shouldered the tools and the wood, went back to the road, and drove home.

3 In the yard, he split the birch again, and he now had four pieces, quarter-round. One of these he cut off to a length of about forty inches. He took that into the shed. He built a fire, and in minutes the room was warm. He sat in his rocking chair and addressed the axe to the quarter-round log—the dark heartwood, the white sapwood. Holding the piece vertically, one end resting on the floor, he cut the heartwood away. He removed the bark and then went rapidly down the sapwood making angled indentations that caused the wood to curve out like petals. He cut them off, and they fell as big chips to the floor. A pile began to grow there as the axe head moved up and down, and what had been by appearance firewood was in a short time converted to lumber—a two-by-three, knotless board that might almost have been sawn in a mill.

4 He then picked up his crooked knife and held its grip in his upturned right hand, the blade poking out to the left. The blade was bent near its outer end (enabling it to move in grooves and hollows where the straight part could not). Both blade and grip

were shaped like nothing I had ever seen. The grip, fashioned for the convenience of a hand closing over it, was bulbous. The blade had no hinge and protruded rigidly—but not straight out. It formed a shallow V with the grip.

5 Vaillancourt held the piece of birch like a violin, sighting along it from his shoulder, and began to carve, bringing the knife upward, toward his chest. Of all the pieces of a canoe, the center thwart is the most complicated in the carving. Looked at from above, it should be broad at the midway point, then taper gradually as it reaches toward the sides of the canoe. Near its ends, it flares out in shoulders that are penetrated by holes, for lashings that will help secure it to the gunwales. The long taper, moreover, is interrupted by two grooved protrusions, where a tumpline can be tied before a portage. The whole upper surface should be flat, but the underside of the thwart rises slightly from the middle outward, then drops again at the ends, the result being that the thwart is thickest in the middle, gradually thinning as it extends outward and thickening again at the gunwales. All of this comes, in the end, to an adroit ratio between strength and weight, not to mention the incidental grace of the thing, each of its features being a mirror image of another. The canoe's central structural element, it is among the first parts set in place. Its long dimension establishes the canoe's width, and therefore many of the essentials of the canoe's design. In portage, nearly all of the weight of the canoe bears upon it.

6 So to me the making of a center thwart seemed a job for a jigsaw, a band saw, a set of chisels, a hammer, a block plane, a grooving plane, calipers, templates, and—most of all—mechanical drawings. One would have thought that anyone assertive enough to try it with a knife alone would at least begin slowly, moving into the wood with caution. Vaillancourt, to the contrary, tore his way in. He brought the knife toward him with such strong, fast, heavy strokes that long splinters flew off the board. "Birch is good stuff to work with," he said. "It's almost as easy to work as cedar. This feels like a hot knife going through butter. I used to use a drawknife. That God-damned thing. You've got to use a vise to hold the work. With the crooked knife, I can work in the woods if I want. I saw an Indian on TV in Canada using one. I got one, and I worked and worked with it to get the knack. Now it almost feels as if it's part of me. If anybody ever comes out with a tool that will rival a crooked knife, I'd like to hear about

it." He sighted along the wood, turned it over, and began whipping splinters off the other side. He said that steel tools had come with the white man, of course, and that most people seemed to imagine that Indian workmanship had improved with steel tools. "But I doubt it," he continued. "With bone and stone tools, it just took longer. The early Indians relied more on abrasion. With the exception of the center thwart, there is no fancy carving in a canoe. It's all flatwork. In fact, I'm doing experiments with bone tools." He stopped carving, reached to a shelf, and picked up a bone awl. "Make two holes with a bone awl in a piece of cedar, take out the wood between the holes with a bone chisel, and you have a mortise for a thwart to fit into." He reached for a piece of cedar (wood debris was all over the shop), made two holes, picked up a wooden mallet and a bone chisel, and made a mortise in the cedar. Then he picked up the long, curving incisor of a beaver. "I made a knife last winter out of a beaver's tooth," he said. "The original crooked knife was made out of a beaver's tooth." He sat down and continued to carve. The strokes were lighter now as he studied the wood, carved a bit, studied the wood, and carved some more. The piece was beginning to look roughly like a thwart, and the gentler motions of the knife were yielding thin, curling shavings that settled down on the bed of chips and splinters around his feet.

7 "Where the crooked knife was, the bark canoe was," he said. "People from Maine recognize the crooked knife. People from New Hampshire do not. All they knew was the drawknife. The God-damned drawknife—what a bummer."

8 The bark canoe was also where the big white birches were, and that excluded a good part of New Hampshire, including Greenville. Vaillancourt goes north to find his bark. The range of the tree—*Betula papyrifera,* variously called the white birch, the silver birch, the paper birch, the canoe birch—forms a swath more than a thousand miles wide (more or less from New York City to Hudson Bay) and reaches westward and northwestward to the Pacific. Far in from the boundaries of this enormous area, though, the trees are unlikely and always have been unlikely to grow large enough for the building of good canoes, and this exclusion includes most of the West, and even the Middle West. The biggest trees and the best of Indian canoes were in what are now New Brunswick, Nova Scotia, Maine, Quebec, and parts of Ontario. Even within this region, the most accomplished craftsmen were concentrated in the east. Of these, the best were the

Malecites. So Henri Vaillancourt builds Malecite canoes. Before all other design factors, he cares most about the artistic appearance of the canoes he builds, and he thinks the best-looking were the canoes of the Malecites. The Malecites lived in New Brunswick and parts of Maine. Vaillancourt builds the Malecite St. John River Canoe and the Malecite St. Lawrence River Canoe. He builds them with modifications, though. Toward the end of the nineteenth century, tribes started copying one another and gave up some of the distinctiveness of their tribal styles, and to varying extents, he said, he has done the same.

9 His carving became even slower now, and he studied the piece carefully before making his moves, but he measured nothing. "There's really no need for feet and inches," he said. "I know more or less what's strong and what isn't. If I want to find the middle of this crosspiece, I can put a piece of bark across it from end to end, and then fold it in half to find the center." He had measured the length—thirty-five inches—and had cut to it exactly. In the spring, when the time came to make the gunwales, he would measure them as well. But that is all he would measure in the entire canoe. According to the prescript passed on by Adney and Chapelle, the center thwart he was working on should taper

> slightly in thickness each way from its center to within 5 inches of the shoulders, which are 30 inches apart. The thickness at a point 5 inches from the shoulder is ¾ inch; from there the taper is quick to the shoulder, which is 5⁄16 inch thick, with a drop to ¼ inch in the tenon. The width, 3 inches at the center, decreases in a graceful curve to within 5 inches of the shoulder, where it is 2 inches, then increases to about 3 inches at the shoulder. The width of the tenon is, of course, 2 inches, to fit the mortise hole in the gunwale.

10 Yet the only instruments Vaillancourt was using to meet these specifications were his eyes.

11 He finished off the tumpline grooves. The thwart appeared to be perfect, but he picked up a piece of broken glass and scraped it gently all over. Fine excelsior came away, and the surface became shiningly smooth. It was noon. He had cut the birch in the woods at half past nine. Now he held the thwart in his hand, turning it this way and that. It was a lovely thing in itself, I thought, for it had so many blendings of symmetry. He said he could have done it in an hour if he had not been talking so much. And he was glad the tree

in the woods had turned into this thwart instead of "all the chintzy two-bit things they make out of birch—clothespins, dowels, toothpicks, Popsicle sticks." As he worked, he had from time to time scooped up handfuls of chips and shavings and fed them into the stove. Even so, the pile was still high around him, and he appeared to be sitting in a cone of snow.

12 He soon added more to the pile. From the rafters he took down a piece of cedar and, with the knife, sent great strips of it flying to the floor. He was now making a stempiece, the canoe part that establishes the profile of the bow or the stern. "Sometimes, when there are, you know, contortions in the grain, you can get into a real rat's nest," he said. "Around a knot, there will be waves in the grain. You cut to the knot from one side, then the other, to get a straight edge. At times like that, I'm tempted just to throw the thing out."

13 The wood he was working now, though, was clear and without complications, and after a short while, in which most of it went to the floor, he had made something that looked very much like a yardstick—albeit a heavy one—a half inch thick. Its corners were all sharp, and it seemed to have been machine-planed. Then he pressed the blade of the crooked knife into one end of the stick and kept pressing just hard enough to split the stick down fifty per cent of its length. He pressed the knife into the end again, near the first cut, and made another split, also stopping halfway. Again and again he split the wood, going far beyond the moment when I, watching him, thought that further splitting would be impossible, would ruin the whole. He split the board thirty-one times—into laminations each a half inch wide and a sixteenth of an inch thick. And all the laminations stopped in the middle, still attached there; from there on, the wood remained solid. "You split cedar parallel to the bark," he commented. "Hickory you can split both ways. There are very few woods you can do that with."

14 He plunged the laminated end of the piece into a bucket of water and left it there for a while, and then he built up the fire with scraps from the floor. In a coffee can he brought water to a boil. He poured it slowly over the laminations, bathing them, bathing them again. Then he lifted the steaming cedar in two hands and bent it. The laminations slid upon one another and formed a curve. He pondered the curve. It was not enough of a curve, he decided. So he bent the piece a little more. "There's an awful lot of it that's just whim," he said. "You vary the stempiece by whim." He liked what he saw now, so he reached for a

strip of basswood bark, tightly wound it around the curve in the cedar, and tied it off. The basswood bark was not temporary. It would stay there, and go into the canoe. Bow or stern, the straight and solid part of the stempiece would run downward from the tip, then the laminated curve would sweep inward, establishing the character of the end—and thus, in large part, of the canoe itself.

Suggestions for Discussion and Writing

1. McPhee notes that Vaillancourt wears a blue oxford-cloth buttondown shirt as he plies his ancient art, and Vaillancourt says that he learned to use the crooked knife by watching an Indian using one on television. What is the purpose of these and other incongruous images in McPhee's narrative?
2. Were any parts of the process unclear to you as you read the essay? Could any passages or sections have been rewritten more simply?
3. Which paragraphs in this essay are primarily narrative? Which are primarily descriptive? How are they amalgamated in order to explain the process of building the canoe?
4. In a real sense, Vaillancourt is building more than a bark canoe. What other significance or meaning does his craftsmanship and its product have?
5. Write an essay in which you describe a process that you know well. Present your thesis as an argument that makes a statement about the subject, and expand your points with descriptive and narrative details. For suggested topics and ideas, see questions 10 and 11 in the exercises on page 155.

STEVEN WEINBERG

The Creation: The First Three Minutes

1 In the beginning, there was an explosion. Not an explosion like those familiar on earth, starting from a definite center and spreading out to engulf more and more of the circumambient air,

but an explosion which occurred simultaneously everywhere, filling all space from the beginning, with every particle of matter rushing apart from every other particle. "All space" in this context may mean either all of an infinite universe, or all of a finite universe which curves back on itself like the surface of a sphere. Neither possibility is easy to comprehend, but this will not get in our way; it matters hardly at all in the early universe whether space is finite or infinite.

2 At about one-hundredth of a second, the earliest time about which we can speak with any confidence, the temperature of the universe was about a hundred thousand million (10^{11}) degrees Centigrade. This is much hotter than in the center of even the hottest star, so hot, in fact, that none of the components of ordinary matter, molecules, or atoms, or even the nuclei of atoms, could have held together. Instead, the matter rushing apart in this explosion consisted of various types of the so-called elementary particles, which are the subject of modern high-energy nuclear physics.

3 One type of particle that was present in large numbers is the electron, the negatively charged particle that flows through wires in electric currents and makes up the outer parts of all atoms and molecules in the present universe. Another type of particle that was abundant at early times is the positron, a positively charged particle with precisely the same mass as the electron. In the present universe, positrons are found only in high-energy laboratories, in some kinds of radioactivity, and in violent astronomical phenomena like cosmic rays and supernovas, but in the early universe the number of positrons was almost exactly equal to the number of electrons. In addition to electrons and positrons, there were roughly similar numbers of various kinds of neutrinos, ghostly particles with no mass or electric charge whatever. Finally, the universe was filled with light. This does not have to be treated separately from the particles—the quantum theory tells us that light consists of particles of zero mass and zero electrical charge known as photons. (Each time an atom in the filament of a light bulb changes from a state of higher energy to one of lower energy, one photon is emitted. There are so many photons coming out of a light bulb that they seem to blend together in a continuous stream of light, but a photoelectric cell can count individual photons, one by one.) Every photon carries a definite amount of energy and momentum depending on the

wavelength of the light. To describe the light that filled the early universe, we can say that the number and the average energy of the photons was about the same as for electrons or positrons or neutrinos.

4 These particles—electrons, positrons, neutrinos, photons—were continually being created out of pure energy, and then after short lives being annihilated again. Their number therefore was not preordained, but fixed instead by a balance between processes of creation and annihilation. From this balance, we can infer that the density of this cosmic soup at a temperature of a hundred thousand million degrees was about four thousand million (4×10^9) times that of water. There was also a small contamination of heavier particles, protons and neutrons, which in the present world form the constituents of atomic nuclei. (Protons are positively charged; neutrons are slightly heavier and electrically neutral.) The proportions were roughly one proton and one neutron for every thousand million electrons or positrons or neutrinos or photons. This number—a thousand million photons per nuclear particle—is the crucial quantity that had to be taken from observation in order to work out the standard model of the universe.

5 As the explosion continued the temperature dropped, reaching thirty thousand million (3×10^{10}) degrees Centigrade after about one-tenth of a second; ten thousand million degrees after about one second; and three thousand million degrees after about fourteen seconds. This was cool enough so that the electrons and positrons began to annihilate faster than they could be re-created out of the photons and neutrinos. The energy released in this annihilation of matter temporarily slowed the rate at which the universe cooled, but the temperature continued to drop, finally reaching one thousand million degrees at the end of the first three minutes. It was then cool enough for the protons and neutrons to begin to form into complex nuclei, starting with the nucleus of heavy hydrogen (or deuterium), which consists of one proton and one neutron. The density was still high enough (a little less than that of water) so that these light nuclei were able rapidly to assemble themselves into the most stable light nucleus, that of helium, consisting of two protons and two neutrons.

6 At the end of the first three minutes the contents of the universe were mostly in the form of light, neutrinos, and antineu-

trinos. There was still a small amount of nuclear material, now consisting of about 73 percent hydrogen and 27 percent helium, and an equally small number of electrons left over from the era of electron-positron annihilation. This matter continued to rush apart, becoming steadily cooler and less dense. Much later, after a few hundred thousand years, it would become cool enough for electrons to join with nuclei to form atoms of hydrogen and helium. The resulting gas would begin under the influence of gravitation to form clumps, which would ultimately condense to form the galaxies and stars of the present universe. However, the ingredients with which the stars would begin their life would be just those prepared in the first three minutes.

7 The standard model sketched above is not the most satisfying theory imaginable of the origin of the universe. There is an embarrassing vagueness about the very beginning, the first hundredth of a second or so. Also, there is the unwelcome necessity of fixing initial conditions, especially the initial thousand-million-to-one ratio of photons to nuclear particles. We would prefer a greater sense of logical inevitability in the theory.

8 For example, one alternative theory that seems philosophically far more attractive is the so-called steady-state model. In this theory, proposed in the late 1940s by Herman Bondi, Thomas Gold, and (in a somewhat different formulation) Fred Hoyle, the universe has always been just about the same as it is now. As it expands, new matter is continually created to fill up the gaps between the galaxies. Potentially, all questions about why the universe is the way it is can be answered in this theory by showing that it is the way it is because that is the only way it can stay the same. The problem of the early universe is banished; there was no early universe.

9 How then did we come to the "standard model"? And how has it supplanted other theories, like the steady-state model? It is a tribute to the essential objectivity of modern astrophysics that this consensus has been brought about, not by shifts in philosophical preference or by the influence of astrophysical mandarins, but by the pressure of empirical data.

10 Can we really be sure of the standard model? Will new discoveries overthrow it and replace the present standard model with some other cosmogony, or even revive the steady-state model? Perhaps. I cannot deny a feeling of unreality in writing

about the first three minutes as if we really know what we are talking about.

11 However, even if it is eventually supplanted, the standard model will have played a role of great value in the history of cosmology. It is now respectable (though only in the last decade or so) to test theoretical ideas in physics or astrophysics by working out their consequences in the context of the standard model. It is also common practice to use the standard model as a theoretical basis for justifying programs of astronomical observation. Thus, the standard model provides an essential common language which allows theorists and observers to appreciate what each other are doing. If some day the standard model is replaced by a better theory, it will probably be because of observations or calculations that drew their motivation from the standard model.

12 [The universe] may go on expanding forever, getting colder, emptier, and deader. Alternatively, it may recontract, breaking up the galaxies and stars and atoms and atomic nuclei back into their constituents. All the problems we face in understanding the first three minutes would then arise again in predicting the course of events in the last three minutes.

Suggestions for Discussion and Writing

1. Examine the first sentence of this selection. What echoes or parallels is Weinberg attempting to establish at the outset? Why?
2. The author refers to "the present universe" (paragraph 3). What is the implication of this phrase?
3. Notice that the narrative process is temporarily halted in paragraphs 3 and 4. What is the purpose of those paragraphs? How does Weinberg combine description with his narrative?
4. Do paragraphs 7 and 8 weaken his hypothesis? Explain.
5. What assumptions does Weinberg make about his audience? Does he dilute his theory in order to accommodate the reader? Or is he writing for the specialist and scientist?
6. How does the last paragraph of this selection offer the reader a sense of "closure" or finality?
7. In an essay that combines narration and description, explain a natural process such as photosynthesis, an earthquake, the acquisition of language, or the aging process in humans.

WAYNE C. BOOTH

What Is an Idea?

1 "I've got an idea; let's go get a hamburger." "All right, now, as sales representatives we must brainstorm for ideas to increase profits." "The way Ray flatters the boss gives you the idea he's bucking for a promotion, doesn't it?" "Hey, listen to this; I've just had an idea for attaching the boat to the top of the car without having to buy a carrier." "The idea of good defense is to keep pressure on the other team without committing errors ourselves." "What did you say that set of books was called? *The Great Ideas?* What does that mean?"

2 The word *idea,* as you can see, is used in a great many ways. In most of the examples above it means something like "intention," "opinion," or "mental image." The "idea" of going for a hamburger is really a mental picture of a possible action, just as the "idea" of a boat carrier is a mental image of a mechanical device. The "ideas" of good defense and Ray the flatterer are really opinions held by the speakers, while the appeal for "ideas" about how to increase profits is really an appeal for opinions (which may also involve mental images) from fellow workers. None of these examples, however, encompasses the meaning of "idea" as it has always been used by those who engage in serious discussions of politics, history, intellectual movements, and social affairs. Even the last example, an allusion to the famous set of books edited by Robert Maynard Hutchins and Mortimer Adler at the University of Chicago, does not yet express an idea; it only directs us toward a source where ideas may be encountered.

3 These uses of "idea" are entirely appropriate in their contexts. Words play different roles at different times. One can "fish" for either trout or compliments, and a scalp, an executive, and a toilet (in the Navy) are all "heads." Usually, these different uses have overlapping, not opposed, meanings. For example, we wouldn't know what fishing for compliments meant unless we already knew what fishing for trout meant; and the "heads" we just referred to are all indications of position or place. In the same way, the different uses of the word *idea* overlap. Even the

most enduring ideas may appear to some as "mere opinion." What, then, does *idea* mean in the context of serious talk, and what keeps some opinions and mental images from being ideas in our sense?

4 Three central features distinguish an idea from other kinds of mental products:

1. An idea is always connected to other ideas that lead to it, follow from it, or somehow support it. Like a family member, an idea always exists amid a network of ancestors, parents, brothers, sisters, and cousins. An idea could no more spring into existence by itself than a plant could grow without a seed, soil, and a suitable environment. For example, the idea that acts of racial discrimination are immoral grows out of and is surrounded by a complex of other, related ideas about the nature of human beings and the nature of moral conduct:
   a. Racial differences are irrelevant to human nature.
   b. The sort of respect that is due to any human being *as* a human being is due equally to *all* human beings.
   c. It is immoral to deny to any human being the rights and privileges due to every human being.

   And so on. You can see that a great many other ideas surround, support, and follow from the leading idea.
2. An idea always has the capacity to generate other ideas. Ideas not only have ancestors and parents, but they make their own offspring. The idea that *racial* discrimination is immoral, for example, is the offspring of the idea that *any* sort of bigotry is wrong.
3. An idea is always capable of yielding more than one argument or position. An idea never has a fixed, once-and-for-all meaning, and it always requires interpretation and discussion. Whenever interpretation is required and discussion permitted, disagreements will exist. Ideas are always to some degree controversial, but the kind of controversy produced by the clash of ideas—unlike the kind of controversy produced by the clash of prejudices—is one in which *reasons* are offered and tested by both sides in the debate. As reasons are considered, positions that seemed fixed turn into ideas that move with argument.

5 In recent years, for example, the idea that racial discrimination is immoral, combined with the idea that past discriminations should be compensated for, has led to the follow-up idea that minority groups should, in some cases, receive preferred treatment, such as being granted admission to medical school with lower scores than those of competing applicants from majority groups. Some people have charged that this is "reverse discrimination," while others advance arguments for and against such positions with great intellectual and moral vigor. Regardless of where you stand on this issue, you can see that interpretations of ideas yield a multiplicity of positions.

6 There are obviously many kinds of mental products that do not qualify as ideas according to these criteria. "Two plus two equals four," for example, is not an idea. Without reference to the ideas that lie behind it, it can neither be interpreted nor used. In and of itself, "two plus two equals four" is simply a brute fact, not an idea. However, as a statement it is clearly the product of ideas: the idea of quantity, the idea that the world can be understood and manipulated in terms of systems of numbers, and so on.

7 Many of our everyday notions, opinions, and pictures of things also fail to qualify as ideas. "I hate John" may be an intelligible utterance—it indicates the feelings of the speaker—but it is not an idea. The "parents" of this utterance lie in the psychology or biography of the speaker, not in other ideas, and it can neither yield its own offspring nor support an argument. "Catholics are sheep," "All communists in government are traitors," "Christianity is the only true religion," "Republicans stink," "Most people on welfare are cheaters," and "Premarital sex is OK if you know what you're doing" are all such non-ideas. With appropriate development or modification, some of these opinions could be turned into ideas, but what keeps them from qualifying as ideas in their present form is that they are only minimally related (and in some instances totally *un*related) to other ideas. One sign that you are being offered mindless, bigoted, or fanatical opinions, not ideas, is the presence of emotion-charged generalizations, unsupported by evidence or argument. Catch words, clichés, and code phrases ("welfare cheaters," "dumb jocks," "a typical woman," "crazy, atheistical scientists") are a sure sign that emotions have shoved ideas out of the picture.

8 A liberal education is an education in ideas—not merely memorizing them, but learning to move among them, balancing one against the other, negotiating relationships, accommodating new arguments, and returning for a closer look. Writing is one of the primary ways of learning how to perform this intricate dance *on one's own.* In American education, where the learning of facts and data is often confused with an education in ideas, thoughtful writing remains one of our best methods for learning how to turn opinions into ideas.

9 The attempt to write well forces us to clarify our thoughts. Because every word in an essay (unlike those in a conversation) can be retrieved in the same form every time, and then discussed, interpreted, challenged, and argued about, the act of putting words down on paper is more deliberate than speaking. It places more responsibility on us, and it threatens us with greater consequences for error. Our written words and ideas can be thrown back in our faces, either by our readers or simply by the page itself as we re-read. We are thus more aware when writing than when speaking that every word is a *choice,* and that it commits us to a meaning in a way that another word would not.

10 One result is that writing forces us to develop ideas more systematically and fully than speaking does. In conversation we can often get away with canyon-sized gaps in our arguments, and we can rely on facial expression, tone, gesture, and other "body language" to fill out our meanings when our words fail. But most of these devices are denied to us when we write. In order to make a piece of writing effective, every essential step must be filled in carefully, clearly, and emphatically. We cannot grab our listeners by the lapel or charm them with our ingratiating smile. The "grabbing" and the "charm" must somehow be put into words, and that always requires greater care than is needed in ordinary conversation.

11 Inexperienced writers often make the mistake of thinking that they have a firmer grasp on their ideas than on their words. They frequently utter the complaint, "I know what I want to say; I just can't find the words for it." This claim is almost always untrue, not because beginning writers are deliberate liars, but because they confuse their intuitive sense that they have *something* to say with the false sense that they already know pre-

cisely what that something is. When a writer is stuck for words, the problem is rarely a problem only of words. Inexperienced writers may think they need larger vocabularies when what they *really* need are clearer ideas and intentions. Being stuck for words indicates that the thought one wants to convey is still vague, unformed, cloudy, and confused. Once you finally discover your concrete meaning, you will discover the proper words for expressing it at the same time. You may revise words later as meanings become *more* clear to you, but no writer ever stands in full possession of an idea without having enough words to express it.

12 Ideas are to writing as strength and agility are to athletic prowess: They do not in themselves guarantee quality, but they are the muscle in all good writing prowess. Not all strong and agile athletes are champions, but all champion athletes are strong and agile. Not everyone who has powerful ideas is a great writer, but it is impossible for any writer even to achieve effectiveness, much less greatness, without them.

Suggestions for Discussion and Writing

1. What is Booth's point: that the word *idea* is widely misused, or that it has several meanings? How do you know?

2. According to Booth, what are you really saying when you claim that you know what you want to say but can't find the words for it?

3. Locate the sentence in which Booth tells you how he intends to approach his definition. Is his definition essentially inclusive or exclusive?

4. Booth uses a variety of methods in his definition. Find one or more paragraphs that show what an idea is *not like,* what it is *like,* what it is *not,* and what it *is.*

5. What method of definition does Booth conclude with (paragraph 12)? Is it an effective technique?

6. How does the author relate ideas to writing and conversation? Is his discussion relevant to the rest of his essay?

7. How satisfactory are the following definitions:

a. "Love is never having to say you're sorry."

b. "Architecture is frozen music."

c. "By the term God, I mean the Deity."

d. "Science is what we know and philosophy is what we don't know." (Bertrand Russell)

8. Using a variety of techniques, define one of the following terms in an essay; because they are abstract, you will have to make your definition specific.

education	morality
love	evil
homesickness	intelligence
patriotism	freedom
beauty	duty

6 Straight and Crooked Thinking: Working with Evidence

All along, you have been working to support your thesis and persuade your reader with evidence. Evidence is an example, or several examples. Your thesis has, in fact, emerged from the evidence, from thinking about the specific things you have experienced, seen, heard, in person, in reading, or on TV. To support that thesis, you have simply turned the process around, bringing in those same specific things, and others, as evidence—descriptive, narrative, and expository. You have been deciding logically on the weight and shape of that evidence, comparing, working out causes and effects, classifying, defining. But your evidence and its connections are always liable to certain logical fallacies that may defeat its persuasiveness.

DEGREES OF EVIDENCE

Write as Close to the Facts as Possible

Facts are the firmest kind of thought, but they are *thoughts* nevertheless—verifiable thoughts about the coal and wheat and other entities of our experience. The whole question of fact comes down to verifiability: things not susceptible of verification leave the realm of factuality. Fact is limited, therefore, to the kinds of things that can be tested by the senses (verified empirically, as the philosophers say) or by inferences from physical data so strong as to allow no other explanation. "Statements of fact" are assertions of a kind provable by referring to experience. The simplest physical facts—that a stone is a stone and that it exists—are so bound into our elementary perceptions of the world that we never think to verify them, and indeed could not verify them beyond gathering testimonials from the group. With less tangible facts, verification is simply doing enough to persuade any reasonable person that the assertion of fact is true, beginning with what our senses can in some way check.

Measuring, weighing, and counting are the strongest empirical verifiers; assertions capable of such verification are the most firmly and quickly demonstrated as factual:

Smith is five feet high and four feet wide.
The car weighs 2300 pounds.
Three members voted for beer.

In the last assertion, we have moved from what we call physical fact to historical fact—that which can be verified by its signs: we have the ballots. Events in history are verified in the same way, although the evidence is scarcer the farther back we go.

Believe What You Write—But Learn the Nature of Belief

Facts, then, are things established by verification. Belief presents an entirely different kind of knowledge: things believed true but yet beyond the reach of sensory verification—a belief in God, for instance. We may infer a Creator from the creation, a Beginning from the beginnings we see around us. But a doubting Thomas will have nothing to touch or see; judging our inferences wrongly drawn, he may prefer to believe in a physical accident, or in a flux with neither beginning nor end. The point is that although beliefs are unprovable, they are not necessarily untrue, and they are not unusable as you discourse with your reader. Many beliefs, of course, have proved false as new evidence turns up. Nevertheless, you can certainly assert beliefs in your writing, establishing their validity in a tentative and probable way, so long as you do not assume you have *proved* them. State your convictions; support them with the best reasons you can find; and don't apologize. But you may wish to qualify your least demonstrable convictions with "I believe," "we may reasonably suppose," "perhaps," "from one point of view," and the like.

Don't Mistake Opinion for Fact

Halfway between fact and belief is *opinion,* a candidate for fact or belief, something you believe true but about whose verification or support you are still uncertain. The difference between fact and opinion is simply a difference in verifiableness. One opinion may eventually prove true, and another false; an opinion may strengthen into belief and then, through verifying tests, into accepted fact, as with Galileo's opinion that the earth moved.

The testing of opinions to discover the facts is, indeed, the central business of argumentation. When you assert something as fact, you indicate (1) that you assume it true and easily verified, and (2) that its truth is generally acknowledged. When you assert something as opinion, you imply some uncertainty about both these things. Here are two common opinions that will probably remain opinions exactly because of such uncertainty:

Girls are brighter than boys.
Men are superior to women.

We know that the terms *brighter* and *superior* have a range of meaning hard to pin down. Even when agreeing upon the tests for numerical and verbal abilities, and for memory and ingenuity, we cannot be sure that we will not miss other kinds of brightness and superiority, or that our tests will measure these things in any thorough way. The range of meaning in our four other terms, moreover, is so wide as virtually to defy verification. We need only ask "At what age?" to illustrate how broad they are. So in these slippery regions of opinion, keep your assertions tentative with *may* and *might* and *perhaps.*

Dispute Your Preferences with Care

Preferences are something else again. They are farther from proof than opinions—indeed, beyond the pale of proof. And yet they are more firmly held than opinions, because they are primarily subjective, sweetening our palates and warming our hearts. *De gustibus non est disputandum:* tastes are not to be disputed. So goes the medieval epigram, from the age that refined the arts of logic. You can't argue successfully about tastes, empirical though they be, because they are beyond empirical demonstration. Are peaches better than pears? Whichever you choose, your choice is probably neither logically defensible nor logically vulnerable. The writer's responsibility is to recognize the logical immunity of preferences, and to qualify them politely with "I think," "many believe," "some may prefer," and so forth.

So go ahead, dispute over tastes, and you may find some solid grounds for them. Shakespeare is greater than Ben Jonson. Subjective tastes have moved all the way up beside fact: the grounds for Shakespeare's margin of greatness have been exhibited, argued, and explored over the centuries, until we accept his superiority, as if empirically verified. Actually, the questions that most commonly concern us are beyond scientific verification. But you can frequently establish your preferences as testable opinions by asserting them reasonably and without unwholesome prejudice, and by using the secondary evidence that other reasonable people agree with you in persuasive strength and number.

ASSESSING THE EVIDENCE

Logical Fallacies: Trust Your Common Sense

From the first, in talking about a valid thesis, about proof, about assumptions and implications and definition, we have been facing logical fallacies—that is, flaws in thought, things that do not add up. Evidence itself raises the biggest question of logic. Presenting any evidence at all faces a logical fallacy that can never be surmounted: no amount of evidence can *logically* prove an assertion because *one* and *some* can never equal *all.* Because the sun has gotten up on time every morning so far is—the logicians tell us—no logical assurance that it will do so tomorrow. Actually, we can take comfort in that fallacy. Since we can never *logically* produce enough evidence for certitude, we can settle for a reasonable amount and call it quits. One piece of evidence all by itself tempts us to cry, "Fallacy! *One* isn't *all* or *every.*" But three or four pieces will probably suit our common sense and calm us into agreement.

Cite Authorities Reasonably

An appeal to some authority to prove your point is really an appeal beyond logic, but not necessarily beyond reason. We naturally turn to authorities to confirm our ideas. "Einstein said" can silence many an objection. But appeals to authority risk four common fallacies. The first is in appealing to the authority outside of his field, even if his field is the universe. After all, the good doctor, of the wispy hair and frayed sweater, was little known for understanding money too.

The second fallacy is in misunderstanding or misrepresenting what the authority really says. Sir Arthur Eddington, if I may appeal to an authority myself, puts the case: "It is a common mistake to suppose that Einstein's theory of relativity asserts that everything is relative. Actually it says, 'There are absolute things in the world but you must look deeply for them. The things that first present themselves to your notice are for the most part relative.' "* If you appeal loosely to Einstein to authenticate an assertion that everything is "relative," you may appeal in vain—since *relative* means relative *to* something else, eventually to some absolute.

The third fallacy is in assuming that one instance from an authority represents him accurately. Arguments for admitting the split infinitive (see 394, 467) to equal status with the unsplit, for instance, often present split constructions from prominent writers. But they do not tell us how many splits a writer avoided, or

* *The Nature of the Physical World* (Ann Arbor: University of Michigan Press, 1958): 23.

how he himself feels about the construction. A friend once showed me a split infinitive in the late Walter Lippmann's column after I had boldly asserted that careful writers like Lippmann never split them. Out of curiosity, I wrote Mr. Lippmann: after all, he might have changed his tune. He wrote back that he had slipped, that he disliked the thing and tried to revise it out whenever it crept in.

The fourth fallacy is deepest: the authority may have faded. New facts have generated new ideas. Einstein has limited Newton's authority. Geology and radioactive carbon have challenged the literal authority of Genesis. Jung has challenged Freud; and Keynes, Marx.

The more eminent the authority, the easier the fallacy. Ask these four questions:

1. Am I citing him outside his field?
2. Am I presenting him accurately?
3. Is this instance really representative?
4. Is he still fully authoritative?

Do not claim too much for your authority, and add other kinds of proof, or other authorities. In short, don't put all your eggs in one basket.

Handle Persistences as You Would Authorities

That an idea's persistence constitutes a kind of unwritten or cumulative authority is also open to logical challenge. Because a belief has persisted, the appeal goes, it must be true. Since earliest times, for example, man has believed in some kind of supernatural beings or Being. Something must be there, the persistence seems to suggest. But the appeal is not logical; the belief could have persisted from causes other than the actuality of divine existence, perhaps only from man's psychological need. As with authority, new facts may vanquish persistent beliefs. The belief that the world was a pancake, persistent though it had been, simply had to give way to Columbus and Magellan. For all this, however, persistence does have considerable strength as an *indication* of validity, to be supported by other reasons.

Inspect Your Documentary Evidence Before Using

Documents are both authoritative and persistent. They provide the only evidence, aside from oral testimony, for all that we know beyond the immediate presence of our physical universe, with its physical remains of the past. Documents point to what has happened, as long ago as Nineveh and Egypt and as recently as the tracings on last hour's blackboard. But documents vary in reliability. You must consider a document's historical context, since factuality may have been of little concern, as with stories of heroes and saints, or with propaganda. You must allow, as with newspapers, for the effects of haste and limited facts. You should consider a document's author, his background, his range of knowledge and belief, his assumptions, his prejudices, his probable motives, his possible tendencies to suppress or slant the facts.

Finally, you should consider the document's data. Are the facts of a kind easily verifiable or easily collected? Indeed, can you present other verification? For example, numerical reports of population can be no more than approximations, and they are hazier the farther back you go in history, as statistical methods slacken. Since the data must have been selected from almost infinite possibilities, does the selection seem reasonably representative? Are your source's conclusions right for the data? Might not the data produce other conclusions? Your own data and conclusions, of course, must also face questioning.

Statistics are particularly persuasive evidence, and because of their psychological appeal, they can be devilishly misleading. To reduce things to numbers seems scientific, incontrovertible, final. But each "1" represents a slightly different quantity, as one glance around a class of 20 students will make clear. Each student is the same, yet entirely different. The "20" is a broad generalization convenient for certain kinds of information: how many seats the instructor will need, how many people are absent, how much the instruction costs per head, and so forth. But clearly the "20" will tell nothing about the varying characteristics of the students or the education. So present your statistics with some caution so that they will honestly show what you want them to show and will not mislead your readers. Averages and percentages can be especially misleading, carrying the numerical generalization one step farther from the physical facts. The truth behind a statement that the average student earns $10 a week could be that nine students earn nothing and one earns $100.

SOME INDUCTIVE TRAPS

Keep Your Hypothesis Hypothetical

Induction and deduction are the two paths of reasoning. Induction is "leading into" (*in ducere,* "to lead in"), thinking through the evidence to some general conclusion. Deduction is "leading away from" some general precept to its particular parts and consequences. All along, you have been *thinking inductively* to find your thesis, and then you have turned the process around, *writing deductively* when you present your thesis and support it with your evidence. Both modes have their uses, and their fallacies.

Induction is the way of science: one collects the facts and sees what they come to. Sir Francis Bacon laid down in 1620 the inductive program in his famous *Novum Organum, sive indicia vera de interpretatione naturae* ("The New Instrument, or true evidence concerning the interpretation of nature"). Bacon was at war with the syllogism; its abstract deductions seemed too rigid to measure nature's subtlety. His new instrument changed the entire course of thought. Before Bacon, the world had deduced the consequences of its general ideas; after Bacon, the world looked around and induced new generalizations from what it saw. Observed facts called the old ideas into question, and theories replaced "truths." As you may know, Bacon died from a cold caught while stuffing a chicken's carcass with snow for an inductive test of refrigeration.

Induction has great strength, but it also has a basic fallacy. The strength is in taking nothing on faith, in having no ideas at all until the facts have suggested them. The fallacy is in assuming that the mind can start blank. Theoretically, Bacon had no previous ideas about refrigeration. Theoretically, he would experiment aimlessly until he noticed consistencies that would lead to the icebox. Actually, from experience, one would already have a hunch, a half-formed theory, that would suggest the experimental tests. Induction, in other words, is always well mixed with deduction. The major difference is in the tentative frame of mind: in making an hypothesis instead of merely borrowing an honored assumption, and in keeping the hypothesis hypothetical, even after the facts seem to have supported it.

Use Analogies to Clarify, Not to Prove

The simplest kind of induction is analogy: because this tree is much like that oak, it too must be some kind of oak. You identify the unknown by its analogy to the known. You inductively look over the similarities until you conclude that the trees are very similar, and therefore the same kind. Analogies are tremendously useful indications of likeness; analogy is virtually our only means of classification, our means of putting things into groups and handling them by naming them. Analogy also illustrates the logical weakness of induction: assuming that *all* characteristics are analogous after finding one or two analogous. We check a few symptoms against what we know of colds and flu, and conclude that we have a cold and flu; but the doctor will add to these a few more symptoms and conclude that we have a virulent pneumonia.

Similarity does not mean total identity, and analogies must always make that shaky assumption, or clearly demonstrate that the mismatching details are unimportant. In your writing, you may use analogy with tremendous effect, as we saw when E. B. White compares Thoreau to a gun-slinging cowboy (139–40). But watch out for the logical gap between *some* and *all.* Make sure that:

1. A reasonably large number of details agree.
2. These details are salient and typical.
3. The misfitting details are insignificant and not typical.

If the brain seems in some ways like a computer, be careful not to assume it is in all ways like a computer. Keep the analogy figurative: it can serve you well, as any metaphor serves, to illustrate the unknown with the known, but not to prove.

Look Before You Leap

The hypothetical frame of mind is the essence of the inductive method, because it acknowledges the logical flaw of induction, namely, the *inductive leap.* No matter how many the facts, or how carefully weighed, a time comes when thought must abandon the details and leap to the conclusion. We leap from the knowledge that *some* apples are good to the conclusion: "[All] apples are good." This leap, say the logicians, crosses an abyss no logic can bridge, because *some* can never guarantee *all*—except as a general *probability.* The major lesson of induction is that *nothing* can be proved, except as a probability. The best we can manage is an *hypothesis,* while maintaining a perpetual hospitality to new facts that might change our theory. This is the scientific frame of mind; it gets as close to substantive truth as we can come, and it keeps us healthily humble before the facts.

Probability is the great limit and guarantee of the generalizations to which we must eventually leap. You know that bad apples are neither so numerous nor so strongly typical that you must conclude: "Apples are unfit for human consumption." You also know what causes the bad ones. Therefore, to justify your leap and certify your generalization, you base your induction on the following three conditions:

1. Your samples are reasonably numerous.
2. Your samples are truly typical.
3. Your exceptions are explainable, and demonstrably not typical.

The inductive leap is always risky because all the data cannot be known. The leap might also be in the wrong direction: more than one conclusion may be drawn from the same evidence. Here, then, is where the inductive frame of mind can help you. It can teach you always to check your conclusions by asking if another answer might not do just as well. Some linguists have concluded that speech is superior to writing because speech has many more "signals" than writing. But from the same facts one might declare writing superior: it conveys the same message with fewer signals.

The shortcomings of induction are many. The very data of sensory observation may be indistinct. Ask any three people to tell how an accident happened, and the feebleness of human observation becomes painfully apparent. If the facts are slippery, the final leap is uncertain. Furthermore, your hypothesis, which must come early to give your investigation some purpose, immediately becomes a *deductive* proposition that not only will guide your selection of facts, but may well distort slightly the facts you select. Finally, as we have seen with statistics and averages, scientific induction relies heavily on mathematics, which requires that qualities be translated into quantities. Neither numbers nor words, those two essential generalizers of our experience, can adequately grasp all our particular diversities. The lesson of induction, therefore, is the lesson of caution. Logically, induction is shot full of holes. But it makes as firm a statement as we can expect about the physical universe and our experience in it. The ultimate beauty of science is perhaps not that it is efficient (and it is), but that it is hypothetical. It keeps our minds open for new hypotheses. The danger lies in thinking it absolute.

The Classic Fallacies

All in all, most fallacies in writing—our own and others'—we can uncover simply by knowing they are lurking and using our heads. We must constantly ask if our words are meaning what they say, and saying what we mean. We must check our assumptions. Then we must ask if we are inadvertently taking *some* for *all,* or making that inductive leap too soon or in an errant direction. But logicians have identified six classic fallacies that sum up most of our muddles:

1. EITHER-OR. You assume only two opposing possibilities: "Either we abolish requirements or education is finished." Education will probably amble on, somewhere in between. Similarly, IF-THEN: "If I work harder on the next paper, then I'll get a better grade." You have overlooked differences in subject, knowledge, involvement, inspiration.
2. OVERSIMPLIFICATION. As with *either-or,* you ignore alternatives. "A student learns only what he wants to learn" ignores all the pressures from parents and society, which in fact account for a good deal of learning.

3. BEGGING THE QUESTION. A somewhat unhandy term: you assume as proved something that really needs proving. "Free all political prisoners" assumes that none of those concerned has committed an actual crime.
4. IGNORING THE QUESTION. The question of whether it is right for a neighborhood to organize against a newcomer shifts to prices of property and taxes.
5. NON SEQUITUR ("IT DOES NOT FOLLOW"). "He's certainly sincere; he must be right." "He's the most popular; he should be president." The conclusions do not reasonably follow from sincerity and popularity.
6. POST HOC, ERGO PROPTER HOC. ("AFTER THIS, THEREFORE BECAUSE OF THIS.") The non sequitur of events: "He stayed up late and therefore won the race." He probably won in spite of late hours, and for other reasons.

EXERCISES

1. *After each of the following assertions, write two or three short questions that will challenge its assumptions, questions like "Good for what? Throwing? Fertilizer?" For example: Girls are brighter than boys. "At what age? In chess? In physics?" In the questions, probe and distinguish among your facts, opinions, beliefs, and preferences.*

1. Men are superior to women.
2. The backfield made some mistakes.
3. Communism means violent repression.
4. Don't trust anyone over thirty.
5. All men are equal.
6. The big companies are ruining the environment.
7. Travel is educational.
8. Our brand of cigarette is free of tar.
9. The right will prevail.
10. A long run is good for you.

2. *Each of the following statements contains at least one fallacious citation of authority. Identify it, and explain how it involves one or several of these reasons: "Outside Field," "Not Accurately Presented," "Not Representative," "Out of Date."*

1. According to Charles Morton, a distinguished seventeenth-century theologian and schoolmaster, the swallows of England disappear to the dark side of the moon in winter.

2. Einstein states that everything is relative.
3. "Nucular" is an acceptable pronunciation of "nuclear." President Eisenhower himself pronounced it this way.
4. War between capitalists and communists is inevitable, as Karl Marx shows.
5. The American economy should be controlled in every detail; after all, economist John Kenneth Galbraith comes out for control.
6. "Fluff is America's finest bubble bath," says Jimmy Connors.

3. *Each of the following statistical statements is fallacious in one or several ways, either omitting something necessary for full understanding or generalizing in unsupported ways. Identify and explain the statistical fallacies.*

1. This car gets thirty-five miles per gallon.
2. Fifty percent of his snapshots are poor.
3. Twenty-nine persons were injured when a local bus skidded on an icy road near Weston and overturned. Two were hospitalized. Twenty-seven were treated and released.
4. Women support this book one hundred percent, but fifty percent of American males are still antifeminist. (In a class of five girls and ten boys, all the girls and five of the boys vote to write about a book entitled *The Stereotyped Female.*)

4. *If baseball is in season, go to the sports page and write a brief explanation of the statistics on batting averages, RBI's, and so forth. Can you find any fallacies—things the statistics do not tell? Or do the same with another sport or subject where statistics are common.*

5. *Explain the following fallacious analogies and inductive leaps.*

1. The brain is like a computer. Scientists have demonstrated that it, like the computer, works through electrical impulses.
2. This girl has ten sweaters; that girl has ten sweaters. They are equally rich in sweaters.
3. At sixty, Kirk retires with investments and savings worth more than $500,000. He has nothing to worry about for the rest of his life.
4. Every time the Boilers play a post-season game, they lose. They will lose this one.
5. English majors are poor mathematicians.
6. I studied hard. I answered every question. None of my answers was wrong. I have read my exam over again and again and can still see no reason for getting only a C.

6. *Name and explain the fallacy in each of the following:*

1. Jones is rich. He must be dishonest.
2. He either worked hard for his money, or he is just plain lucky.

3. The best things in life are free, like free love.
4. Sunshine breeds flies, because when the sun shines the flies come out.
5. If they have no bread, let them eat cake. Cake is both tastier and richer in calories.
6. This is another example of American imperialism.
7. Smith's canned-soup empire reaches farther than the Roman empire.
8. *Chips* is America's most popular soap. It is clearly the best.
9. The draft is illegal. It takes young men away from their education and careers at the most crucial period of their lives. They lose thousands of dollars' worth of their time.
10. Women are the most exploited people in the history of the world.

Readings

Evidence—its use and misuse—supplies the underpinnings in the following essays. The feminist writer Barbara Ehrenreich offers evidence from a variety of sources to demonstrate that a "new man" is emerging. Harvard paleontologist Stephen Jay Gould shows that even scientists are not immune to the follies and fallacies of careless reasoning. The eminent mathematician, historian, and humanist Jacob Bronowski illustrates precivilized Old Testament tribal life by following a tribe of modern nomads. All of these writers have garnered their evidence inductively and present it to us at different points along the inductive path, beginning with the questions they and others had asked, or with assertions gathered along the trail.

BARBARA EHRENREICH

A Feminist's View of the New Man

1 There have been waves of "new women" arriving on cue almost every decade for the last 30 years or so—from the civic-minded housewife, to the liberated single, to the dressed-for-success executive. But men, like masculinity itself, were thought to be made of more durable stuff. Change, if it came at all, would come only in response to some feminine—or feminist—initiative.

2 In the 1970's, for example, it had become an article of liberal faith that a new man would eventually rise up to match the new

feminist woman, that he would be more androgynous than any "old" variety of man, and that the change, which was routinely expressed as an evolutionary leap from John Wayne to Alan Alda, would be an unambiguous improvement.

3 Today, a new man is at last emerging, and I say this as someone who is not much given to such announcements. A new man, like a new sexuality or a new conservatism, is more likely to turn out to be a journalistic artifact than a cultural sea change.

4 But this time something has happened, both to our common expectations of what constitutes manhood and to the way many men are choosing to live.

5 I see the change in the popular images that define masculinity, and I see it in the men I know, mostly in their thirties, who are conscious of possessing a sensibility and even a way of life that is radically different from that of their fathers. These men have been, in a word, feminized, but without necessarily becoming more feminist. In fact, I do not think that those of us who are feminists either can or, for the most part, would want to take credit for the change.

6 Taking his mid-1950's progenitor as a benchmark, the most striking characteristic of the new man is that he no longer anchors his identity in his role as family breadwinner. He may *be* the family breadwinner, or imagine becoming one someday, but his ability to do so has ceased to be the urgent and necessary proof of his maturity or of his heterosexuality. In fact, he may postpone or avoid marriage indefinitely—which is why the women's magazines complain so much about the male "lack of commitment" and "refusal to grow up."

7 But if the old responsibilities have declined, the pressure is not off: The old man expressed his status through his house and the wife who presided over it; the new man expects to express his status through his own efforts and is deeply anxious about the self he presents to the world. Typically, he is concerned—some might say obsessed—with his physical health and fitness. He is an avid and style-conscious consumer, not only of clothes but of food, home furnishings, and visible displays of culture. Finally, and in a marked reversal of the old masculinity, he is concerned that people find him, not forbearing or strong, but genuine, open, and sensitive.

8 What accounts for this change in men? Or, perhaps I should ask more broadly, for this change in our notion of masculinity—

a change that affects not only single, affluent young men but potentially the married, middle-aged, and financially immobile male? Sheldon Kotel, a Long Island accountant in his early forties, who was my host on a local radio talk show, attributes any change in men to a prior revolution among women. From the early 1970's, he says, "you could see what was happening with women, and we had to get our act together, too. They didn't want to be in their traditional role anymore, and I didn't want to go on being a meal ticket for some woman."

9 Certainly the new man's unwillingness to "commit himself," in the old-fashioned sense, could be interpreted as a peevish reaction to feminist women—just as his androgynous bent could be interpreted as a positive adjustment, an attempt, as the advocates of men's liberation would say, to "get in touch with one's feminine side." Spokesmen for men's liberation, from Warren Farrell in the early 1970's to Donald H. Bell, whose book, *Being a Man: The Paradox of Masculinity,* was published in 1982, depict themselves and their fellows as wrestling with the challenge of feminism—giving up a little privilege here, gaining a little sensitivity there, to emerge more "whole" and "self-nurturing."

10 But, for the most part, the new men one is likely to encounter today in our urban singles' enclaves (or on the pages of a men's fashion magazine) bear no marks of arduous self-transformation. No ideological struggle—pro- or antifeminist—seems to have shaped their decision to step out of the traditional male role; in a day-to-day sense, they simply seem to have other things on their minds.

11 So I do not think there is a one-word explanation—like feminism—for the new manhood. Rather, I would argue, at least a part of what looks new has been a long time in the making and predates the recent revival of feminism by many decades. Male resistance to marriage, for example, is a venerable theme in American culture, whether in the form of low humor (Li'l Abner's annual Sadie Hawkins Day escape from Daisy Mae) or high art (the perpetual bachelorhood of heroes like Ishmael or the Deerslayer). As Leslie Fiedler argued in 1955 in *An End to Innocence,* the classics of American literature are, by and large, propaganda for boyish adventure rather than the "mature heterosexuality" so admired by mid-twentieth-century psychoanalysts.

12 The sources of male resentment are not hard to find: In a frontier society, women were cast as the tamers and civilizers of

men; in an increasingly urban, industrial society, they became, in addition, the financial dependents of men. From a cynical male point of view, marriage was an arrangement through which men gave up their freedom for the dubious privilege of supporting a woman. Or, as H. L. Mencken put it, marriage was an occasion for a man "to yield up his liberty, his property and his soul to the first woman who, in despair of finding better game, turns her appraising eye upon him." After all, the traditional female contributions to marriage have been menial, like housework, or intangible, like emotional support. The husband's traditional contribution, his wage or at least a good share of it, was indispensable, measurable and, of course, portable—whether to the local tavern or the next liaison.

13 But before male resentment of marriage could become anything more than a cultural undercurrent of grumbling and misogynist humor, three things had to happen. First, it had to become not only physically possible but reasonably comfortable for men to live on their own. In nineteenth-century homes, even simple tasks like making breakfast or laundering a shirt could absorb long hours of labor. Bachelorhood was a privileged state, sustained by servants or a supply of maiden sisters; the average man either married or settled for boardinghouse life. As a second condition for freedom from marriage, men had to discover better ways of spending their money than on the support of a family. The historic male alternatives were drinking and gambling, but these have long been associated, for good reason, with precipitate downward mobility. Third, the penalties levied against the nonconforming male—charges of immaturity, irresponsibility, and latent sexual deviancy—had to be neutralized or inverted.

14 Within the last few decades, all of these conditions for male freedom have been met. Domestic appliances, plus a rapid rise in the number of apartment dwellings and low-price restaurants made it possible for a man of average means to contemplate bachelorhood as something other than extended vagrancy. As Philip Roth observed of the 1950's in *My Life as a Man,* it had become entirely feasible—though not yet acceptable—for a young man "to eat out of cans or in cafeterias, sweep his own floor, make his own bed, and come and go with no binding legal attachments." In addition, that decade saw two innovations that boosted the potential autonomy of even the most domestically incompetent males—frozen foods and drip-dry clothes.

15 Perhaps more important, the consumer-goods market, which had focused on a bland assemblage of family-oriented products, began to show the first signs of serious segmentation. *Playboy*'s success in the 1950's instigated a revival of sophisticated men's magazines (sophisticated, that is, compared with *True, Police Gazette,* or *Popular Mechanics*) that delivered an audience of millions of independent-minded men to the advertisers of liquor, sports cars, stereo equipment, and vacations.

16 No sooner had the new, more individualistic male life style become physically possible and reasonably attractive than it began also to gain respectability. Starting in the 1960's, expert opinion began to retreat from what had been a unanimous endorsement of marriage and traditional sex roles. Psychology, transformed by the human-potential movement, switched from "maturity" as a standard for mental health to the more expansive notion of "growth." "Maturity" had been a code word, even in the professional literature, for marriage and settling down; "growth" implied a plurality of legitimate options, if not a positive imperative to keep moving from one insight or experience to the next. Meanwhile, medicine—alarmed by what appeared to be an epidemic of male heart disease—had begun to speak of men as the "weaker sex" and to hint that men's greater vulnerability was due, in part, to the burden of breadwinning.

17 The connection was scientifically unwarranted, but it cast a lasting shadow over conventional sex roles: The full-time homemaker, who had been merely a parasite on resentful males, became a potential accomplice to murder, with the hard-working, role-abiding breadwinner as her victim. By the 1970's, no salvo of male resentment—or men's liberation—failed to mention that the cost of the traditional male role was not only psychic stagnation and sexual monotony, but ulcers, heart disease, and an early death.

18 Today, the old aspersions directed at the unmarried male have largely lost their sting. Images of healthy, hard-working men with no apparent attachments abound in the media, such as, for example, the genial-looking bicyclist in the advertisement for *TV Guide,* whose caption announces invitingly, "Zero Dependents."

19 Perhaps most important, a man can now quite adequately express his status without entering into a lifelong partnership with a female consumer. The ranch house on a quarter-acre of

grass is still a key indicator of social rank, but it is not the only one. A well-decorated apartment, a knowledge of wines, or a flair for cooking can be an equally valid proof of middle-class (or upper-middle-class) membership, and these can now be achieved without the entanglement of marriage or the risk of being thought a little "queer."

20 Certainly feminism contributed to the case against the old style of male conformity. On the ideological front, the women's movement popularized the sociological vocabulary of "roles"—a linguistic breakthrough that highlighted the social artifice involved in masculinity, as we had known it, as well as femininity. More practically, feminists envisioned a world in which neither sex would be automatically dependent and both might be breadwinners. Betty Friedan speculated that "perhaps men may live longer in America when women carry more of the burden of the battle with the world, instead of being a burden themselves," and Gloria Steinem urged men to support the cause because they "have nothing to lose but their coronaries." Yet feminism only delivered the *coup de grâce* to the old man, who married young, worked hard, withheld his emotions, and "died in the harness." By the time of the feminist revival in the late 1960's and 70's, American culture was already prepared to welcome a new man, and to find him—not caddish or queer—but healthy and psychologically enlightened.

21 But if the new man's resistance to commitment grows out of longstanding male resentment, there are other features of the new manhood that cannot be explained as a product of the battle of the sexes, no matter which side is presumed to have taken the initiative. Married or single, the preoccupations of these men suggest anxiety rather than liberation, and I think the anxiety stems from very real and relatively recent insecurities about class.

22 The professional-managerial middle class, which is the breeding ground for social ideals like the new man or new woman, has become an embattled group. In the 1950's and 60's, young men of this class could look forward to secure, high-status careers, provided only that they acquired some credentials and showed up for work. Professional-level job slots were increasing, along with the expansion of corporate and governmental administrative apparatuses, and jobs in higher education increased to keep pace with the growing demand for managerial and "mental" workers.

23 Then came the long economic downturn of the 1970's, and whole occupations—from public administration to college history teaching—closed their ranks and lost ground. One whole segment of formerly middle-class, educated youth drifted downward to become taxi drivers, waiters, or carpenters. As other people crowded into the most vocationally promising areas—medicine, law, management—those too became hazardously overpopulated. According to recent studies of the "disappearing middle class," the erstwhile middle-class majority is tumbling down and out (both because of a lack of jobs and because those that remain have not held their own against inflation), while a minority is scrambling up to become the new high-finance, high-tech gentry. Our new men are mainly in the latter category, or are at least holding on by their fingernails.

24 Times of rapid class realignment magnify the attention paid to class insignia—the little cues that tell us who is a social equal and who is not. In the prosperous 1960's and early 70's, the counterculture had temporarily blurred class lines among American men, mixing Ivy League dropouts with young veterans, hip professionals with unschooled street kids. Avant-garde male fashion was democratic: Blue jeans, gold chains, and shoulder-length hair could equally well be affected by middle-aged psychiatrists, young truck drivers, or off-duty tax lawyers. Thanks to Army-surplus chic and its rock-star embellishments, there was no sure way to distinguish the upward bound from the permanently down and out.

25 In the insecure 1980's, class lines are being hastily redrawn, and many features of the new manhood can best be understood as efforts to stay on the right side of the line separating "in" from "out," and upscale from merely middle class. The new male consumerism, for example, is self-consciously elitist: Italian-knit sweaters and double-breasted blazers have replaced the voluntary simplicity of flannel shirts and denim jackets. *Esquire* announced a "return to elegant dressing" that excludes not only the polyester set but the rumpled professor and any leftover bohemians.

26 Consumer tastes are only the most obvious class cues that define the new man and set him off, not only from the old white-collar man but from the less fortunate members of his own generation. Another is his devotion to physical exercise, especially in its most solitary and public form—running. Running is a new

activity, dating from the 1970's, and it is solidly upscale. Fred Lebow, the president of the New York Road Runners Club, describes the average marathon runner as a male, "34 years old, college educated, physically fit, and well-off," and a *New York Times* poll found that 46 percent of the participants in the 1983 New York City Marathon earned more than $40,000 a year (85 percent of the participants were male). The old man smoked, drank martinis to excess, and puttered at golf. The new man is a nonsmoker (among men, smoking is becoming a blue-collar trait), a cautious drinker, and, if not a runner, a patron of gyms and spas.

27 I would not argue that men run in order to establish their social status—certainly not at a conscious level. Running is one manifestation of the general obsession with fitness that gripped the middle class in the 1970's and for which there is still no satisfactory sociological explanation. On one level, running is a straightforward response to the cardiac anxiety that has haunted American men since the 1950's; it may also be a response to the occupational insecurity of the 1970's and 80's. Then, too, some men run to get away from their wives—transforming Rabbit Angstrom's cross-country dash in the final scene of John Updike's *Rabbit Run* into an acceptable daily ritual. Donald Bell says he took up running (and vegetarianism) "to escape somewhat from the pain and frustration which I felt in this less than perfect marriage."

28 But, whatever the individual motivations, running has become sufficiently identified as an upper-middle-class habit to serve as a reliable insignia of class membership: Running is public testimony to a sedentary occupation, and it has all but replaced the more democratic sports, such as softball and basketball, that once promoted interclass male mingling.

29 Finally, there is that most promising of new male traits—sensitivity. I have no hesitation about categorizing this as an upscale class cue if only because new men so firmly believe that it is. For more than a decade, sensitivity has been supposed to be the inner quality that distinguishes an educated, middle-class male from his unregenerate blue-collar brothers: "They" are Archie Bunkers; "we" are represented by his more liberal, articulate son-in-law. As thoughtful a scholar as Joseph H. Pleck, program director of the Wellesley College Center for Research on Women, who has written extensively on the male sex role, simply

restates (in a 1976 *Journal of Social Issues*) the prejudice that blue-collar men are trapped in the "traditional" male role, "where interpersonal and emotional skills are relatively undeveloped."

30 No one, of course, has measured sensitivity and plotted it as a function of social class, but Judith Langer, a market researcher, reports that, in her studies, it is blue-collar men who express less "traditional" or "macho" values, both in response to products and in speaking of their relationships with women. "Certainly I'm not suggesting that *only* blue-collar men show such openness," she concludes, "but rather that the stereotype of blue-collar workers can be limited."

31 To the extent that some special form of sensitivity is located in educated and upwardly mobile males, I suspect it may be largely a verbal accomplishment. The vocabulary of sensitivity, at least, has become part of the new masculine politesse; certainly no new man would admit to being insensitive or willfully "out of touch with his feelings." Quite possibly, as sensitivity has spread, it has lost its moorings in the therapeutic experience and come to signify the heightened receptivity associated with consumerism: a vague appreciation that lends itself to aimless shopping.

32 None of these tastes and proclivities of the new man serve to differentiate him from the occasional affluent woman of his class. Women in the skirted-suit set tend to postpone marriage and child-bearing; to work long hours and budget their time scrupulously; to follow fashions in food and clothing, and to pursue fitness, where once slimness would have sufficed. As Paul Fussell observes in "Class: A Guide Through the American Status System," the upper-middle class—and I would include all those struggling to remain in the upper part of the crumbling middle class—is "the most 'role-reversed' of all." And herein lies one of the key differences between the old and the new versions of the American ideal of masculinity: The old masculinity defined itself against femininity and expressed anxiety—over conformity or the rat race—in metaphors of castration. The new masculinity seems more concerned to preserve the tenuous boundary between the classes than to delineate distinctions between the sexes. Today's upper-middle-class or upwardly mobile male is less terrified about moving down the slope toward genderlessness than he is about simply moving down-scale.

33 The fact that the new man is likely to remain single well into his prime career years—or, if married, is unlikely to be judged by

his wife's appearance and tastes—only intensifies his status consciousness. The old man of the middle class might worry about money, but he could safely leave the details of keeping up with the Joneses to his wife. He did not have to comprehend casseroles or canapés, because she would, nor did he have to feel his way through complex social situations, since sensitivity also lay in her domain. But our new man of the 1980's, married or not, knows that he may be judged solely on the basis of his own savoir-faire, his ability to "relate," his figure and possibly his muscle tone. Without a wife, or at least without a visible helpmeet, he has had to appropriate the status-setting activities that once were seen as feminine. The androgynous affect is part of making it.

34 The question for feminists is: Is this new man what we wanted? Just a few years ago, feminists were, on the whole, disposed to welcome any change in a direction away from traditional manhood. Betty Friedan, in *The Second Stage,* saw "the quiet movement of American men" as "a momentous change in their very identity as men, going beyond the change catalyzed by the women's movement," and she suggested that it might amount to a "massive, evolutionary development."

35 That was written in a more innocent time, when feminists were debating the "Cinderella complex," as Colette Dowling termed women's atavistic dependencies on men, rather than the "Peter Pan syndrome," which is how one recent best seller describes the male aversion to commitment. In recent months, there has been a small flurry of feminist attacks on the new male or on assorted new-male characteristics.

36 *The Washington City Paper* carried a much-discussed and thoroughly acid article on "Wormboys," described by writer Deborah Laake as men who are "passive" in relation to women, who "shrink from marriage" and children, and "cannot be depended on during tough times." According to one woman she quotes, these new men are so fearful of commitment that they even hesitate to ask a woman out to dinner: "They're more interested in saying, 'Why don't you meet me for a drink?' because it implies so much less commitment on their part." I wouldn't exaggerate the extent of the backlash, but it has been sufficient to send several male colleagues my way to ask, with nervous laughter, whether I was writing a new contribution to the "war on wimps."

37 I don't blame them for being nervous. My generation of feminists insisted that men change, but we were not always directive—or patient—enough to say how. We applauded every sign of male sensitivity or growth as if it were an evolutionary advance. We even welcomed the feminization of male tastes, expecting that the man who was a good cook and a tasteful decorator at twenty-five would be a devoted father and partner in midlife. We did not understand that men were changing along a trajectory of their own and that they might end up being less like what we *are* than like what we were once expected to be—vain and shallow and status-conscious.

38 But since these are times when any hint of revisionism easily becomes grist for conservatism, it is important to emphasize that if we don't like the new male, neither are we inclined to return to the old one. If the new man tends to be a fop, the old man was (and is), at worst, a tyrant and a bully. At best, he was merely dull, which is why, during the peak years of male conformity, when the test of manhood lay in being a loyal breadwinner, so many of us lusted secretly for those few males—from James Dean and Elvis Presley to Jack Kerouac—who represented unattainable adventure. In our fantasies, at least, we did not want to enslave men, as *Playboy*'s writers liked to think, but to share the adventure.

39 Today, thanks to the women's movement, we have half a chance: Individualism, adventure—that "battle with the world" that Friedan held out to women more than twenty years ago—is no longer a male prerogative. But if it is to be a shared adventure, then men will have to change, and change in ways that are not, so far, in evidence. Up until now, we have been content to ask them to become more like women—less aggressive, more emotionally connected with themselves and others. That message, which we once thought revolutionary, has gotten lost in the androgynous drift of the consumer culture. It is the marketplace that calls most clearly for men to be softer, more narcissistic and receptive, and the new man is the result.

40 So it is not enough, anymore, to ask that men become more like women; we should ask instead that they become more like what both men and women *might* be. My new man, if I could design one, would be capable of appreciation, sensitivity, intimacy—values that have been, for too long, feminine. But he would also be capable of commitment, to use that much-abused word, and I mean by that commitment not only to friends and

family but to a broad and generous vision of how we might all live together. As a feminist, I would say that vision includes equality between men and women and also—to mention a social goal that seems almost to have been forgotten—equality among men.

Suggestions for Discussion and Writing

1. Why did many women believe that men would change "only in response to some feminine—or feminist—initiative" (paragraph 1)? Isn't such an idea presumptuous on the part of women?
2. What do John Wayne and Alan Alda represent, respectively (paragraph 2)?
3. A common warning often heard among young people during the 1960's and early 1970's in this country was, "Don't trust anyone over thirty!" On the basis of paragraph 7 and other sections of her essay, is Ehrenreich guilty of similar age stereotyping?
4. If a man refuses to "get in touch with one's feminine side" (paragraph 9) and is "out of touch with his feelings" (paragraph 31), is he a male chauvinist, according to the author? According to you? If you are a woman, would you marry such a man? Explain.
5. According to the author, why have males resented marriage? Why is it easier for them to "avoid commitment" today? What does she think of single men?
6. Ehrenreich mentions running as one of the obsessions of the upper-middle-class male. Can you think of others? Do you participate in any of them? Do you think of yourself as upper-middle-class?
7. Does the author like the "new male"? How do you know?
8. The author links the second paragraph with the first by the connective "for example." Underline several other words and phrases that help to tie one paragraph to another in this essay.
9. What kind of evidence does Ehrenreich offer her reader? How many of her arguments are based on facts? How many are beliefs and opinions?
10. Assess the author's evidence. Does she commit any logical fallacies? Who are the authorities that she cites? What documentary evidence does she provide?
11. If you disagree with Ehrenreich—if you believe that the "new

man" exists only in the imagination of a few optimistic women—write an essay disposing of her argument. Support your position with evidence, not merely beliefs and opinions.

12. Try your hand at defining one of the following terms: "the new sexuality"; "the new woman"; "macho." Give your reader as much factual evidence as possible to support your ideas.

STEPHEN JAY GOULD

Wide Hats and Narrow Minds

1 In 1861, from February to June, the ghost of Baron Georges Cuvier haunted the Anthropological Society of Paris. The great Cuvier, Aristotle of French biology (an immodest designation from which he did not shrink), died in 1832, but the physical vault of his spirit lived on as Paul Broca and Louis Pierre Gratiolet squared off to debate whether or not the size of a brain has anything to do with the intelligence of its bearer.

2 In the opening round, Gratiolet dared to argue that the best and brightest could not be recognized by their big heads. (Gratiolet, a confirmed monarchist, was no egalitarian. He merely sought other measures to affirm the superiority of white European males.) Broca, founder of the Anthropological Society and the world's greatest craniometrician, or head measurer, replied that "study of the brains of human races would lose most of its interest and utility" if variation in size counted for nothing. Why, he asked, had anthropologists spent so much time measuring heads if the results had no bearing upon what he regarded as the most important question of all—the relative worth of different peoples:

> Among the questions heretofore discussed within the Anthropological Society, none is equal in interest and importance to the question before us now. . . . The great importance of craniology has struck anthropologists with such force that many among us have neglected the other parts of our science in order to devote ourselves almost exclusively to the study of skulls. . . . In such data, we hope to find some information relevant to the intellectual value of the various human races.

3 Broca and Gratiolet battled for five months and through nearly two hundred pages of the published bulletin. Tempers flared. In the heat of battle, one of Broca's lieutenants struck the lowest blow of all: "I have noticed for a long time that, in general, those who deny the intellectual importance of the brain's volume have small heads." In the end, Broca won, hands down. During the debate, no item of information had been more valuable to Broca, none more widely discussed or more vigorously contended, than the brain of Georges Cuvier.

4 Cuvier, the greatest anatomist of his time, the man who revised our understanding of animals by classifying them according to function—how they work—rather than by rank in an anthropocentric scale of lower to higher. Cuvier, the founder of paleontology, the man who first established the fact of extinction and who stressed the importance of catastrophes in understanding the history both of life and the earth. Cuvier, the great statesman who, like Talleyrand, managed to serve all French governments, from revolution to monarchy, and die in bed. (Actually, Cuvier passed the most tumultuous years of the revolution as a private tutor in Normandy, although he feigned revolutionary sympathies in his letters. He arrived in Paris in 1795 and never left.) F. Bourdier, a recent biographer, describes Cuvier's corporeal ontogeny, but his words also serve as a good metaphor for Cuvier's power and influence: "Cuvier was short and during the Revolution he was very thin; he became stouter during the Empire; and he grew enormously fat after the Restoration."

5 Cuvier's contemporaries marveled at his "massive head." One admirer affirmed that it "gave to his entire person an undeniable cachet of majesty and to his face an expression of profound meditation." Thus, when Cuvier died, his colleagues, in the interests of science and curiosity, decided to open the great skull. On Tuesday, May 15, 1832, at seven o'clock in the morning, a group of the greatest doctors and biologists of France gathered to dissect the body of Georges Cuvier. They began with the internal organs and, finding "nothing very remarkable," switched their attention to Cuvier's skull. "Thus," wrote the physician in charge, "we were about to contemplate the instrument of this powerful intelligence." And their expectations were rewarded. The brain of Georges Cuvier weighed 1,830 grams, more than 400 grams above average and 200 grams larger than any nondiseased brain previously weighed. Unconfirmed reports

and uncertain inference placed the brains of Oliver Cromwell, Jonathan Swift, and Lord Byron in the same range, but Cuvier had provided the first direct evidence that brilliance and brain size go together.

6 Broca pushed his advantage and rested a good part of his case on Cuvier's brain. But Gratiolet probed and found a weak spot. In their awe and enthusiasm, Cuvier's doctors had neglected to save either his brain or his skull. Moreover, they reported no measures on the skull at all. The figure of 1,830 g for the brain could not be checked; perhaps it was simply wrong. Gratiolet sought an existing surrogate and had a flash of inspiration: "All brains are not weighed by doctors," he stated, "but all heads are measured by hatters, and I have managed to acquire, from this new source, information which, I dare to hope, will not appear to you as devoid of interest." In short, Gratiolet presented something almost bathetic in comparison with the great man's brain: he had found Cuvier's hat! And thus, for two meetings, some of France's greatest minds pondered seriously the meaning of a worn bit of felt.

7 Cuvier's hat, Gratiolet reported, measured 21.8 cm in length and 18.0 cm in width. He then consulted a certain M. Puriau, "one of the most intelligent and widely known hatters of Paris." Puriau told him that the largest standard size for hats measured 21.5 by 18.5 cm. Although very few men wore a hat so big, Cuvier was not off scale. Moreover, Gratiolet reported with evident pleasure, the hat was extremely flexible and "softened by very long usage." It had probably not been so large when Cuvier bought it. Moreover, Cuvier had an exceptionally thick head of hair, and he wore it bushy. "This seems to prove quite clearly," Gratiolet proclaimed, "that if Cuvier's head was very large, its size was not absolutely exceptional or unique."

8 Gratiolet's opponents preferred to believe the doctors and refused to grant much weight to a bit of cloth. More than twenty years later, in 1883, G. Hervé again took up the subject of Cuvier's brain and discovered a missing item: Cuvier's head had been measured after all, but the figures had been omitted from the autopsy report. The skull was big indeed. Shaved of that famous mat of hair, as it was for the autopsy, its greatest circumference could be equaled by only 6 percent of "scientists and men of letters" (measured in life with their hair at that) and zero percent of domestic servants. As for the infamous hat, Hervé

pleaded ignorance, but he did cite the following anecdote: "Cuvier had a habit of leaving his hat on a table in his waiting room. It often happened that a professor or a statesman tried it on. The hat descended below their eyes."

9 Yet, just as the doctrine of more-is-better stood on the verge of triumph, Hervé snatched potential defeat from the jaws of Broca's victory. Too much of a good thing can be as troubling as a deficiency, and Hervé began to worry. Why did Cuvier's brain exceed those of other "men of genius" by so much? He reviewed both details of the autopsy and records of Cuvier's frail early health and constructed a circumstantial case for "transient juvenile hydrocephaly," or water on the brain. If Cuvier's skull had been artificially enlarged by the pressure of fluids early during its growth, then a brain of normal size might simply have expanded—by decreasing in density, not by growing larger—into the space available. Or did an enlarged space permit the brain to grow to an unusual size after all? Hervé could not resolve this cardinal question because Cuvier's brain had been measured and then tossed out. All that remained was the magisterial number, 1,830 grams. "With the brain of Cuvier," wrote Hervé, "science has lost one of the most precious documents it ever possessed."

10 On the surface, this tale seems ludicrous. The thought of France's finest anthropologists arguing passionately about the meaning of a dead colleague's hat could easily provoke the most misleading and dangerous inference of all about history—a view of the past as a domain of naïve half-wits, the path of history as a tale of progress, and the present as sophisticated and enlightened.

11 But if we laugh with derision, we will never understand. Human intellectual capacity has not altered for thousands of years so far as we can tell. If intelligent people invested intense energy in issues that now seem foolish to us, then the failure lies in our understanding of their world, not in their distorted perceptions. Even the standard example of ancient nonsense—the debate about angels on pinheads—makes sense once you realize that theologians were not discussing whether five or eighteen would fit, but whether a pin could house a finite or an infinite number. In certain theological systems, the corporeality or noncorporeality of angels is an important matter indeed.

12 In this case, a clue to the vital importance of Cuvier's brain for nineteenth-century anthropology lies in the last line of Broca's

statement, quoted above: "In such data, we hope to find some information relevant to the intellectual value of the various human races." Broca and his school wanted to show that brain size, through its link with intelligence, could resolve what they regarded as the primary question for a "science of man"—explaining why some individuals and groups are more successful than others. To do this, they separated people according to a priori convictions about their worth—men versus women, whites versus blacks, "men of genius" versus ordinary folks—and tried to demonstrate differences in brain size. The brains of eminent men (literally males) formed an essential link in their argument—and Cuvier was the *crème de la crème.* Broca concluded:

> In general, the brain is larger in men than in women, in eminent men than in men of mediocre talent, in superior races than in inferior races. Other things equal, there is a remarkable relationship between the development of intelligence and the volume of the brain.

13 Broca died in 1880, but disciples continued his catalog of eminent brains (indeed, they added Broca's own to the list—although it weighed in at an undistinguished 1,484 grams). The dissection of famous colleagues became something of a cottage industry among anatomists and anthropologists. E.A. Spitzka, the most prominent American practitioner of the trade, cajoled his eminent friends: "To me the thought of an autopsy is certainly less repugnant than I imagine the process of cadaveric decomposition in the grave to be." The two premier American ethnologists John Wesley Powell and W. J. McGee made a wager over who had the larger brain—and Spitzka contracted to resolve the issue for them posthumously. (It was a toss-up. The brains of Powell and McGee differed very little, no more than varying body size might require.)

14 By 1907, Spitzka could present a tabulation of 115 eminent men. As the list grew in length, ambiguity of results increased apace. At the upper end, Cuvier was finally overtaken when Turgenev broke the 2,000-gram barrier in 1883. But embarrassment and insult stalked the other end. Walt Whitman managed to hear the varied carols of America singing with only 1,282 g. Franz Josef Gall, a founder of phrenology—the original "science" of judging mental worth by the size of localized brain areas—could

muster only 1,198 g. Later, in 1924, Anatole France almost halved Turgenev's 2,012 and weighed in at a mere 1,017 g.

15 Spitzka, nonetheless, was undaunted. In an outrageous example of data selected to conform with a priori prejudice, he arranged, in order, a large brain from an eminent white male, a bushwoman from Africa, and a gorilla. (He could easily have reversed the first two by choosing a larger black and a smaller white.) Spitzka concluded, again invoking the shade of Georges Cuvier: "The jump from a Cuvier or a Thackeray to a Zulu or a Bushman is no greater than from the latter to the gorilla or the orang."

16 Such overt racism is no longer common among scientists, and I trust that no one would now try to rank races or sexes by the average size of their brains. Yet our fascination with the physical basis of intelligence persists (as it should), and the naïve hope remains in some quarters that size or some other unambiguous external feature might capture the subtlety within. Indeed, the crassest form of more-is-better—using an easily measured quantity to assess improperly a far more subtle and elusive quality—is still with us. And the method that some men use to judge the worth of their penises or their automobiles is still being applied to brains. This essay was inspired by recent reports on the whereabouts of Einstein's brain. Yes, Einstein's brain was removed for study, but a quarter century after his death, the results have not been published. The remaining pieces—others were farmed out to various specialists—now rest in a Mason jar packed in a cardboard box marked "Costa Cider" and housed in an office in Wichita, Kansas. Nothing has been published because nothing unusual has been found. "So far it's fallen within normal limits for a man his age," remarked the owner of the Mason jar.

17 Did I just hear Cuvier and Anatole France laughing in concert from on high? Are they repeating a famous motto of their native land: *plus ça change, plus c'est la même chose* ("the more things change, the more they remain the same"). The physical structure of the brain must record intelligence in some way, but gross size and external shape are not likely to capture anything of value. I am, somehow, less interested in the weight and convolutions of Einstein's brain than in the near certainty that people of equal talent have lived and died in cotton fields and sweatshops.

Suggestions for Discussion and Writing

1. How convincing is "the first direct evidence that brilliance and brain size go together" (paragraph 5)? What is Gould *really* saying here?
2. What is the most dangerous and misleading inference of all about history, according to Gould? Why is it dangerous?
3. Why were Spitzka's choices "an outrageous example of data selected to conform with a priori prejudice" (paragraph 15)? Why was his conclusion racist?
4. Gould hopes "that no one would now try to rank races or sexes by the average size of their brains" (paragraph 16). Is he right? Are there other systems equally fallacious that are still employed?
5. Comment on the structure of the first three sentences in paragraph 4.
6. Explain Gould's reference to the quotation at the end of paragraph 4.
7. What is the point of the anecdote concerning Einstein's brain?
8. Why did Gould portray Cuvier and Anatole France laughing (paragraph 17)? What does each represent?
9. List the classical fallacies committed by the scientists mentioned in this essay. Explain how each went wrong.
10. What kinds of evidence have led Gould to his conclusion that the size and the shape of the brain are not significant? What type of evidence does he seem to lean on more heavily?
12. Write an essay in which you examine and dispose of a once widely held notion. Like Gould, quote the supporters of the belief and their arguments. Show how they erred and how their evidence failed to support their conclusions.

JACOB BRONOWSKI

The Harvest of the Seasons

1 The history of man is divided very unequally. First there is his biological evolution: all the steps that separate us from our ape ancestors. Those occupied some millions of years. And then there is his cultural history: the long swell of civilization that separates us from the few surviving hunting tribes of Africa, or

from the food-gatherers of Australia. And all that second, cultural gap is in fact crowded into a few thousand years. It goes back only about twelve thousand years—something over ten thousand years, but much less than twenty thousand. From now on, I shall only be talking about those last twelve thousand years which contain almost the whole ascent of man as we think of him now. Yet the difference between the two numbers, that is, between the biological time-scale and the cultural, is so great that I cannot leave it without a backward glance.

2 It took at least two million years for man to change from the little dark creature with the stone in his hand, *Australopithecus* in Central Africa, to the modern form, *Homo sapiens.* That is the pace of biological evolution—even though the biological evolution of man has been faster than that of any other animal. But it has taken much less than twenty thousand years for *Homo sapiens* to become the creatures that you and I aspire to be: artists and scientists, city builders and planners for the future, readers and travellers, eager explorers of natural fact and human emotion, immensely richer in experience and bolder in imagination than any of our ancestors. That is the pace of cultural evolution; once it takes off, it goes as the ratio of those two numbers goes, at least a hundred times faster than biological evolution.

3 Once it takes off: that is the crucial phrase. Why did the cultural changes that have made man master of the earth begin so recently? Twenty thousand years ago, man in all parts of the world that he had reached was a forager and a hunter, whose most advanced technique was to attach himself to a moving herd as the Lapps still do. By ten thousand years ago that had changed, and he had begun in some places to domesticate some animals and to cultivate some plants; and that is the change from which civilization took off. It is extraordinary to think that only in the last twelve thousand years has civilization, as we understand it, taken off. There must have been an extraordinary explosion about 10,000 B.C.—and there was. But it was a quiet explosion. It was the end of the last Ice Age.

4 We can catch the look and, as it were, the smell of the change in some glacial landscape. Spring in Iceland replays itself every year, but it once played itself over Europe and Asia when the ice retreated. And man, who had come through incredible hardships, had wandered up from Africa over the last million years, had battled through the Ice Ages, suddenly found the ground

flowering and the animals surrounding him, and moved into a different kind of life.

5 It is usually called the "agricultural revolution." But I think of it as something much wider, the biological revolution. There was intertwined in it the cultivation of plants and the domestication of animals in a kind of leap-frog. And under this ran the crucial realization that man dominates his environment in its most important aspect, not physically but at the level of living things—plants and animals. With that there comes an equally powerful social revolution. Because now it became possible—more than that, it became necessary—for man to settle. And this creature that had roamed and marched for a million years had to make the crucial decision: whether he would cease to be a nomad and become a villager. We have an anthropological record of the struggle of conscience of a people who make this decision: the record is the Bible, the Old Testament I believe that civilization rests on that decision. As for people who never made it, there are few survivors. There are some nomad tribes who still go through these vast transhumance journeys from one grazing ground to another: the Bakhtiari in Persia, for example. And you have actually to travel with them and live with them to understand that civilization can never grow up on the move.

Everything in nomad life is immemorial. The Bakhtiari have always travelled alone, quite unseen. Like other nomads, they think of themselves as a family, the sons of a single founding-father. (In the same way the Jews used to call themselves the children of Israel or Jacob.) The Bakhtiari take their name from a legendary herdsman of Mongol times, Bakhtyar. The legend of their own origin that they tell of him begins,

> And the father of our people the hill-man, Bakhtyar, came out of the fastness of the southern mountains in ancient times. His seed were as numerous as the rocks on the mountains, and his people prospered.

6 The biblical echo sounds again and again as the story goes on. The patriarch Jacob had two wives, and had worked as a herdsman for seven years for each of them. Compare the patriarch of the Bakhtiari:

> The first wife of Bakhtyar had seven sons, fathers of the seven brother lines of our people. His second wife had four sons. And our sons shall take for wives the daughters from their father's brothers' tents, lest the flocks and tents be dispersed.

As with the children of Israel, the flocks were all-important; they are not out of the mind of the storyteller (or the marriage counsellor) for a moment.

7 Before 10,000 B.C., nomad peoples used to follow the natural migration of wild herds. But sheep and goats have no natural migrations. They were first domesticated about ten thousand years ago—only the dog is an older camp follower than that. And when man domesticated them, he took on the responsibility of nature; the nomad must lead the helpless herd.

8 The role of women in nomad tribes is narrowly defined. Above all, the function of women is to produce men-children; too many she-children are an immediate misfortune, because in the long run they threaten disaster. Apart from that, their duties lie in preparing food and clothes. For example, the women among the Bakhtiari bake bread—in the biblical manner, in unleavened cakes on hot stones. But the girls and the women wait to eat until the men have eaten. Like the men, the lives of the women center on the flock. They milk the herd, and they make a clotted yoghourt from the milk by churning it in a goatskin bag on a primitive wooden frame. They have only the simple technology that can be carried on daily journeys from place to place. The simplicity is not romantic; it is a matter of survival. Everything must be light enough to be carried, to be set up every evening and to be packed again every morning. When the women spin wool with their simple ancient devices, it is for immediate use, to make the repairs that are essential on the journey—no more.

9 It is not possible in the nomad life to make things that will not be needed for several weeks. They could not be carried. And in fact the Bakhtiari do not know how to make them. If they need metal pots, they barter them from settled peoples or from a caste of gypsy workers who specialize in metals. A nail, a stirrup, a toy, or a child's bell is something that is traded from outside the tribe. The Bakhtiari life is too narrow to have time or skill for specialization. There is no room for innovation, because there is not time, on the move, between evening and morning, coming and going all their lives, to develop a new device or a new thought—not

even a new tune. The only habits that survive are the old habits. The only ambition of the son is to be like the father.

10 It is a life without features. Every night is the end of a day like the last, and every morning will be the beginning of a journey like the day before. When the day breaks, there is one question in everyone's mind: Can the flock be got over the next high pass? One day on the journey, the highest pass of all must be crossed. This is the pass Zadeku, twelve thousand feet high on the Zagros, which the flock must somehow struggle through or skirt in its upper reaches. For the tribe must move on, the herdsman must find new pastures every day, because at these heights grazing is exhausted in a single day.

11 Every year the Bakhtiari cross six ranges of mountains on the outward journey (and cross them again to come back). They march through snow and the spring flood water. And in only one respect has their life advanced beyond that of ten thousand years ago. The nomads of that time had to travel on foot and carry their own packs. The Bakhtiari have pack-animals—horses, donkeys, mules—which have only been domesticated since that time. Nothing else in their lives is new. And nothing is memorable. Nomads have no memorials, even to the dead. (Where is Bakhtyar, where was Jacob buried?) The only mounds that they build are to mark the way at such places as the Pass of the Women, treacherous but easier for the animals than the high pass.

12 The spring migration of the Bakhtiari is a heroic adventure; and yet the Bakhitari are not so much heroic as stoic. They are resigned because the adventure leads nowhere. The summer pastures themselves will only be a stopping place—unlike the children of Israel, for them there is no promised land. The head of the family has worked seven years, as Jacob did, to build a flock of fifty sheep and goats. He expects to lose ten of them in the migration if things go well. If they go badly, he may lose twenty out of that fifty. Those are the odds of the nomad life, year in and year out. And beyond that, at the end of the journey, there will still be nothing except an immense, traditional resignation.

13 Who knows, in any one year, whether the old when they have crossed the passes will be able to face the final test: the crossing of the Bazuft River? Three months of melt-water have swollen the river. The tribesmen, the women, the pack animals, and the flocks are all exhausted. It will take a day to manhandle the flocks across the river. But this, here, now is the testing day. Today is

the day on which the young become men, because the survival of the herd and the family depends on their strength. Crossing the Bazuft River is like crossing the Jordan; it is the baptism to manhood. For the young man, life for a moment comes alive now. And for the old—for the old, it dies.

14 What happens to the old when they cannot cross the last river? Nothing. They stay behind to die. Only the dog is puzzled to see a man abandoned. The man accepts the nomad custom; he has come to the end of his journey, and there is no place at the end. . . .

Suggestions for Discussion and Writing

1. What seems to account for the vast difference between the biological time scale and the cultural time scale?
2. Explain the first sentence of the third paragraph.
3. What had to happen before humans could get settled? Is the process still going on?
4. How would you explain the similarity between the stories of Bakhtyar and Jacob? What is your guess about their historicity?
5. In what sense is everything in nomad life "immemorial" (paragraph 5)?
6. Is Bronowski writing for a scholarly audience or for the interested laypeople? How do you know?
7. Explain how the first paragraph sets up the framework for the entire essay.
8. Bronowski advances a theory that attempts to explain why man has only recently become master of the earth. Phrase that theory in your own words.
9. What kinds of evidence does Bronowski offer his reader? How reliable is it?
10. Write an essay in which you compare the place of men and women in the Bakhtiari and U.S. societies. You could also bring in something from Ehrenreich to good advantage.

7
Writing Good Sentences

All this time you have been writing sentences, as naturally as breathing, and perhaps with as little variation. Now for a close look at the varieties of the sentence. Some varieties can be shaggy and tangled indeed. But they are all offshoots of the simple active sentence, the basic English genus *John hits Joe,* with action moving straight from subject through verb to object.

This subject-verb-object sentence can be infinitely grafted and contorted, but there are really only two general varieties of it: (1) the "loose, or strung-along," in Aristotle's phrase, and (2) the periodic. English naturally runs "loose," or "cumulative." Our thoughts are by nature strung along from subject through verb to object, with whatever comes to mind simply added as it comes. The loose sentence puts its subject and verb early. But we can also use the periodic sentence characteristic of our Latin and Germanic ancestry, where ideas hang in the air like girders until all interconnections are locked by the final word, at the period: *John, the best student in the class, the tallest and most handsome, hits Joe.* A periodic sentence, in other words, is one that suspends its meaning until the end, usually with subject and verb widely separated, and the verb as near the end as possible.

So we have two varieties of the English sentence. The piece-by-piece and the periodic species simply represent two ways of thought: the first, the natural stringing of thoughts as they come; the second, the more careful contrivance of emphasis and suspense.

THE SIMPLE SENTENCE

Use the Simple Active Sentence, Loosely Periodic

Your best sentences will be hybrids of the loose and the periodic. First, learn to use active verbs *(John* HITS *Joe),* which will keep you within the simple active pattern with all parts showing (subject-verb-object), as opposed to a verb in the passive voice *(Joe* IS HIT *by John),* which puts everything backwards and uses more words. Then learn to give your native strung-along sentence a touch of periodicity and suspense.

Any change in normal order can give you unusual emphasis, as when you move the object ahead of the subject:

> **That I like.**
> **The house itself she hated, but the yard was grand.**
> **Nature I loved; and next to Nature, Art.**

Most often, we expect our ideas one at a time, in normal succession—*John hits Joe*—and with anything further added, in proper sequence, at the end—*a real haymaker.* Change this fixed way of thinking, and you immediately put your reader on the alert for something unusual. Consequently, some of your best sentences will be simple active ones sprung wide with phrases coloring subject, verb, object, or all three, in various ways. You may, for instance, effectively complicate the subject:

> **King Lear, proud, old, and childish, probably aware that his grip on the kingdom is beginning to slip, devises a foolish plan.**

Or the verb:

> **A good speech usually begins quietly, proceeds sensibly, gathers momentum, and finally moves even the most indifferent audience.**

Or the object:

Her notebooks contain marvelous comments on the turtle in the back yard, the flowers and weeds, the great elm by the drive, the road, the earth, the stars, and the men and women of the village.

COMPOUND AND COMPLEX SENTENCES

Learn the Difference Between Compound and Complex Sentences

You make a compound sentence by linking together simple sentences with a coordinating conjunction *(and, but, or, nor, yet, still, for, so)* or with a colon or a semicolon. You make a complex one by hooking lesser sentences onto the main sentence with *that, which, who,* or one of the many other subordinating connectives like *although, because, where, when, after, if.* The compound sentence *coordinates,* treating everything on the same level; the complex *subordinates,* putting everything else somewhere below its one main self-sufficient idea. The compound links ideas one after the other, as in the basic simple sentence; the complex is a simple sentence elaborated by clauses instead of merely by phrases. The compound represents the strung-along way of thinking; the complex usually represents the periodic.

Avoid Simple-Minded Compounds

Essentially the compound sentence *is* simple-minded, a set of clauses on a string—a child's description of a birthday party, for instance: "We got paper hats and we pinned the tail on the donkey and we had chocolate ice cream and Randy sat on a piece of cake and I won third prize." *And . . . and . . . and.*

But this way of thinking is always useful for pacing off related thoughts, and for breaking the staccato of simple statement. It often briskly connects cause and effect: "The clock struck one, and down he run." "The solipsist relates all knowledge to his own being, and the demonstrable commonwealth of human nature dissolves before his dogged timidity." The compound sentence is built on the most enduring of colloquial patterns—the simple sequence of things said as they occur to the mind—it has the pace, the immediacy, and the dramatic effect of talk. Hemingway, for instance, often gets all the numb tension of a shell-shocked mind by reducing his character's thoughts all to one level, in sentences something like this: "It was a good night and I sat at a table and . . . and . . . and. . . ."

Think of the compound sentence in terms of its conjunctions—the words that yoke its clauses—and of the accompanying punctuation. Here are three basic groups of conjunctions that will help you sort out and punctuate your compound thoughts.

Group I. *The three common coordinating conjunctions:* and, but, *and* or (nor). *Put a comma before each.*

> **I like her, and I don't mind saying so.**
> **Art is long, but life is short.**
> **Win this point, or the game is lost.**

Group II. *Conjunctive adverbs:* therefore, moreover, however, nevertheless, consequently, furthermore. *Put a semicolon before, and a comma after each.*

> **Nations indeed seem to have a kind of biological span like human life, from rebellious youth, through caution, to decay; consequently, predictions of doom are not uncommon.**

Group III. *Some in-betweeners—*yet, still, so*—which sometimes take a comma, sometimes a semicolon, depending on your pace and emphasis.*

> **We long for the good old days, yet we never include the disadvantages.**
> **People long for the good old days; yet they rarely take into account the inaccuracy of human memory.**
> **The preparation had been halfhearted and hasty, so the meeting was wretched.**
> **Rome declined into the pleasures of its circuses and couches; so the tough barbarians conquered.**

Try Compounding Without Conjunctions

Though the conjunction usually governs its compound sentence, two powerful coordinators remain—the semicolon and the colon alone. For contrasts, the semicolon is the prince of coordinators:

Semicolon **The dress accents the feminine; the pants suit speaks for freedom.**

Golf demands the best of time and space; tennis, the best of personal energy.

The government tries to get the most out of taxes; the individual tries to get out of the most taxes.

The colon similarly pulls two "sentences" together without blessing of conjunction, period, or capital. But it signals amplification, not contrast: the second clause explains the first.

Colon **A house with an aging furnace costs more than the asking price suggests: twenty dollars more a month in fuel means about one hundred sixty dollars more a year.**

A growing population means more business: more business will exhaust our supply of ores in less than half a century.

Sports at any age are beneficial: they keep your pulses hopping.

Learn to Subordinate

You probably write compound sentences almost without thinking. But the subordinations of the complex usually require some thought. Indeed, you are ranking closely related thoughts, arranging the lesser ones so that they bear effectively on your main thought. You must first pick your most important idea. You must then change mere sequence into subordination—ordering your lesser thoughts "sub," or below, the main idea. The childish birthday sentence, then, might come out something like this:

After we got paper hats and ate chocolate ice cream, after Randy sat on a piece of cake and everyone pinned the tail on the donkey, I WON THIRD PRIZE.

You do the trick with connectives—with any word, like *after* in the sentence above, indicating time, place, cause, or other qualification.

> ***If*** **they try,** ***if*** **they fail, THEY ARE STILL GREAT** ***because*** **their spirit is unbeaten.**

You daily achieve subtler levels of subordination with the three relative pronouns *that, which, who,* and with the conjunction *that. That, which,* and *who* connect thoughts so closely related as to seem almost equal, but actually each tucks a clause (subject-and-verb) into some larger idea:

> **The car,** ***which*** **runs perfectly, is not worth selling.**
> **The car** ***that*** **runs perfectly is worth keeping.**
> **He thought** ***that*** **the car would run forever.**
> **He thought [*that* omitted but understood] the car would run forever.**

Relative Pronoun

Subordinating Conjunction

But the subordinating conjunctions and adverbs *(although, if, because, since, until, where, when, as if, so that)* really put subordinates in their places. Look at *when* in this sentence of E. B. White's from *Charlotte's Web:*

> **Next morning** ***when*** **the first light came into the sky and the sparrows stirred in the trees,** ***when*** **the cows rattled their chains and the rooster crowed and the early automobiles went whispering along the road, Wilbur awoke and looked for Charlotte.**

Adverbs

Here the simple *when,* used only twice, has regimented five subordinate clauses, all of equal rank, into their proper station below that of the main clause, "Wilbur awoke and looked for Charlotte." You can vary the ranking intricately and still keep it straight:

> ***Although*** **some claim** ***that*** **time is an illusion,** ***because*** **we have no absolute chronometer,** ***although*** **the mind cannot effectively grasp time,** ***because*** **the mind itself is a kind of timeless presence almost oblivious to seconds and hours,** ***although*** **the time of our solar system may be only an instant in the universe at large, WE STILL CANNOT QUITE DENY** ***that***

Subordinating Conjunctions

some progression of universal time is passing over us, *if* only we could measure it.

Complex sentences are, at their best, really simple sentences gloriously delayed and elaborated with subordinate thoughts. The following beautiful and elaborate sentence from the Book of Common Prayer is all built on the simple sentence "draw near":

> **Ye who do truly and earnestly repent you of your sins, and are in love and charity with your neighbors, and intend to lead a new life, following the commandments of God, and walking from henceforth in his holy ways, draw near with faith, and take this holy sacrament to your comfort, and make your humble confession to Almighty God, devoutly kneeling.**

Even a short sentence may be complex, attaining a remarkably varied suspense. Notice how the simple statement "I allowed myself" is skillfully elaborated in this sentence by the late Wolcott Gibbs of *The New Yorker:*

> **Twice in my life, for reasons that escape me now, though I'm sure they were discreditable, I allowed myself to be persuaded that I ought to take a hand in turning out a musical comedy.**

Try for Still Closer Connections: Modify

Your subordinating *if*'s and *when*'s have really been modifying—that is, limiting—the things you have attached them to. But there is a smoother way. It is an adjectival sort of thing, a shoulder-to-shoulder operation, a neat trick with no need for shouting, a stone to a stone with no need for mortar. You simply put clauses and phrases up against a noun, instead of attaching them with a subordinator. This sort of modification includes the following constructions, all using the same close masonry: (1) appositives, (2) relatives understood, (3) adjectives-with-phrase, (4) participles, (5) absolutes.

Appositives. Those phrases about shoulders and tricks and stones, above, are all in apposition with *sort of thing,* and they are grammatically subordinate to it. *Apposition* means "put to" or "add to"—putting an equivalent beside, like two peas in a pod —hence these phrases are nearly coordinate and interchangeable. They are compressions of a series of sentences ("It is an adjectival sort of thing. It is a neat trick . . . ," and so forth) set side by side, "stone to stone." Mere contact does the work of the verb *is* and its subject *it.* English often does the same with subordinate clauses, omitting the *who is* or *that is* and putting the rest directly into apposition. "The William who is the Conqueror" becomes "William the Conqueror." "The Jack who is the heavy hitter" becomes "Jack the heavy hitter." These, incidentally, are called "restrictive" appositions, because they restrict to a particular designation the nouns they modify, setting this William and this Jack apart from all others (with no separating commas). Similarly, you can make nonrestrictive appositives from nonrestrictive clauses, clauses that simply add information (between commas). "Smith, who is a man to be reckoned with, . . ." becomes "Smith, a man to be reckoned with, . . ." "Jones, who is our man in Liverpool, . . ." becomes "Jones, our man in Liverpool, . . ." Restrictive or nonrestrictive, close contact neatly makes your point.

Relatives Understood. You can often achieve the same economy, as I have already hinted, by omitting the relative pronouns *that, which,* and *who* with their verbs, thus gaining a compression both colloquial and classic:

> **A comprehension [that is] both colloquial and classic. . . .**
> **The house, [which was] facing north, had a superb view.**
> **The specimens [that] he had collected. . . .**
> **The girl [whom] he [had] left behind. . . .**

Adjectives-with-Phrase. This construction is also appositive and adjectival. It is neat and useful:

> **The law was passed,** ***thick with provisions and codicils, heavy with implications.***
> **There was the lake,** ***smooth in the early-morning air.***

Participles. Participles—when acting as adjectives—are extremely supple subordinates. Consider this sequence of six simple sentences:

> **He had been thrown.**
> **He had accepted.**
> **He felt a need.**
> **He demanded money.**
> **He failed.**
> **He chose not to struggle.**

Now see how Richard Wright, in *Native Son,* subordinates the first five of these to the sixth with participles. He elaborates the complete thought into a forceful sentence that runs for eighty-nine words with perfect clarity:

> ***Having been thrown*** **by an accidental murder into a position where he had sensed a possible order and meaning in his relations with the people about him;** ***having accepted*** **the moral guilt and responsibility for that murder because it had made him feel free for the first time in his life;** ***having felt*** **in his heart some obscure need to be at home with people and** ***having demanded*** **ransom money to enable him to do it—*****having*** **done all this and** ***failed,*** **he chose not to struggle any more.**

These participles have the same adjectival force:

> **Dead to the world,** ***wrapped*** **in sweet dreams,** ***untroubled*** **by bills, he slept till noon.**

Notice that the participles operate exactly as the adjective *dead* does.

Beware of dangling participles. They may trip you, as they have tripped others. The participle, with its adjectival urge, may grab the first noun that comes along, with shocking results:

> **Bowing to the crowd, the bull caught him unawares.**
> **Observing quietly from the bank, the beavers made several errors in judgment.**
> **Squandering everything at the track, the money was never repaid.**

What we need is a list of teachers broken down alphabetically.

Move the participle next to its intended noun or pronoun; you will have to supply this word if inadvertence or the passive voice has omitted it entirely. Recast the sentence for good alignment when necessary. You may also save the day by changing a present participle to a past, as in the third example below, or, perhaps better, by activating the sentence, as in the fourth example:

The bull caught him unawares as he bowed to the crowd.
Observing quietly from the bank, they saw the beavers make several errors in judgment.
Squandered at the track, the money was never repaid.
Having squandered everything at the track, he never repaid the money.
What we need is an alphabetical list of teachers.

Gerunds, which look like present participles but act as nouns, are also good economizers. The two sentences "He had been thrown" and "It was unpleasant" can become one, with a gerund as subject: "*Having been thrown* was unpleasant." Gerunds also serve as objects of verbs and prepositions:

She hated *going* home.
By *driving* carefully, they increased their mileage.

Absolutes. The absolute phrase has a great potential of polished economy. It stands grammatically "absolute" or alone, modifying only through proximity, like an apposition. Many an absolute is simply a prepositional phrase with the preposition dropped:

He ran up the stairs, [with] *a bouquet of roses under his arm,* and rang the bell.
She walked slowly, [with] *her camera ready.*

But the ablative absolute (*ablative* means "removed") is absolutely removed from the main clause, modifying only by proximity. If you have had some Latin, you will probably remember this construction as some kind of brusque condensation, something like "*The road completed,* Caesar moved his camp." But it survives in the best of circles. Somewhere E. B. White admits to feeling particularly good one morning, just having brought off an especially fine ablative absolute. And it is actually more common than you may suppose. A recent newspaper article stated that "the Prince had fled the country, *his hopes of a negotiated peace shattered.*" The *hopes shattered* pattern (noun plus participle) marks the ablative absolute (also called, because of the noun, a "nominative absolute"). The idea might have been more conventionally subordinated: "since his hopes were shattered" or "with his hopes shattered." But the ablative absolute accomplishes the subordination with economy and style.

Take a regular subordinate clause: "*When* the road *was* completed." Cut the subordinator and reduce the verb. You now have an ablative absolute, a phrase that stands absolutely alone, shorn of both its connective *when* and its full predication *was:* "*The road completed,* Caesar moved his camp." Basically a noun and a participle, or noun and adjective, it is a kind of grammatical shorthand, a telegram: *ROAD COMPLETED CAESAR MOVED*—most said in fewest words, speed with high compression. This is its appeal and its power.

The cat stopped, ***its back arched, its eyes frantic.***
All things considered, **the plan would work.**
The ***dishes washed,*** **the** ***baby bathed*** **and** ***asleep,*** **the last** ***ashtray emptied,*** **they could at last relax.**

PARALLEL CONSTRUCTION

Use Parallels to Strengthen Equivalent Ideas

No long complex sentence will hold up without parallel construction. Paralleling can be very simple. Any word will seek its own kind, noun to noun, adjective to adjective, infinitive to infinitive. The simplest series of things automatically runs parallel:

shoes and ships and sealing wax
I came, I saw, I conquered

to be or not to be
a dull, dark, and soundless day
mediocre work, cowardly work, disastrous work

But they very easily run out of parallel too, and this you must learn to prevent. The last item especially may slip out of line, as in this series: "friendly, kind, unobtrusive, and *a bore*" (boring). The noun *bore* has jumped off the track laid by the preceding parallel adjectives. Your train of equivalent ideas should all be of the same grammatical kind to carry their equivalence clearly—to strengthen it: either parallel adjectives, *friendly, kind, unobtrusive,* and *boring,* or all nouns, *a friend, a saint, a diplomat,* and *a bore.* Your paralleling articles and prepositions should govern a series as a whole, or should accompany *every* item:

a hat, cane, pair of gloves, and mustache
a hat, a cane, a pair of gloves, and a mustache
by land, sea, or air
by land, by sea, or by air

Verbs also frequently intrude to throw a series of adjectives (or nouns) out of parallel:

FAULTY: He thought the girl was *attractive, intelligent,* and *knew* how to make him feel needed.
IMPROVED: He thought the girl was *attractive, intelligent,* and *sympathetic,* knowing how to make him feel needed.

Watch the Paralleling of Pairs

Pairs should be pairs, not odds and ends. Notice how the faulty pairs in these sentences have been corrected:

She liked *the lawn and gardening* (the lawn and the garden).
They were *all athletic or big men on campus* (athletes or big men on campus).
They wanted *peace without being disgraced* (peace without dishonor).
He was *shy but a creative boy* (shy but creative).

Check your terms on both sides of your coordinating conjunctions *(and, but, or)* and see that they match:

> **Orientation week seems both worthwhile [adjective] and ~~a~~ necessary [adj.] ~~necessity~~ [noun].**
>
> **He prayed that they would leave and ^that the telephone would not ring.**

Learn to Use Paralleling Coordinators

The sentence above about "Orientation week" has used one of a number of useful (and tricky) parallel constructions: *both-and; either-or; not only-but also; not-but; first-second-third; as well as.* This last one is similar to *and,* a simple link between two equivalents, but it often causes trouble:

> **One should take care of one's physical self [noun]** ***as well as*** **being [participle] able to read and write.**

Again, the pair should be matched: "one's *physical self* as well as one's *intellectual self,*" or "one's physical *self* as well as one's *ability* to read and write"—though this second is still slightly unbalanced, in rhetoric if not in grammar. The best cure would probably extend the underlying antithesis, the basic parallel:

> **One should take care of one's physical self as well as one's intellectual self, of one's ability to survive as well as to read and write.**

With the *either-or*'s and the *not only-but also*'s, you continue the principle of pairing. The *either* and the *not only* are merely signposts of what is coming: two equivalents linked by a coordinating conjunction *(or* or *but).* Beware of putting the signs in the wrong place—too soon for the turn:

> **He either is an absolute piker or a fool!**
>
> **Neither in time nor space. . . .**
>
> **He not only likes the girl but the family, too.**

In these examples, the thought got ahead of itself, as in talk. Just make sure that the word following each of the two coordinators is of the same kind, preposition for preposition, article for article, adjective for adjective—for even with signs well placed, the parallel can skid:

> **The students are not only organizing [present participle]**
> **discussing**
> **social activities, but also are ~~interested~~ [passive construction] ~~in~~ political questions.**

Put identical parts in parallel places; fill in the blanks with the same parts of speech: "not only ———, but also ———."

Beginning with *Not only,* a common habit, always takes more words as it duplicates subject and verb, inviting a comma splice and frequently misaligning a parallel:

> **POOR:** ***Not only*** **is man limited in his mind and in his position in the universe, he is also limited in his physical powers.**
> **IMPROVED: Man is limited** ***not only*** **in his mind and in his position in the universe,** ***but also*** **in his physical powers.** [*21 words for 23*]

The following sentence avoids the comma splice but still must duplicate subject and verb:

> **POOR:** ***Not only*** **are the names similar, but the two men share some similarities of character.**
> **IMPROVED: The two men share similarities** ***not only*** **in name** ***but*** **in character.** [*12 words for 15*]

The following experienced writer avoids the usual comma splice with a semicolon but makes a dubious parallel:

> **POOR:** ***Not only*** **was the right badly splintered into traditional conservatives, economic liberals, and several other factions; the Communists were the weakest they had been in half a century.**
> **IMPROVED: The right was badly splintered . . . , and the Communists. . . .**

You similarly parallel the words following numerical coordinators:

Numerical Coordinates

However variously he expressed himself, he unquestionably thought, first, *that* everyone could get ahead; second, *that* workers generally were paid more than they earned; and, third, *that* laws enforcing a minimum wage were positively undemocratic.

For a number of reasons, he decided (1) *that* he did not like it, (2) *that* she would not like it, (3) *that* they would be better off without it. [Note that the parentheses around the numbers operate exactly as any parentheses, and need no additional punctuation.]

My objections are obvious: (1) *it* is unnecessary, (2) *it* costs too much, and (3) *it* won't work.

In parallels of this kind, *that* is usually the problem, since you may easily, and properly, omit it when there is only one clause and no confusion:

> **. . . he unquestionably thought everyone could get ahead.**

If second and third clauses occur, as your thought moves along, you may have to go back and put up the first signpost:

> **that**
> **. . . he unquestionably thought ^everyone could get ahead, that workers . . . , and that laws. . . .**

Enough of *that.* Remember simply that equivalent thoughts demand parallel constructions. Notice the clear and massive strategy in the following sentence from the concluding chapter of Freud's last book, *An Outline of Psychoanalysis.* Freud is not only summing up the previous discussion, but also expressing the quintessence of his life's work. He is pulling everything together in a single sentence. Each of the parallel *which* clauses gathers up, in proper order, an entire chapter of his book (notice the parallel force in repeating *picture,* and the summarizing dash):

> **The picture of an ego which mediates between the id and the external world, which takes over the instinctual demands of the former in order to bring them to satisfaction, which perceives things in the latter and uses them as memories, which, intent upon its self-preservation, is on guard against excessive claims from both directions, and which is governed in all its decisions by the injunctions of a modified**

> **pleasure principle—this picture actually applies to the ego only up to the end of the first period of childhood, till about the age of five.**

Such precision is hard to match. This is what parallel thinking brings—balance and control and an eye for sentences that seem intellectual totalities, as if struck out all at once from the uncut rock. Francis Bacon's sentences can seem like this (notice how he drops the verb after establishing his pattern):

> **For a crowd is not company, and faces are but a gallery of pictures, and talk but a tinkling cymbal, where there is no love.**
> **Reading maketh a full man; conference a ready man; and writing an exact man.**

Commas would work well in the second example (see 410–11):

> **Reading maketh a full man; conference, a ready man; and writing, an exact man.**

THE LONG AND SHORT OF IT

Your style will emerge once you can manage some length of sentence, some intricacy of subordination, some vigor of parallel, and some play of long against short, of amplitude against brevity. Try the very long sentence, and the very short. Short sentences are meatiest:

> **Money talks.**
> **The mass of men lead lives of quiet desperation.**
> **The more selfish the man, the more anguished the failure.**

Experiment with the Fragment

The fragment is close to conversation. It is the laconic reply, the pointed afterthought, the quiet exclamation, the telling question. Try to cut and place it clearly (usually at beginnings and ends of paragraphs) so as not to lead your reader to expect a full sentence, or to suspect a poor writer:

But no more.
First, a look behind the scenes.
No, not really.
Enough of that.

The fragment, of course, usually counts as an error. The reader expects a sentence and gets only a fragment of one: you leave him hanging in air, waiting for the second shoe to fall, or the voice to drop, with the thought completed, at the period. The *rhetorical* fragment—the effective and persuasive one—leaves him satisfied: *Of course.* The *grammatical* fragment leaves him unsatisfied: *When the vote was counted.* A question hangs in the air: *what* happened? who won? who got mad? But the point here about rhetorical fragments is to use their short, conversational staccato as one of your means to vary the rhythm of your long and longer sentences, playing long against short.

Develop a Rhythm of Long and Short

The conversational flow between long and short makes a passage move. Study the subordinations, the parallels, and the play of short and long in this elegant passage of Virginia Woolf's—after you have read it once for sheer enjoyment. She is writing of Lord Chesterfield's famous letters to Philip Stanhope, his illegitimate son:

Subordinate, Long

But while we amuse ourselves with this brilliant nobleman and his views on life we are aware, and the letters owe much of their fascination to this consciousness, of a dumb yet substantial figure on the farther side of the page.

Short, Long

Philip Stanhope is always there. It is true that he says nothing, but we feel his presence in Dresden, in Berlin, in Paris, opening the letters and pouring over them and looking dolefully at the thick packets which have been accumulating year after year since he was a child of seven.

Short, Shorter; Longer, Long

He had grown into a rather serious, rather stout, rather short young man. He had a taste for foreign politics. A little serious reading was rather to his liking. And by every post the letters came—urbane, polished, brilliant, imploring and commanding him

to learn to dance, to learn to carve, to consider the management of his legs, and to seduce a lady of fashion. He did his best. He worked very hard in the school of the Graces, but their service was too exacting. He sat down halfway up the steep stairs which lead to the glittering hall with all the mirrors. He could not do it. He failed in the House of Commons; he subsided into some small post in Ratisbon; he died untimely. He left it to his widow to break the news which he had lacked the heart or the courage to tell his father—that he had been married all these years to a lady of low birth, who had borne him children.

Short; Longer

Short
Parallels Long

The Earl took the blow like a gentleman. His letter to his daughter-in-law is a model of urbanity. He began the education of his grandsons. . . .*

Short; Longer

Those are some sentences to copy. We immediately feel the rhythmic play of periodic and loose, parallel and simple, long and short. Such orchestration takes years of practice, but you can always begin.

EXERCISES

1. *Give each of the following sentences a touch of periodicity (that is, suspense) by changing the normal word order, by adding interruptive words or phrases, or by complicating one of the three principal elements of the sentence: the subject, the verb, the object.*

EXAMPLE *She made her way along the smoldering roof.*

Carefully at first, then with reckless steps, she made her way along the peak of the smoldering roof.

1. Commune residents are often escapees from solidly middle-class families.
2. Old friends are often shocked and embarrassed when they meet after years of separation and find they now have little in common.
3. Some firemen began carrying guns when they were frightened by the chaos of the riots.
4. The bottleneck in education is that the teacher can listen and respond to no more than one student at a time.
5. The car wheezed to a stop.

---

*From *The Second Common Reader* by Virginia Woolf, copyright 1932 by Harcourt Brace Jovanovich, Inc.; renewed 1960 by Leonard Woolf. Reprinted by permission of the publisher.

2. *Write six compound sentences, two with* and, *two with* but, *two with* or (nor). *Try to get as grand a feeling of consequence as possible with your* and's: *"Empires fall, and the saints come marching in."*
3. *Write three compound sentences using conjunctive adverbs, on the pattern: "———; therefore, ———." Punctuate carefully with semicolon and comma.*
4. *Write three compound sentences in which the link is the semicolon alone. Try for meaningful contrasts.*

   EXAMPLE *The county wants the new expressway; the city wants to renew its streets.*

5. *Write three compound sentences in which the link is a colon. Try to make the second half of the compound explain the first.*

   EXAMPLE *His game was ragged: he went into sand traps four times, and into the trees five.*

6. *Here are some pairs of sentences. Convert them into complex sentences, trying to use a variety of subordinators.*

   1. He couldn't go on. He was just too tired.
   2. The crime commission recommended a number of such programs. Federal funds have been made available for putting them into operation.
   3. We can probably never perfect the process beyond its present state. We should still try.
   4. Most schools are just now starting courses in computers for freshmen. To evaluate those programs will take several years.
   5. On small farms, labor was not specialized. On medium farms, labor was partially specialized. But large farms carefully divided their workers into teams of specialists.

7. *Streamline the following sentences by using appositives:*

   1. The security guard, who must have been a very frightened man, fired point-blank into the crowd.
   2. Professor Stanley, who is now associate vice-president and director of business operations, has been named a vice-president at the University of Nebraska.
   3. The book, which has been a best-seller for several months, will be made into a movie.
   4. American social mores have undergone staggering changes since the early 1950's. These changes are so great in quality and number as to constitute a virtual revolution.
   5. The Globe Theatre, which was immediately acclaimed the best designed and appointed playhouse in London, was completed in 1599.

8. *Consolidate the following sentences, using adjectival phrases and absolutes rather than subordinate clauses.*

1. The young girl cowered in the corner. There was pure terror in her eyes.
2. This construction is also appositional and adjectival. It is a neat trick for the beginning writer to remember.
3. Its deck was splintered and peeling. Its rigging was nearly all frayed and rotted. The boat obviously hadn't been cared for at all.
4. Griswell had neither eaten nor slept, and when he stumbled into the bar he was trembling with fatigue.
5. The ladder was sagging with his weight, and at last it collapsed.

9. *Keeping an eye out for dangling participles, revise the following sentences by transforming as many verbs as reasonably possible into participles.*

1. Apparently the boxer thought the bell had sounded. He dropped his guard, and he was immediately knocked out.
2. He settled into a Bohemian life in the French quarter. He started publishing in all the appropriate little magazines. And at last he found himself presiding over a colony of artists and writers.
3. The prisoners were obviously angered by the news that no guards were fired. They felt cheated and betrayed. And so on August 4 they seized three guards as hostages to force the warden to reconsider.
4. Dalton Trumbo was blacklisted in Hollywood; he was vilified in the press; and he was forced to write scripts under an assumed name until nearly 1960.
5. The student-designed rocket functioned perfectly. It rose one hundred miles above the earth, flew for ten minutes, traveled some fifty miles down range, and splashed down precisely on target.

10. *Try turning the phrases and subordinate clauses in the following sentences into absolutes.*

1. With examinations coming and with the temperature dropping, students are beginning to show up at the health service with all sorts of nebulous ailments, most of them purely imagined.
2. Ted left the room, leaving his things still scattered over the floor.
3. Even though the tank was filled with gas and the ignition was working perfectly, the engine still wouldn't start.
4. Even though the stock market had collapsed, and fifteen percent of the workers were jobless, Hoover nonetheless felt the economy would eventually right itself without tinkering.
5. When his three minutes were up, he deposited another quarter.

11. *Correct the faulty parallelism in the following sentences from students' papers, and clean up any wordiness you find.*

1. A student follows not only a special course of training, but among his studies and social activities finds a liberal education.
2. Either the critics attacked the book for its triteness, or it was criticized for its lack of organization.
3. This is not only the case with the young voters of the United States but also of the adult ones.
4. Certain things are not actually taught in the classroom. They are learning how to get along with others, to depend on oneself, and managing one's own affairs.
5. Knowing Greek and Roman antiquity is not just learning to speak their language but also their culture.

12. *Write an imitation of the passage from Virginia Woolf on 262–63, choosing your own subject but matching the pattern, lengths, and rhythms of her sentences, sentence for sentence, if you can. At any rate, aim toward effective rhythms of long and short.*

Readings

The essays in this section present the many faces of the English sentence in a variety of poses: long and short, periodic and loose, simple, compound, and complex. Abraham Lincoln's magnificent thoughts in troubled times still resound for today's reader. E. B. White, a modern master of the sentence, limns the limitations and pleasures of the essayist. William Manchester's portrait of the greatest Englishman of the twentieth century recaptures the drama and suspense of England's darkest hour. Finally, Woody Allen's parody reminds us that the ritual we have all endured—the graduation address—does not have to be a sober occasion.

ABRAHAM LINCOLN

The Gettysburg Address *

1 Four score and seven years ago our fathers brought forth [,up]on this continent, a new nation, conceived in [liberty] Liberty, and dedicated to the proposition that [“]all men are created equal.[”]

---

*Lincoln twice revised the first draft of his famous address, delivered November 19, 1863. I have bracketed his deletions and underscored his additions, comparing his final fair copy (the “Bliss” copy) against his first two drafts. Lincoln added the phrase *who fought here* and the word *advance* (indicated in italics) for publication some time after the event. See Joseph Tausek, *The True Story of the Gettysburg Address* (New York: Lincoln MacVeagh, The Dial Press, 1933), facsimile foldout facing p. 36, and *Abraham Lincoln's Gettysburg Address: the First and Second Drafts Now in the Library of Congress* (Washington D.C.: U.S. Government Printing Office, 1950).

2 Now we are engaged in a great civil war, testing whether that nation, or any nation so conceived, and so dedicated, can long endure. We are met on a great battle-field of that war. We have come to dedicate a portion of [it] that field, as a final resting place for those who [died here, that the] here gave their lives that that nation might live. [This we may, in all propriety do.] It is altogether fitting and proper that we should do this.

3 But, in a larger sense, we can not dedicate—we can not consecrate—we can not hallow—this ground. The brave men, living and dead, who struggled here, have [hallowed] consecrated it, far above our poor power to add or detract. The world will little note, nor long remember what we say here [; while], *but* it can never forget what they did here. It is [rather] for us, the living [to stand here ‖ we here be dedicated], rather, to be dedicated here to the unfinished work which they *who fought here* have thus far so nobly [carried on] *advanced.* It is rather for us to be here dedicated to the great task remaining before us—that from these honored dead we take increased devotion to that cause for which they [here] gave the last full measure of devotion— that we here highly resolve that these dead shall not have died in vain—that [the] this nation, under God, shall have a new birth of freedom—and that government of the people, by the people, for the people, shall not perish from the earth.

Suggestions for Discussion and Writing

1. Throughout his speech, Lincoln alludes to the kinship of life and death. Find several such examples, and explain how they strengthen his central theme. Why are these images appropriate to the time and place of his address?
2. Why didn't Lincoln say "eighty" instead of "fourscore" in his opening sentence? What tone does such Biblical language establish? Find other examples of elevated language.
3. Lincoln's speech, though brief, can be divided into three sections. The first describes the occasion, the second dedicates the ground, and the last draws a conclusion by calling on his hearers to dedicate themselves to the preservation of the Union. Locate the specific sentences that comprise each section.
4. Among the rhetorical devices Lincoln uses in his address are antithesis and parallelism, as illustrated in the following:

(antithesis) The world will little *note*
nor long *remember* what *we say* here
but it can never *forget* what *they did* here.
(parallelism) government *of the people, by the people, for the people.*

Find several other instances of these devices, as well as others mentioned in this chapter. What does he do with *dedicate*?

5. Pick out Lincoln's shortest sentence and his longest sentence. How are they effective?
6. To get something of Lincoln's rhythm (and to have some fun), try a parody of the famous address in your own terms: "Not quite a score and five weeks ago, I brought myself forth in freshman composition. . . ."

ABRAHAM LINCOLN

Second Inaugural Address [March 4, 1865]

Fellow countrymen:

1 At this second appearing to take the oath of the presidential office, there is less occasion for an extended address than at the first. Then a statement somewhat in detail of the course to be pursued seemed very fitting and proper; now, at the expiration of four years, during which public declarations have constantly been called forth concerning every point and place of the great contest which still absorbs attention and engrosses the energies of the nation, little that is new could be presented. The progress of our arms, upon which all else chiefly depends, is as well known to the public as to myself. It is, I trust, reasonably satisfactory and encouraging to all. With a high hope for the future, no prediction in that regard is ventured. On the occasion corresponding to this four years ago, all thoughts were anxiously directed to an impending civil war. All dreaded it. All sought to avoid it. While the Inaugural Address was being delivered from this place, devoted altogether to saving the Union without war, the insurgent agents were

in the city seeking to destroy it without war—seeking to dissolve the Union, and divide the effects by negotiating. Both parties deprecated war, but one of them would make war rather than let it perish, and war came. One eighth of the whole population were colored slaves, not distributed generally over the Union, but located in the Southern part. These slaves contributed a peculiar and powerful interest. All knew the interest would somehow cause war. To strengthen, perpetuate, and extend this interest was the object for which the insurgents would rend the Union by war, while the government claimed no right to do more than restrict the territorial enlargement of it. Neither party expected the magnitude or duration which it has already attained; neither anticipated that the cause of the conflict might cease even before the conflict itself should cease. Each looked for an easier triumph and a result less fundamental and astonishing. Both read the same Bible and pray to the same God. Each invokes His aid against the other. It may seem strange that any man should dare to ask a just God's assistance in wringing bread from the sweat of other men's faces; but let us judge not, that we be not judged. The prayer of both should not be answered; that of neither has been answered fully, for the Almighty has His own purposes. "Woe unto the world because of offenses, for it must needs be that offense come; but woe unto that man by whom the offense cometh." If we shall suppose American slavery one of those offenses which, in the providence of God, must needs come, but which, having continued through His appointed time, He now wills to remove, and that He gives to both North and South this terrible war, as was due to those by whom the offense came, shall we discern that there is any departure from those divine attributes which believers in the living God always ascribe to Him? Fondly do we hope, fervently do we pray, that this mighty scourge of war may speedily pass away; yet if it be God's will that it continue until the wealth piled by bondsmen by two hundred and fifty years' unrequited toil shall be sunk, and until every drop of blood drawn with the lash shall be paid by another drawn with the sword, as was said three thousand years ago, so still it must be said that the judgments of the Lord are true and righteous altogether.

2 With malice toward none, with charity for all, with firmness in the right, as God gives us to see the right, let us strive on to finish the work we are in, to bind up the nation's wounds, to care for him who shall have borne the battle, and for his widow and

orphans; to do all which may achieve and cherish a just and a lasting peace among ourselves and with all nations.

Suggestions for Discussion and Writing

1. Lincoln, elected before the Civil War broke out in 1860 and reelected in 1864, says that "there is less occasion for an extended address" this second time. Why?
2. Rewrite Lincoln's last sentence in your own words ("With malice toward none . . .").
3. Compare Lincoln's address with Ronald Reagan's second inaugural address or with the inaugural address of another recent president. How do the addresses compare in terms of content and style?
4. Many politicians invoke God's blessing in their speeches. What is Lincoln saying about God's role in the Civil War?
5. See what you can do with two sentences patterned on Lincoln's last two: "Fondly do we hope, fervently do we pray, that this awful scourge of a midterm. . . ."

E. B. WHITE

The Essayist

1 The essayist is a self-liberated man, sustained by the childish belief that everything he thinks about, everything that happens to him, is of general interest. He is a fellow who thoroughly enjoys his work, just as people who take bird walks enjoy theirs. Each new excursion of the essayist, each new "attempt," differs from the last and takes him into new country. This delights him. Only a person who is congenitally self-centered has the effrontery and the stamina to write essays.

2 There are as many kinds of essays as there are human attitudes or poses, as many essay flavors as there are Howard Johnson ice creams. The essayist arises in the morning and, if he has work to do, selects his garb from an unusually extensive wardrobe: he can pull on any sort of shirt, be any sort of person, according to his

mood or his subject matter—philosopher, scold, jester, raconteur, confidant, pundit, devil's advocate, enthusiast. I like the essay, have always liked it, and even as a child was at work, attempting to inflict my young thoughts and experiences on others by putting them on paper. I early broke into print in the pages of *St. Nicholas.* I tend still to fall back on the essay form (or lack of form) when an idea strikes me, but I am not fooled about the place of the essay in twentieth-century American letters—it stands a short distance down the line. The essayist, unlike the novelist, the poet, and the playwright, must be content in his self-imposed role of second-class citizen. A writer who has his sights trained on the Nobel Prize or other earthly triumphs had best write a novel, a poem, or a play, and leave the essayist to ramble about, content with living a free life and enjoying the satisfactions of a somewhat undisciplined existence. (Dr. Johnson called the essay "an irregular, undigested piece"; this happy practitioner has no wish to quarrel with the good doctor's characterization.)

3 There is one thing the essayist cannot do, though—he cannot indulge himself in deceit or in concealment, for he will be found out in no time. Desmond MacCarthy, in his introductory remarks to the 1928 E. P. Dutton & Company edition of Montaigne, observes that Montaigne "had the gift of natural candour. . . ." It is the basic ingredient. And even the essayist's escape from discipline is only a partial escape: the essay, although a relaxed form, imposes its own disciplines, raises its own problems, and these disciplines and problems soon become apparent and (we all hope) act as a deterrent to anyone wielding a pen merely because he entertains random thoughts or is in a happy or wandering mood.

4 I think some people find the essay the last resort of the egoist, a much too self-conscious and self-serving form for their taste; they feel that it is presumptuous of a writer to assume that his little excursions or his small observations will interest the reader. There is some justice in their complaint. I have always been aware that I am by nature self-absorbed and egoistical; to write of myself to the extent I have done indicates a too great attention to my own life, not enough to the lives of others. I have worn many shirts, and not all of them have been a good fit. But when I am discouraged or downcast I need only fling open the door of my closet, and there, hidden behind everything else, hangs the mantle of Michel de Montaigne, smelling slightly of camphor.

Suggestions for Discussion and Writing

1. Look up the etymology of *essay* and then explain why White puts *attempt* in quotation marks in the first sentence.
2. Why, as the author laments, does the essayist not have the status or recognition of the novelist or poet? Should he?
3. According to White, what are some of the constraints that the essay imposes on its practitioner?
4. White says that the essayist may adopt a variety of roles: "philosopher, scold, jester, raconteur, confidant, pundit, devil's advocate, enthusiast." Which role has he assumed in this essay? What other roles can you think of that the essayist sometimes assumes?
5. White implies that the essay is rambling and formless. Does his essay conform to that description?
6. Select several essays in this book and analyze their style by using White's analogy of the writer's wardrobe. In each case, what shirt did the writer put on? How do you know?
7. One of White's techniques for achieving variety is to alternate the short sentence with the long. In the first paragraph, for example, he inserts a short sentence to contrast with those surrounding it ("This delights him"). Another technique is to add a touch of periodicity by suspending a key idea until the end; the last sentence in the first paragraph is an example. Find other examples of these and other techniques (such as subordination and parallelism) used in White's essay that add variety to his sentences.
8. If you find satisfaction in something that others find trivial or even meaningless, write an essay explaining your interest in it. As you write, aim for a mix of sentence structures and patterns.

WILLIAM MANCHESTER

The Lion at Bay: Winston Spencer Churchill

1 The French had collapsed. The Dutch had been overwhelmed. The Belgians had surrendered. The British army, trapped, fought free and fell back toward the Channel ports,

converging on a fishing town whose name was then spelled Dunkerque.

2 Behind them lay the sea.

3 It was England's greatest crisis since the Norman conquest, vaster than those precipitated by Philip II's Spanish Armada, Louis XIV's triumphant armies, or Napoleon's invasion barges massed at Boulogne. This time Britain stood alone. If the Germans crossed the Channel and established uncontested beachheads, all would be lost, for it is a peculiarity of England's island that its southern weald is indefensible against disciplined troops. In A.D. 61, Queen Boudicca of the Iceni rallied the tribes of East Anglia and routed the Romans at Colchester, Saint Albans, and London (then Londinium), cutting the Ninth Legion to pieces and killing seventy thousand. But because the nature of the southern terrain was unsuitable for the construction of strongpoints, new legions under Paulinus, arriving from Gaul, crushed the revolt, leaving the grief-stricken queen to die by her own hand.

4 Now the 220,000 Tommies at Dunkirk, Britain's only hope, seemed doomed. On the Flanders beaches they stood around in angular, existential attitudes, like dim purgatorial souls awaiting disposition. There appeared to be no way to bring more than a handful of them home. The Royal Navy's vessels were inadequate. King George VI has been told that they would be lucky to save 17,000. The House of Commons was warned to prepare for "hard and heavy tidings." Then, from the streams and estuaries of Kent and Dover, a strange fleet appeared: trawlers and tugs, scows and fishing sloops, lifeboats and pleasure craft, smacks and coasters, the island ferry *Gracie Fields*; Tom Sopwith's America's Cup challenger *Endeavour*; even the London fire brigade's firefloat *Massey Shaw*—all of them manned by civilian volunteers: English fathers, sailing to rescue England's exhausted, bleeding sons.

5 Even today what followed seems miraculous. Not only were Britain's soldiers delivered; so were French support troops: a total of 338,682 men. But wars are not won by fleeing from the enemy. And British morale was still unequal to the imminent challenge. These were the same people who, less than a year earlier, had rejoiced in the fake peace bought by the betrayal of Czechoslovakia at Munich. Most of their leaders and most of the press remained craven. It had been over a thousand years since

Alfred the Great had made himself and his countrymen one and sent them into battle transformed. Now in this new exigency, confronted by the mightiest conqueror Europe had ever known, England looked for another Alfred, a figure cast in a mold which, by the time of the Dunkirk deliverance, seemed to have been forever lost.

6 England's new leader, were he to prevail, would have to stand for everything England's decent, civilized Establishment had rejected. They viewed Adolf Hitler as the product of complex social and historical forces. Their successor would have to be a passionate Manichaean who saw the world as a medieval struggle to the death between the powers of good and the powers of evil, who held that individuals are responsible for their actions and that the German dictator was therefore wicked. A believer in martial glory was required, one who saw splendor in the ancient parades of victorious legions through Persepolis and could rally the nation to brave the coming German fury. An embodiment of fading Victorian standards was wanted: a tribune for honor, loyalty, duty, and the supreme virtue of action; one who would never compromise with iniquity, who could create a sublime mood and thus give men heroic visions of what they were and might become. Like Adolf Hitler he would have to be a leader of intuitive genius, a born demagogue in the original sense of the word, a believer in the supremacy of his race and his national destiny, an artist who knew how to gather the blazing light of history into his prism and then distort it to his ends, an embodiment of inflexible resolution who could impose his will and his imagination on his people—a great tragedian who understood the appeal of martyrdom and could tell his followers the worst, hurling it to them like great hunks of bleeding meat, persuading them that the year of Dunkirk would be one in which it was "equally good to live or to die"—who could if necessary be just as cruel, just as cunning, and just as ruthless as Hitler but who could win victories without enslaving populations, or preaching supernaturalism, or foisting off myths of his infallibility, or destroying, or even warping, the libertarian institutions he had sworn to preserve. Such a man, if he existed, would be England's last chance.

7 In London there was such a man.

8 Now at last, at last, his hour had struck. He had been waiting in Parliament for forty years, had grown bald and gray in his

nation's service, had endured slander and calumny only to be summoned when the situation seemed hopeless to everyone except him. His youngest daughter, seventeen-year-old "Mary the Mouse"—her family nickname—had been sunning herself at Chartwell, their country home in Kent, during the first hours of the German breakthrough, when the music on her portable radio had been interrupted by a BBC bulletin: "His Majesty the King has sent for Mr. Winston Churchill and asked him to form a government." Mary, who adored her father, prayed for him and assumed that he would save England. So, of course, did he. But among those who fully grasped the country's plight, that was a minority view. The Conservative party leadership, the men of Munich, still controlled the government—Lord Halifax, Sir Horace Wilson, Sir Kingsley Wood, Sir John Simon, Sir Samuel Hoare, and, of course, Churchill's predecessor as prime minister, Neville Chamberlain, who detested him and everything he represented. Even George VI hadn't wanted Chamberlain to quit No. 10 Downing Street; he thought his treatment had been "grossly unfair." The King suggested Halifax as his successor. Labour's erratic Stafford Cripps had already come out for Halifax. That suited the Tory hierarchy, but only a coalition could govern the nation, and the National Executive of the Labour party, meeting in a basement room of the Highcliff Hotel in Bournemouth, sent word that they would serve under no Conservative except Churchill. So Chamberlain persuaded the reluctant King to choose the man neither wanted.

9 Not that it seemed to matter much. Churchill had said that "the Germans are always either at your throat or at your feet," and as a hot May melted into a hotter June it appeared that their stranglehold was now unbreakable. Hitler was master of Europe. No one, not even Caesar, had stood so securely upon so glittering a pinnacle. The Führer told Göring: "The war is finished. I'll come to an understanding with England." On May 28, the first day of the Dunkirk evacuation, Halifax, speaking for the Conservative leadership, had told Churchill that a negotiated peace was England's only alternative. Now, as the new prime minister's foreign secretary and a member of his War Cabinet, the Yorkshire nobleman was quoted by the United Press as inviting "Chancellor Hitler to make a new and more generous peace offer." It was, he said, the only reasonable course, the only decision a stable man of sound judgment could reach.

10 He was quite right. But Winston Churchill was not a reasonable man. He was about as sound as the Maid of Orleans, a comparison he himself once made—"It's when I'm Joan of Arc that I get excited." Even more was he an Elijah, an Isaiah; a prophet. Deep insight, not stability, was his forte. To the War Cabinet he said, "I have thought carefully in these last days whether it was part of my duty to consider entering into negotiations with that man," and concluded: "If this long island story of ours is to end at last, let it end only when each one of us lies choking in his own blood upon the ground." He spoke to them, to the House, and then to the English people as no one had before or ever would again. He said: "I have nothing to offer but blood, toil, tears, and sweat." Another politician might have told them: "Our policy is to continue the struggle; all our forces and resources will be mobilized." This is what Churchill said:

> Even though large tracts of Europe and many old and famous states have fallen or may fall into the grip of the Gestapo and all the odious apparatus of Nazi rule, we shall not flag or fail. We shall go on to the end. We shall fight in France, we shall fight on the seas and oceans, we shall fight with growing confidence and growing strength in the air, we shall defend our island, whatever the cost may be, we shall fight on the beaches, we shall fight on the landing grounds, we shall fight in the fields and in the streets, we shall fight in the hills; we shall never surrender.

11 "Behind us," he said, ". . . gather a group of shattered states and bludgeoned races: the Czechs, the Poles, the Danes, the Norwegians, the Belgians, the Dutch—upon all of whom a long night of barbarism will descend, unbroken even by a star of hope, unless we conquer, as conquer we must, as conquer we shall." That was the language of the Elizabethans, and of a particular Elizabethan, the greatest poet in history: "This England never did, nor never shall, / Lie at the proud foot of a conqueror."

12 Now, fired by the conviction which could only belong to one who had faced down inner despair, Churchill defied the "celestial grins" of Britain's enemies, said peace feelers would "be viewed with the greatest disfavor by me," and said he contemplated the future "with stern and tranquil gaze." Free En-

glishmen, he told his people, would be more than a match for the "deadly, drilled, docile, brutish mass of the Hun soldiery plodding on like a swarm of crawling locusts." But he warned his family to prepare for invaders. His son's bride Pamela protested: "But Papa, What can *I* do?" He growled: "You can always get a carving knife from the kitchen and take one with you, can't you?" To the demoralized French he declared: "Whatever you may do, we shall fight on forever and ever and ever." General Maxime Weygand replied by asking what would happen if a hundred Nazi divisions landed at Dover. Churchill told him: *"Nous les frapperons sur la tête"*—they would be hit on the head as they crawled ashore. Visiting Harrow, he heard the boys sing an old school song rewritten in his honor:

> Not less we praise in darker days
> The Leader of our Nation,
> And Churchill's name shall win acclaim
> From each new generation.

He suggested a change. "Darker," he said, should be "sterner." These were no dark days, he told them. Indeed, they would be remembered as great days, provided this "island race" followed his watchword: "Never, never, never, never give in."

13 And so he saved Western civilization when men considered its redemption worth any price. The Nazi stain was spreading into the Balkans, into the Middle East, into Brazil; the German-American Bund was staging mass rallies in Madison Square Garden; the *New York Times* reported in front-page headlines: URUGUAY ON GUARD FOR FIFTH COLUMN, NAZIS TAKE BOLD TONE IN ECUADOR, and ARGENTINE NAZIS RALLY. Men who think of themselves as indispensable are almost always wrong, but Winston Churchill was surely that then. He was like the lion in Revelation, "the first beast," with "six wings about him" and "full of eyes within." In an uncharacteristically modest moment on his eightieth birthday he said: "It was the nation and the race dwelling all round the globe that had the lion's heart; I had the luck to be called upon to give the roar." It wasn't that simple. The spirit, if indeed within them, lay dormant until he became prime minister and they, kindled by his soaring prose, came to see themselves as he saw them and emerged a people transformed, the admiration of free men everywhere.

Suggestions for Discussion and Writing

1. How does Manchester prepare the reader for the appearance of Churchill in his essay? What (or whom) is Churchill compared to?
2. What is the purpose of the allusions to Joan of Arc, Elijah, and Isaiah? How do they and the other allusions contribute to the portrait of Churchill that Manchester is preparing?
3. How does Manchester give a historical perspective to the crisis he describes? Note, for example, paragraph 3; what kind of framework is the author constructing?
4. The staccato movement of the sentences in the opening paragraph is followed by a single-sentence paragraph. What effect is achieved by this sentence pattern? What is the author's intent?
5. Note the last sentence of paragraph 4. How does Manchester keep it from becoming confusing or lulling, despite its length?
6. Select one of your heroes from history and attempt a similar sketch. Try to match your sentence structure with the mood, pace, and overall effect that you are trying to achieve.

WOODY ALLEN

My Speech to the Graduates

1 More than any other time in history, mankind faces a crossroads. One path leads to despair and utter hopelessness. The other, to total extinction. Let us pray we have the wisdom to choose correctly. I speak, by the way, not with any sense of futility, but with a panicky conviction of the absolute meaninglessness of existence which could easily be misinterpreted as pessimism. It is not. It is merely a healthy concern for the predicament of modern man. (Modern man is here defined as any person born after Nietzsche's edict that "God is dead," but before the hit recording "I Wanna Hold Your Hand.") This "predicament" can be stated in one of two ways, though certain linguistic philosophers prefer to reduce it to a mathematical equation where it can be easily solved and even carried around in the wallet.

2 Put in its simplest form, the problem is: How is it possible

to find meaning in a finite world given my waist and shirt size? This is a very difficult question when we realize that science has failed us. True, it has conquered many diseases, broken the genetic code, and even placed human beings on the moon, and yet when a man of eighty is left in a room with two eighteen-year-old cocktail waitresses nothing happens. Because the real problems never change. After all, can the human soul be glimpsed through a microscope? Maybe—but you'd definitely need one of those very good ones with two eyepieces. We know that the most advanced computer in the world does not have a brain as sophisticated as that of an ant. True, we could say that of many of our relatives, but we only have to put up with them at weddings or special occasions. Science is something we depend on all the time. If I develop a pain in the chest I must take an X-ray. But what if the radiation from the X-ray causes me deeper problems? Before I know it, I'm in for surgery. Naturally, while they're giving me oxygen an intern decides to light on a cigarette. The next thing you know I'm rocketing over the World Trade Center in bedclothes. Is this science? True, science has taught us how to pasteurize cheese. And true, this can be fun in mixed company—but what of the H-bomb? Have you ever seen what happens when one of those things falls off a desk accidentally? And where is science when one ponders the eternal riddles? How did the cosmos originate? How long has it been around? Did matter begin with an explosion or by the word of God? And if by the latter, could He not have begun it just two weeks earlier to take advantage of some of the warmer weather? Exactly what do we mean when we say man is mortal? Obviously it's not a compliment.

3 Religion, too, has unfortunately let us down. Miguel de Unamuno writes blithely of the "eternal persistence of consciousness," but that is no easy feat. Particularly when reading Thackeray. I often think how comforting life must have been for early man because he believed in a powerful, benevolent Creator who looked after all things. Imagine his disappointment when he saw his wife putting on weight. Contemporary man, of course, has no such peace of mind. He finds himself in the midst of a crisis of faith. He is what we fashionably call "alienated." He has seen the ravages of war, he has known natural catastrophes, he has been to singles bars. My good friend Jacques Monod spoke often of the randomness of the cosmos. He believed everything in existence

occurred by pure chance with the possible exception of his breakfast, which he felt certain was made by his housekeeper. Naturally belief in a divine intelligence inspires tranquillity. But this does not free us from our human responsibilities. Am I my brother's keeper? Yes. Interestingly, in my case I share that honor with the Prospect Park Zoo. Feeling godless then, what we have done is made technology God. And yet can technology really be the answer when a brand new Buick, driven by my close associate, Nat Persky, winds up in the window of Chicken Delight causing hundreds of customers to scatter? My toaster has never once worked properly in four years. I follow the instructions and push two slices of bread down in the slots and seconds later they rifle upward. Once they broke the nose of a woman I loved very dearly. Are we counting on nuts and bolts and electricity to solve our problems? Yes, the telephone is a good thing—and the refrigerator—and the air conditioner. But not every air conditioner. Not my sister Henny's, for instance. Hers makes a loud noise and still doesn't cool. When the man comes over to fix it, it gets worse. Either that or he tells her she needs a new one. When she complains, he says not to bother him. This man is truly alienated. Not only is he alienated, but he can't stop smiling.

4 The trouble is, our leaders have not adequately prepared us for a mechanized society. Unfortunately our politicians are either incompetent or corrupt. Sometimes both on the same day. The Government is unresponsive to the needs of the little man. Under five-seven, it is impossible to get your Congressman on the phone. I am not denying that democracy is still the finest form of government. In a democracy at least, civil liberties are upheld. No citizen can be wantonly tortured, imprisoned, or made to sit through certain Broadway shows. And yet this is a far cry from what goes on in the Soviet Union. Under their form of totalitarianism, a person merely caught whistling is sentenced to thirty years in a labor camp. If, after fifteen years, he still will not stop whistling they shoot him. Along with this brutal fascism we find its handmaiden, terrorism. At no other time in history has man been so afraid to cut into his veal chop for fear that it will explode. Violence breeds more violence, and it is predicted that by 1990 kidnapping will be the dominant mode of social interaction. Overpopulation will exacerbate problems to the breaking point. Figures tell us there are already more people on earth than we need to move even the heaviest piano. If we do not call a halt to

breeding, by the year 2000 there will be no room to serve dinner unless one is willing to set the table on the heads of strangers. Then they must not move for an hour while we eat. Of course energy will be in short supply, and each car owner will be allowed only enough gasoline to back up a few inches.

5 Instead of facing these challenges, we turn to distractions like drugs and sex. We live in far too permissive a society. Never before has pornography been this rampant. And those films are lit so badly! We are a people who lack defined goals. We have never learned to love. We lack leaders and coherent programs. We have no spiritual center. We are adrift in the cosmos wreaking monstrous violence on one another out of frustration and pain. Fortunately, we have not lost our sense of proportion. Summing up, it is clear the future holds great opportunities. It also holds pitfalls. The trick will be to avoid the pitfalls, seize the opportunities, and get back home by six o'clock.

Suggestions for Discussion and Writing

1. Despite his humor, is Allen singling out any particular targets in our society for his satire? How do you know?
2. Explain the allusions to Nietzsche, de Unamuno, and Monod. How do they serve Allen's purpose?
3. What is the modern "predicament" that Allen is concerned with in his parody? Is he serious? What examples does he offer to support his argument?
4. Find several examples of Allen's use of exaggeration and understatement. Does he get carried away to make his reader laugh, or is the humor justified?
5. Is the last paragraph of this essay primarily serious, or is he laughing to the very end?
6. One of the sources of Allen's humor is the unexpected punch line that deflates a serious idea. Locate several examples of this technique.
7. Write your own graduation speech to the graduates of your high school. Try to maintain an ironic or satiric tone throughout the speech.

8 Correcting Wordy Sentences

Now let us contemplate evil—or at least the innocently awful, the bad habits that waste our words, fog our thoughts, and wreck our delivery. Our thoughts are naturally roundabout, our phrases naturally secondhand. Our satisfaction in merely getting something down on paper naturally blinds us to our errors and ineptitudes. It hypnotizes us into believing we have said what we meant, when our words actually say something else: "Every seat in the house was filled to capacity." Two ways of expressing your thought, two clichés, have collided: *every seat was taken* and *the house was filled to capacity.* Cut the excess wordage, and the absurd accident vanishes: "Every seat was taken." Good sentences come from constant practice in correcting the bad.

Count Your Words

Writing is devilish; the general sin is wordiness. We put down the first thought that comes, we miss the best order, and we then need lengths of *is*'s, *of*'s, *by*'s, and *which*'s—words virtually meaningless in themselves—to wire our meaningful words together again. Look for the two or three words that carry your meaning; then see if you can rearrange them to speak for themselves, cutting out all the little useless wirings:

> **This is the young man who was elected to be president by the class. [This is the young man the class elected president.**

Or: **The class elected this young man president.** *9 words, or 7 words, for 14*]

See if you can't promote a noun into a verb, and cut overlaps in meaning:

Last week, the gold stampede in Europe reached near panic proportions. [Last week, Europe's gold speculators almost *stampeded. 7 words for 11*]

Frequently you can reduce tautologies (467):

each separate incident	**each incident**
many different ways	**many ways**
dash quickly	**dash**

As these examples show, the basic cure for wordiness is to count the words in any suspected sentence or phrase—and to make each word count. If you can rephrase to save even one word, your sentence will be clearer. And seek the active verb: *John* HITS *Joe.*

Shun the Passive Voice

The passive voice is more wordy and deadly than most people imagine, or it would not be so persistent.

It was voted that there would be a drive for the cleaning up of the people's park. [*passive voice—17 words*]
We [the town, the council] voted a drive to clean up the people's park. [*active voice—10 or 11 words, depending on subject*]

The passive voice puts the cart before the horse: the object of the action first, then the harnessing verb, running backwards, then the driver forgotten, and the whole contraption at a standstill. The passive voice is simply "passive" action, the normal action backwards: object-verb-subject (with the true subject usually forgotten) instead of subject-verb-object—*Joe is hit by John* instead of *John hits Joe.*

The passive voice liquidates and buries the active individual, along with most of the awful truth. Our massed, scientific, and bureaucratic society is so addicted to it that you must constantly alert yourself against its drowsy, impersonal pomp. The simple English sentence is active; it *moves* from subject through verb to object: "The dean's office has turned down your proposal." But the impersonal bureau emits instead a passive smokescreen, and the student sees no one at all to help him:

> **It has been decided that your proposal for independent study is not sufficiently in line with the prescribed qualifications as outlined by the college in the catalog.**

Committees always write this way, and the effect on academic writing, as the professor goes from committee to desk to classroom, is astounding. "It was moved that a meeting would be held," the secretary writes, to avoid pinning the rap on anybody. So writes the professor, so writes the student.

I reluctantly admit that the passive voice has certain uses. In fact, your meaning sometimes demands the passive voice; the agent may be better under cover—insignificant, or unknown, or mysterious. The active "Shrapnel hit him" seems to belie the uncanny impersonality of "He was hit by shrapnel." The broad forces of history similarly demand the passive: "The West was opened in 1848." Moreover, you may sometimes need the passive voice to place your true subject, the hero of the piece, where you can modify him conveniently: "Joe was hit by John, who, in spite of all. . . ." And sometimes it simply is more convenient: "This subject-verb-object sentence can be infinitely contorted." You can, of course, find a number of passive constructions in this book, which preaches against them, because they can also space out a thought that comes too fast and thick. In trying to describe periodic sentences, for instance (246), I changed "until all interconnections lock in the final word" (active) to ". . . are locked by the final word" (passive). The *lock* seemed too tight, especially with *in,* and the locking seemed contrary to the ways buildings *are built.* Yes, the passive has its uses.

But it is wordy. It puts useless words in a sentence. Its dullness derives as much from its extra wordage as from its impersonality. The best way to prune is with the active voice, cutting the passive and its fungus as you go. Notice the effect on these typical and real samples:

PASSIVE: Public concern *has* also *been given* a tremendous impetus *by* the findings of the Hoover Commission on the federal government, and "little Hoover" commissions to survey the organizational structure and functions of many state governments *have been established.*

ACTIVE: The findings of the Hoover Commission on federal government *have* also greatly stimulated public concern, and many states *have established* "little Hoover" commissions to survey their governments. [*27 words for 38*]

PASSIVE: The algal mats *are made up of* the interwoven filaments of several genera.

ACTIVE: The interwoven filaments of several genera *make up* the algal mats. [*11 words for 13*]

PASSIVE: Many of the remedies *would* probably *be shown to be* faith cures.

ACTIVE: Many of the remedies *were* probably faith cures. [*8 words for 12*]

PASSIVE: Anxiety and emotional conflict *are lessened* when latency sets in. The total personality *is oriented* in a repressive, inhibitory fashion so as to maintain the barriers, and what Freud has called "psychic dams," against psychosexual impulses.

ACTIVE: When latency sets in, anxiety and emotional conflict *lessen.* The personality *inhibits* itself, maintaining its barriers—Freud's "psychic dams"—against psychosexual impulses. [*22 words for 36*]

Check the Stretchers

To be, itself, frequently ought not to be:

He seems [to be] upset about something.
She considered him [to be] perfect.
This appears [to be] difficult.

Above all, keep your sentences awake by not putting them into those favorite stretchers of the passivists, *There is . . . which, It is . . . that,* and the like:

Moreover, [there is] one segment of the population [which] never seeks employment.
[There are] many women [who] never marry.

> **[There] is nothing wrong with it. [Nothing is. . . .]**
> **[It is] his last book [that] shows his genius best.**
> **[It is] this [that] is important.**

Cut every *it* not referring to something. Next to activating your passive verbs, and cutting the passive *there is*'s and *it is*'s, perhaps nothing so improves your prose as to go through it systematically also deleting every *to be,* every *which, that, who,* and *whom* not needed for utter clarity or for spacing out a thought. All your sentences will feel better.

Beware the Of-and-Which Disease

The passive sentence frequently breaks out in a rash of *of*'s and *which*'s, and even the active sentence may suffer. Diagnosis: something like sleeping sickness. *With*'s, *in*'s, *to*'s and *by*'s also inflamed. Surgery imperative. Here is an actual case:

> **Many biological journals, especially those *which* regularly publish new scientific names, now state *in* each issue the exact date *of* publication *of* the preceding issue. *In* dealing *with* journals *which* do not follow this practice, or *with* volumes *which* are issued individually, the biologist often needs *to* resort *to* indexes . . . *in order to* determine the actual date *of* publication *of* a particular name.**

Note *of publication of* twice over, and the three *which*'s. The passage is a sleeping beauty. The longer you look at it, the more useless little attendants you see. Note the inevitable passive voice *(which are issued)* in spite of the author's active efforts. The *of*'s accompany extra nouns, *publication* repeating *publish,* for instance. Remedy: (1) eliminate *of*'s and their nouns, (2) change *which* clauses into participles, (3) change nouns into verbs. You can cut more than a third of this passage without touching the sense (39 words for 63):

> **Many biological journals, especially those regularly *publishing* new scientific names, now give the date of each preceding issue. With journals not *following* this practice, and with some books, the biologist must turn to indexes . . . *to date* a particular name.**

I repeat: you can cut most *which*'s, one way or another, with no loss of blood. Participles can modify their antecedents directly, since they are verbal adjectives, without an intervening *which:* "a car *which was* going south" is "a car going south"; a train *which is* moving" is "a moving train." Similarly with the adjective itself: "a song *which was* popular last year" is "a song popular last year"; "a person *who is* attractive" is "an attractive person." Beware of this whole crowd: *who are, that was, which are.*

If you need a relative clause, remember *that. Which* has almost completely displaced it in labored writing. *That* is still best for restrictive clauses, those necessary to definition: "A house that faces north is cool" (a participle would save a word: "A house facing north is cool"). *That* is tolerable; *which* is downright oppressive. *Which* should signal the nonrestrictive clause (the afterthought): "The house, which faces north, is a good buy." Here you need *which.* Even restrictive clauses must turn to *which* when complicated parallels arise. "He preaches the brotherhood of man *that* everyone affirms" elaborates like this: "He preaches the brotherhood of man *which* everyone affirms, *which* all the great philosophies support, but *for which* few can make any immediate concession." Nevertheless, if you need relatives, a *that* will often ease your sentence and save you from the *which*'s.

Verbs and their derivatives, especially present participles and gerunds, can also help to cure a string of *of*'s. Alfred North Whitehead, usually of clear mind, once produced this linked sausage: "Education is the acquisition *of* the art *of* the utilization *of* knowledge." Anything to get around the three *of*'s and the three heavy nouns would have been better: "Education instills the art of using knowledge"—"Education teaches us to use knowledge well." Find an active verb for *is the acquisition of,* and shift *the utilization of* into some verbal form: the gerund *using,* or the infinitive *to use.* Shun the *-tion*'s! Simply change your surplus *-tion*'s and *of*'s—along with your *which* phrases—into verbs, or verbals *(to use, learning).* You will save words, and activate your sentences.

Avoid "The Use Of"

In fact, both *use,* as a noun, and *use,* as a verb, are dangerously wordy words. Since *using* is one of our most basic concepts, other words in your sentence will already contain it.

> **He uses rationalization. [He rationalizes.]**
> **He uses the device of foreshadowing. [He foreshadows.]**
> **Through [the use of] logic, he persuades.**
> **His [use of] dialogue is effective.**

The utilization of and *utilize* are only horrendous extremes of the same pestilence, to be stamped out completely.

Break the Noun Habit

Passive writing adores the noun, modifying nouns with nouns in pairs, and even in denser clusters—which then become official jargon. Break up these logjams, let the language flow, make one noun of the pair an adjective:

> ***Teacher militancy* is not as marked in Pittsburgh. [*Teachers* are not so *militant* in Pittsburgh.** *7 words for 8*]

Or convert one noun to a verb:

> ***Consumer demand* is falling in the area of services. [Consumers *are demanding* fewer services.** *5 words for 9*]

Of course, nouns have long served English as adjectives: as in "*rail*road," "*railroad* station," "*court*house," and "*noun* habit." But modern prose has aggravated the tendency beyond belief; and we get such monstrosities as *child sex education course* and *child sex education curriculum publication deadline reminder*—whole strings of nothing but nouns. Education, sociology, and psychology produce the worst noun-stringers, the hardest for you not to copy if you take these courses. But we have all caught the habit. The nouns *level* and *quality*, used as adjectives, have produced a rash of redundancies. A meeting of "high officials" has now unfortunately become a meeting of "high-*level* officials." The "finest cloth" these days is always "finest *quality* cloth." Drop those two redundant nouns and you will make a good start, and will sound surprisingly original. In fact, using the noun *quality* as an adjective has become almost obsessive—*quality food, quality wine, quality service, quality entertainment, high-quality drilling equipment*—blurring all distinctions of *good, fine, excellent, superb, superior,* in one dull and inaccurate cliché. A good rule: DON'T USE NOUNS AS ADJECTIVES. You can drop many an excess noun:

WORDY	DIRECT
advance notice	notice
long in size	long

WORDY	DIRECT
puzzling in nature	puzzling
of an indefinite nature	indefinite
of a peculiar kind	peculiar
in order to	to
by means of	by
in relation to	with
in connection with	with
1986-model car	1986 car
at this point in time	at this time; now

Wherever possible, find the equivalent adjective:

of great importance	important
highest significance level	highest significant level
government spending	governmental spending
reaction fixation	reactional fixation
teaching excellence	excellent teaching
encourage teaching quality	encourage good teaching

Or change the noun to its related participle:

advance placement	advanced placement
uniform police	uniformed police
poison arrow	poisoned arrow

Or make the noun possessive:

reader interest	reader's interest
veterans insurance	veterans' insurance

Or try a cautious *of:*

color lipstick	color of lipstick
significance level	level of significance

Of all our misused nouns, *type* has become particularly pestilential and trite. Advertisers talk of *detergent-type cleansers* instead of *detergents;* educators, of *apprentice-type situations* instead of *apprenticeships;* newspapermen, of *fascist-type organizations* instead of *fascistic organizations.* We have forgotten that making the individual stand for the type is the simplest and oldest of metaphors: "Give us this day our daily bread." A twentieth-century supplicant might have written "bread-type food."

The active sentence transmits the message by putting each word unmistakably in its place, a noun as a noun, an adjective as an adjective, with the verb—no stationary *is*—really carrying the mail. Recently, after a flood, a newspaper produced this apparently succinct and dramatic sentence: **Dead animals cause water pollution.** (The word *cause,* incidentally, indicates wasted words.) That noun *water* as an adjective throws the meaning off and takes 25 percent more words than the essential active message: **Dead animals pollute water.** As you read your way into the sentence, it seems to say *dead animals cause water* (which is true enough), and then you must readjust your thoughts to accommodate *pollution.* The simplest change is from *water pollution* (noun-noun) to *polluted water* (adjective-noun), clarifying each word's function. But the supreme solution is to make *pollute* the verb it is, and the sentence a simple active message in which no word misspeaks itself. Here are the possibilities, in a scale from most active and clearest to most passive and wordiest, which may serve to chart your troubles if you get tangled in causes and nouns:

Dead animals pollute water.
Dead animals cause polluted water.
Dead animals cause water pollution.
Dead animals are a factor in causing the pollution of water.
Dead animals are a serious factor in causing the water pollution situation.
Dead farm-type animals are a danger factor in causing the post-flood clearance and water pollution situation.

So the message should now be clear. Write simple active sentences, outmaneuvering all passive eddies, all shallow *is*'s, *of*'s, *which*'s, and *that*'s, all overlappings, all rocky clusters of nouns: they take you off your course, delay your delivery, and wreck many a straight and gallant thought.

Avoid Excessive Distinctions and Definitions

Too many distinctions, too many nouns, and too much Latin make pea soup:

> **Reading is a processing skill of symbolic reasoning sustained by the interfacilitation of an intricate hierarchy of substrata factors that have been mobilized as a psychological working system and pressed into service in accordance with the purpose of the reader.**

This comes from an educator, with the wrong kind of education. He is saying:

> **Reading is a process of symbolic reasoning aided by an intricate network of ideas and motives. [*16 words for 40*]**

Except with crucial assumptions and implications (see 149–54), try *not* to define your terms. If you do, you are probably either evading the toil of finding the right word, or defining the obvious:

> **Let us agree to use the word signal as an abbreviation for the phrase "the simplest kind of sign." (This agrees fairly well with the customary meaning of the word "signal.")**

That came from a renowned semanticist, an authority on the meanings of words. The customary meaning of a word *is* its meaning, and uncustomary meanings come only from careful punning. Don't underestimate your readers, as this semanticist did.

The definer of words is usually a bad writer. Our semanticist continues, trying to get his signals straight and grinding out about three parts sawdust to every one of meat. In the following excerpt, I have bracketed his sawdust. Read the sentence first as he wrote it: then read it again, omitting the bracketed words:

> **The moral of such examples is that all intelligent criticism [of any instance] of language [in use] must begin with understanding [of] the motives [and purposes] of the speaker [in that situation].**

Here, each of the bracketed phrases is already implied in the others. Attempting to be precise, the writer has beclouded himself. Naturally, the speaker would be "in that situation"; naturally, a sampling of language would be "an instance" of language "in use." *Motives* may not be *purposes,* but the difference here is insignificant. Our semanticist's next sentence deserves some kind of immortality. He means "Muddy language makes trouble":

> **Unfortunately, the type of case that causes trouble in practice is that in which the kind of use made of language is not transparently clear. . . .**

Clearly, transparency is hard. Writing is hard. It requires constant attention to meanings, and constant pruning. Count your words, and make your words count.

EXERCISES

1. *Clear up the blurred ideas, and grammar, in these sentences from students' papers and official prose, making each word say what it means, and counting your words to make sure your version has fewer.*

1. Tree pruning may be done in any season of the year. [11 words]
2. After reading a dozen books, the subject is still as puzzling as ever. [13]
3. The secret teller vote used in the past was this time a recorded teller vote. [15]
4. The courses listed herein are those which meet the college-level requirements which were stated above. [16]
5. Records can be used in the Audio Room by individual students for their suggested listening assignments. [16]
6. My counter was for refunds for which the customer had already paid for. [13]
7. Entrance was gained by means of the skylight. [8]
8. The reason we give this test is because we are anxious to know whether or not you have reflexes that are sufficiently fast to allow you to be a safe worker. [31]

2. *Find in your textbooks two or three passages suffering from the passive voice, the of-and-which disease, the the-use-of contagion, and the noun habit ("which shows the effect of age and intelligence level upon the use of the reflexes and the emergence of child behavior difficulties") and rewrite them in clear English.*

3. *Recast these sentences in the active voice, clearing out all passive constructions, saving as many words as you can, and indicating the number saved:*

1. The particular topic chosen by the instructor for study in his section of English 2 must be approved by the Steering Committee. [Start with "The Steering Committee," and don't forget the economy of an apostrophe-*s*. I managed 14 words for 22.]
2. Avoidance of such blunders should not be considered a virtue for which the student is to be commended, any more than he would be praised for not wiping his hands on the tablecloth or polishing his shoes with the guest towels. [Begin "We should not"; try *avoiding* for *avoidance*. I dropped *virtue* as redundant and scored 27 for 41.]
3. The first respect in which too much variation seems to exist is in the care with which writing assignments are made. ["First, care in assigning"—8 for 21.]
4. The remaining variations that will be mentioned are concerned not with the assignment of papers but with the marking and grading of them. ["Finally, I shall mention"—14 for 23.]
5. The difference between restrictives and nonrestrictives can also be better approached through a study of the different contours that mark the utterance of the two kinds of elements than through confusing attempts to differentiate the two by meaning. ["One can differentiate restrictives"—I managed 13 for 38. The writer is dead wrong, incidentally: meaning is the true differentiator. See 401–03.]

4. *Eliminate the italicized words in the following passages, together with all their accompanying wordiness, indicating the number of words saved (my figures again are merely guides; other solutions that come close are quite good).*

1. *There is* a certain tendency to defend one's own position *which* will cause the opponent's argument to be ignored. [13 for 19]
2. *It is* the other requirements *that* present obstacles, some *of which* may prove insurmountable in the teaching of certain subjects. [11 for 20]
3. In the sort of literature-centered course being discussed here, *there is* usually a general understanding *that* themes will be based on the various literary works *that* are studied, the theory being *that* both the instruction in literature and *that* in writing will be made more effective by this interrelationship. [21 for 50]
4. The person *whom* he met was an expert *who was* able to teach the fundamentals quickly. [13 for 16]
5. They will take a pride *which is* wholly justifiable in being able to command a prose style *that is* lucid and supple. [13 for 22]

5. *To culminate this chapter, clear up the wordiness, especially the italicized patches, in these two official statements, one from an eminent linguist, one from an eminent publisher.*

1. The work *which is* reported *in this* study *is* an investigation *of* language *within* the social context *of* the community *in which it is spoken. It is* a study *of* a linguistic structure *which is* unusually complex, but no more than the social structure *of* the city *in which it* functions. [I tried two versions, as I chased out the *which*'s; 29 for 52, and 22 for 52.]
2. Methods *which are* unique to the historian *are illustrated* throughout the volume *in order* to show how history *is written* and how historians work. The historian's approach to his subject, *which* leads to the asking of provocative questions and to a new understanding of complex events, situations, and personalities *is probed.* The manner *in which* the historian reduces masses of chaotic fact—and occasional fancy—to reliable meaning, and the way *in which* he formulates explanations and tests them *is examined and clarified* for the student. *It is its* emphasis on historical method *which* distinguishes this book from other source readings in western civilization. The problems *which are examined* concern *themselves with* subjects *which are dealt with by* most courses in western civilization. [66 for 123. The all-time winner from a student is 45 words.]

9
Words

Here is the word. Sesquipedalian or short, magniloquent or low, Latin or Anglo-Saxon, Celtic, Danish, French, Spanish, Indian, Hindustani, Dutch, Italian, Portuguese, Choctaw, Swahili, Chinese, Hebrew, Turkish, Greek—English contains them all, a million words at our disposal, if we are disposed to use them. No language is richer than English. But our spoken vocabularies average only about 2800 words, our expository vocabularies probably fewer than 8000. We all have a way to go to possess our heritage.

VOCABULARY

Build Your Stock Systematically

If you can increase your hoard, you increase your chances of finding the right word when you need it. Read as widely as you can, and look words up the second or third time you meet them. I once knew a man who swore he learned three new words a day from his reading by using each at least once in conversation. I didn't ask him about *polyphiloprogenitive* or *antidisestablishmentarianism.* It depends a little on the crowd. But the idea is sound. The bigger the vocabulary, the more various the ideas one can get across with it—the more the shades and intensities of meaning.

The big vocabulary also needs the little word. The vocabularian often stands himself on a Latin cloud and forgets the Anglo-Saxon ground—the common ground between him and his audience. So do not forget the little things, the *stuff, lint, get, twig, snap, go, mud, coax.* Hundreds of small words not in immediate vogue can refresh your vocabulary. The Norse and Anglo-Saxon adjectives in *-y (muggy, scrawny, drowsy)* for instance, rarely appear in sober print. The minute the beginner tries to sound dignified, in comes a misty layer of words a few feet off the ground and nowhere near heaven, the same two dozen or so, most of them verbs. One or two will do no harm, but any accumulation is fatal—words like *depart* instead of *go:*

accompany—go with
appeared—looked *or* seemed
arrive—come
become—get
cause—make
cease—stop
complete—finish
continue—keep on
delve—dig
discover—find
indicate—say
locate—find
manner—way
place—put
possess—have
prepare—get ready
questioned—asked
receive—get
relate—tell
remain—stay
remove—take off
retire—go to bed
return—go back
secure—get
transform—change
verify—check

Through the centuries, English has added Latin derivatives alongside the Anglo-Saxon words already there, keeping the old with the new: after the Anglo-Saxon *deor* (now *deer*) came the *beast* and then the *brute,* both from Latin through French, and the *animal* straight from Rome. We have the Anglo-Saxon *cow, sheep,* and *pig* alongside Latin (through French) *beef, mutton,* and *pork.* Although we use more Anglo-Saxon in assembling our sentences *(to, by, with, though, is),* well over half our total vocabulary comes one way or another from Latin. The things of this world tend to be Anglo-Saxon *(man, house, stone, wind, rain);* the abstract qualities, Latin and French *(value, duty, contemplation).*

Most of our big words are Latin and Greek. Your reading acquaints you with them; your dictionary will show you their prefixes and roots. Learn the common prefixes and roots (see Exercise 3 at the end of this chapter), and you can handle all kinds of foreigners at first encounter; *con-cession* (going along with), *ex-clude* (lock out), *pre-fer* (carry before), *sub-version* (turning under), *trans-late* (carry across), *claustro-phobia* (dread of being locked in), *hydro-phobia* (dread of water), *ailuro-philia* (love of cats), *megalo-cephalic* (big-headed), *micro-meter* (little measurer). You can even, for fun, coin a word to suit the occasion: *megalopede* (big-footed). You can remember that *intramural* means "within the (college) walls," and that "intermural sports," which is the frequent mispronunciation and misspelling, would mean something like "wall battling wall," a physical absurdity.

Besides owning a good dictionary, you should refer, with caution, to a thesaurus, a treasury of synonyms ("together-names"), in which you can find the word you couldn't think of; the danger lies in raiding this treasury too enthusiastically. Checking for meaning in a dictionary will help assure that you have expanded, not distorted, your vocabulary.

ABSTRACT AND CONCRETE

Learn Their Powers, Separate and Combined

Every good stylist has perceived, in one way or another, the distinction between the abstract and the concrete. Tangible things—things we can touch—are "concrete"; their qualities, along with all our emotional, intellectual, and spiritual states, are "abstract." The rule for a good style is to be as concrete as you can, to illustrate tangibly your general propositions, to use *shoes* and *ships* and *sealing wax* instead of *commercial concomitants.*

But abstraction, a "drawing out from," is the very nature of thought. Thought moves from concrete to abstract. In fact, *all* words are abstractions. *Stick* is a generalization of all sticks, the crooked and the straight, the long and the short, the peeled and the shaggy. No word fits its object like a glove, because words are not things: words represent ideas of things. They are the means by which we class eggs and tents and trees so that we can handle them as ideas—not as actual things but as *kinds* or *classes* of things.

Abstract words can attain a power of their own, as the rhetorician heightens attention to their meanings. This ability, of course, does not come easily or soon. I repeat, you need to be as concrete as you can, to illustrate tangibly, to pin your abstractions down to specifics. But once you have learned this, you can move on to the rhetoric of abstraction, which is a kind of squeezing of abstract words for their specific juice.

Lincoln does exactly this when he concentrates on *dedication* six times within the ten sentences of his dedication at Gettysburg: "We have come to *dedicate*. . . . It is rather for us to be here *dedicated*. . . ." Similarly, Eliot refers to "faces/Distracted from distraction by distraction" *(Four Quartets)*. Abstractions can, in fact, operate beautifully as specifics: "As a knight, Richard the Lion-Hearted was a *triumph;* as a king, he was a *disaster.*" Many rhetorical patterns likewise concentrate on abstract essences:

> **. . . tribulation works patience, and patience experience, and experience hope. (Rom. v.3–4)**
> **The humble are proud of their humility.**
> **Care in your youth so you may live without care.**

An able writer like Samuel Johnson can make a virtual poetry of abstractions, as he alliterates and balances them against each other (I have capitalized the alliterations and italicized the balances):

> **Dryden's performances were always hasty, either *Excited* by some *External occasion*, or *Extorted* by some *domestic necessity;* he *ComPosed without Consideration* and *Published without Correction.***

Notice especially how *excited* ("called forth") and *extorted* ("twisted out"), so alike in sound and form, so alike in making Dryden write, nevertheless contrast their opposite essential meanings.

So before we disparage abstraction, we should acknowledge its rhetorical power; and we should understand that it is an essential distillation, a primary and natural and continual mental process. Without it, we could not make four of two and two. So we make abstractions of abstractions to handle bigger and bigger groups of ideas. *Egg* becomes *food,* and *food* becomes *nourish-*

ment. We also classify all the psychic and physical qualities we can recognize: *candor, truth, anger, beauty, negligence, temperament.* But because our thoughts drift upward, we need always to look for the word that will bring them nearer earth, that will make our abstractions seem visible and tangible, that will make them graspable—mentioning a *handle,* or a *pin,* or an *egg,* alongside our abstraction, for instance.

But the writer's ultimate skill perhaps lies in making a single object represent its whole abstract class. I have paired each abstraction below with its concrete translation:

> ***Friendliness* is the salesman's best asset.**
> ***A smile* is the salesman's best asset.**
>
> ***Administration of proper proteins* might have saved John Keats.**
> ***A good steak* might have saved John Keats.**
>
> **To *understand* the world by *observing all of its geological details. . . .***
> **To *see* the world in *a grain of sand. . . .***

METAPHOR

Bring Your Words to Life

As you have probably noticed, I frequently use metaphors—the most useful way of making our abstractions concrete. The word is Greek for "transfer" *(meta* equals *trans* equals *across; phor* equals *fer* equals *ferry).* Metaphors illustrate our general ideas at a single stroke. Many of our common words are metaphors, *grasp* for "understanding," for instance, which compares the mind to something with hands, *transferring* the physical picture of the clutching hand to the invisible mental act.

Metaphor seems to work at about four levels, each with a different clarity and force. Suppose you wrote "he swelled and displayed his finery." You have transferred to a man the qualities of a peacock to make his appearance and personality vivid. You have chosen one of the four ways to make this transfer:

I. SIMILE:	**He was like a peacock.**
	He displayed himself as a peacock does.
	He displayed himself as if he were a peacock.
II. PLAIN METAPHOR:	**He was a peacock.**
III. IMPLIED METAPHOR:	**He swelled and displayed his finery.**
	He swelled and ruffled his plumage.
	He swelled, ruffling his plumage.
IV. DEAD METAPHOR:	**He strutted.**

I. Simile. The simile is the most obvious form the metaphor can take, and hence would seem elementary. But it has powers of its own, particularly where the writer seems to be trying urgently to express the inexpressible, comparing his subject to several different possibilities, no one wholly adequate. In *The Sound and the Fury,* Faulkner thus describes two jaybirds (my italics):

> **[they] whirled up on the blast *like gaudy scraps of cloth or paper* and lodged in the mulberries, . . . screaming into the wind that *ripped* their harsh cries onward and away *like scraps of paper or of cloth* in turn.**

The simile has a high poetic energy. D. H. Lawrence uses it frequently, as here in *The Plumed Serpent* (my italics):

> **The lake was quite black, *like a great pit.* The wind suddenly blew with violence, with a strange ripping sound in the mango trees, *as if some membrane in the air were being ripped.***

II. Plain Metaphor. The plain metaphor makes its comparison in one imaginative leap. It is shorthand for "as if he were a peacock"; it pretends, by exaggeration *(hyperbole),* that he *is* a peacock. We move instinctively to this kind of exaggerated comparison as we try to convey our impressions with all their emotional impact. "He was a maniac at Frisbee," we might say, or "a dynamo." The metaphor is probably our most common figure of speech: *the pigs, the swine, a plum, a gem, a phantom of delight, a shot* *in the arm.* It may be humorous or bitter; it may be simply and aptly visual: "The road was a ribbon of silver." Thoreau extends a metaphor through several sentences in one of his most famous passages:

> **Time is but a stream I go a-fishing in. I drink at it; but while I drink I see the sandy bottom and detect how shallow it is. Its thin current slides away, but eternity remains. I would drink deeper; fish in the sky, whose bottom is pebbly with stars.**

III. Implied Metaphor. The implied metaphor is even more widely used. It operates most often among the verbs, as in *swelled, displayed,* and *ruffled,* the verbs suggesting "peacock." Most ideas can suggest analogues of physical processes or natural history. Give your television system *tentacles* reaching into every home, and you have compared TV to an octopus, with all its lethal and wiry suggestions. You can have your school spirit *fall below zero,* and you have implied that your school spirit is like temperature, registered on a thermometer in a sudden chill. Malcolm Cowley writes metaphorically about Hawthorne's style, first in a direct simile *(like a footprint)* and then in a metaphor implying that phrases are people walking at different speeds:

> **He dreamed in words, while walking along the seashore or under the pines, till the words fitted themselves to his stride. The result was that his eighteenth-century English developed into a natural, a *walked,* style, with a phrase for every step and a comma after every phrase like a footprint in the sand. Sometimes the phrases hurry, sometimes they loiter, sometimes they march to drums.***

IV. Dead Metaphor. The art of resuscitation is the metaphorist's finest skill. It comes from liking words and paying attention to what they say. Simply add onto the dead metaphor enough implied metaphors to get the circulation going again: *He strutted, swelling and ruffling his plumage. He strutted* means by itself "walked in a pompous manner." By bringing the metaphor back to life, we keep the general meaning but also restore the physical picture of a peacock puffing up and spreading his feathers. We recognize

---

* *The Portable Hawthorne* (New York: Viking, 1948).

strut concretely and truly for the first time. We know the word, and we know the man. We have an image of him, a posture strongly suggestive of a peacock.

Perhaps the best dead metaphors to revive are those in proverbial clichés. See what Thoreau does (in his *Journal*) with *spur of the moment:*

> **I feel the spur of the moment thrust deep into my side. The present is an inexorable rider.**

Or again, when in *Walden* he speaks of wanting "to improve *the nick of time,* and notch it on my stick too," and of not being *thrown off the track* "by every nutshell and mosquito's wing that falls on the rails." In each case, he takes the proverbial phrase literally and physically, adding an attribute or two to bring the old metaphor back alive.

You can go too far, of course. Your metaphors can be too thick and vivid, and the obvious pun brings a howl of protest. I have myself advised scholars against metaphors because they are so often overworked and so often tangled in physical impossibilities, becoming "mixed" metaphors. "The violent population explosion has paved the way for new intellectual growth" looks pretty good—until you realize that explosions do not pave, and that new vegetation does not grow up through solid pavement. Changing *paved* to *cleared* would clear the confusion. The metaphor, then, is your most potent device. It makes your thought concrete and your writing vivid. It tells in an instant how your subject looks to you. But it is dangerous. It should be quiet, almost unnoticed, with all details agreeing, and all absolutely consistent with the natural universe.

ALLUSION

Illuminate the Dim with a Familiar Light

Allusions also illustrate your general idea by referring it to something else, making it take your reader as Grant took Richmond, making you the Mickey Mantle of the essay, or the Mickey Mouse.

Allusions depend on common knowledge. Like the metaphor, they illustrate the remote with the familiar—a familiar place, or event, or personage. "He looked . . . like a Japanese Humphrey Bogart," writes William Bittner of French author Albert Camus, and we instantly see a face like the one we know so well (a glance at Camus's picture confirms this allusion as surprisingly accurate). Perhaps the most effective allusions depend on a knowledge of literature. When Thoreau writes that "the winter of man's discontent was thawing as well as the earth," we get a secret pleasure from recognizing this as an allusive borrowing from the opening lines of Shakespeare's *Richard III:* "Now is the winter of our discontent / Made glorious summer by this sun of York." Thoreau flatters us by assuming we are as well read as he. We need not catch the allusion to enjoy his point, but if we catch it, we feel a sudden fellowship of knowledge with him. We now see the full metaphorical force, Thoreau's and Shakespeare's both, heightened as it is by our remembrance of Richard Crookback's twisted discontent, an allusive illustration of all our pitiful resentments now thawing with the spring.

Allusions can also be humorous. The hero of Peter De Vries's "The Vale of Laughter," alluding to Lot's wife looking back on Sodom (Gen. 19.26) as he contemplates adultery for a moment, decides on the path toward home and honor:

> **If you look back, you turn into a pillar of salt. If you look ahead, you turn into a pillar of society.**

DICTION

Reach for Both the High and the Low

"What we need is a mixed diction," said Aristotle, and his point remains true twenty-three centuries and several languages later. The aim of style, he says, is to be clear but distinguished. For clarity, we need common, current words; but, used alone, these are commonplace, and as ephemeral as everyday talk. For distinction, we need words not heard every minute, unusual words, large words, foreign words, metaphors; but, used alone, these become bogs, vapors, or at worst, gibberish. What we need is a diction that weds the popular with the dignified, the clear current with the sedgy margins of language and thought.

Not too low, not too high; not too simple, not too hard—an easy breadth of idea and vocabulary. English is peculiarly well endowed for this Aristotelian mixture. The long abstract Latin words and the short concrete Anglo-Saxon ones give you all the range you need. For most of your ideas, you can find Latin and Anglo-Saxon partners. In fact, for many ideas, you can find a whole spectrum of synonyms from Latin through French to Anglo-Saxon, from general to specific—from *intrepidity* to *fortitude* to *valor* to *courage* to *bravery* to *pluck* to *guts.* Each of these *denotes* or specifies the same thing: being brave. But each has a different *connotation,* or aura of meaning (see Glossary, 438). You can choose the high word for high effect, or you can get tough with Anglo-Saxon specifics. But you do not want all Anglo-Saxon, and you must especially guard against sobriety's luring you into all Latin. Tune your diction agreeably between the two extremes.

Indeed, the two extremes generate incomparable zip when tumbled side by side, as in *incomparable zip, inconsequential snip, megalomaniacal creep,* and the like. Rhythm and surprise conspire to set up the huge adjective first, then to add the small noun, like a monumental kick. Here is a passage from Edward Dahlberg's *Can These Bones Live,* which I opened completely at random to see how the large fell with the small (my italics):

> **Christ walks on a *visionary sea;* Myshkin . . . has his ecstatic premonition of infinity when he has an *epileptic fit.* We know the inward size of an artist by his *dimensional thirsts.* . . .**

This mixing of large Latin and small Anglo-Saxon, as John Crowe Ransom has noted, is what gives Shakespeare much of his power:

> **This my hand will rather**
> **The multitudinous seas incarnadine,**
> **Making the green one red.**

The short Anglo-Saxon *seas* works sharply between the two magnificent Latin words, as do the three short Anglo-Saxons that bring the big passage to rest, contrasting the Anglo-Saxon *red* with its big Latin kin, *incarnadine.* William Faulkner, who soaked himself in Shakespeare, gets much the same power from the same mixture. He is describing a very old Negro woman in *The Sound and the Fury* (the title itself comes from Shakespeare's *Macbeth,* the source of the *multitudinous seas* passage). She has been fat, but now she is wrinkled and completely shrunken except for her stomach:

> **. . . a paunch almost dropsical, as though muscle and tissue had been courage or fortitude which the days or the years had consumed until only the indomitable skeleton was left rising like a ruin or a landmark above the somnolent and impervious guts. . . .**

The impact of that short, ugly Anglo-Saxon word *guts,* with its slang metaphorical pun, is almost unbearably moving. And the impact would be nothing, the effect slurring, without the grand Latin preparation.

A good diction takes work. It exploits the natural, but does not come naturally. It demands a wary eye for the way meanings sprout, and it demands the courage to prune. It has the warmth of human concern. It is a cut above the commonplace, a cut above the inaccuracies and circumlocutions of speech, yet within easy reach. Clarity is the first aim; economy, the second; grace, the third; dignity, the fourth. Our writing should be a little strange, a little out of the ordinary, a little beautiful, with words and phrases not met every day but seeming as right and natural as grass. A good diction takes care and cultivation.

It can be overcultivated. It may seem to call attention to itself rather than to its subject. Suddenly we are aware of the writer at work, and a little too pleased with himself, reaching for the elegant cliché and the showy phrase. Some readers find this very fault with my own writing, though I do really try to saddle my maverick love of metaphor. If I strike you in this way, you can use me profitably as a bad example along with the following passage. I have italicized elements that individually may have a certain effectiveness, but that cumulatively become mannerism, as if the writer were watching himself gesture in a mirror. Some of his phrases are redundant; some are trite. Everything is somehow cozy and grandiose, and a little too nautical:

> ***There's*** **little excitement** ***ashore*** **when merchant ships from** ***faraway*** **India, Nationalist China, or Egypt** ***knife through*** **the** ***gentle swells*** **of Virginia's Hampton Roads. This** ***unconcern*** **may simply reflect the** ***nonchalance*** **of people who live by** ***one of the world's great seaports.*** **Or perhaps** ***it's just*** **that** ***folk*** **who** ***dwell*** **in the** ***home towns*** **of atomic submarines and Mercury astronauts are not likely to be impressed by a visiting freighter,** ***from however distant a realm. . . . Upstream a bit*** **and also** ***to port,*** **the mouth of the Elizabeth River leads to Portsmouth and a major naval shipyard.** ***To starboard lies*** **Hampton, where at Langley Air Force Base the National Aeronautics and Space Administration prepares to send a man** ***into the heavens.***

EXERCISES

1. *As a warmup, clear the preceding example of its overdone phrases.*

2. *Revise the following sentences to make them more vivid and distinct by replacing as many of the abstract terms as possible with concrete terms.*

1. For the better part of a year, he was without gainful employment.
2. Of the students who go to college outside their own state, seventy percent do not go back after completing their studies.
3. A sizable proportion of those people who use long-distance movers are large-corporation employees whose moving expenses are entirely underwritten by their companies.
4. His great-grandfather once ran successfully for high public office, but he never served because his opponent mortally wounded him in a duel with pistols.
5. There was a severe disturbance in Jackson prison one day in the spring —convicts, armed with makeshift weapons, took some of the prison personnel hostage.
6. Her husband had one extramarital relationship after another and finally disappeared with a hotel dining room employee in one of our larger midwestern cities.
7. Rejected by the military because of an impairment of his vision, Ernest became a journalist with a midwestern newspaper.
8. Disadvantaged people are often maltreated by the very social-service agencies ostensibly designed to help them.
9. The newspaper reported that a small foreign car had overturned on the expressway just north of town.
10. The new contract offers almost no change in the fringe-benefit package.

3. *Look up in your dictionary six of the Latin and Greek constituents listed below. Illustrate each with several English derivatives closely translated, as in these two examples:* con *(with)*—convince *(conquer with),* conclude *(shut with),* concur *(run with);* chron- *(time)*—chronic *(lasting a long time),* chronicle *(a record of the time),* chronometer *(time-measurer).*

LATIN: *a- (ab-), ad-, ante-, bene-, bi-, circum-, con-, contra-, di- (dis-), e- (ex-), in- (two meanings), inter-, intra-, mal-, multi-, ob-, per-, post-, pre-, pro-, retro-, semi-, sub- (sur-), super-, trans-, ultra-.*

GREEK: *a- (an-), -agogue, allo-, anthropo-, anti-, apo-, arch-, auto-, batho-, bio-, cata-, cephalo-, chron-, -cracy, demo-, dia-, dyna-, dys-, ecto-, epi-, eu-, -gen, geo-, -gon, -gony, graph-, gyn-, hemi-, hepta-, hetero-, hexa-, homo-, hydr-, hyper-, hypo-, log-, mega-, -meter, micro-, mono-, morph-, -nomy, -nym, -pathy, penta-, -phagy, phil-, -phobe (ia), -phone, poly-, pseudo-, psyche-, -scope, soph-, stereo-, sym- (syn-), tele-, tetra-, theo-, thermo-, tri-, zoo-.*

4. *Revise the following sentences so as to clear up the illogical or unnatural connections in their metaphors and similes.*

1. The violent population explosion has paved the way for new intellectual growth.
2. The book causes a shock, like a bucket of icy water suddenly thrown on a fire.
3. The whole social fabric will become unstuck.
4. The tangled web of Jack's business crumbled under its own weight.
5. His last week had mirrored his future, like a hand writing on the wall.
6. The recent economic picture, which seemed to spell prosperity, has wilted beyond repair.
7. They were tickled to death by the thunderous applause.
8. Stream of consciousness fiction has gone out of phase with the new castles in the air of fantasy.
9. The murmured protests drifted from the convention floor to the podium, cracking the façade of his imperturbability.
10. Richard was ecstatic with his success. He had scaled the mountain of difficulties and from here on out he could sail with the breeze.

5. *Write a sentence for each of the following dead metaphors, bringing it to life by adding implied metaphorical detail, as in "She* bridled, *snorting and tossing her mane," or by adding a simile, as in "He was* dead *wrong, laid out like a corpse on a slab."*

dead center, pinned down, sharp as a tack, stick to, whined, purred, reflected, ran for office, yawned, take a course.

6. *Write a sentence for each of the following, in which you allude either humorously or seriously to:*

1. A famous—or infamous—person (Caesar, Napoleon, Barnum, Lincoln, Stalin, Picasso, Bogart)
2. A famous event (the Declaration of Independence, the Battle of Waterloo, the landing on Plymouth Rock, the Battle of the Bulge, the signing of the Magna Carta, Custer's Last Stand, the Watergate break-in)
3. A notable place (Athens, Rome, Paris, London Bridge, Jerusalem, the Vatican)
4. This famous passage from Shakespeare, by quietly borrowing some of its phrases:

> To be, or not to be—that is the question:
> Whether 'tis nobler in the mind to suffer
> The slings and arrows of outrageous fortune,
> Or to take arms against a sea of troubles,
> And by opposing end them.

7. *Write a paragraph in which you mix your diction as effectively as you can, with the big Latin word and the little Anglo-Saxon, the formal word and just the right touch of slang, working in at least two combinations of the extremes, on the pattern of* multitudinous seas, diversionary thrust, incomparable zip, *underlining these for your instructor's convenience.*

8. *Write a* TERRIBLE ESSAY. *Have some fun with this perennial favorite, in which you reinforce your sense for clear, figurative, and meaningful words by writing the muddiest and wordiest essay you can invent, gloriously working out all your bad habits. Organize in the usual way, with a thesis, a good beginning, middle, and end, but parody the worst kind of sociological and bureaucratic prose. Here are the rules:*

1. Put EVERYTHING in the passive voice.
2. Modify nouns *only* with nouns, preferably in strings of three or four, never with adjectives. *governmental spending* becomes *government level spending;* an *excellent idea* becomes *quality program concept.*
3. Use only big abstract nouns—as many *-tion*'s as possible.
4. Use no participles: not *dripping faucets* but *faucets which drip;* and use as many *which*'s as possible.
5. Use as many words as possible to say the least.
6. Work in as many trite and wordy expressions as possible: *needless to say, all things being equal, due to the fact that, in terms of, as far as that is concerned.*
7. Sprinkle heavily with *-wise*-type and *type*-type expressions, and say *hopefully* every three or four sentences.

8. Compile and use a basic terrible vocabulary: *situation, aspect, function, factor, phase, process, procedure, utilize, the use of,* and so on. The class may well cooperate in this.

9. *Refine your sense of diction and meanings still further by writing an* IRONIC ESSAY, *saying the opposite of what you mean, as in "The party was a dazzling success," "The Rockheads are the solidest group in town," "Our team is the best in the West."*

Readings

The power of the word is aptly demonstrated by the four writers in this section. Using the rhetorical power of abstraction yet pinning their abstractions down to specifics, they clothe their ideas in words that give their writing clarity, economy, grace, and dignity. Good diction takes care and cultivation, and William Zinsser alerts his readers to the verbal weeds that can sprout overnight. Richard Selzer wields words as deftly as he does his scalpel as he explains why a surgeon wants to write. In lucid, measured prose that exhibits the classical virtues of harmony, balance, and elegance, George Will skewers the followers of astrology. Finally, in an essay as applicable today as when it was written in 1946, George Orwell laments the decline of clarity and honesty in language.

WILLIAM ZINSSER

Clutter

1 Fighting clutter is like fighting weeds—the writer is always slightly behind. New varieties sprout overnight, and by noon they are part of American speech. It only takes a John Dean testifying on TV to have everyone in the country saying "at this point in time" instead of "now."

2 Consider all the prepositions that are routinely draped onto verbs that don't need any help. Head up. Free up. Face up to. We no longer head committees. We head them up. We don't face problems anymore. We face up to them when we can free up a

few minutes. A small detail, you may say—not worth bothering about. It *is* worth bothering about. The game is won or lost on hundreds of small details. Writing improves in direct ratio to the number of things we can keep out of it that shouldn't be there. "Up," in "free up," shouldn't be there. It's not only unnecessary; it's silly. Can we picture anything being freed *up*? The writer of clean English must examine every word that he puts on paper. He will find a surprising number that don't serve any purpose.

3 Take the adjective "personal," as in "a personal friend of mine," "his personal feeling," or "her personal physician." It is typical of the words that can be eliminated nine times out of ten. The personal friend has come into the language to distinguish him from the business friend, thereby debasing not only language but friendship. Someone's feeling *is* his personal feeling—that's what "his" means. As for the personal physician, he is that man so often summoned to the dressing room of a stricken actress so that she won't have to be treated by the impersonal physician assigned to the theater. Someday I'd like to see him identified as "her doctor."

4 Or take those curious intervals of time like the short minute. "Twenty-two short minutes later she had won the final set." Minutes are minutes, physicians are physicians, friends are friends. The rest is clutter.

5 Clutter is the laborious phrase which has pushed out the short word that means the same thing. These locutions are a drag on energy and momentum. Even before John Dean gave us "at this point in time," people had stopped saying "now." They were saying "at the present time," or "currently," or "presently" (which means "soon"). Yet the idea can always be expressed by "now" to mean the immediate moment ("now I can see him"), or by "today" to mean the historical present ("today prices are high"), or simply by the verb "to be" ("it is raining"). There is no need to say "at the present time we are experiencing precipitation."

6 Speaking of which, we are experiencing considerable difficulty getting *that* word out of the language now that it has lumbered in. Even your dentist will ask if you are experiencing any pain. If he were asking one of his own children he would say, "Does it hurt?" He would, in short, be himself. By using a more pompous phrase in his professional role he not only sounds more important; he blunts the painful edge of truth. It is the language of the airline stewardess demonstrating the oxygen mask that will

drop down if the plane should somehow run out of air. "In the extremely unlikely possibility that the aircraft should experience such an eventuality," she begins—a phrase so oxygen-depriving in itself that we are prepared for any disaster, and even gasping death shall lose its sting.

7 Clutter is the ponderous euphemism that turns a slum into a depressed socioeconomic area, a salesman into a marketing representative, a dumb kid into an underachiever and a bad kid into a pre-delinquent. (The Albuquerque public schools announced a program for "delinquent and pre-delinquent boys.")

8 Clutter is the official language used by the American corporation—in the news release and the annual report—to hide its mistakes. When a big company recently announced that it was "decentralizing its organizational structure into major profit-centered businesses" and that "corporate staff services will be aligned under two senior vice-presidents" it meant that it had had a lousy year.

9 Clutter is the language of the interoffice memo ("the trend to mosaic communication is reducing the meaningfulness of concern about whether or not demographic segments differ in their tolerance of periodicity") and the language of computers ("we are offering functional digital programming options that have built in parallel reciprocal capabilities with compatible third generation contingencies and hardware").

10 Clutter is the language of the Pentagon throwing dust in the eyes of the populace by calling an invasion a "reinforced protective reaction strike" and by justifying its vast budgets on the need for "credible second-strike capability" and "counterforce deterrence." How can we grasp such vaporous doubletalk? As George Orwell pointed out in "Politics and the English Language," an essay written thirty years ago but cited with amazing frequency during the Vietnam years of Johnson and Nixon, "In our time, political speech and writing are largely the defense of the indefensible. . . . Thus political language has to consist largely of euphemism, question-begging, and sheer cloudy vagueness." Orwell's warning that clutter is not just a nuisance but a deadly tool did not turn out to be inoperative. By the 1960's his words had come true in America.

11 I could go on quoting examples from various fields—every profession has its growing arsenal of jargon to fire at the layman and hurl him back from its walls. Recently I received a brochure

from a foundation which used the verb "potentialize." But the list would be depressing and the lesson tedious. The point of raising it now is to serve notice that clutter is the enemy, whatever form it takes. It slows the reader and robs the writer of his personality, making him seem pretentious.

12 Beware, then, of the long word that is no better than the short word: "numerous" (many), "facilitate" (ease), "individual" (man or woman), "remainder" (rest), "initial" (first), "implement" (do), "sufficient" (enough), "attempt" (try), "referred to as" (called), and hundreds more. Beware, too, of all the slippery new fad words for which the language already has equivalents: overview and quantify, optimize and maximize, parameter and interpersonal, input and throughput, peer group and paradigm, public sector and private sector. Avoid trendy words like "trendy." They are all weeds that will smother what you write.

13 Nor are all the weeds as obvious as these. Once alerted, anybody can see that compatible third-generation contingencies and reinforced protective reaction strikes are heavy weights to attach to any sentence. More insidious are the little growths of perfectly ordinary words with which we explain how we propose to go about our explaining, or which inflate a simple preposition or conjunction into a whole windy phrase.

14 "I might add," "It should be pointed out," "It is interesting to note that"—how many sentences begin with these dreary clauses announcing what the writer is going to do next? If you might add, add it. If it should be pointed out, point it out. If it is interesting to note, *make* it interesting. Being told that something is interesting is the surest way of tempting the reader to find it dull; are we not all stupefied by what follows when someone says, "This will interest you"? As for the inflated prepositions and conjunctions, they are the innumerable phrases like "with the possible exception of" (except), "for the reason that" (because), "he totally lacked the ability to" (he couldn't), "she was unable to give any information beyond the fact that" (she said).

15 Clutter takes more forms than you can shake twenty sticks at. Prune it ruthlessly. Be grateful for everything that you can throw away. Re-examine each sentence that you put on paper. Is every word doing new and useful work? Can any thought be expressed with more economy? Is anything pompous or pretentious or faddish? Are you hanging on to something useless just because you think it's beautiful? Remember Thoreau:

> Our life is frittered away by detail. . . . Instead of a million count half-a-dozen, and keep your accounts on your thumb-nail. . . . Let us spend one day as deliberately as Nature and not be thrown off the track by every nutshell and mosquito's wing that falls on the rails.

16 Simplify, simplify.

Suggestions for Discussion and Writing

1. What simile does Zinsser introduce in his opening paragraph? Why is it apt? Does he sustain it throughout his essay?
2. Zinsser gives examples of clutter in paragraph 7. Add additional examples that you have read or heard.
3. In general, why are most people wordy in their speech but more economical in their written language?
4. What gives paragraphs 7–10 their unity?
5. If you disagree with Zinsser with regard to any term he attacks, write an essay defending the word. You may believe, for example, that *to free up* conveys a meaning distinct from *to free.* As you write, make certain that none of your sentences or paragraphs becomes overrun with clutter.

RICHARD SELZER

The Art of Surgery

1 Someone asked me why a surgeon would write. Why, when the shelves are already too full? They sag under the deadweight of books. To add a single adverb is to risk exceeding the strength of the boards. A surgeon should abstain. A surgeon, whose fingers are more at home in the steamy gulleys of the body than they are tapping the dry keys of a typewriter. A surgeon, who feels the slow slide of intestines against the back of his hand and is no more alarmed than were a family of snakes taking their comfort from such an indolent rubbing. A surgeon, who palms the human heart as though it were some captured bird.

2 Why should he write? Is it vanity that urges him? There is glory enough in the knife. Is it for money? One can make too much money. No. It is to search for some meaning in the ritual of surgery, which is at once murderous, painful, healing, and full of love. It is a devilish hard thing to transmit—to find, even. Perhaps if one were to cut out a heart, a lobe of the liver, a single convolution of the brain, and paste it to a page, it would speak with more eloquence than all the words of Balzac. Such a piece would need no literary style, no mass of erudition or history, but in its very shape and feel would tell all the frailty and strength, the despair and nobility of man. What? Publish a heart? A little piece of bone? Preposterous. Still I fear that is what it may require to reveal the truth that lies hidden in the body. Not all the undressings of Rabelais, Chekhov, or even William Carlos Williams have wrested it free, although God knows each one of those doctors made a heroic assault upon it.

3 I have come to believe that it is the flesh alone that counts. The rest is that with which we distract ourselves when we are not hungry or cold, in pain or ecstasy. In the recesses of the body I search for the philosophers' stone. I know it is there, hidden in the deepest, dampest cul-de-sac. It awaits discovery. To find it would be like the harnessing of fire. It would illuminate the world. Such a quest is not without pain. Who can gaze on so much misery and feel no hurt? Emerson has written that the poet is the only true doctor. I believe him, for the poet, lacking the impediment of speech with which the rest of us are afflicted, gazes, records, diagnoses, and prophesies.

4 I invited a young diabetic woman to the operating room to amputate her leg. She could not see the great shaggy black ulcer upon her foot and ankle that threatened to encroach upon the rest of her body, for she was blind as well. There upon her foot was a Mississippi Delta brimming with corruption, sending its raw tributaries down between her toes. Gone were all the little web spaces that when fresh and whole are such a delight to loving men. She could not see her wound, but she could feel it. There is no pain like that of the bloodless limb turned rotten and festering. There is neither unguent nor anodyne to kill such a pain yet leave intact the body.

5 For over a year I trimmed away the putrid flesh, cleansed, anointed, and dressed the foot, staving off, delaying. Three times each week, in her darkness, she sat upon my table, rocking back

and forth, holding her extended leg by the thigh, gripping it as though it were a rocket that must be steadied lest it explode and scatter her toes about the room. And I would cut away a bit here, a bit there, of the swollen blue leather that was her tissue.

6 At last we gave up, she and I. We could no longer run ahead of the gangrene. We had not the legs for it. There must be an amputation in order that she might live—and I as well. It was to heal us both that I must take up knife and saw, and cut it off. And when I could feel it drop from her body to the table, see the blessed *space* appear between her and that leg, I too would be well.

7 Now it is the day of the operation. I stand by while the anesthetist administers the drugs, watch as the tense familiar body relaxes into narcosis. I turn then to uncover the leg. There, upon her kneecap, she has drawn, blindly, upside down for me to see, a face; just a circle with two ears, two eyes, a nose, and a smiling upturned mouth. Under it she has printed SMILE, DOCTOR. Minutes later I listen to the sound of the saw, until a little crack at the end tells me it is done.

8 So I have learned that man is not ugly, but that he is Beauty itself. There is no other his equal. Are we not all dying, none faster or more slowly than any other? I have become receptive to the possibilities of love (for it is love, this thing that happens in the operating room), and each day I wait, trembling in the busy air. Perhaps today it will come. Perhaps today I will find it, take part in it, this love that blooms in the stoniest desert.

9 All through literature the doctor is portrayed as a figure of fun. Shaw was splenetic about him; Molière delighted in pricking his pompous medicine men, and well they deserved it. The doctor is ripe for caricature. But I believe that the truly great writing about doctors has not yet been done. I think it must be done *by* a doctor, one who is through with the love affair with his technique, who recognizes that he has played Narcissus, raining kisses on a mirror, and who now, out of the impacted masses of his guilt, has expanded into self-doubt, and finally into the high state of wonderment. Perhaps he will be a nonbeliever who, after a lifetime of grand gestures and mighty deeds, comes upon the knowledge that he has done no more than meddle in the lives of his fellows, and that he has done at least as much harm as good. Yet he may continue to pretend, at least, that there is nothing to fear, that death will not come, so long as people ask it of him.

Later, after his patients have left, he may closet himself in his darkened office, sweating and afraid.

10 A writing doctor would treat men and women with equal reverence. For what is the "liberation" of either sex to him who knows the diagrams, the inner geographies of each? I love the solid heft of men as much as I adore the heated capaciousness of women—women in whose penetralia is found the repository of existence. I would have them glory in that. Women are physics and chemistry. They are matter. It is their bodies that inform of the frailty of men. We have not their cellular, enzymatic wisdom. Man is albuminoid, proteinaceous, laked pearl; woman is yolky, ovoid, rich. Both are exuberant bloody growths. I would use the defects and deformities of each for my sacred purpose of writing, for I know that it is the marred and scarred and faulty that are subject to grace. I would seek the soul in the facts of animal economy and profligacy. Yes, it is the exact location of the soul that I am after. The smell of it is in my nostrils. I have caught glimpses of it in the body diseased. If only I could tell it. Is there no mathematical equation that can guide me? So much pain and pus equals so much truth? It is elusive as the whippoorwill that one hears calling incessantly from out the night window, but which, nesting as it does low in the brush, no one sees. No one but the poet, for he sees what no one else can. He was born with the eye for it.

11 Once I thought I had it: Ten o'clock, one night; the end room off a long corridor in a college infirmary; my last patient of the day; degree of exhaustion suitable for the appearance of a vision, some manifestation. The patient is a young man recently returned from Guatemala, from the excavation of Mayan ruins. His left upper arm wears a gauze dressing which, when removed, reveals a clean punched-out hole the size of a dime. The tissues about the opening are swollen and tense. A thin brownish fluid lips the edge, and now and then a lazy drop of the overflow spills down the arm. An abscess, inadequately drained. I will enlarge the opening to allow better egress of the pus. Nurse, will you get me a scalpel and some . . .

12 What happens next is enough to lay Francis Drake avomit in his cabin. No explorer ever stared in wilder surmise than I into that crater from which there now emerges a narrow gray head whose sole distinguishing feature is a pair of black pincers. The head sits atop a longish flexible neck arching now this way, now

that, testing the air. Alternately it folds back upon itself, then advances in new boldness. And all the while, with dreadful rhythmicity, the unspeakable pincers open and close. Abscess? Pus? Never. Here is the lair of a beast at whose malignant purpose I could but guess. A Mayan devil, I think, that would soon burst free to fly about the room, with horrid blanket-wings and iridescent scales, raking, pinching, injecting God knows what acid juice. And even now the irony does not escape me, the irony of my patient as excavator excavated.

13 With all the ritual deliberation of a high priest I advance a surgical clamp toward the hole. The surgeon's heart is becoming a bat hanging upside down from his rib cage. The rim achieved—now thrust—and the ratchets of the clamp close upon the empty air. The devil has retracted. Evil mocking laughter bangs back and forth in the brain. More stealth. Lying in wait. One must skulk. Minutes pass, perhaps an hour. . . . A faint disturbance in the lake, and once again the thing upraises, further and further, hovering. Acrouch, strung, the surgeon is one with his instrument; there is no longer any boundary between its metal and his flesh. They are joined in a single perfect tool of extirpation. It is just for this that he was born. Now—thrust—and clamp—and yes. Got him!

14 Transmitted to the fingers comes the wild thrashing of the creature. Pinned and wriggling, he is mine. I hear the dry brittle scream of the dragon, and a hatred seizes me, but such a detestation as would make of Iago a drooling sucktit. It is the demented hatred of the victor for the vanquished, the warden for his prisoner. It is the hatred of fear. Within the jaws of my hemostat is the whole of the evil of the world, the dark concentrate itself, and I shall kill it. For mankind. And, in so doing, will open the way into a thousand years of perfect peace. Here is Surgeon as Savior indeed.

15 Tight grip now . . . steady, relentless pull. How it scrabbles to keep its tentacle-hold. With an abrupt moist plop the extraction is complete. There, writhing in the teeth of the clamp, is a dirty gray body, the size and shape of an English walnut. He is hung everywhere with tiny black hooklets. Quickly . . . into the specimen jar of saline . . . the lid screwed tight. Crazily he swims round and round, wiping his slimy head against the glass, then slowly sinks to the bottom, the mass of hooks in frantic agonal wave.

16 "You are going to be all right," I say to my patient. "We are *all* going to be all right from now on."

17 The next day I take the jar to the medical school. "That's the larva of the warble fly," says a pathologist. "The fly usually bites a cow, and deposits its eggs beneath the skin. There, the egg develops into the larval form which, when ready, burrows its way to the outside through the hide, and falls to the ground. In time it matures into a full-grown warble fly. This one happened to bite a man. It was about to come out on its own, and, of course, it would have died."

18 The words *imposter, sorehead, servant of Satan* spring to my lips. But now he has been joined by other scientists. They nod in agreement. I gaze from one gray eminence to another, and know the mallet-blow of glory pulverized. I tried to save the world, but it didn't work out.

19 No, it is not the surgeon who is God's darling. He is the victim of vanity. It is the poet who heals with his words, stanches the flow of blood, stills the rattling breath, applies poultice to the scalded flesh.

20 Did you ask me why a surgeon writes? I think it is because I wish to be a doctor.

Suggestions for Discussion and Writing

1. As Chapter 1 of this book points out (page 1), writing helps us catch our ideas and realize our thoughts. What is Selzer trying to discover about himself in his essay? Does he find it?
2. What does Selzer mean when he says, "[I]t is the flesh alone that counts"? What does the body become a symbol for? Relate this idea to paragraph 8 ("for it is love, this thing that happens in the operating room").
3. Selzer admits that the doctor is caricatured in literature. What is there about the profession that makes the doctor a ripe target?
4. Why would a doctor experience "impacted masses of . . . guilt" (paragraph 9)? Is this an indictment of the medical profession, or a testimony to its sensitivity?
5. The description of the operation in paragraphs 11–15 is gruesome, even gross. What was Selzer's intention in presenting such graphic details? What do the operation, the patient, and the larva symbolize?

6. Explain how the allusions to Francis Drake (paragraph 12) and Iago (paragraph 14) are appropriate.
7. How does the tone of the pathologist's explanation in paragraph 17 differ from the tone in the preceding paragraphs? What deliberate contrast is Selzer trying to establish?
8. Selzer's word choice establishes his tone early in the essay. Notice, for example, the sinister use of "invited" in the first sentence of paragraph 4, "the steamy gulleys of the body" and "the slow slide of intestines" in paragraph 1. Find other examples of specific diction that support the tone and mood of this piece.
9. Write an essay in which you explain to your reader (and to yourself) why you do something: why you play the guitar, enjoy photography, or ride a motorcycle. To illuminate your ideas, dramatize specific moments or events in carefully chosen words.

GEORGE F. WILL

The Astrological Impulse

1 Some intergalactically famous scientists, including eighteen Nobel laureates, have directed some delicate railery against the nonsense called astrology:

2 "It is simply a mistake to imagine that the forces exerted by stars and planets at the moment of birth can in any way shape our futures. Neither is it true that the position of distant heavenly bodies make certain days or periods more favorable to particular kinds of action, or that the sign under which one was born determines one's compatibility or incompatibility with other people."

3 That astrology is preposterous is, of course, obvious to everyone except people with stupendous capacities for the willful suspension of disbelief. But such people are not apt to pay attention to what real scientists say.

4 "One would imagine," say the scientists from the depth of their innocence, "in this day of widespread enlightenment and education, that it would be unnecessary to debunk beliefs based

on magic and superstition." But there is a telling tension between the scientists' belief that enlightenment is widespread, and their correct assessment that "acceptance of astrology pervades modern society" and contributes "to the growth of irrationalism and obscurantism." Actually, the fact that astrology is a huge and high-growth industry says something unflattering about human beings, and about our times.

5 There is an instinct, implanted deep in the human constitution: when people feel or want to feel intimations of immortality, they look up, beyond Gothic spires, beyond mountain tops, to the stars which seem, unlike people, timeless and autonomous. Astrology is a manifestation of that instinct.

6 Some people just must believe that the celestial order they think they see has some mysterious significance, and involves some overmastering intention that involves them. Of course there is more than a little vanity in the notion that we wee creatures are somehow connected to those heavenly bodies. This is a way of sneaking in through the back door a belief expelled through the front door in the sixteenth century—the belief that we are the center of a caring universe.

7 As the science of astronomy matured, we learned that the stars are not all that orderly and timelessness. Indeed, there is a lot of wobbling and banging around in the infinitesimal fraction of the universe we observe. We know more about the heavens than the Babylonians did when preparing their star charts, and we know that the heavens are as susceptible to change as is (*pace* Kant) the moral law.

8 Astrology has a distant, parasitic relationship with perhaps the most beautiful science, astronomy. Astronomy has helped kill the parasite, at least among people open to evidence. But astrology lives on as a specious psychology, enabling people to classify themselves, for whatever pleasure that brings them.

9 Astrology is the sort of anti-intellectual intellectuality that flourishes in an unsettled age, especially among people foreign to learning but respectful, after a fashion, of what they fancy is learning. Especially since the early 1960's, the world has become a strange place to many Americans who sense a new and distressing unpredictability. Before then it was—or at least they liked to think it was—possible to know the kind of world that was just over the horizon of the future. Astrology bestows on its believers a

sense of being not quite completely adrift on turbulent seas. It is odd but true that many people find it soothing to believe that they are under the predictable sway of stars.

10 Astrology is as old as the hills, but is, in its bizarre fashion, in tune with a major theme of modernist thought. The giants among the makers of the modern mind—Darwin, Marx, Freud—differed on many things, but not on this theme: human beings are subject to common forces. To the extent that people today believe that knowledge is power, it is because they think knowledge enables them to elude or at least swim with those forces, whatever they are. Astrology is an attempt at such powerful knowledge.

11 The distressed scientists insist, "We must all face the world, and we must realize that our futures lie in ourselves, and not in the stars." But there is no "must" about it.

[September 17, 1975]

Suggestions for Discussion and Writing

1. According to Will, why do so many people believe in astrology? What is the pleasure that it brings to its followers?
2. How do you know from the tone of the first paragraph that Will is having a bit of fun?
3. How was "the belief that we are the center of a caring universe" (paragraph 6) expelled "through the front door in the sixteenth century"? What historical or scientific event is Will alluding to? Do some people still cling to the belief?
4. How does Will link astrology with Darwin, Marx, and Freud? What did each of these thinkers believe about man?
5. Will's dominant tone is that of detached amusement. Find sentences that convey this impression.
6. Comment on Will's use of slang and standard English. Is it effective, or does it detract from his essay?
7. Explain the last sentence in Will's essay.
8. Select a widespread belief that you regard as quackery, and write an essay debunking it. Avoid sarcasm and heavy-handed arguments; instead, try to show your reader how silly the idea is. Aim for variety in the length and structure of your sentences.

GEORGE ORWELL

Politics and the English Language

1 Most people who bother with the matter at all would admit that the English language is in a bad way, but it is generally assumed that we cannot by conscious action do anything about it. Our civilization is decadent and our language—so the argument runs—must inevitably share in the general collapse. It follows that any struggle against the abuse of language is a sentimental archaism, like preferring candles to electric light or hansom cabs to aeroplanes. Underneath this lies the half-conscious belief that language is a natural growth and not an instrument which we shape for our own purpose.

2 Now, it is clear that the decline of a language must ultimately have political and economic causes: it is not due simply to the bad influence of this or that individual writer. But an effect can become a cause, reinforcing the original cause and producing the same effect in an intensified form, and so on indefinitely. A man may take to drink because he feels himself to be a failure, and then fail all the more completely because he drinks. It is rather the same thing that is happening to the English language. It becomes ugly and inaccurate because our thoughts are foolish, but the slovenliness of our language makes it easier for us to have foolish thoughts. The point is that the process is reversible. Modern English, especially written English, is full of bad habits which spread by imitation and which can be avoided if one is willing to take the necessary trouble. If one gets rid of these habits, one can think more clearly, and to think clearly is a necessary first step towards political regeneration: so that the fight against bad English is not frivolous and is not the exclusive concern of professional writers. I will come back to this presently, and I hope that by that time the meaning of what I have said here will have become clearer. Meanwhile, here are five specimens of the English language as it is now habitually written.

3 These five passages have not been picked out because they

are especially bad—I could have quoted far worse if I had chosen—but because they illustrate various of the mental vices from which we now suffer. They are a little below the average, but are fairly representative samples. I number them so that I can refer back to them when necessary:

(1) I am not, indeed, sure whether it is not true to say that the Milton who once seemed not unlike a seventeenth-century Shelley had not become, out of an experience ever more bitter in each year, more alien [*sic*] to the founder of that Jesuit sect which nothing could induce him to tolerate.

Professor Harold Laski (Essay in *Freedom of Expression*)

(2) Above all, we cannot play ducks and drakes with a native battery of idioms which prescribes such egregious collocations of vocables as the Basic *put up with* for *tolerate* or *put at a loss* for *bewilder.*

Professor Lancelot Hogben *(Interglossa).*

(3) On the one side we have the free personality: by definition it is not neurotic, for it has neither conflict nor dream. Its desires, such as they are, are transparent, for they are just what institutional approval keeps in the forefront of consciousness; another institutional pattern would alter their number and intensity; there is little in them that is natural, irreducible, or culturally dangerous. But *on the other side,* the social bond itself is nothing but the mutual reflection of these self-secure integrities. Recall the definition of love. Is not this the very picture of a small academic? Where is there a place in this hall of mirrors for either personality or fraternity?

Essay on psychology in *Politics* (New York)

(4) All the "best people" from the gentlemen's clubs, and all the frantic fascist captains, united in common hatred of Socialism and bestial horror of the rising tide of the mass revolutionary movement, have turned to acts of provocation, to foul incendiarism, to medieval legends of poisoned wells, to legalize their own destruction of proletarian organizations, and rouse the agitated petty-bourgeoisie to chauvinistic fervor on behalf of the fight against the revolutionary way out of the crisis.

Communist pamphlet

(5) If a new spirit *is* to be infused into this old country, there is one thorny and contentious reform which must be tackled, and that is the humanization and galvanization of the B.B.C. Timidity here will bespeak cancer and atrophy of the soul. The heart of Britain may be sound and of strong beat, for instance, but the British lion's roar at present is like that of Bottom in Shakespeare's *Midsummer Night's Dream*—as gentle as any sucking dove. A virile new Britain cannot continue indefinitely to be traduced in the eyes or rather ears, of the world by the effete languors of Langham Place, brazenly masquerading as "standard English." When the Voice of Britain is heard at nine o'clock, better far and infinitely less ludicrous to hear aitches honestly dropped than the present priggish, inflated, inhibited, school-ma'amish arch braying of blameless bashful mewing maidens!

Letter in *Tribune*

4 Each of these passages has faults of its own, but, quite apart from avoidable ugliness, two qualities are common to all of them. The first is staleness of imagery; the other is lack of precision. The writer either has a meaning and cannot express it, or he inadvertently says something else, or he is almost indifferent as to whether his words mean anything or not. The mixture of vagueness and sheer incompetence is the most marked characteristic of modern English prose, and especially of any kind of political writing. As soon as certain topics are raised, the concrete melts into the abstract and no one seems to think of turns of speech that are not hackneyed: prose consists less and less of *words* chosen for the sake of their meaning, and more and more of *phrases* tacked together like the sections of a prefabricated henhouse. I list below, with notes and examples, various of the tricks by means of which the work of prose-construction is habitually dodged:

DYING METAPHORS

5 A newly invented metaphor assists thought by evoking a visual image, while on the other hand a metaphor which is technically "dead" (e.g., *iron resolution*) has in effect reverted to being an ordinary word and can generally be used without loss of vivid-

ness. But in between these two classes there is a huge dump of worn-out metaphors which have lost all evocative power and are merely used because they save people the trouble of inventing phrases for themselves. Examples are: *ring the changes on, take up the cudgels for, toe the line, ride roughshod over, stand shoulder to shoulder with, play into the hands of, no axe to grind, grist to the mill, fishing in troubled waters, on the order of the day, Achilles' heel, swan song, hotbed.* Many of these are used without knowledge of their meaning (what is a "rift," for instance?), and incompatible metaphors are frequently mixed, a sure sign that the writer is not interested in what he is saying. Some metaphors now current have been twisted out of their original meaning without those who use them even being aware of the fact. For example, *toe the line* is sometimes written *tow the line.* Another example is *the hammer and the anvil,* now always used with the implication that the anvil gets the worst of it. In real life it is always the anvil that breaks the hammer, never the other way about: a writer who stopped to think what he was saying would be aware of this, and would avoid perverting the original phrase.

OPERATORS OR VERBAL FALSE LIMBS

6 These save the trouble of picking out appropriate verbs and nouns, and at the same time pad each sentence with extra syllables which give it an appearance of symmetry. Characteristic phrases are: *render inoperative, militate against, make contact with, be subjected to, give rise to, give grounds for, have the effect of, play a leading part (role) in, make itself felt, take effect, exhibit a tendency to, serve the purpose of, etc., etc.* The keynote is the elimination of simple verbs. Instead of being a single word, such as *break, stop, spoil, mend, kill,* a verb becomes a *phrase,* made up of a noun or adjective tacked on to some generalpurpose verb such as *prove, serve, form, play, render.* In addition, the passive voice is wherever possible used in preference to the active, and noun constructions are used instead of gerunds *(by examination of* instead of *by examining).* The range of verbs is further cut down by means of the *-ize* and *de-* formation, and the banal statements are given an appearance of profundity by means of the *not un-* formation. Simple conjunctions and prepositions are replaced by such phrases as *with respect to,*

having regard to, the fact that, by dint of, in view of, in the interests of, on the hypothesis that; and the ends of sentences are saved from anticlimax by such resounding commonplaces as *greatly to be desired, cannot be left out of account, a development to be expected in the near future, deserving of serious consideration, brought to a satisfactory conclusion,* and so on and so forth.

PRETENTIOUS DICTION

7 Words like *phenomenon, element, individual* (as noun), *objective, categorical, effective, virtual, basic, primary, promote, constitute, exhibit, exploit, utilize, eliminate, liquidate,* are used to dress up simple statements and give an air of scientific impartiality to biased judgments. Adjectives like *epoch-making, epic, historic, unforgettable, triumphant, age-old, inevitable, inexorable, veritable,* are used to dignify the sordid processes of international politics, while writing that aims at glorifying war usually takes on an archaic color, its characteristic words being: *realm, throne, chariot, mailed fist, trident, sword, shield, buckler, banner, jackboot, clarion.* Foreign words and expressions such as *cul de sac, ancien régime, deus ex machina, mutatis mutandis, status quo, gleichshaltung, weltanschauung,* are used to give an air of culture and elegance. Except for the useful abbreviations *i.e., e.g.,* and *etc.,* there is no real need for any of the hundreds of foreign phrases now current in English. Bad writers, and especially scientific, political, and sociological writers, are nearly always haunted by the notion that Latin or Greek words are grander than Saxon ones, and unnecessary words like *expedite, ameliorate, predict, extraneous, deracinated, clandestine, subaqueous* and hundreds of others constantly gain ground from their Anglo-Saxon opposite numbers. The jargon peculiar to Marxist writing (*hyena, hangman, cannibal, petty bourgeois, these gentry, lacquey, flunkey, mad dog, White Guard,* etc.) consists largely of words and phrases translated from Russian, German, or French; but the normal way of coining a new word is to use a Latin or Greek root with the appropriate affix and, where necessary, the *-ize* formation. It is often easier to make up words of this kind (*deregionalize, impermissible, extramarital, nonfragmentatory*, and so forth) than to think up the English words that will cover one's meaning. The result, in general, is an increase in slovenliness and vagueness.

MEANINGLESS WORDS

8 In certain kinds of writing, particularly in art criticism and literary criticism, it is normal to come across long passages which are almost completely lacking in meaning. Words like *romantic, plastic, values, human, dead, sentimental, natural, vitality,* as used in art criticism, are strictly meaningless in the sense that they not only do not point to any discoverable object, but are hardly ever expected to do so by the reader. When one critic writes, "The outstanding feature of Mr. X's work is its living quality," while another writes, "The immediately striking thing about Mr. X's work is its peculiar deadness," the reader accepts this as a simple difference of opinion. If words like *black* and *white* were involved, instead of the jargon words *dead* and *living,* he would see at once that language was being used in an improper way. Many political words are similarly abused. The word *Fascism* has now no meaning except in so far as it signifies "something not desirable." The words *democracy, socialism, freedom, patriotic, realistic, justice,* have each of them several different meanings which cannot be reconciled with one another. In the case of a word like *democracy,* not only is there no agreed definition, but the attempt to make one is resisted from all sides. It is almost universally felt that when we call a country democratic we are praising it: consequently the defenders of every kind of régime claim that it is a democracy, and fear that they might have to stop using the word if it were tied down to any one meaning. Words of this kind are often used in a consciously dishonest way. That is, the person who uses them has his own private definition, but allows his hearer to think he means something quite different. Statements like *Marshal Pétain was a true patriot, The Soviet Press is the freest in the world, The Catholic Church is opposed to persecution,* are almost always made with intent to deceive. Other words used in variable meanings, in most cases more or less dishonestly, are: *class, totalitarian, science, progressive, reactionary, bourgeois, equality.*

9 Now that I have made this catalogue of swindles and perversions, let me give another example of the kind of writing that they lead to. This time it must of its nature be an imaginary one. I am going to translate a passage of good English into modern English of the worst sort. Here is a well-known verse from *Ecclesiastes:*

> I returned and saw under the sun, that the race is not to the swift, nor the battle to the strong, neither yet bread to the wise, nor yet riches to men of understanding, nor yet favour to men of skill; but time and chance happeneth to them all.

Here it is in modern English:

> Objective consideration of contemporary phenomena compels the conclusion that success or failure in competitive activities exhibits no tendency to be commensurate with innate capacity, but that a considerable element of the unpredictable must invariably be taken into account.

10 This is a parody, but not a very gross one. Exhibit (3), above, for instance, contains several patches of the same kind of English. It will be seen that I have not made a full translation. The beginning and ending of the sentence follow the original meaning fairly closely, but in the middle the concrete illustrations—race, battle, bread—dissolve into the vague phrase "success or failure in competitive activities." This had to be so, because no modern writer of the kind I am discussing—no one capable of using phrases like "objective consideration of contemporary phenomena"—would ever tabulate his thoughts in that precise and detailed way. The whole tendency of modern prose is away from concreteness. Now analyze these two sentences a little more closely. The first contains forty-nine words but only sixty syllables, and all its words are those of everyday life. The second contains thirty-eight words of ninety syllables: eighteen of its words are from Latin roots, and one from Greek. The first sentence contains six vivid images, and only one phrase ("time and chance") that could be called vague. The second contains not a single fresh, arresting phrase, and in spite of its ninety syllables it gives only a shortened version of the meaning contained in the first. Yet without a doubt it is the second kind of sentence that is gaining ground in modern English. I do not want to exaggerate. This kind of writing is not yet universal, and outcrops of simplicity will occur here and there in the worst-written page. Still, if you or I were told to write a few lines on the uncertainty of human fortunes, we should probably come much nearer to my imaginary sentence than to the one from *Ecclesiastes.*

11 As I have tried to show, modern writing at its worst does not

consist in picking out words for the sake of their meaning and inventing images in order to make the meaning clearer. It consists in gumming together long strips of words which have already been set in order by someone else, and making the results presentable by sheer humbug. The attraction of this way of writing is that it is easy. It is easier—even quicker once you have the habit—to say *In my opinion it is a not unjustifiable assumption that* than to say *I think.* If you use ready-made phrases, you not only don't have to hunt about for words; you also don't have to bother with the rhythms of your sentences, since these phrases are generally so arranged as to be more or less euphonious. When you are composing in a hurry—when you are dictating to a stenographer, for instance, or making a public speech—it is natural to fall into a pretentious, Latinized style. Tags like *a consideration which we should do well to bear in mind* or *a conclusion to which all of us would readily assent* will save many a sentence from coming down with a bump. By using stale metaphors, similes, and idioms, you save much mental effort, at the cost of leaving your meaning vague, not only for your reader but for yourself. This is the significance of mixed metaphors. The sole aim of a metaphor is to call up a visual image. When these images clash—as in *The Fascist octopus has sung its swan song, the jackboot is thrown into the melting pot*—it can be taken as certain that the writer is not seeing a mental image of the objects he is naming; in other words he is not really thinking. Look again at the examples I gave at the beginning of this essay. Professor Laski (1) uses five negatives in fifty-three words. One of these is superfluous, making nonsense of the whole passage, and in addition there is the slip *alien* for *akin,* making further nonsense, and several avoidable pieces of clumsiness which increase the general vagueness. Professor Hogben (2) plays ducks and drakes with a battery which is able to write prescriptions, and, while disapproving of the everyday phrase *put up with,* is unwilling to look *egregious* up in the dictionary and see what it means. (3), if one takes an uncharitable attitude towards it, is simply meaningless: probably one could work out its intended meaning by reading the whole of the article in which it occurs. In (4), the writer knows more or less what he wants to say, but an accumulation of stale phrases chokes him like tea leaves blocking a sink. In (5), words and meaning have almost parted company. People who write in this manner usually have a general emotional meaning—they dislike one thing and want to express solidarity with another—but they are not interested in the detail of what they are saying. A scrupulous writer, in every sentence that he writes, will ask himself at least four questions, thus: What am I trying to say? What words will express it? What image or idiom will make it clearer? Is this image fresh enough to have an effect? And he will probably ask himself two more: Could I put it more shortly? Have I said anything that is avoidably ugly? But you are not obliged to go to all this trouble. You can shirk it by simply throwing your mind open and letting the ready-made phrases come crowding in. They will construct your sentences for you—even think your thoughts for you, to a certain extent—and at need they will perform the important service of partially concealing your meaning even from yourself. It is at this point that the special connection between politics and the debasement of language becomes clear.

12 In our times it is broadly true that political writing is bad writing. Where it is not true, it will generally be found that the writer is some kind of rebel, expressing his private opinions and not a "party line." Orthodoxy, of whatever color, seems to demand a lifeless, imitative style. The political dialects to be found in pamphlets, leading articles, manifestos, White Papers, and the speeches of under-secretaries do, of course, vary from party to party, but they are all alike in that one almost never finds in them a fresh, vivid, home-made turn of speech. When one watches some tired hack on the platform mechanically repeating the familiar phrases—*bestial atrocities, iron heel, bloodstained tyranny, free peoples of the world, stand shoulder to shoulder*—one often has a curious feeling that one is not watching a live human being but some kind of dummy, a feeling which suddenly becomes stronger at moments when the light catches the speaker's spectacles and turns them into blank discs which seem to have no eyes behind them. And this is not altogether fanciful. A speaker who uses that kind of phraseology has gone some distance towards turning himself into a machine. The appropriate noises are coming out of his larynx, but his brain is not involved as it would be if he were choosing his words from himself. If the speech he is making is one that he is accustomed to make over and over again, he may be almost unconscious of what he is saying, as one is when one utters the responses in church. And this reduced state of consciousness, if not indispensable, is at any rate favorable to political conformity.

13 In our time, political speech and writing are largely the de-

fense of the indefensible. Things like the continuance of British rule in India, the Russian purges and deportations, the dropping of the atom bombs on Japan, can indeed be defended, but only by arguments which are too brutal for most people to face, and which do not square with the professed aims of political parties. Thus political language has to consist largely of euphemism, question-begging, and sheer cloudy vagueness. Defenseless villages are bombarded from the air, the inhabitants driven out into the countryside, the cattle machine-gunned, the huts set on fire with incendiary bullets: this is called *pacification.* Millions of peasants are robbed of their farms and sent trudging along the roads with no more than they can carry: this is called *transfer of population* or *rectification of frontiers.* People are imprisoned for years without trial, or shot in the back of the neck or sent to die of scurvy in Arctic lumber camps: this is called *elimination of unreliable elements.* Such phraseology is needed if one wants to name things without calling up mental pictures of them. Consider for instance some comfortable English professor defending Russian totalitarianism. He cannot say outright, "I believe in killing off your opponents when you can get good results by doing so." Probably, therefore, he will say something like this:

14 "While freely conceding that the Soviet régime exhibits certain features which the humanitarian may be inclined to deplore, we must, I think, agree that a certain curtailment of the right to political opposition is an unavoidable concomitant of transitional periods, and that the rigors which the Russian people have been called upon to undergo have been amply justified in the sphere of concrete achievement."

15 The inflated style is itself a kind of euphemism. A mass of Latin words falls upon the facts like soft snow, blurring the outlines and covering up all the details. The great enemy of clear language is insincerity. When there is a gap between one's real and one's declared aims, one turns as it were instinctively to long words and exhausted idioms, like a cuttlefish squirting out ink. In our age there is no such thing as "keeping out of politics." All issues are political issues, and politics itself is a mass of lies, evasions, folly, hatred, and schizophrenia. When the general atmosphere is bad, language must suffer. I should expect to find—this is a guess which I have not sufficient knowledge to verify—that the German, Russian, and Italian languages have all deteriorated in the last ten or fifteen years, as a result of dictatorship.

16 But if thought corrupts language, language can also corrupt

thought. A bad usage can spread by tradition and imitation, even among people who should and do know better. The debased language that I have been discussing is in some ways very convenient. Phrases like *a not unjustifiable assumption, leaves much to be desired, would serve no good purpose, a consideration which we should do well to bear in mind,* are a continuous temptation, a packet of aspirins always at one's elbow. Look back through this essay, and for certain you will find that I have again and again committed the very faults I am protesting against. By this morning's post I have received a pamphlet dealing with conditions in Germany. The author tells me that he "felt impelled" to write it. I open it at random, and here is almost the first sentence that I see: "(The Allies) have an opportunity not only of achieving a radical transformation of Germany's social and political structure in such a way as to avoid a nationalistic reaction in Germany itself, but at the same time of laying the foundations of a co-operative and unified Europe." You see, he "feels impelled" to write—feels, presumably, that he has something new to say—and yet his words, like cavalry horses answering the bugle, group themselves automatically into the familiar dreary pattern. This invasion of one's mind by ready-made phrases *(lay the foundations, achieve a radical transformation)* can only be prevented if one is constantly on guard against them, and every such phrase anaesthetizes a portion of one's brain.

17 I said earlier that the decadence of our language is probably curable. Those who deny this would argue, if they produced an argument at all, that language merely reflects existing social conditions, and that we cannot influence its development by any direct tinkering with words and constructions. So far as the general tone or spirit of a language goes, this may be true, but it is not true in detail. Silly words and expressions have often disappeared, not through any evolutionary process but owing to the conscious action of a minority. Two recent examples were *explore every avenue* and *leave no stone unturned,* which were killed by the jeers of a few journalists. There is a long list of flyblown metaphors which could similarly be got rid of if enough people would interest themselves in the job; and it should also be possible to laugh the *not un-* formation out of existence, to reduce the amount of Latin and Greek in the average sentence, to drive out foreign phrases and strayed scientific words, and, in general, to make pretentiousness unfashionable. But all these are minor

points. The defense of the English language implies more than this, and perhaps it is best to start by saying what it does *not* imply.

18 To begin with it has nothing to do with archaism, with the salvaging of obsolete words and turns of speech, or with the setting up of a "standard English" which must never be departed from. On the contrary, it is especially concerned with the scrapping of every word or idiom which has outworn its usefulness. It has nothing to do with correct grammar and syntax, which are of no importance so long as one makes one's meaning clear, or with the avoidance of Americanisms, or with having what is called a "good prose style." On the other hand, it is not concerned with fake simplicity and the attempt to make written English colloquial. Nor does it even imply in every case preferring the Saxon word to the Latin one, though it does imply using the fewest and shortest words that will cover one's meaning. What is above all needed is to let the meaning choose the word, and not the other way about. In prose, the worst thing one can do with words is to surrender to them. When you think of a concrete object, you think wordlessly, and then, if you want to describe the thing you have been visualizing you probably hunt about till you find the exact words that seem to fit. When you think of something abstract, you are more inclined to use words from the start, and unless you make a conscious effort to prevent it, the existing dialect will come rushing in and do the job for you, at the expense of blurring or even changing your meaning. Probably it is better to put off using words as long as possible and get one's meaning as clear as one can through pictures or sensations. Afterwards one can choose—not simply *accept*—the phrases that will best cover the meaning, and then switch round and decide what impression one's words are likely to make on another person. This last effort of the mind cuts out all stale or mixed images, all prefabricated phrases, needless repetitions, and humbug and vagueness generally. But one can often be in doubt about the effect of a word or a phrase, and one needs rules that one can rely on when instinct fails. I think the following rules will cover most cases:

(i) Never use a metaphor, simile, or other figure of speech which you are used to seeing in print.
(ii) Never use a long word where a short one will do.

(iii) If it is possible to cut a word out, always cut it out.
(iv) Never use the passive where you can use the active.
(v) Never use a foreign phrase, a scientific word, or jargon word if you can think of an everyday English equivalent.
(vi) Break any of these rules sooner than say anything outright barbarous.

These rules sound elementary, and so they are, but they demand a deep change in attitude in anyone who has grown used to writing in the style now fashionable. One could keep all of them and still write bad English, but one could not write the kind of stuff that I quoted in those five specimens at the beginning of this article.

19 I have not here been considering the literary use of language, but merely language as an instrument for expressing and not for concealing or preventing thought. Stuart Chase and others have come near to claiming that all abstract words are meaningless, and have used this as a pretext for advocating a kind of political quietism. Since you don't know what Fascism is, how can you struggle against Fascism? One need not swallow such absurdities as this, but one ought to recognize that the present political chaos is connected with the decay of language, and that one can probably bring about some improvement by starting at the verbal end. If you simplify your English, you are freed from the worst follies of orthodoxy. You cannot speak any of the necessary dialects, and when you make a stupid remark, its stupidity will be obvious, even to yourself. Political language—and with variations this is true of all political parties, from Conservatives to Anarchists—is designed to make lies sound truthful and murder respectable, and to give an appearance of solidity to pure wind. One cannot change this all in a moment, but one can at least change one's own habits, and from time to time one can even, if one jeers loudly enough, send some worn-out and useless phrase—some *jackboot, Achilles' heel, hotbed, melting pot, acid test, veritable inferno,* or other lump of verbal refuse—into the dustbin where it belongs.

Suggestions for Discussion and Writing

1. Orwell claims that "the decline of a language must ultimately have political and economic causes" (paragraph 2). Cite some

examples that would support his statement. Are there other causes that he might be ignoring?

2. Paragraph 11 offers a list of questions for the writer to ask himself, and paragraph 18 contains a list of rules for the writer to follow. Do they overlap? Do they contradict any of his ideas expressed elsewhere in this essay? Has he omitted any important rules?
3. Can you update Orwell's list of pretentious diction (paragraph 7)?
4. What is wrong with the five passages Orwell quotes in paragraph 13?
5. Do you agree with his statement that grammar and syntax are unimportant as long as the meaning of the passage is clear? Provide examples to illustrate or challenge his statement.
6. The author states that his essay contains the very faults he is protesting (paragraph 16). Can you find examples?
7. Orwell's essay is in three parts. The first part consists of paragraphs 1–15. What are the second and third parts? What is the topic of each? How are they linked?
8. Underline several of Orwell's transitions, and explain how they tie his essay together.
9. Where does Orwell place his thesis sentence in this essay? Where does he confront the objections that he thinks his readers might have?
10. Describe Orwell's personality as it is projected in the first several paragraphs of this essay.
11. Who is Orwell's audience as he probably imagined them? Are they the practitioners of the vices he attacks?
12. What is a dying metaphor? How would you recognize one? Can you add to the examples that Orwell provides?
13. Examine several of Orwell's similes and metaphors, showing how they illustrate his discussion or thesis.
14. Orwell mentions several euphemisms in paragraph 13. By drawing on Watergate and Vietnam, update his paragraph.
15. Write an essay in which you use the following sentence from Orwell as your thesis statement: "In our time, political speech and writing are largely the defense of the indefensible."
16. Select the jargon of a particular occupation such as computers or the aerospace industry, and show how it has enriched or debased our language.
17. How much is the reader (rather than the *writer*) to blame for the abundance of meaningless writing today? Write an essay in which you describe the typical reader.
18. Compare the prose style and sensitivity to language of two

recent presidents: Harry Truman and Dwight Eisenhower, for example, or John F. Kennedy and Jerry Ford.

19. Write an essay urging clearer and simpler language in one of the courses you are taking. Support your case by citing egregious examples from your textbooks.

20. Analyze a recent political speech according to Orwell's principles.

10
Research

Now to consolidate and advance. Instead of eight or nine hundred words, you will write three thousand. Instead of a self-propelled debate or independent literary analysis, you will write a scholarly argument. You will also learn to use the library, and to take notes and give footnotes. You will learn the ways of scholarship. You will learn to acknowledge your predecessors as you distinguish yourself, to make not only a bibliography, but a contribution.

The research paper is very likely not what you think it is. *Research* is searching again. You are looking, usually, where others have looked before; but you hope to see something they have not. Research is not combining a paragraph from the *Encyclopaedia Britannica* and a paragraph from *The Book of Knowledge* with a slick pinch from *Time.* That's robbery. Nor is it research even if you carefully change each phrase and acknowledge the source. That's drudgery. Even in some high circles, I am afraid, such scavenging is called research. It is not. It is simply a cloudier condensation of what you have done in school as a "report"—sanctioned plagiarism to teach something about ants or Ankara, a tedious compiling of what is already known. That such material is new to you is not the issue: it is already in the public stock.

CHOOSING YOUR SUBJECT

Pick Something That Interests You

First get yourself a subject. You need not shake the world. Such subjects as "Subsidized College Football," "Small College Versus Big University," "Excluding the Press from Trials," or the changing valuation of a former best seller well suit the research paper. Bigger subjects, of course, will try your mettle: nuclear power, abortion, federal funding, endangered species as against public need. The whole question of governmental versus private endeavor affords many lively issues for research and decision, perhaps in your own locality and your local newspaper.

You can stir your own interests and turn up a number of good ideas for research by reading the newspapers—*The Christian Science Monitor* is especially fruitful—and by browsing the current magazines such as *Time, Newsweek, Psychology Today, Scientific American, Atlantic Monthly, Saturday Review,* and many another. Other good sources are interviews on TV, film documentaries, and even arguments in the coffee shop or bar.

Work with a Thesis

Once you have spotted a subject that interests you, lean toward your inclination about it and write it into a tentative thesis sentence. Though tentative, any stand *for* or *against* will save you time in further searching, and help you establish manageable bounds.

Since you will be dealing mostly with facts in the public stock and with ideas with other people's names on them, what can you do to avoid copycatting? You move from facts and old ideas to new ideas. In other words, you begin by inquiring what is *already* known about a subject, then, as you collect inferences and judgments, you begin to perceive fallacies, to form conclusions of your own, to reinforce or to change your working thesis. Here the range is infinite. Every old idea needs new assertion. Every new assertion needs judgment. Here you are in the area of values, where everyone is in favor of virtue but in doubt about what is virtuous. Your best area of research is in some controversial issue, where you can add, and document, a new judgment of "right" or "wrong." I have put it bluntly to save you from drowning in slips of paper.

Unless you have a working hypothesis to keep your purpose alive as you collect, or at least a clear question to be answered, you may collect forever, forever hoping for a purpose. If you have a thesis, you will learn—and then overcome—the temptations of collecting only the supporting evidence and ignoring the obverse facts and whispers of conscience. If further facts and good arguments persuade you to the other side, so much the better. You will be the stronger for it.

Persuade Your Reader You Are Right

You do not search primarily for facts. You do not aim to summarize everything ever said on the subject. You aim to persuade your reader that the thesis you believe in is right. You persuade him by (1) letting him see that you have been thoroughly around the subject and that you know what is known of it and thought of it, (2) showing him where the wrongs are wrong, and (3) citing the rights as right. *Your* opinion, *your* thesis, is what you are showing; all your quotations from all the authorities in the world are subservient to *your* demonstration. You are the reigning authority. You have, for the moment, the longest perspective and the last word. So, pick a thesis, and move into the library.

USING THE LIBRARY

Start with the Encyclopedias

Find the *Encyclopaedia Britannica,* and you are well on your way. The *Britannica* will survey your subject and guide you to your sources. It is not, usually, a basic source in itself, but each article will refer you, at the end, to several authorities. If someone's initials appear at the end, look them up in the contributors' list. The author of the article is an authority himself; you should mention him in your paper, and also look him up to see what books he has written on the subject. Furthermore, the contributors' list will name several works, which will swell your bibliography and aid your research. The index will also refer you to data scattered through all the volumes. Under "Medicine," for instance, it directs you to such topics as "Academies," "Hypnotism," "Licensing," "Mythology," and so on. The *Encyclopedia Americana, Collier's Encyclopedia,* and *Chambers's Encyclopaedia,* though less celebrated, will here and there challenge *Britannica's* reign, and the one-volume *Columbia Encyclopedia* is a fine shorter reference.

The World Almanac and Book of Facts, a paperbacked lode of news and statistics (issued yearly since 1868), can provide a factual nugget for almost any subject. Other good ones are *Webster's Biographical Dictionary* and *Webster's New Geographical Dictionary;* their concise entries lead quickly to thousands of people and places. And don't overlook the atlases: *The Times Atlas of the World, The National Atlas of the United States.* Another treasure-trove is *The Oxford English Dictionary* (twelve volumes and supplement—abbreviated *OED* in footnotes), which gives the date a word, like *highwayman,* first appeared in print, and traces changing usages through the years.

Explore your library's reference works. You will find many encyclopedias, outlines, atlases, and dictionaries providing more intensive coverage than the general works on the arts, history, philosophy, literature, the social sciences, the natural sciences, business, and the technologies. Instructors in subjects you may be exploring can guide you to the best references.

Next Find the Card Catalog

The catalog's 3 × 5 cards list all the library's holdings—books, magazines, newspapers, atlases—and alphabetize (1) authors, (2) publications, and (3) general subjects, from *A* to *Z.* You will find *John Adams* and *The Anatomy of Melancholy* and *Atomic Energy,* in that order, in the *A* drawers. Page 343 illustrates the three kinds of cards (filed alphabetically) on which the card catalog will list the same book—by author, by subject, and by title.

You will notice that the bottom of the card shows the Library of Congress's cataloging number (Q175.W6517) and the number from the older, but still widely used, Dewey Decimal System (501). Your library will use one or the other to make its own "call number," typed in the upper left hand corner of its cards—the number you will put on your slip when you sign out the book.

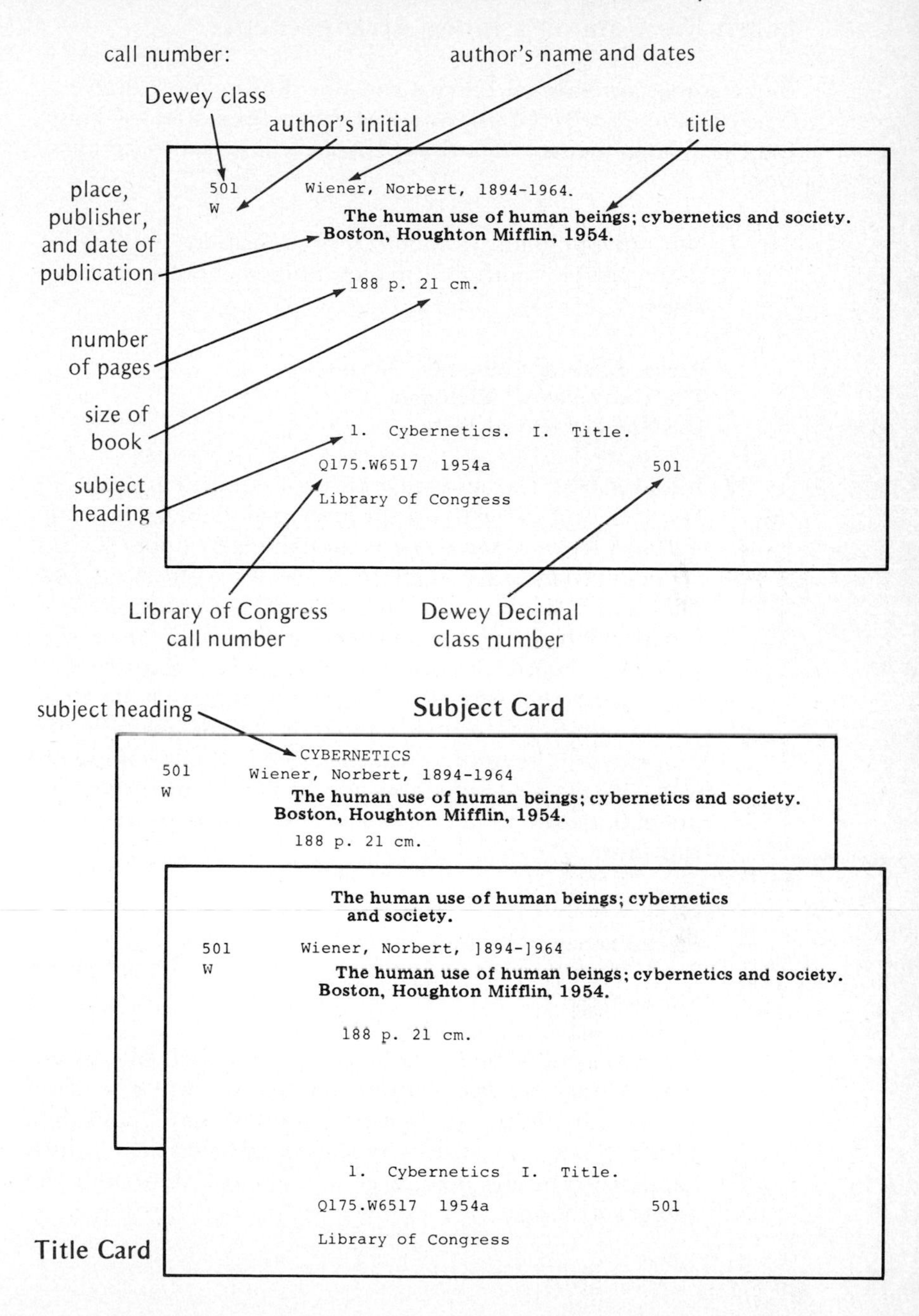
Author Card: the "Main Entry"
call number:
Dewey class
author's initial
author's name and dates
title
place, publisher, and date of publication
number of pages
size of book
subject heading
501
W
Wiener, Norbert, 1894-1964.
The human use of human beings; cybernetics and society.
Boston, Houghton Mifflin, 1954.
188 p. 21 cm.
1. Cybernetics. I. Title.
Q175.W6517 1954a
501
Library of Congress
Library of Congress call number
Dewey Decimal class number
Subject Card
subject heading
CYBERNETICS
501
W
Wiener, Norbert, 1894-1964
The human use of human beings; cybernetics and society.
Boston, Houghton Mifflin, 1954.
188 p. 21 cm.
The human use of human beings; cybernetics and society.
501
W
Wiener, Norbert,]894-]964
The human use of human beings; cybernetics and society.
Boston, Houghton Mifflin, 1954.
188 p. 21 cm.
1. Cybernetics I. Title.
Q175.W6517 1954a
501
Library of Congress
Title Card

Learn the Catalog's Inner Arrangements

Since some alphabetical entries run on, drawer after drawer—*New York City, New York State, New York Times,* for instance—knowing the arrangements *within* these entries will help you find your book.

1. Not only men and women but organizations and institutions can be "authors" if they publish books or magazines.

   Parke, Davis & Company, Detroit
   The University of Michigan
   U.S. Department of State

2. Initial *A, An, The,* and their foreign equivalents (*Ein, El, Der, Une,* and so forth) are ignored in alphabetizing a title: *A Long Day in a Short Life* is alphabetized under *L.* But French surnames are treated as if they were one word: *De la Mare* as if *Delamare, La Rochefoucauld* as if *Larochefoucauld.*
3. Cards are usually alphabetized *word by word: Stock Market* comes before *Stockard* and *Stockbroker.* "Short before long" is another way of putting it, meaning that *Stock* and all its combinations with separate words precede the longer words beginning with *Stock-.* Whether a compound word is one or two makes the apparent disorder. Hyphenations are treated as two words. The sequence would run thus:

   Stock
   Stock-Exchange Rulings
   Stock Market
   Stockard

4. Cards on one subject are arranged alphabetically by author. Under *Anatomy,* for instance, you will run from "Abernathy, John" to "Yutzy, Simon Menno," and then suddenly run into a title—*An Anatomy of Conformity*—which happens to be the next large alphabetical item after the subject *Anatomy.*

5. Identical names are arranged in the order (a) person, (b) titles and places, as they fall alphabetically.

Washington, Booker T.
Washington, George
Washington (State)
Washington, University of
Washington, D.C.
Washington Square **[by Henry James]**

"Washington," the state, precedes the other "Washingtons" because "State" (which appears on the card only in parentheses) is not treated as part of its name. The University of Washington precedes "Washington, D.C." because no words or letters actually follow the "Washington" of its title.

6. Since *Mc, M',* and *Mac* are all filed as if they were *Mac,* they go by the letter following them: *M'Coy, McDermott, Machinery, MacKenzie.*
7. Other abbreviations are also filed as if spelled out: *Dr. Zhivago* would be filed as if beginning with *Doctor; St. Joan* as if with *Saint; Mrs. Miniver* as if with *Mistress*—except that many libraries now alphabetize *Mr.* and *Mrs.* as spelled, and *Ms.* has found its place in the alphabetizing.
8. Saints, popes, kings, and people are filed, in that order, by name and not by appellation (do not look under *Saint* for St. Paul, nor under *King* for King Henry VIII). The order would be:

Paul, Saint
Paul VI, Pope
Paul I, Emperor of Russia
Paul, Jean

9. An author's books are filed first by collected works, then by individual titles. Different editions of the same title follow chronologically. Books *about* an author follow the books *by* him.

That is the system. Now you can thumb through the cards filed under your subject—"Cancer," or "Television," or "Melville"—to see what books your library has on it, and you can look up any authorities your encyclopedia has mentioned. Two or three of the most recent books will probably give you all you want, because each of these will refer you, by footnote and bibliography, to important previous works.

Find the Indexes to Periodicals and Newspapers

Indexes to periodicals do for articles what the card catalog does for books. Some index by subjects only, others by subjects and authors. Begin with the *Reader's Guide to Periodical Literature*—an index of articles (and portraits and poems) in more than one hundred magazines. Again, take the most recent issue, look up your subject, and make yourself a bibliographical card for each title—spelling out the abbreviations of titles and dates according to the key just inside the cover. If you don't spell them out fully, your cards may be mysteries to you when you sit down to write. You can drop back a few issues and years to collect more articles; and if your subject belongs to the recent past (after 1907), you can drop back to the right year and track your subject forward. (*Poole's Index to Periodical Literature* provides similar guidance to American and English periodicals from 1802 to 1906).

You can do the same with the *New York Times Index,* beginning with 1913. It will probably lead you to news that appeared in any paper. The *Social Sciences Index* and the *Humanities Index* do for scholarly journals what the *Reader's Guide* does for the popular ones. (These two *Indexes* were the *International Index* [until 1965] and the *Social Sciences and Humanities Index* [until 1974].) If you are searching for an essay that may be in a book rather than a magazine, your guide is the *Essay and General Literature Index.* Add to these the *Book Review Digest* (since 1905), the *Biography Index* (which nicely collects scattered references), and the *Current Biography Index,* and you will probably need no more. But if you should need more, consult Constance M. Winchell's *Guide to Reference Books,* which is also a valuable guide to encyclopedias and dictionaries.

MAKING YOUR CARDS

Before you start toward the library, get some 3 × 5 cards for your bibliography. Plan on some ten or fifteen sources for your three thousand words of text. As you pick up an author or two, and some titles, start a bibliographical card for each: *one card for each title.* Leave space to the left to put in the call number later, and space at the top for a label of your own, if needed. Put the author (last name first) on one line, and the title of his work on the next, leaving space to fill in the details of publication when you get to the work itself—for books, place of publication, publisher, and date; for magazine articles, volume number, date, and pages. Italicize (that is, underscore) titles of books and magazines; put titles of articles *within* books and magazines in quotation marks. The card catalog will supply the call numbers, and much of the other publishing data you need; but check and complete all your publishing data when you finally get the book or magazine in your hands, putting a light ✓ in pencil to assure yourself that your card is authoritative, that quotations are word for word and all your publishing data accurate, safe to check your finished paper against. Get the author's name as it appears on the title page, adding details in brackets, if helpful: Smith, D[elmar] P[rince]. Get all the information, to save repeated trips to the library. You will simplify some of the publishing data for your "Works Cited" (see 374–75), but get it all down now to be sure.

Take Brief Notes

Some people abhor putting notes on bibliographical cards. A separate card for bibliography and other cards for notes—written only on one side for ease of manipulation and viewing—are certainly more orderly and thorough. But the economy of taking notes directly on bibliographical cards is, I have found, well worth the slight clutter. Limiting yourself to what you can put on the front and back of one bibliographical card will restrain your notes to the sharp and manageable. You can always add another note card if you must. If you find one source offering a number of irresistible quotations, put each one separately on a 3 × 5 card (with author's name on each), so you can rearrange them later for writing.

However you do it, keep your notes brief. Read quickly, with an eye for the general idea and the telling point. Holding a clear thesis in mind will guide and limit your note taking. Some of your sources will need no more than the briefest summary: "Violently opposed, recommends complete abolition." This violent and undistinguished author will appear in your paper only among several others in a single footnote to one of your sentences: "Opposition, of course, has been tenacious and emphatic.[2]"

Suppose you are writing a paper affirming that animals can talk (as the student in our sample did, 363–75). You find that Herbert Terrace says "No"(372). Here is a perfect piece of opposition, a *con,* to set your thesis against, to explain and qualify. But don't copy too much. Summarize the author's point, jot down some facts you might use, and copy down directly, within distinct quotation marks, only the most quotable phrases: "There isn't anything that even hints at language" (see our sample, 368).

Take care with page numbers. When your passage runs from one page to the next—from 29 over onto 30, for instance—put "(29–30)" after it, *but also mark the exact point where the page changed.* You might want to use only part of the passage and then be uncertain as to which of the pages contained it. An inverted L-bracket and the number "30" after the last word of page 29, will do nicely: "All had **30** occurred earlier." Do the same even when the page changes in midword with a hyphen: "having con- **21** vinced no one."

When preparing a research paper on a piece of literature, you would also make a bibliographical card for the edition you are using, and would probably need a number of note cards for summaries and quotations from the work itself—one card for each item, for convenience in sorting.

Take Care Against Plagiarism

If you borrow an idea, cite your source. If you have an idea of your own and then discover that someone has beaten you to it, swallow your disappointment and cite your predecessor. Or you can get back some of your own by saying, in a footnote, "I discover that Smith agrees with me on this point," explaining, if possible, what Smith has overlooked, or his differing emphasis. Your "Works Cited" will list Smith's article for all future reference. A danger lies in copying out phrases from your source as you summarize what it says, and then incorporating them in your essay, without remembering that those phrases are not yours. The solution is, again, to take down and mark quotations accurately in your notes, to summarize succinctly *in your own words,* as far away from the original as possible, and always to credit your sources.

YOUR FIRST DRAFT

Plot Your Course

Formal outlines, especially those made too early in the game, can take more time than they are worth, but a long paper with notes demands some planning. First, draft a beginning paragraph, incorporating your thesis. Then read through your notes, arranging them roughly in the order you think you will use them, getting the opposition off the street first. If your thesis is strongly argumentative, you can sort into three piles: *pro*'s, *con*'s, and *in-between*'s (often simple facts). Now, by way of outline, you can simply make three or four general headings on a sheet of paper, with ample space between, in which you can jot down your sources in the order, *pro* and *con,* that is best for your argument. Our paper on animal speech would block out something like this:

I. Animals use language.

PRO	CON
	Only spontaneous cries (De Vore)
But differing signals (Pilbeam, Seyfarth)	

II. Volition (Lyn Miles)

PRO	CON
	But Hediger—deception widespread. Chimps lack speech centers. Clever Hans (Hahn)

III. Understanding
Much evidence in general
Peg the poodle (Hahn)
Dolphins (Parfit, Lilly)

But Norris (Parfit)

Herman (Parfit)

IV. Talking apes (Witmer Furness, Hayes, Laidler)

V. Ameslan (Gardners)
"George smell Roger" (Miles)
"Roger tickle Lucy" (Linden)
Patterson

But Terrace and Nim

Fred the cockatoo (Terry)

Outline More Fully for the Finished Product

You can easily refine this rough blocking into a full topic outline, one that displays your points logically, not necessarily in the actual sequence of your writing. You can make this outline best after your first draft has stretched and squeezed your material into handsomer shape. The principle of outlining is to rank equivalent headings—keeping your headings all as nouns, or noun phrases, to make the ranks apparent as in the full outline of our sample paper (363).

But *begin to write soon.* You have already begun to write, of course, in getting your thesis down on paper, and then drafting a first paragraph to hold it. Now that you have blocked out your argument or your course, however roughly, plunge into your first draft.

Put in Your References as You Go

The Modern Language Association of America, in conformity with many journals in the social sciences and sciences, recommends a system of citations that simplifies your job considerably. A list of "Works Cited" at the end of your paper—the usual bibliography—now replaces all footnotes merely identifying a work. Previously, on first mention, you would have made the following footnote:

> [1]**Irven De Vore, *Primate Behavior: Field Studies of Monkeys and Apes* (New York: Holt, Rinehart and Winston, 1965), p. 598.**

Now you save all that for your "Works Cited," where you would have had to repeat it anyway. You skip the footnote altogether, putting in your paper no more than the author's name and the page number, omitting the old and unnecessary *p.*:

> **Irven De Vore, for instance, concludes that primates' cries express no more than emotional states and degrees of arousal (598). Samuelson believes. . . .**

If you have two Walds, simply include their first names or initials. If Wald has two works, devise two convenient short titles: Wald claims (*Apes* 5) that . . . , but he later admits some significant variations ("Simians" 121). More details on the new system will follow in a moment. But the old problem of handling footnotes and numbering them in your first draft has vanished. All you do is mention your author's name—last name alone suffices—and then add the page number in parenthesis where you usually would have put a footnote number. Now you limit your footnotes to your own commentary or explanation, which of course may include other authors and even quotations handled in the same way. These few footnotes you may type directly into your draft, surrounding them with triple parentheses: (((. . .)))—the easiest distinction you can make.

YOUR FINAL DRAFT

Reset Your Long Quotations

Your final draft will change in many ways, as the rewriting polishes up your phrases and turns up new and better ideas. But some changes are merely presentational. The triple parentheses of your first draft will disappear, along with the quotation marks around the *long* quotations, since you will single-space and indent, *without quotation marks,* all quotations of more than fifty words, to simulate the appearance of a printed page. You will do the same with shorter quotations, if you want to give them special emphasis, and also with passages of poetry. Some instructors prefer, and some handbooks recommend, that you double space your long inset quotations, setting them off by triple spacing, above and below, as you would in an essay submitted for publication.

Differentiate Those Page Numbers

Notice that you cite, or quote, in three different ways: (1) indirect quotation or reference, (2) direct quotation in your running text, (3) direct quotation set apart from your running text and single-spaced. Accordingly, you punctuate the page-parenthesis in three slightly different ways.

1. With an indirect quotation or reference, you simply include the parenthesis, like any parenthesis, *within* the sentence, or within the phrase—that is, *before* any and all punctuation marks:

. . . as Anderson (291) and others believe, but not. . . .

. . . as others, including Anderson (291), believe.

Anderson believes the evidence inconclusive (291).

2. With a direct quotation in your running text, put the page-parenthesis *after* the closing quotation mark but *before* the punctuation, thus including the parenthesis within *your* sentence.

He thinks them "quite daffy" (213), but concedes. . . .

As Belweather says, "Many of these proposals for investigation are quite daffy" (213).

3. But when you inset and single-space a quotation, you *omit* quotation marks, and put the page-parenthesis *after* the final period and a few spaces farther along—with no period following it:

. . . a culture, a commonly shared, learned, and remembered history as a group, which it transmits through the generations. (218)

What if an author has more than one work? I repeat for clarity. Simply devise a short label for each. Suppose Samuelson has both a book and an article you want to cite—I'm making these up: *Physiological Differences in Simian Primates* and "The Oral and Nasal Physiology of *Pongo Pygmaeus.*" Your reference then might read: Samuelson finds the neocortex inadequate for language (*Physiological* 291), and ". . . the larynx is too high" ("Oral" 13).

THE DETAILS OF "WORKS CITED"

Handle with care so that your readers can find what you found, and you too can find it again. Note that the new system condenses most publishers' names: "Holt, Rinehart and Winston" becomes "Holt"; "Dunne Press, Inc." becomes "Dunne"; "Alfred D. Knopf" became "Knopf." Spacing is like this:

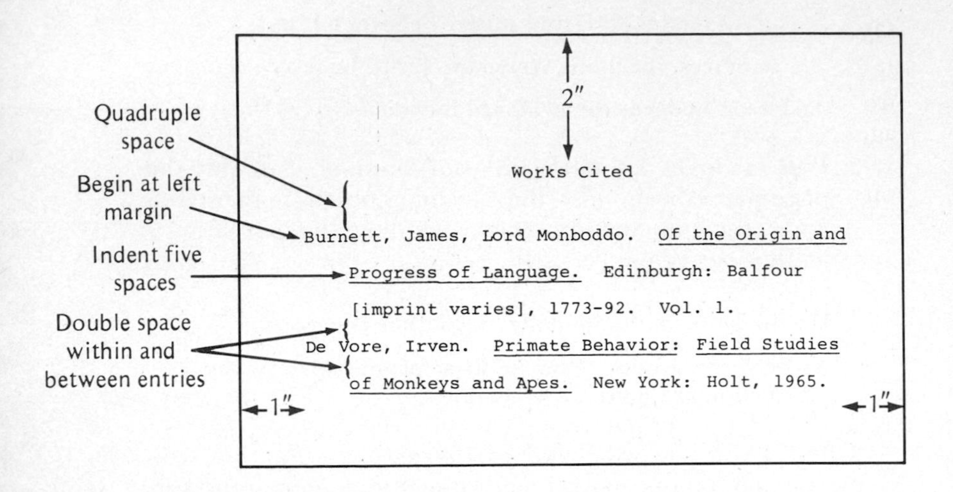

Books

You indicate books that give no place or date of publication as follows:

Segal, Annette. *The Question of Rights.* N.p.: Bell, n.d.

When listing other works by the same author, use three hyphens and a period instead of repeating the name:

Two Authors; More Than One Entry for Same Author(s)

Jones, Bingham, and Samuel Maher. *The Kinescopic Arts and Sciences.* Princeton: Little House, 1970.

---. "Television and Vision: The Case for Governmental Control." *Independent Review* 7 (1969): 18–31.

Jones and Maher also wrote the second entry, which alphabetizes second with its *T* following the *K* of *Kinescopic.* If Jones alone had written "Television and Vision," it would come first, with his name in full, and the "Kinescopic" entry would follow as it stands.

Books that are monographs in a series look like this:

Thornbury, Ethel Margaret. *Henry Fielding's Theory of the Comic Prose Epic.* Univ. of Wisconsin Studies in Language and Literature, no. 37. Madison, Wis.: U. of Wisconsin P., 1931.

Magazines

With scholarly journals that number their pages consecutively throughout the year, you give volume number, the year, and the pages an article covers, with no comma following title and all in Arabic numbers, but with spaces between numbers and punctuations:

> **Solovyov, Vladimir. "The Paradox of Russian Vodka." *Michigan Quarterly Review* 21 (1982): 406–19.**

With weekly and monthly magazines that begin numbering their pages anew with each issue, give the full date:

> **Hahn, Emily. "Getting Through to Others." Part 1. *The New Yorker* 17 Apr. 1978: 38–103.**

Newspapers

Newspaper articles sometimes need more detail. Alphabetize by title—by *Trouble* in the following item:

> **"The Trouble with Fiction" (editorial). *New York Times* 10 Apr. 1984: 4.8.**

You have added "editorial" in parenthesis after the quotation marks but before the period. Here again the full date is necessary. The "4.8" indicates "Section 4, page 8." With newspapers that letter their sections—*A, B, C, D*—give the letter and page-number, just as it appears in the newspaper—8*B* or *D*-4.

If the article has a by-line, you include the author. If the article is mostly an interview with one authority, bracket that authority as your key, since you will be quoting him in your essay:

> **[Mills, Jay.] "Chipmunks Are Funny People." Associated Press News Release. *Back Creek Evening Star* 15 Oct. 1983: D4, D8.**

Source Within Source

When you find a useful quotation, or a complete essay, within another source or collection, include both in your "Works Cited."

Caldwell, Abraham B. "The Case for a Streaming Consciousness." ***American Questioner*** **62 (1979): 37–49. Qtd. Mendenhall.**

You then also cite Mendenhall fully in your "Works Cited."

Small, David R. "The Telephone and Urbanization." In ***Annals of American Communication:*** **401–18.**

Again, cite the *Annals* fully in your "Works Cited." You may simplify citations of articles in encyclopedias.

Peters, Arnold. "Medicine." ***Encyclopaedia Britannica.*** **11th ed. 1911.**

"Jackal." ***Encyclopaedia Britannica: Micropaedia.*** **1980 ed.**

You need neither volume nor page numbers in alphabetized encyclopedias, only the edition you are citing. The entry on "Medicine" was initialed "A.P.," and you have looked up the author's name in the contributors' list. The article on the "Jackal" was anonymous, to be alphabetized in your "Works Cited" under *J*.

Editions

Alphabetize editions by the author's name, but cite the editor:

Shakespeare, William. ***Romeo and Juliet.*** **In** ***An Essential Shakespeare.*** **Ed. Russell Fraser. New York: Prentice-Hall, 1972.**

But alphabetize by the editor, when you have referred to his introduction and notes:

Cowley, Malcolm, ed. ***The Portable Hawthorne.*** **With introduction and notes. New York: Viking, 1948.**

Quackenbush, Colby. Afterword ***The Scarlet Letter.*** **By Nathaniel Hawthorne. New York: Dunne, 1983.**

In the second entry, Quackenbush has contributed only an "Afterword" with no editor specified, and you have referred only to his remarks. If, on the other hand, you quote from both the novel and Quackenbush, you would list by *Hawthorne:*

Hawthorne, Nathaniel. *The Scarlet Letter.* With afterword by Colby Quackenbush. New York: Dunne, 1983.

Other Details

Gillies, George L. "Henry Smith's 'Electra.'" *Speculation* 2 (1881): 490–98.

This example shows where to put the period when the title of an article ends in a quotation. The original title would have had double quotation marks around the poem.

Schwartz, P[aul] F[riedrich]. *A Quartet of Thoughts.* New York: Appleton, 1943.

[Lewes, George H.] "Percy Bysshe Shelley." *Westminster Review* 35 (1841): 303–44.

These entries bracket useful details not appearing in the published work. Keep famous initials as initials: T. S. Eliot, H. G. Wells, D. H. Lawrence.

Pamphlets and other oddities require common sense:

"The Reading Problem." Mimeographed pamphlet. Center City, Arkansas: Concerned Parents Committee, 25 Dec. 1979.

Racial Integration.* House Committee on Health, Education, and Welfare, U. S. Congress, 101st Cong., 2nd sess., 1969, H. Rep. 391 to accompany H. R. 6128.

Briefly include the details to help others hunt them down.

Recordings, films, and tapes also require some ingenuity. Do not cite microfilms and other reproductions of things in print. Simply cite the book, article, or newspaper as if you had it in hand. But other media are forms of publication in themselves, to be cited as clearly as possible if you use them. The American Library Association recommends the following ways of citation.†

---

*For recalcitrant cases, the current edition of *Style Manual,* U. S. Government Printing Office, is helpful.

†Eugene B. Fleischer, *Style Manual for Citing Microform and Nonprint Media* (Chicago: American Library Association, 1978).

DISC

O'Neill, Eugene. *Long Day's Journey into Night.* Sound Recording. Caedmon, 1972. 3 discs TRS350. Disc 3, Side 2.

CASSETTE

Bogard, Charles. *"Ree-deep, ribbid": Herpetologist Charles Bogard Studies the Frog and Its Call.* Sound Recording. Center for Cassette Studies, 1971. Cassette 010 13460.

Other non-print items follow the same pattern, with the square brackets containing "[Motion Picture]" or "[Filmstrip]" to indicate the kind.

Omit Unnecessary Abbreviations

DO NOT USE these old favorites:

ibid.—*ibidem* ("in the same place"), meaning the title and page recently cited. Instead, *use the author's last name and page,* preferably phrased as part of your text: ". . . as Claeburn also makes clear (28)."

op. cit.—*opere citato* ("in the work cited"), meaning a work referred to again after several others have intervened. Again, *use the author's last name and page:* ". . . too small for vocalization (Adams 911)."

loc. cit.—*loco citato* ("in the place cited"). Simply repeat the page number: ". . . as Smith says (31). He cites, however, some notable exceptions (31)."

p., pp.—"page, pages." These old standbys are now redundant: *Omit them completely.* As we have seen, the number alone within parentheses suffices in the text, as it does in "Works Cited" as well.

l., ll.—"line, lines." These you would probably not need anyway, since they concern certain kinds of literary and textual scholarship, but, as you see, they are confusing, since they look like the numerals 1 and 11. If you ever need them, just write "line" and "lines."

Use Only the Convenient Abbreviations

The following conventional abbreviations remain useful (do *not* italicize them):

cf.—*confer* ("bring together," or "compare"); do not use for "see."

et al.—*et alii* ("and others"); does not mean "and all"; use after the first author in multiple authorships: "Ronald Elkins et al."

Two more Latin terms, also not italicized, are equally handy:

passim—Not an abbreviation, but a Latin word meaning "throughout the work; here and there." Use when a writer makes the same point in many places within a single work; use also for statistics you have compiled from observations and tables scattered throughout his work.

sic—a Latin word meaning "so"; "this is so"; always in brackets—[sic]—because used only within quotations following some misspelling or other surprising detail to show that it really was there, was "so" in the original and that the mistake is not yours.

Other useful abbreviations are:

c. or **ca.**	*circa,* "about" (c. 1709)
ch., chs.	chapter, chapters, with Arabic numerals, "ch. 12."
ed.	edited by, edition, editor
ms., mss.	manuscript, manuscripts
n.d.	no date given
n.p.	no place of publication given
rev.	revised
tr., trans.	translated by
vol., vols.	volume, volumes (use only with books: *Forsyte Saga,* vol. 3.)

A footnote using some of these might go like this:

[3]See Donald Allenberg et al., *Population* 308–12; cf. Weiss 60. Dillon, passim, takes a position even more conservative than Weiss's. See also A. H. Hawkins 71–83 and ch. 10. Records sufficient for broad comparisons begin only ca. 1850.

Abbreviate Books of the Bible, Even the First Time

The Bible and its books, though capitalized as ordinary titles, are never italicized. Spell them out in your running text: "The Bible begins with Genesis." You refer to them also directly in your text, within parentheses—abbreviated, with no commas, and with Arabic numerals: Mark 16.6; Jer. 4.24; 1 Sam. 18.33. No comma—only a space—separates name from numbers; periods separate the numbers, *with no spacing.* The dictionary gives the accepted abbreviations: Gen., Exod., Lev., Deut. Make biblical references like this:

> **There is still nothing new under the sun (Eccl. 1.9); man still does not live by bread alone (Matt. 4.4).**
>
> **As Ecclesiastes tells us, "there is no new thing under the sun" (1.9).**

Abbreviate Plays and Long Poems After First Mention

After first mention, handle plays and long poems like biblical citations. Your "Works Cited" will contain the edition you are using. Italicize the title (underscore on typewriter or in handwriting): Merch. 2.4.72–75 (this is *The Merchant of Venice,* Act II, scene iv, lines 72–75), Caesar 5.3.6, Ham. 1.1.23; Iliad 9.93 (=Book IX, line 93), PL 4.918 (=*Paradise Lost,* Book IV, line 918). Notice: no comma between short-title and numbers; periods and no spaces between numbers. Use the numbers alone if you have already mentioned the title, or have clearly implied it, as in repeated quotations from the same work.

For the most part, I have based these instructions on the *MLA Handbook for Writers of Research Papers,* second edition (1984), compiled by the Modern Language Association of America following the customs for work in literature and the humanities. The social and natural sciences use slightly different conventions; for papers in the social and natural sciences, consult your instructor about the correct style, or style manual, to follow.

A good general manual is the current edition of Kate L. Turabian, *A Manual for Writers of Term Papers, Theses, and Dissertations* (Chicago and London: The University of Chicago Press). A larger reference popular with scholars is *A Manual of Style* (the "Chicago Style Manual"), also published by the University of Chicago Press. Both the *MLA Handbook* and the Chicago *Manual* list other manuals for the various disciplines—engineering, geology, linguistics, psychology, and medicine, for example.

SAMPLE RESEARCH PAPER

Here is a complete research paper, with everything laid out in typescript and properly spaced, as if you had done it. The writer has followed out his own interest in pets, as anyone might explore an interest in automobiles, kites, piccolos, or whatever. The writer has found a lively argumentative area, right down the alley of his personal curiosity about his dog's eloquent but speechless communication. The back of the first page shows note-cards for his first three citations, each one different: (1) a summarized reference, (2) a full quotation, single-spaced and inset, (3) a brief quotation followed by summarized information.

Our paper combines title-page with outline. Perhaps more common is the separate title-page. Notice especially how the two footnotes contain only authorial amplification (367, 369), and how the writer easily refers to his sources, both in his footnotes and in his text. To set up a separate title-page, center the title four inches down from the top, with capitals and small letters—NOT all in capitals:

Can Animals Talk?

[quadruple space]

Sherman Clark

[12 to 15 lines of space]

English 123

Mr. Baker

4 June 1985

Notice also the spacing of "Works Cited," with the hanging indentation five spaces in for clear distinction, but otherwise everything double-spaced (374–75). Anonymous titles fall into alphabetical place among the alphabetized authors, with no "Anon." crowding them all in at first.

Sherman Clark
English 123
Mr. Baker
April 16, 1984

Can Animals Talk?

Thesis: Although many remain skeptical, evidence shows that animals are to some extent capable of comprehending and using human language.

I. Communication
    A. Natural communication
        1. Spontaneous general cries
        2. Differentiated cries
            a. Vervet monkeys' warnings
            b. Vervet monkeys' conversational grunts
    B. Volitional communication
        1. Deceptive signals
        2. Trained signals
            a. Clever Hans's failure
            b. Peg's success
II. Animals' vocal language
    A. Natural vocal language
        1. Lilly's dolphins
        2. Norris's denial
    B. Trained vocal language
        1. Herman's dolphins
        2. Talking apes
            a. Witmer, Furness, Hayes, Laidler
            b. Physical deficiency
III. Animals' sign language
    A. Natural gestures
    B. Trained gestures
        1. The Gardners and Washoe
        2. Patterson's vocal and sign evidence
        3. Terrace's skepticism
IV. The cockatoo's spontaneous sentence

Chimp Talk. Con

Monkey-cries and those of other non-human primates are involuntary, representing only immediate emotions and different intensities of arousal.

De Vore 158✓

Baboons. Pro

"Almost all behavior in monkeys and apes involves a mixture of the learned and the innate; almost all behavior is under some genetic control in that its development is channelled -- although the amount of channelling varies. Thus all baboons of one species will grow up producing much the same range of vocalizations; however, the same sound may have subtly different meanings for members of different troops of the same species."✓

Pilbeam 111✓

Monkey-cries. Pro

Field studies "suggest that these natural signals may be more specific and wordlike than anyone ever imagined."✓ 17
Tom Struhsaker discovered vervet cries:

(1) raspy bark - leopard - take to trees.
(2) short stacatto grunts - eagle - look up, then dive for cover (bushes, grass).
(3) high-pitched chutter - snake - all stand and scan grass.

Seyfarth 17✓

Can Animals Talk?

My Golden Retriever speaks for food. He tells any of my family what he wants, whether just to go out or to go for a walk. Everything about him--his different whines, his eyes and the wrinkles between, his ears, his tail--conveys the message. Some people similarly feel that horses can almost talk. In fact, researchers have discovered distinctive cries in birds, wolves, and monkeys, and have even taught chimpanzees to use language on computers. Although many remain skeptical, a formidable body of evidence now shows that some animals can use and comprehend language.

Opening Invitation

(Funneling to)

Thesis

The case against non-human linguistic comprehension rests on defining it as the ability to generate new sentences. But clearly animals communicate in vocal sounds. Their cries tell clearly of discovered food or danger. But are these language? The skeptics answer, "No." Irven De Vore, for instance, concludes that primates' cries express only emotional states and degrees of arousal (158), not the rational detachment of a linguistic concept.

Opposition: Con

Back to Pro

Con

Source Cited with Page in Parenthesis

But others find something very like language in non-human primates. David Pilbeam observes that

Topic Sentence (Pro)

> . . . all baboons of one species will grow up producing much the same range of vocalizations; however,

Page in Parenthesis Without Period After

> the same sound may have subtly different meanings for members of different troops of the same species. (111)

Robert Seyfarth says of vervet monkeys in Africa: their

Quotation Marks, Page in Parenthesis, Period After

"natural signals may be more specific and more wordlike than anyone ever imagined" (17). Vervets have three alarms. A raspy bark for a leopard sends the troop into the trees. Short staccato grunts for eagles send everyone into the brush. A high-pitched chutter for a snake brings all to

Same Page Repeated

their hind legs to scan the grass (17). By playing their recorded alarms, Seyfarth demonstrated that the sounds alone, not an actual snake or leopard, sent the message.

Further Evidence

Browsing vervets also make four different grunts, meaning: (1) "You are dominant; I approach cautiously"; (2) "You are subordinate, but need not move off"; (3) "We move into an open plain"; (4) "Another group approaches" (18).

Topic Sentence (Con)

Pro

The problem of volition--of intending a meaning--remains open to interpretation. Lyn Miles reports volitional "language" in chimpanzees. Bruno wanted a hose his cage-mate had. He went to the door and uttered the chimpanzee's alarm. His companion dropped the hose and ran to see while Bruno captured the hose (15). Nevertheless, H. Hediger

Con

questions that teaching chimpanzees signs to get what they want is language, particularly the computerized system known as "Yerkish." He points out that the animal brain

3
S. Clark
Eng. 123

lacks the human speech center, the Broca's Area and the Wernicke Area (443), and that deceptive signals, which seem to indicate volition, are widespread in creatures far below the rational threshold. Female glowworms emit the female signal of another species to catch and eat their incoming males. Polar foxes and many birds give alarms to scare their colleagues from choice morsels (441-42).

Hediger suspects the "Clever Hans Effect," frequently mentioned in criticizing animals' linguistic achievements. Clever Hans, a German horse, mystified the late nineteenth century by tapping out numbers and picking out words until his examiners discovered that he followed his questioners' inadvertent signals--slight signs of satisfaction at his reaching the right number of taps or nuzzling the right placard.[1] Hediger sees little more than a clever animal's sensing a human animal's involuntary signs to get what he wants.

Further Opposition (Con)

Nevertheless, evidence that animals can understand human language is plentiful. Emily Hahn cites Mrs. Elizabeth Mann Borgese, daughter of Thomas Mann (54-59), most

Topic Sentence Switching Back to Pro

[1] See Hahn, 46-48. Wilhelm van Osten, a mathematician, trained Hans and exhibited him privately in Berlin. Hans would nod or shake his head to yes-no questions, would indicate "up" or "down," would translate into a code of hoof-taps answers concerning letters, musical tones, and names of playing cards.

Amplifying Footnote

Evidence: Specific Illustration

notably her testing of an Italian poodle named Peg. To avoid Clever-Hansing, Mrs. Borgese took a child's picture book, faced it away from her, and opened it at random. She marked the place, closed the book, and asked Peg, in her native Italian, "Did you see what I showed you?" Peg barked three times, her "Yes." She then chose from her cards "CAVALLI," or "horses." Mrs. Borgese opened the book at her marker and discovered a picture of two work horses. Peg could not only spell but tell plurals from singulars.

Additional Evidence: Expert Opinion

Opinion: Con

This is training, which discounts Peg's natural ability to talk. But Dr. John C. Lilly believes that dolphins have a language, culture, oral history, philosophy, and system of ethics, as he told Michael Parfit (76). Kenneth Norris disagrees: "There isn't anything that even hints at language" (Parfit 77).

Return to Pro

Nevertheless, Louis Herman is demonstrating the dolphin's linguistic capacity. He has created a computerized code of whistles that his dolphins understand and use. One dolphin has a vocabulary of twenty-five nouns, adjectives, and verbs. Herman throws a ball into the pool. The dolphin whistles "ball." Herman whistles him to push the ball to a floating plastic pipe, then to push the pipe to the ball, demonstrating a grasp of subjects and verbs that

5
S. Clark
Eng. 123

bridges the gap between word and sentence (Parfit 79).

Apes have been taught to speak. In 1909, Lightner Witmer trained a chimpanzee to say "mama," though the *ah* was only whispered (179-205). In 1916, William H. Furness taught a female orangutan to say "papa" and "cup" (283-84). Beginning in 1947 with a three-day-old, Cathy and Keith Hayes taught their chimpanzee Viki three words in thirty difficult months: "mama," "papa," and "cup." After six years, they had added no more than "up," and Viki's discrimination was far from accurate and not always forthcoming (67, 108, 136, 240).[2]

Historical Evidence

Contemporary Evidence

By limiting the environment and following Furness's method of molding lips, tongue, and breath, Keith Laidler in England has accomplished more with his infant orangutan, Cody: four distinct words, for the naturally taciturn ape, at the age of fifteen months in less than eight months of training: *kuh*, from the larynx with mouth open ("a drink"); *puh*, from pouted lips, unvoiced ("pick me up"); *fuh*, from teeth over lower lip ("solid food"); and *thuh*, from tongue between teeth ("brush me," which Cody also used for "I'm

[2] Linden reports once that Viki achieved four words (15), and once that she was able "laboriously to produce seven words" (68). But he gives no source, misspells Viki "Vicki," and finally refers to the Hayeses as "Keith and Virginia" (244). Laidler (36, 162) agrees that Viki's limit was four.

Footnote Discussing Conflicting Evidence

sorry"). Cody became more than 70% accurate on most days, and even invented sheesh for "come follow" (123-30, 144-45, 161-65).

But, in spite of limited success, Viki showed the way to sign language. R. Allen and Beatrice Gardner noticed in films that Viki was fluent in gestures as she agonized with words. Hence their famous experiments in teaching the female chimpanzee, Washoe, American Sign Language, or "Ameslan," which led to many similar projects. The Gardners reinforced the chimpanzee's natural asking gesture, the hand extended, palm up. They taught Washoe to flex her wrist upward and back for the Ameslan sign "give me." In Ameslan, both hands extended side by side, palms down, then rotated outward, signify "open," which Washoe learned to ask for opening doors and turning on faucets. She can generate new words like "water bird" for "swan." Her responses show a sense of syntax and an urge to communicate independent of physical needs. Hearing a dog bark, she made two Ameslan signs, pointing to her ear for "hear," slapping her thigh for "dog." She was saying "I hear a dog" (664-72).

Most Recent Evidence

Though ape-Ameslan omits the finger-spelling that augments human signing, each animal and person has a name-sign, usually his finger-spelt initial combined with a characteristic gesture like pushing back the hair or touching the moustache. Eugene Linden tells of watching Roger Fouts reversing the chimpanzee Lucy's habitual "Roger tickle Lucy." Lucy, puzzled, signed, "No, Roger tickle Lucy." Fouts signed back, "No, Lucy tickle Roger." Linden "could see comprehension brighten in Lucy's eyes" as she responded and enjoyed successive turn-abouts (99). Finally, Lyn Miles tells of a chimpanzee, Allee, signing to a trainer named George as another trainer (evidently Fouts again) approached smoking a pipe, "George smell Roger"--not only an original sentence but a remark showing sympathetic understanding of another, which is a good conceptual step beyond a simple "I want," or even "I smell" (15).

Francine Patterson's work with her two gorillas, Koko and Michael, reveals even more remarkable verbal ability. Patterson, unlike the chimpanzee people, combines spoken English with Ameslan. With a computer that generates a female voice, Koko will punch keys to enunciate "want apple eat" when shown an apple ("Conversation" 465). Koko also can rhyme, signing "hair bear" and "all ball," and pointing to a pig in a series of toys when asked what rhymes with "big" (Education 141). She also makes spontaneous metaphors, like "red mad gorilla" when angry.

Futher Evidence

Title Given When Author Has Two Works Cited

Her junior partner, Michael, also generates sentences.

When a teacher asked what he had been doing, he repeatedly signed anger, hit, mouth, red, hair, and woman to tell of a red-haired woman's fisticuffs in an office across the way, which Michael and Koko had watched from their window. When asked about a bird, Michael signed bird good cat chase eat red trouble cat eat bird, clearly another narrative of what he had seen (172-73).

Argument (Con)

Herbert S. Terrace challenges Patterson for Clever-Hansing and wishful interpretation. He raised from infancy a male chimpanzee named Nim Chimsky in honor of Noam Chomsky, the Cartesian linguist who disbelieves in animals' language. After four years, Terrace returned Nim to his center of origin in Oklahoma believing that Nim could form sentences. But after studying his evidence, he concluded that Nim was just another clever behaviorist doing what he must to get what he wanted. Nim's sign-sentences, Terrace believes, were probably only "separate words related to a particular situation but not to each other" (169-70). Unlike a child, Nim would frequently interrupt a question, showing that he was not following the signaled sequence as a sentence. Unlike a child's lengthening sentences, Nim's remained an average of only 1.5 signs. The most Terrace will admit is that chimpanzees "can master some aspects of human language" (226).

9
S. Clark
Eng. 123

Nevertheless, some animals in human environment have managed conceptual language: for instance, a cockatoo named Fred, one of those birds proverbial for mindless parroting. His trainer had prepared him for a TV serial in which an actor was to carry him around upside down:

Further Evidence: Pro

> "Fred started screaming at the top of his lungs, 'Stop! Stop! Don't hurt Fred!' He yelled this through the entire scene . . . and it was on a first-time basis. He had never been taught those words before. He put that phrase together all by himself." (Terry B-7)

An intense emotion had produced not an animal's emotive cry but spontaneous human sentences.

Clearly, then, animals have demonstrated themselves capable of language, in a human environment and under intense training. In the wild, with their keener senses, environmental awareness, and involuntary signals, animals have little need for conversation. But human communication, too, relies to a considerable extent on context, on tiny signals of mood, on smiles, nervous tics, and gestures. We are probably closer to the animals than we think, and the whistling dolphins, talking Freds, and signing Washoes have shown that they sometimes can in fact talk to us on our own ground.

Thesis Restated

Clincher

10
S. Clark
Eng. 123

Works Cited

De Vore, Irven. Primate Behavior: Field Studies of Monkeys and Apes. New York: Holt, 1965.

Furness, W. H. "Observations on the Mentality of Chimpanzees and Orang-utans." Proceedings of the American Philosophical Society (Philadelphia: Am. Philos. Soc., 1916) 65: 281-90.

Gardner, R. Allen, and Beatrice T. Gardner. "Teaching Sign Language to a Chimpanzee." Science 165 (1969): 664-72.

Hahn, Emily. "Getting Through to Others." Part 1. The New Yorker 17 Apr. 1978: 38-103.

Hayes, Cathy. The Ape in Our House. New York: Harper, 1951.

Hediger, H[eini]. "Do You Speak Yerkish? The Newest Colloquial Language with Chimpanzees." In Sebeok and Sebeok: 441-47.

Laidler, Keith. The Talking Ape. New York: Stein and Day, 1980.

Linden, Eugene. Apes, Men, and Language. New York: Saturday Review Press; Dutton, 1974.

[Miles, Lyn]. "Chimpanzees Chat in Sign Language." Associated Press Release. Ann Arbor News 14 Nov. 1975: 15.

11
S. Clark
Eng. 123

Montagu, Ashley. Man and Aggression. 2nd ed. New York: Oxford, 1973.

Parfit, Michael. "Are Dolphins Trying to Say Something, Or Is It All Much Ado About Nothing?" Smithsonian 11 (1980): 72-81.

Patterson, Francine. "Conversation with a Gorilla." National Geographic Magazine 15 (1978): 438-65.

______, and Eugene Linden. The Education of Koko. New York: Holt, 1981.

Pilbeam, David. "An Idea We Could Live Without: The Naked Ape." Discovery 7 (1971). Rpt. in Ashley Montagu: 110-121.

Sebeok, Thomas A., and Jean Umiker Sebeok, eds. Speaking of Apes: A Critical Anthology of Two-Way Communication with Man. New York and London: Plenum, 1980.

Seyfarth, Robert. "Talking with Monkeys and Great Apes." International Wildlife 12 (1982): 12-18.

Terrace, Herbert S. Nim. New York: Knopf, 1978.

Terry, Sara. "All This and a Cockatoo Too!" Christian Science Monitor Service. Ann Arbor News 5 Mar. 1978: B-7.

Witmer, Lightner. "A Monkey with Mind." The Psychological Clinic [Philadelphia] 3 (1909): 179-205.

EXERCISES

1. *Consult the current* World Almanac and Book of Facts *for the date of some memorable event: the sinking of the* Titanic *or the* Lusitania, *Lindbergh's flight over the Atlantic, the United States' entry into war, the founding of the United Nations, the great stock-market crash, or the like. Now go to another collection, like* Facts on File, *and some of the other almanacs and yearbooks for the year of your event; write an essay entitled, let us say, "1929"—a synopsis of the monumental and the quaint for that year, as lively and interesting as you can make it.*
2. *Look up some event of the recent past (after 1913) in the* New York Times Index. *Write a paper on how the event is reported in the* Times *and in the other newspapers available in your library.*
3. *Choose a subject like the origin of man, the PLO, apartheid—anything that interests you—and compile a bibliographical list of the articles given in the* Reader's Guide, *beginning with the most recent issue and going backward in time until you have eight or ten titles. You may have to look under several headings, such as "archeology," "anthropology," and "evolution," for the origin of man; under "Israel," "Lebanon," and others in addition to "PLO" itself; and under "South Africa," "racism," and "apartheid" itself for apartheid. Then look in the scholarly* Indexes *(see 346), and make another bibliographical listing of your subject for the same period. Which articles appear in the* Humanities *or* Social Sciences Index *(or both) only? Which articles appear in the* Reader's Guide *only? Which appear in both the* Indexes *and the* Guide? *Write a brief commentary about the differences in coverage in these two (or three) indexes. What does comparing them tell you about research?*
4. *In the* Essay and General Literature Index, *look up three essays published in anthologies between 1965 and 1969 on Gerard Manley Hopkins, recording each entry and then following it by full data on the book, with call number, from the card catalog.*
5. *Select some well-known literary work:* Walden, David Copperfield, Huckleberry Finn, Alice in Wonderland, The Wind in the Willows, A Farewell to Arms. *Describe how thoroughly it is cataloged by your library. Check cards for author, title, and subject. How many editions does the library have? Is the work contained within any* Works? *How many cards treat it as a subject? Does your library own a first edition? This last may require that you find the date of the first edition by looking up your author in an encyclopedia, checking available books about him, and perhaps checking in the British Library's* General Catalogue of Printed Books, *or, for a twentieth-century book,* United States Catalog of Printed Books, *or* Cumulative Book Index *to discover the earliest cataloging.*

11
A Writer's Grammar

Theories of grammar have proliferated in the twentieth century, but the familiar nouns, verbs, adjectives, and other entities persist simply because they are the most handy. In spite of certain leaks in the system, traditional grammar can give writers the most help when they need it. Grammar tells us how sentences fit together meaningfully. On paper, we can see where the meanings slide. Here are some typical sliding sentences, each with slippage noted, each slippage discussed on the text pages given at the right.

They **study hard, but** ***you*** **do not have to work all the time. [*You* does not agree with *They*.]**	391–92
Holden ***goes*** **to New York and** ***learned*** **about life. [*Learned* does not agree in tense with *goes*.]**	386
A ***citizen*** **should support the government, but** ***they*** **should also be free to criticize it. [*They* does not agree with *citizen*.]**	391–92
The ***professor*****, as well as the students,** ***were*** **glad the course was over. [*Were* does not agree with *professor*.]**	382–84
As ***he looked up*****, a** ***light could be seen*** **in the window. [The subject has shifted awkwardly from *he* to *light*, and the verbal construction from active to passive.]**	387

Now we knew: it was *him.* [*Him* does not agree in case with the subject, *it.*] 388

Let's keep this between you and *I.* [*I* cannot be the object of *between.*] 389

Can you and Shirley play doubles next Sunday with *Bob and I?* [*I* cannot be the object of *with—with I?*] 389

They accuse William Singleton Stone and *I* of mismanaging their accounts. [*I* cannot be the object of a verb—*accuse I?*] 389

The students always elect *whomever* is popular. [*Whomever* cannot be the subject of the verb *is.*] 388

She hated *me* leaving so early. [She hated not *me* but the *leaving.*] 390

***Bill* told *Fred* that *he* failed the exam. [*He* can mean either *Bill* or *Fred.*]** 394

***Each* of the laborers performed *their* task. [*Each* and *their* disagree in number.]** 391

***Father* felt *badly.* [*Badly* describes Father's competence, not his condition.]** 392

He *spoke friendly.* [The verb requires an adverb, like *warmly,* and *friendly,* though ending in *-ly,* is an adjective, not an adverb.] 392

She said *on Tuesday* she *would call.* [The position of *on Tuesday* confuses the times of *saying* and *calling.*] 393–94

***Walking* to class, her *book* slipped from her grasp. [*Walking* refers illogically to *book.*]** 394

While *playing* the piano, the *dog* sat by me and howled. [Dogs don't usually play pianos.] 394

With each of these, you sense that something is wrong. With a little thought you can usually find the trouble. But what to do may not be so readily apparent. We first need to understand something of the basic structure of grammar.

Know the Basic Parts of Speech

The parts of speech are the elements of the sentence. A grasp of the basic eight—nouns, pronouns, verbs, adjectives, adverbs, prepositions, conjunctions, and interjections—will give you a sense of the whole.

Nouns. Nouns name something. A *proper noun* names a particular person, place, or thing. A *common noun* names a general class of things; a common noun naming a group as a single unit is a *collective noun.* A phrase or clause functioning as a noun is a *noun phrase* or a *noun clause.* Here are some examples:

PROPER: **George, Cincinnati, Texas, Europe, Declaration of Independence**
COMMON: **stone, tree, house, girl, artist, nation, democracy**
COLLECTIVE: **committee, family, quartet, herd, navy, clergy, kind**
NOUN PHRASE: ***Riding the surf* takes stamina.**
NOUN CLAUSE: ***What you say* may depend on *how you say it.***

Pronouns. As their name indicates, pronouns stand "for nouns." The noun a pronoun represents is called its *antecedent.* Pronouns may be classified as follows:

PERSONAL *(standing for persons):* **I, you, he, she, we, they; me, him, her, us, them; his, our, and so on**
POSSESSIVE *(indicating ownership):* **my, mine, yours, his, hers, ours, theirs, whose, its—notice that none of them takes the usual possessive apostrophe-*s: ours* not our's, *its* not it's.**
REFLEXIVE *(turning the action back on the doer):* **I hurt *myself.* They enjoy *themselves.***
INTENSIVE *(emphasizing the doer):* **He *himself* said so.**
RELATIVE *(linking subordinate clauses):* **who, which, that, whose, whomever, whichever, and so on**
INTERROGATIVE *(beginning a question):* **who, which, what**
DEMONSTRATIVE *(pointing to things):* **this, that, these, those, such**
INDEFINITE *(standing for indefinite numbers of persons or things):* **any, each, few, some, anyone, no one, everyone, somebody, and so on**
RECIPROCAL *(plural reflexives):* **each other, one another**

Note that pronouns describing nouns function as adjectives:

> PRONOUNS: ***Few*** **would recognize** ***this.***
> PRONOUNS AS ADJECTIVES: ***Few*** **readers would recognize** ***this*** **allusion.**

Verbs. Verbs express actions or states of being, present, past, or future. A verb may be *transitive,* requiring an object to complete the thought, or *intransitive,* requiring no object for completeness. Some verbs can function either transitively or intransitively. *Linking verbs* link the subject to a state of being.

> TRANSITIVE: **He** ***put*** **his feet on the chair. She** ***sold*** **her old car. They** ***sang*** **a sad old song. She** ***lays*** **carpets.**
> INTRANSITIVE: **He** ***smiled.*** **She** ***cried.*** **They** ***sang*** **like birds. They** ***are coming.*** **He** ***lies*** **down.**
> LINKING: **He** ***is*** **happy. She** ***feels*** **angry. This** ***looks*** **bad. It** ***is*** **she.**

Adjectives. Adjectives narrow and specify nouns or pronouns. An *adjectival phrase* or *adjectival clause* functions in a sentence as a single adjective would.

> ADJECTIVES: **The** ***red*** **house faces west. He was a** ***handsome*** **devil. The** ***old haunted*** **house was** ***empty.*** **We saw a** ***dancing*** **bear. We walked at a** ***leisurely*** **pace.** ***These*** **books belong to** ***that*** **student. [In the last example, demonstrative pronouns serve as adjectives.]**
> ADJECTIVAL PHRASE: **He had reached the end** ***of the book.***
> ADJECTIVAL CLAUSE: **Here is the key** ***that unlocks the barn.***

Articles, which point out nouns, are classified with adjectives. *The,* the "definite" article, points to specific persons or things; *A* and *an,* the "indefinite" articles, point out persons or things as members of groups.

> ARTICLES: ***The*** **hunter selected** ***a*** **rifle from** ***an*** **assortment.**

Adverbs. Adverbs describe verbs, adjectives, or other adverbs, completing the ideas of *how, how much, when,* and *where.* An *adverbial phrase* or *adverbial clause* functions as a single adverb would.

ADVERBS: Though *slightly* fat, he runs *quickly* and plays *extremely well.* She runs *fast.*
ADVERBIAL PHRASE: He left *after the others.* He spoke *with vigor.*
ADVERBIAL CLAUSE: She lost the gloves *after she left the store.*

Certain forms of verbs, alone or in phrases, serve as nouns, adjectives, and adverbs. *Participles* act as adjectives. *Present participles* are verbs plus *-ing,* and *past participles* are regular verbs plus *-ed* (see 455 for *Irregular verbs*). *Gerunds,* like present participles, are verbs plus *-ing* but work as nouns; past participles occasionally function as nouns, also. *Infinitives—to* plus a verb—serve as nouns, adjectives, or adverbs. Unlike participles and gerunds, infinitives can have subjects, which are always in the objective case.

PRESENT PARTICIPLES: *Feeling* miserable and *running* a fever, she took to her bed. [adjectives]
PAST PARTICIPLES: The nurses treated the *wounded* soldier. [adjective] The nurses treated the *wounded.* [noun]
GERUND PHRASE: *His going* ended the friendship. [noun, subject of sentence]
INFINITIVES: *To err* is human; *to forgive,* divine. [nouns, subjects of sentence]
I saw *him* [to] go. [phrase serving as noun, object of *saw; him* subject of *to go*]
Ford is the man *to watch.* [adjective]
Coiled, the snake waited *to strike.* [adverb]

Prepositions. A preposition links a noun or pronoun to another word in the sentence. A preposition and its object form a *prepositional phrase,* which acts as an adjective or adverb:

BY *late afternoon,* Williams was exhausted. [as adverb, modifying *was exhausted*]
He walked TO *his car* and drove FROM *the field.* [as adverbs, modifying *walked* and *drove*]
The repairman opened the base OF *the telephone.* [as adjective, modifying *base*]

Conjunctions. Conjunctions join words, phrases, and clauses. *Coordinating* conjunctions—*and, but, or, nor, yet, so, still, for*—join equals:

Mary *and* I won easily.
Near the shore *but* far from home, the bottle floated.
He was talented, *yet* he failed.
Could you take Karl *and* me water-skiing.

Subordinating conjunctions attach clauses to the basic subject-and-verb:

***Since* it was late, they left.**
He worked hard *because* he needed an *A*.
They stopped *after* they reached the spring.

Interjections. Interjections interrupt the usual flow of the sentence to emphasize feelings:

But, *oh,* the difference to me.
Mr. Dowd, *alas,* has ignored the evidence.
The consumer will suddenly discover that, *ouch,* his dollar is cut in half.

AGREEMENT: NOUNS AND VERBS

Make Your Verb and Its Subject Agree

Match singulars with singulars, plurals with plurals. First, find the verb, since that names the action—*sways* in the following sentence: "The poplar tree *sways* in the wind, dropping yellow leaves on the lawn." Then ask *who* or *what* sways, and you have your simple subject: *tree,* a singular noun. Then make sure that your singular subject matches its singular verb. (A reminder: contrary to nouns, the majority of singular verbs end in *s*—the actor performs; actors perform.) You will have little trouble except when subject and verb are far apart, or when the number of the subject itself is doubtful. (Is *family* singular or plural? What about *none?* What about *neither he nor she?*)

Subject and Verb Widely Separated

FAULTY: ***Revision* of their views about markets and averages *are* mandatory.**

REVISED: ***Revision* of their views about markets and averages *is* mandatory.**

Sidestep the plural constructions that fall between your singular subject and its verb:

Mistaken Plurals

FAULTY: **The *attention* of the students *wander* out the window.**
REVISED: **The *attention* of the students *wanders* out the window.**

FAULTY: **The *plaster*, as well as the floors, *need* repair.**
REVISED: **The *plaster*, as well as the floors, *needs* repair.**

Collective nouns *(committee, jury, herd, group, family, kind, quartet)* are single units (plural in British usage); give them singular verbs, or plural members:

Collective Nouns

FAULTY: **Her *family were* ready.**
REVISED: **Her *family was* ready.**

FAULTY: **The *jury have disagreed* among themselves.**
REVISED: **The *jurors have disagreed* among themselves.**

FAULTY: **These *kind* of muffins *are* delicious.**
REVISED: ***These muffins are* delicious.**
REVISED: ***This kind* of muffin *is* delicious.**

Watch out for the indefinite pronouns—*each, neither, anyone, everyone, no one, none, everybody, nobody.* Each of these is (not *are*) singular in idea, yet each one flirts with the crowd from which it singles out its idea: each of *these,* either of *them,* none of *them.* Give all of them singular verbs.

Indefinite Pronouns

***None* of these men *is* a failure.**
***None* of the class, even the best prepared, *wants* the test.**
***Everybody,* including the high-school kids, *goes* to Andy's Drive-In.**
***Neither* the right nor the left *supports* the issue.**

None of them are is very common. From Shakespeare's time to ours, it has persisted alongside the more precise *none of them is,* which seems to have the edge in careful prose.

When one side of the *either-or* contrast is plural, you have a problem, conventionally solved by matching the verb to the nearer noun:

"Either-Or"

Either the players or the coach *is* bad.

Since *players is* disturbs some feelings for plurality, the best solution is probably to switch your nouns:

> **Either the coach or the players *are* bad.**

When both sides of the contrast are plural, the verb is naturally also plural:

> **Neither the rights of man nor the needs of the commonwealth *are* relevant to the question.**

Don't let a plural noun in the predicate lure you into a plural verb:

> FAULTY: **His most faithful rooting *section are* his family and his girl.**
> REVISED: **His most faithful rooting *section is* his family and his girl.**
> REVISED: **His family and his girl *are* his best rooting section.**

ALIGNING THE VERBS

Verbs have *tense* (past, present, future), *mood* (indicative, imperative, subjunctive), and *voice* (active, passive). These can sometimes slip out of line, as your thought slips, so a review should be useful here:

Use the Tense That Best Expresses Your Idea

Each tense (from Latin *tempus,* meaning time) has its own virtues for expressing what you want your sentences to say. Use the *present tense,* of course, to express present action: "Now she *knows.* She *is leaving.*" Use the present also for habitual action: "He *sees* her every day," and for describing literary events: "Hamlet *finds* the king praying, but he *is* unable to act; he *lets* the opportunity slip." And use the present tense to express timeless facts: "The Greeks knew the world *is* round." The present can also serve for the future: "Classes begin next Monday." Apply the *past tense* to all action before the present:

> **One day I *was watching* television when the phone *rang;* it *was* the police.**
> **In the center of the cracked façade, the door *sagged;* rubble *lay* all around the foundations.**

Use the *future tense* for action expected after the present:

> **He *will finish* it next year.**
> **When he *finishes* next year, . . . [The present functioning as future]**
> **He *is going to finish* it next year. [The "present progressive" *is going* plus an infinitive, like to *finish,* commonly expresses the future.]**

Use the *present perfect tense* for action completed ("perfected") but relevant to the present moment:

> **I *have gone* there before.**
> **He *has sung* forty concerts.**
> **She *has driven* there every day.**

Use the *past perfect tense* to express "the past of the past":

> **"When we *arrived* [past], they *had finished* [past perfect]."**

Similarly, use the *future perfect tense* to express "the past of the future":

> **When we *arrive* [future], they *will have finished* [future perfect].**
> **You *will have worked* thirty hours by Christmas. [future perfect].**
> **The flare *will signal* [future] that he *has started* [perfect].**

Set your tense, then move your reader clearly forward or back from it as your thought requires:

Shifting tenses

> **Hamlet *finds* the king praying. He *had sworn* instant revenge the night before, but he *will achieve* it only by accident and about a week later. Here he *is* unable to act; he *loses* his best opportunity.**

But avoid mixtures like this: "Hamlet *finds* the king praying, but he *was* unable to act; he *let* the opportunity slip." Here, all the verbs should be in the present, corresponding to *finds*.

Confusing the past tense of *lie* with the verb *lay* is a frequent error. *Lie* is intransitive, taking no object: *Lie* down; I *lie* down; I *lay* down yesterday; I have *lain* down often. *Lay* is transitive, taking an object: I *lay* carpets; I *laid* one yesterday; I have *laid* them often. When someone says incorrectly "He is *laying* down," ask yourself the impudent questions "Who is Down?" or "Is he laying goosefeathers?"—and you might remember to say, and write: "He is *lying* down."

Keep Your Moods in Mind

The *indicative mood,* which indicates matters of fact (our usual verb and way of writing), and the *imperative mood,* which commands ("Do this," "Keep your moods in mind"), will give you no trouble. The *subjunctive mood,* which expresses an action or condition not asserted as actual fact, occasionally will. The conditional, provisional, wishful, suppositional ideas expressed by the subjunctive are usually subjoined (*subjunctus,* "yoked under") in subordinate clauses. The form of the verb is often plural, and often in past tense, even though the subject is singular, and the condition present or future.

He looked as if he *were* confident.
If I *were* you, Miles, I would ask her myself.
If this *be* error, and upon me [*be*] proved. . . .
***Had* he *been* sure, he would have said so.**
I demand that he *make* restitution.
I move that the nominations *be closed,* and that the secretary *cast* a unanimous ballot.

Don't let *would have* (colloquial *would've*) seep into your conditional clause from your main clause:

FAULTY: **If he *would have known,* he never would have said that.**
REVISED: **If he *had known,* he never would have said that.**
REVISED: ***Had* he *known,* he never would have said that.**

Be careful not to write *would of* or *should of* for *would have (would've)* or *should have (should've).*

"Would've"

Don't Mix Active and Passive Voice

One parting shot at our friend the passive. Avoid misaligning active with passive in the same sentence:

> **As he *entered* the room, muttering *was heard* [he *heard*].**
> **After they *laid out* the pattern, electric shears *were used* [they *used* electric shears].**

Mixed voices

You can also think of this as an awkward shift of subject, from *he* to *muttering,* from *they* to *shears.* Here is a slippery sample, where the subject stays the same:

> FAULTY: **This plan *reduces* taxes and *has been used* successfully in three other cities.**
> REVISED: **This plan *reduces* taxes and *has been* successful in three other cities.**
> REVISED: **This plan *reduces* taxes and *has proved* workable in three other cities.**

Past tense; not passive voice

REFERENCE OF PRONOUNS

Match Your Pronouns to What They Stand For

Pronouns stand for *(pro)* nouns. They *refer* to nouns already expressed *(antecedents),* or they stand for conceptions (people, things, ideas) already established or implied, as in "*None of them* is perfect." Pronouns must agree with the singular and plural ideas they represent, and stand clearly as subjects or objects.

When a relative pronoun *(who, which, that)* is the subject of a clause, it takes a singular verb if its antecedent is singular, a plural verb if its antecedent is plural:

Phil is the only *one* of our swimmers WHO *has* won three gold medals. [The antecedent is *one,* not *swimmers.*]
Phil is one of the best *swimmers* WHO *have* ever been on the team. [The antecedent is *swimmers,* not *one.*]

Pronouns may stand either as subjects or objects of the action, and their form changes accordingly.

Use Nominative Pronouns for Nominative Functions

Those pronouns in the predicate that refer to, or complement, the subject are troublesome; keep them nominative:

Subjective Complement

He discovered that it was *I.*
It was *they* who signed the treaty.

Another example is that of the pronoun in *apposition* with the subject (that is, *positioned near, applied to,* and meaning the same thing as, the subject):

Apposition with Subject

***We* students would rather talk than sleep.**

After *than* and *as,* the pronoun is usually the subject of an implied verb:

Implied Verb

She is taller than *I* [am].
You are as bright as *he* [is].
She loves you as much as *I* [do].

But note: "She loves you as much as [she loves] *me.*" Match your pronouns to what they stand for, subjects for subjects, objects for objects. (But a caution: use an objective pronoun as the subject of an infinitive. See 381, 390).

Use a nominative pronoun as subject of a noun clause. This is the trickiest of pronominal problems, because the subject of the clause also looks like the object of the main verb:

FAULTY: **The sergeant asked *whomever* did it to step forward.**
REVISED: **The sergeant asked *whoever* did it to step forward.**

Similarly, parenthetical remarks like *I think, he says,* and *we believe* often make pronouns seem objects when they are actually subjects:

FAULTY: Ellen is the girl *whom* I think *will succeed.*
REVISED: Ellen is the girl *who* I think *will succeed.*

Use Objective Pronouns for Objective Functions

Compound objects give most of the trouble. Try the pronoun by itself: "invited *me,*" "sent *him,*" and so forth. These are all correct:

Compound Objects

The mayor invited my wife and *me* to dinner. [*not* my wife and *I*]
Between *her* and *me,* an understanding grew.
They sent it to Stuart and *him.*
. . . for you and *me.*

Again, *see if the pronoun would stand by itself* ("for I"? No, *for me*):

FAULTY: The credit goes to *he* who tries. ["to he"?]
REVISED: The credit goes to *him* who tries.

Pronouns in apposition with objects must themselves be objective:

Apposition with Object

FAULTY: The mayor complimented us both—Bill and *I.*
REVISED: The mayor complimented us both—Bill and *me.*

FAULTY: She gave the advice specifically to us—Helen and *I.*
REVISED: She gave the advice specifically to us—Helen and *me.*

FAULTY: Between us—Elaine and *I*—an understanding grew.
REVISED: Between us—Elaine and *me*—an understanding grew.

FAULTY: He would not think of letting *we* girls help him.
REVISED: He would not think of letting *us* girls help him.

Notice this one:

FAULTY: **Will you please help Leonard and *I* find the manager?**
REVISED: **Will you please help Leonard and *me* find the manager?**

Leonard and me are objective both as objects of the verb *help* and as subjects of the shortened infinitive *to find.* Subjects of infinitives are always in the objective case, as in "She saw *him* go"; "She helped *him* find his keys."

Use a Possessive Pronoun Before a Gerund

Since gerunds are *-ing* words used as nouns, the pronouns attached to them must say what they mean:

FAULTY: **She disliked *him* hunting.**
REVISED: **She disliked *his* hunting.**

The object of her dislike is not *him* but *hunting.*

Keep Your Antecedents Clear

If an antecedent is missing, ambiguous, vague, or remote, the pronoun will suffer from "faulty reference."

MISSING: **In Texas *they* produce a lot of oil.**
REVISED: **Texas produces a lot of oil.**

AMBIGUOUS: **Paul smashed into a girl's *car who* was visiting his sister.**
REVISED: **Paul smashed into the car of a *girl* visiting his sister.**

VAGUE: **Because Ann had never spoken before an audience, she was afraid of *it.***
REVISED: **Because Ann had never spoken before an audience, she was afraid.**

REMOTE: **The castle was built in 1537. The rooms and furnishings are carefully kept up, but the entrance is now guarded by a coin-fed turnstile. *It* still belongs to the Earl.**

REVISED: **The castle, which still belongs to the Earl, was built in 1537. The rooms and furnishings are carefully kept up, but the entrance is now guarded by a coin-fed turnstile.**

This poses a special problem, especially when heading a sentence ("This is a special problem"). Many good stylists insist that every *this* refer back to a specific noun—*report* in the following example:

The commission submitted its *report. This* proved windy, evasive, and ineffectual.

"This"

Others occasionally allow (as I do) a more colloquial *this,* referring back more broadly:

The commission submitted its report. This ended the matter.

Give an Indefinite or General Antecedent a Singular Pronoun

FAULTY: ***Each* of the students hoped to follow in *their* teacher's footsteps.**

REVISED: ***Each* of the students hoped to follow in *his* [or *his or her*] teacher's footsteps.**

REVISED: ***All* of the students hoped to follow in *their* teacher's footsteps. [Here, we have a single class.]**

FAULTY: **If the *government* dares to face the new philosophy, *they* should declare *themselves.***

REVISED: **If the *government* dares to face the new philosophy, *it* should declare *itself.***

Keep Person and Number Consistent

Don't slip from person to person *(I* to *they);* don't fall among singulars and plurals—or you will get bad references:

FAULTY: **_They_ have reached an age when _you_ should know better.**
REVISED: **_They_ have reached an age when _they_ should know better.**

FAULTY: **A motion _picture_ can improve upon a book, but _they_ usually do not.**
REVISED: **A motion _picture_ can improve upon a book, but _it_ usually does not.**

MODIFIERS MISUSED AND MISPLACED

Keep Your Adjectives and Adverbs Straight

The adjective sometimes wrongly crowds out the adverb: "He played a *real* conservative game." And the adverb sometimes steals the adjective's place, especially when the linking verb looks transitive but isn't *(feels, looks, tastes, smells),* making the sense wrong: "He feels *badly*" (adverb) means incompetence, not misery. The cure is to modify your nouns with adjectives, and everything else with adverbs:

He played a _really_ conservative game. [adverb]
He feels _bad._ [adjective]
This tastes _good._ [adjective]
I feel _good._ [adjective—spirit]
I feel _well._ [adjective—health]
This works _well._ [adverb]

Some words serve both as adjectives and adverbs: *early, late, near, far, hard, only, little, right, wrong, straight, well, better, best, fast,* for example, to be squeezed for their juice.

Think _little_ of _little_ things.

Near is a hard case, serving as an adjective *(the near future)* and as an adverb of place *(near the barn),* and then also trying to serve for *nearly,* the adverb of degree:

FAULTY: We are nowhere *near* knowledgeable enough.
REVISED: We are not *nearly* knowledgeable enough.

FAULTY: It was a *near* treasonous statement.
REVISED: It was a *nearly* treasonous statement.

FAULTY: With Dodge, he has a tie of *near*-filial rapport.
REVISED: With Dodge, he has an *almost* filial rapport.

Slow has a long history as an adverb, but *slowly* keeps the upper hand in print. Notice that adverbs usually go after, and adjectives before:

The *slow* freight went *slowly.*

Make Your Comparisons Complete

Ask yourself "Than what?"—when you find your sentences ending with a *greener* (adjective) or a *more smoothly* (adverb):

FAULTY: The western plains are *flatter.*
REVISED: The western plains are *flatter than* those east of the Mississippi.

FAULTY: He plays more *skillfully.*
REVISED: He plays more *skillfully than* most boys his age.

FAULTY: Jane told her more than Ellen.
REVISED: Jane told her more than she told Ellen.

FAULTY: His income is lower than a *busboy.*
REVISED: His income is lower than a *busboy's.*

Don't Let Your Modifiers Squint

Some modifiers squint in two directions at once. Place them to modify one thing only.

FAULTY: They agreed *when both sides ceased fire* to open negotiations.
REVISED: They agreed to open negotiations *when both sides ceased fire.*

FAULTY: **Several delegations *we know* have failed.**
REVISED: ***We know* that several delegations have failed.**

FAULTY: **They hoped to try *thoroughly* to understand.**
REVISED: **They hoped to try to understand *thoroughly*.**

FAULTY: **He resolved to *dependably* develop plans.**
REVISED: **He resolved to develop *dependable* plans.**

Don't Let Your Modifiers or References Dangle

The *-ing* words (the gerunds and participles) tend to slip loose from the sentence and dangle, referring to nothing or the wrong thing.

FAULTY: **Going home, the walk was slippery. [participle]**
REVISED: **Going home, I found the walk slippery.**

FAULTY: **When getting out of bed, his toe hit the dresser. [gerund]**
REVISED: **When getting out of bed, he hit his toe on the dresser.**

Infinitive phrases also can dangle badly:

FAULTY: **To think clearly, some logic is important.**
REVISED: **To think clearly, you should learn some logic.**

Any phrase or clause may dangle:

FAULTY: **When only a freshman [phrase], Jim's history teacher inspired him.**
REVISED: **When Jim was only a freshman, his history teacher inspired him.**

FAULTY: **After he had taught thirty years [clause], the average student still seemed average.**
REVISED: **After he had taught thirty years, he found the average student still average.**

EXERCISES

1. *Straighten out these disagreements and misalignments:*

1. These kinds of questions are sheer absurdities.
2. Conservatism, as well as liberalism, are summonses for change in American life, as we know it.
3. Neither the make of his car nor the price of his stereo impress us.
4. Her family were bitter about it.
5. The grazing ground of both the antelope and the wild horses are west of this range.
6. The campus, as well as the town, need to wake up.
7. The extinction of several species of whales are threatened.
8. None of the group, even Smith and Jones, want to play.
9. If I would have studied harder, I would have passed.
10. First he investigated the practical implications, and then the moral implications that were involved were examined.

2. *Revise these faulty pronouns, and their sentences where necessary:*

1. None of us are perfect.
2. Doug is the only one of the boys who always stand straight.
3. He took my wife and I to dinner.
4. She disliked him whistling the same old tune.
5. He will give the ticket to whomever wants it: he did it for you and I.
6. My mother insists on me buying my own clothes: the average girl likes their independence.

3. *Straighten out these adjectives and adverbs:*

1. The demonstration reached near riot proportions.
2. It smells awfully.
3. The dress fitted her perfect.
4. He has a reasonable good chance.
5. His car had a special built engine.

4. *Complete and adjust these partial thoughts.*

1. He swims more smoothly.
2. The pack of a paratrooper is lighter than a soldier.
3. The work of a student is more intense than his parents.

5. *Unsquint these modifiers:*

1. She planned on the next day to call him.
2. They asked after ten days to be notified.
3. The party promised to completely attempt reform.
4. Several expeditions we know have failed.

6. *Mend these danglers:*

1. What we need is a file of engineers broken down by their specialties.
2. Following the games on television, the batting average of every player was at his fingertips.
3. When entering the room, the lamp fell over.
4. After he arrived at the dorm, his father phoned.

7. *Correct the following:*

1. No one likes dancing backward all their lives.
2. His pass hit the wide receiver real good.
3. The ball was laying under the bench.
4. If they would of come earlier, they would of seen everything.
5. I feel badly about it.

8. *Cure the following:*

1. The professor as well as the students were glad the course was over.
2. We study hard at State, but you do not have to work all the time.
3. As he looked up, a light could be seen in the window.
4. A citizen should support the government, but they should also be free to criticize it.
5. She hated me leaving so early.
6. This is one of the best essays that has been submitted.

12
Punctuation, Spelling, Capitalization

Punctuation gives the silent page some of the breath of life. It marks the pauses and emphases with which a speaker points his meaning. Loose punctuators forget what every good writer knows: that even silent reading produces an articulate murmur in our heads, that language springs from the breathing human voice, that the beauty and meaning of language depend on what the written word makes us *hear,* on the sentence's tuning of emphasis and pause. Commas, semicolons, colons, periods, and other punctuation transcribe our meaningful pauses to the printed page.

THE PERIOD: MARKING THE SENTENCE

A period marks a sentence, a subject completed in its verb:

She walked.

A phrase—which lacks a verb, though it may contain a verb *form* (see 381)—subordinates this idea, making it *depend* on some other main clause:

***While walking,* she thought.**

A subordinate clause does the same, making the whole original sentence subordinate:

***While she walked,* she thought.**

Like a period, and a question mark, an exclamation mark marks a sentence, but much more emphatically: *Plan to revise!* Use it sparingly if you want it to count rhetorically.

Take special care not to break off a phrase or clause with a period, making a fragment that looks like a sentence but isn't (unless you intend a rhetorical fragment—see 261–62), and don't use the comma as a period (see 407).

FAULTY: **She dropped the cup. Which had cost twenty dollars.**
REVISED: **She dropped the cup, which had cost twenty dollars.**

FAULTY: **He swung furiously, the ball sailed into the lake.**
REVISED: **He swung furiously. The ball sailed into the lake.**

THE COMMA

Here are the four basic commas:

I. THE INTRODUCER—after introductory phrases and clauses.
II. THE COORDINATOR—between "sentences" joined by *and, but, or, nor, yet, so, still, for.*
III. THE INSERTER—a PAIR around any inserted word or remark.
IV. THE LINKER—when adding words, phrases, or clauses.

I. The Introducer. A comma after every introductory word or phrase makes your writing clearer, more alive with the breath and pause of meaning:

Indeed, the idea failed.
After the first letter, she wrote again.
In the autumn of the same year, he went to Paris.

Without the introductory comma, your reader frequently expects something else:

After the first letter she wrote, she. . . .
In the autumn of the same year he went to Paris, he. . . .

But beware! What looks like an introductory phrase or clause may actually be the subject of the sentence *and should take no comma.* A comma can break up a good marriage of subject and verb. The comma in each of these is an interloper, and should be removed:

That handsome man in the ascot tie, is the groom.
The idea that you should report every observation, is wrong.
The realization that we must be slightly dishonest to be truly kind, comes to all of us sooner or later.

If your clause-as-subject is unusually long, or confusing, you may relieve the pressure by inserting some qualifying remark after it, between two commas:

The idea that you should report every observation, ***however insignificant,*** **is wrong.**
The realization that we must be slightly dishonest to be truly kind, ***obviously the higher motive,*** **comes to all of us sooner or later.**

II. The Coordinator. Between "sentences" joined by coordinate conjunctions. You will often see the comma omitted when your two clauses are short: "He hunted and she fished." But nothing is wrong with "He hunted, and she fished." The comma, in fact, shows the slight pause you make when you say it.

Think of the "comma-and" **(, and)** as a unit equivalent to the period. The period, the semicolon, and the "comma-and" **(, and)** all designate independent clauses—independent "sentences"—but give different emphases:

. **He was tired. He went home.**
; **He was tired; he went home.**
, and **He was tired, and he went home.**

A comma tells your reader that another subject and predicate are coming:

He hunted the hills and dales.
He hunted the hills, and she fished in the streams.
She was naughty but nice.
She was naughty, but that is not our business.
Wear your jacket or coat.
Wear your jacket, or you will catch cold.
It was strong yet sweet.
It was strong, yet it was not unpleasant.

Of course, you may use a comma in *all* the examples above if your sense demands it. The contrasts set by *but, or,* and *yet* often urge a comma, and the even stronger contrasts with *not* and *either-or* demand a comma, whether or not full predication follows:

It was strong, yet sweet.
It was a battle, not a game.
. . . either a bird in the hand, or two in the bush.

Commas signal where you would pause in speaking.

The meaningful pause also urges an occasional comma in compound predicates, usually not separated by commas:

He granted the usual permission and walked away.
He granted the usual permission, and walked away.

Both are correct. In the first sentence, however, the granting and walking are perfectly routine, and the temper unruffled. In the second, some kind of emotion has forced a pause, and a comma, after *permission.* Similarly, meaning itself may demand a comma between the two verbs:

He turned and dropped the vase.
He turned, and dropped the vase.

In the first sentence, he turned the vase; in the second, himself. Your **, and** in compound predicates suggests some touch of drama, some meaningful distinction, or afterthought.

You need a comma before *for* and *still* even more urgently. Without the comma, their conjunctive meaning changes; they assume their ordinary roles, *for* as a preposition, *still* as an adjective or adverb:

She liked him still. . . . [That is, either *yet* or *quiet!*]
She liked him, still she could not marry him.
She liked him for his money.
She liked him, for a good man is hard to find.

An observation: *for* is the weakest of all the coordinators. Almost a subordinator, it is perilously close to *because. For* can seem moronic if cause and effect are fairly obvious: "She liked him, for he was kind." Either make a point of the cause by full subordination—"She liked him *because* he was kind"—or flatter the reader with a semicolon: "She liked him; he was kind." *For* is effective only when the cause is somewhat hard to find: "Blessed are the meek, for they shall inherit the earth."

To summarize the basic point about the comma as coordinator: put a comma before the coordinator *(, and , but , or , nor , yet , so , still , for)* when joining independent clauses, and add others necessary for emphasis or clarity.

III. The Inserter. Put a PAIR of commas around every inserted word, phrase, or clause—those expressions that seem parenthetical and are called "nonrestrictive." When you cut a sentence in two to insert something necessary, you need to tie off *both* ends, or your sentence will die on the table:

Abilene, Kansas looks promising. [, Kansas,]
When he packs his bag, however he goes. [, however,]
The car, an ancient Packard is still running. [, an ancient Packard,]
April 10, 1985 is agreeable as a date for final payment. [, 1985,]
John Jones, Jr. is wrong. [, Jr.,]
I wish, Sandra you would do it. [, Sandra,]

You do not mean that 1985 is agreeable, nor are you telling John Jones that Junior is wrong. Such parenthetical insertions need a PAIR of commas:

> **The case,** ***nevertheless,*** **was closed.**
> **She will see,** ***if she has any sense at all,*** **that he is right.**
> **Sam,** ***on the other hand,*** **may be wrong.**
> **Note,** ***for example,*** **the excellent brushwork.**
> **John Jones,** ***M.D.,*** **and Bill Jones,** ***Ph.D.,*** **doctored the punch to perfection.**
> **He stopped at Kansas City,** ***Missouri,*** **for two hours.**

The same rule applies to all *nonrestrictive* remarks, phrases, and clauses—all elements simply additive, explanatory, and hence parenthetical:

> **John,** ***my friend,*** **will do what he can.**
> **Andy,** ***his project sunk, his hopes shattered,*** **was speechless.**
> **The taxes,** ***which are reasonable,*** **will be paid.**
> **That man,** ***who knows,*** **is not talking.**

Think of *nonrestrictive* as "nonessential" to your meaning, hence set off by commas. Think of *restrictive* as essential and "restricting" your meaning, hence not set off at all (use *which* for nonrestrictives, *that* for restrictives; see 288).

> **RESTRICTIVES:**
> **The taxes that are reasonable will be paid.**
> **Southpaws who are superstitious will not pitch on Friday nights.**
> **The man who knows is not talking.**
>
> **NONRESTRICTIVES:**
> **The taxes, which are reasonable, will be paid.**
> **Southpaws, who are superstitious, will not pitch on Friday nights.**
> **The man, who knows, is not talking.**

The difference between restrictives and nonrestrictives is one of meaning, and the comma-pair signals that meaning. How many grandmothers do I have in the first sentence below (restrictive)? How many in the second (nonrestrictive)?

My grandmother who smokes pot is ninety.
My grandmother, who smokes pot, is ninety.

In the first sentence, I still have two grandmothers, since I am distinguishing one from the other by my restrictive phrase (no commas) as the one with the unconventional habit. In the second sentence, I have but one grandmother, about whom I am adding an interesting though nonessential, nonrestrictive detail within a pair of commas. Read the two aloud, and you will hear the difference in meaning, and how the pauses at the commas signal that difference. Commas are often optional, of course. The difference between a restictive and a nonrestrictive meaning may sometimes be very slight. For example, you may take our recent bridegroom either way (but not halfway):

That handsome man, in the ascot tie, is the groom. [nonrestrictive]
That handsome man in the ascot tie is the groom. [restrictive]

Your meaning will dictate your choice. But use **PAIRS** of commas or none at all. Never separate subject and verb, or verb and object, with just one comma.

Some finer points. One comma of a pair enclosing an inserted remark may coincide with, and, in a sense, overlay, a comma "already there":

In each box, a bottle was broken.
In each box, however, a bottle was broken.

The team lost, and the school was sick.
The team lost, in spite of all, and the school was sick.

The program will work, but the cost is high.
The program will work, of course, but the cost is high.

Between the coordinate clauses, however, a semicolon might have been clearer:

The team lost, in spite of all; and the school was sick.
The program will work, of course; but the cost is high.

Beware: *however,* between commas, cannot substitute for *but,* as in the perfectly good sentence: "He wore a hat, *but* it looked terrible." You would be using a comma where a full stop (period or semicolon) should be:

> **WRONG:**
> **He wore a hat, however, it looked terrible.**
>
> **RIGHT** *(notice the two meanings):*
> **He wore a hat; however, it looked terrible.**
> **He wore a hat, however; it looked terrible.**

But a simple **, but** avoids both the ambiguity of the floating *however* and the ponderosity of anchoring it with a semicolon, fore or aft: "He wore a hat, but it looked terrible."

Another point. *But* may absorb the first comma of a pair enclosing an introductory remark (although it need not do so):

> **At any rate, he went.**
> **But, at any rate, he went.**
> **But at any rate, he went.**
> **But [,] if we want another party, we had better clean up.**
> **The party was a success, but [,] if we want another one, we had better clean up.**

But avoid a comma *after* "but" in sentences like this:

> **I understand your argument, but [,] I feel your opponent has a stronger case.**

Treat the "he said" and "she said" of dialogue as a regular parenthetical insertion, within commas, and without capitalizing, unless a new sentence begins:

> **"I'm going," he said, "whenever I get up enough nerve."**
> **"I'm going," he said. "Whenever I get up enough nerve, I'm really going."**

And American usage puts the comma *inside* ALL quotation marks:

> **"He is a nut," she said.**
> **She called him a "nut," and walked away.**

Finally, the comma goes after a parenthesis, never before:

> **On the day of her graduation (June 4, 1985), the weather turned broiling hot.**

IV. The Linker. This is the usual one, linking on additional phrases and afterthoughts:

> **They went home, having overstayed their welcome.**
> **The book is too long, overloaded with examples.**

It also links items in series. Again, the meaningful pause demands a comma:

> **words, phrases, or clauses in a series**
> **to hunt, to fish, and to hike**
> **He went home, he went upstairs, and he could remember nothing.**
> **He liked oysters, soup, roast beef, and song.**

Put a linker before the concluding *and.* By carefully separating all elements in a series, you keep alive a final distinction long ago lost in the daily press, the distinction Virginia Woolf makes (see 262): "urbane, polished, brilliant, imploring and commanding him. . . ." *Imploring and commanding* is syntactically equal to each one of the other modifiers in the series. If Woolf customarily omitted the last comma, as she does not, she could not have reached for that double apposition. The muscle would have been dead. These other examples of double apposition will give you an idea of its effectiveness:

> **They cut out his idea, root and branch.**
> **He lost all his holdings, houses and lands.**
> **He loved to tramp the woods, to fish and hunt.**

A comma makes a great deal of difference, of sense and distinction.

But adjectives in series, as distinct from nouns in series, change the game a bit. Notice the difference between the following two strings of adjectives:

a good, unexpected, natural rhyme
a good old battered hat

With adjectives in series, only your sense can guide you. If each seems to modify the noun directly, as in the first example above, use commas. If each seems to modify the total accumulation of adjectives and noun, as with *good* and *old* in the second phrase, do not use commas. Say your phrases aloud, and put your commas in the pauses that distinguish your meaning.

Finally, a special case. Dramatic intensity sometimes allows you to join clauses with commas instead of conjunctions:

She sighed, she cried, she almost died.
I couldn't do it, I tried, I let them all get away.
It passed, it triumphed, it was a good bill.
I came, I saw, I conquered.

The rhetorical intensity of this construction—the Greeks called it *asyndeton*—is obvious. The language is breathless, or grandly emphatic. As Aristotle once said, it is a person trying to say many things at once. The subjects repeat themselves, the verbs overlap, the idea accumulates a climax. By some psychological magic, the clauses of this construction usually come in three's. The comma is its sign. But unless you have a stylistic reason for such a flurry of clauses, go back to the normal comma and conjunction, the semicolon, or the period.

FRAGMENTS, COMMA SPLICES, AND RUN-ONS

These are the most persistent problems in using the comma—either missing it or misusing it. The rhetorical fragment, as we have seen (262), may have great force: "So what." But the grammatical one needs repairing with a comma:

FAULTY: **She dropped the cup. Which had cost twenty dollars.**
REVISED: **She dropped the cup, which had cost twenty dollars.**

FAULTY: **He does not spell everything out. But rather hints that something is wrong, and leaves the rest up to the reader.**

REVISED: **He does not spell everything out, but rather hints . . . , and leaves. . . .**

FAULTY: **. . . and finally, the book is obscure. Going into lengthy discussions and failing to remind the reader of the point.**

REVISED: **. . . and finally, the book is obscure, going into lengthy discussion. . . .**

FAULTY: **Yet here is her husband treating their son to all that she considers evil. Plus the fact that the boy is offered beer.**

REVISED: **Yet here is her husband treating their son to all that she considers evil, especially beer.**

FAULTY: **He points out that one never knows what the future will bring. Because it is actually a matter of luck.**

REVISED: **He points out that one never knows what the future will bring, because it is actually a matter of luck.**

FAULTY: **They are off. Not out of their minds exactly but driven, obsessed.**

REVISED: **They are off, not out of their minds exactly, but driven, obsessed.**

Beware the Comma Splice, and the Run-On

The comma splice is the beginner's most common error, the opposite of the fragment—putting a comma where we need a period rather than putting a period where we need a comma—splicing two sentences together with a comma:

The comma splice is a common error, it is the opposite of a fragment. Comma Splice

Of course, you will frequently see comma splices, particularly in fiction and dialogue, where writers are conveying colloquial speed and the thoughts come tumbling fast. Some nonfiction writers borrow this same speed here and there in their prose. But you should learn to recognize these as comma splices and generally avoid them because they may strike your reader as the errors of innocence. Like the rhetorical fragment, a comma splice between short clauses can be most effective (see *asyndeton,* 406): "If speech and cinema are akin to music, writing is like architecture; *it endures, it has weight.*"*

The run-on sentence (fortunately less common) omits even the splicing comma, running one sentence right on to another without noticing:

Run-On **The comma splice is a common error it is the opposite of a fragment.**

Here the writer is in deeper trouble, having somehow never gotten the feel of a sentence as based on subject and verb, and thus needing special help. But most of us can see both the comma splice and run-on as really being two sentences, to be restored as such:

The comma splice is a common error. It is the opposite of a fragment.

Or to be coordinated by adding a conjunction after the comma:

The comma splice is a common error, and it is. . . .

Or to be subordinated by making the second sentence a phrase:

The comma splice is a common error, the opposite. . . .

Here are some typical comma splices:

She cut class, it was boring.
The class was not merely dull, it was useless.
Figures do not lie, they mislead.
He was more than satisfied, he was delighted.

Each of these pulls together a pair of closely sequential sentences. But a comma without its *and* or *but* will not hold the coordination. Either make them the sentences they are:

*Italics added. Richard Lloyd-Jones, "What We May Become," *College Composition and Communication* 33 (1952): 205.

She cut class. It was boring.
Figures do not lie. They mislead.

Or coordinate them with a colon or dash (with a semicolon *only* if they contrast sharply):

The class was not merely dull: it was useless.
He was more than satisfied—he was delighted.

Or subordinate in some way:

She cut class because it was boring.
The class was not merely dull but useless.
More than satisfied, he was delighted.

Here are some more typical splices, all from one set of papers in advanced freshman composition dealing with Shakespeare's *The Tempest.* I have circled the comma where the period should be:

She knows nothing of the evil man is capable of, to her every man is beautiful.
The question of his sensibility hovers, we wonder if he is just.
Without a doubt, men discourage oppression, they strive to be free.
Ariel is civilized society, besides being articulate, he has direction and order.
Stephano and Trinculo are the comics of the play, never presented as complete characters, they are not taken seriously.

You will accidentally splice with a comma most frequently when adding a thought (a complete short sentence) to a longer sentence:

The book describes human evolution in wholly believable terms, comparing the social habits of gorillas and chimpanzees to human behavior, it is very convincing. [Either ". . . believable terms. Comparing . . . ," or "human behavior. It. . . ."]

Conjunctive adverbs (*however, therefore, nevertheless, moreover, furthermore,* and others) may also cause comma splices and trouble:

She continued teaching, however her heart was not in it.

Here are three mendings:

She continued teaching, but her heart was not in it.
She continued teaching; however, her heart was not in it.
She continued teaching; her heart, however, was not in it.

Similarly, transitional phrases *(in fact, that is, for example)* may splice your sentences together:

He disliked discipline, that is, he really was lazy.

You can strengthen the weak joints like this:

He disliked discipline; that is, he really was lazy.
He disliked discipline, that is, anything demanding.

SEMICOLON AND COLON

Use the semicolon only where you could also use a period, unless desperate. This dogmatic formula, which I shall loosen up in a moment, has saved many a punctuator from both despair and a reckless fling of semicolons. Confusion comes from the belief that the semicolon is either a weak colon or a strong comma. It is most effective as neither. It is best, as we have seen (250), in pulling together and contrasting two independent clauses that could stand alone as sentences:

The dress accents the feminine. The pants suit speaks for freedom.

Semicolon **The dress accents the feminine; the pants suit speaks for freedom.**

This compression and contrast by semicolon can go even farther, allowing us to drop a repeated verb in the second element (note also how the comma marks the omission):

Golf demands the best of time and space; tennis demands the best of personal energy.

Golf demands the best of time and space; tennis, the best of personal energy.
Tragedy begins with the apple; comedy, with the banana peel.*

Use a semicolon with a transitional word *(moreover, therefore, then, however, nevertheless)* to signal close contrast and connection:

He was lonely, blue, and solitary; moreover, his jaw ached.

Used sparingly, the semicolon emphasizes your crucial contrasts; used recklessly, it merely clutters your page. *Never* use it as a colon: its effect is exactly opposite. A colon, as in the preceding sentence, signals the meaning to go ahead; a semicolon, as in this sentence, stops it. The colon is a green light; the semicolon is a stop sign.

Consequently, a wrong semicolon frequently makes a fragment. *Use a semicolon only where you could also use a period*—forget the exceptions—or you will make semicolon-fragments like the italicized phrases following the erroneous semicolons circled below:

The play opens on a dark street in New York City; ***one streetlight giving the only illumination.***
The geese begin their migration in late August or early September; ***some groups having started, in small stages, a week or so earlier.***

Each of those semicolons should have been a comma.

Of course, you may occasionally need a semicolon to unscramble a long line of phrases and clauses, especially those in series and containing internal commas:

Composition is hard because we often must discover our ideas by writing them out, clarifying them on paper; because we must also find a clear and reasonable order for ideas the mind presents simultaneously; and because we must find, by trial and error, exactly the right words to convey our ideas and our feelings about them.

The colon waves the traffic on through the intersection: "Go right ahead," it says, "and you will find what you are looking for."

---

*Adapted from Guy Davenport, *Life,* 27 Mar. 1970: 12.

The colon emphatically and precisely introduces a series, the clarifying detail, the illustrative example, and the formal quotation:

Colon **The following players will start: Corelli, Smith, Jones, Baughman, and Stein.**
Pierpont lived for only one thing: money.
In the end, it was useless: Adams really was too green.
We remember Sherman's words: "War is hell."

PARENTHESIS AND DASH

The dash says aloud what the parenthesis whispers. Both enclose interruptions too extravagant for a pair of commas to hold. The dash is the more useful—since whispering tends to annoy—and will remain useful only if not overused. It can serve as a conversational colon. It can set off a concluding phrase—for emphasis. It can bring long introductory matters to focus, concluding a series of parallel phrases: "—all these are crucial." It can insert a full sentence—a clause is really an incorporated sentence—directly next to a key word. The dash allows you to insert—with a kind of shout!—an occasional exclamation. You may even insert—and who would blame you?—an occasional question. The dash affords a structural complexity with all the tone and alacrity of talk.

With care, you can get much the same power from a parenthesis:

Many philosophers have despaired (somewhat unphilosophically) of discovering any certainties whatsoever.
Thus did Innocent III (we shall return to him shortly) inaugurate an age of horrors.
But in such circumstances (see page 34), be cautious.
Delay had doubled the costs (a stitch in time!), so the plans were shelved.

But dashes seem more generally useful, and here are some special points. When one of a pair of dashes falls where a comma would be, it absorbs the comma:

If one wanted to go, he certainly could.
If one wanted to go—whether invited or not—he certainly could.

Not so with the semicolon:

He wanted to go—whether he was invited or not; she had more sense.

To indicate the dash, type two hyphens (--) flush against the words they separate—not one hyphen between two spaces, nor a hyphen spaced to look exactly like a hyphen.

Put commas and periods *outside* a parenthetical group of words (like this one), even if the parenthetical group could stand alone as a sentence (see the preceding "Innocent III" example). (But if you make an actual full sentence parenthetical, put the period inside.)

Change has had its way with the parenthesis around numbers. Formal print and most guides to writing, including this one, still hold to the full parenthesis:

Numbered Items

The sentence really has only two general varieties: (1) the "loose" or strung-along, in Aristotle's phrase, and (2) the periodic.
He decided (1) that he did not like it, (2) that she would not like it, and (3) that they would be better off without it.

Popular print now omits the first half of the parenthesis:

. . . decided 1) that he did not like it, 2) that she. . . .

But for your papers—keep the full parenthesis.

BRACKETS

Brackets indicate your own words inserted or substituted within a quotation from someone else: "Byron had already suggested that [they] had killed John Keats." You have substituted "they" for "the gentlemen of the *Quarterly Review*" to suit your own context; you do the same when you interpolate a word of explanation: "Byron had already suggested that the gentlemen of the *Quarterly Review* [especially Croker] had killed John Keats." *Do not use parentheses:* they mark the enclosed words as part of the original quotation. Don't claim innocence because your typewriter lacks brackets. Just leave spaces and draw them in later, or type slant lines and tip them with pencil or with the underscore key: *[. . .]*

In the example below, you are pointing out with a *sic* (Latin for "so" or "thus"), which you should not italicize, that you are reproducing an error exactly as it appears in the text you are quoting:

> **"On no occassion [sic] could we trust them."**

Similarly you may give a correction after reproducing the error:

> **"On the twenty-fourth [twenty-third], we broke camp."**
> **"In not one instance [actually, Baldwin reports several instances] did our men run under fire."**

Use brackets when you need a parenthesis within a parenthesis:

> **(see Donald Allenberg, *The Future of Television* [New York, 1973]: 15–16)**

Your instructor will probably put brackets around the wordy parts of your sentences, indicating what you should cut:

> **In fact, [the reason] he liked it [was] because it was different.**

QUOTATION MARKS AND ITALICS

Put quotation marks around quotations that "run directly into your text" (like this), but *not* around quotations set off from the text and indented. You normally inset poetry, as it stands, without quotation marks:

> **An aged man is but a paltry thing,**
> **A tattered coat upon a stick, unless**
> **Soul clap its hands and sing. . . .**

But if you run it into your text, use quotation marks, with virgules (slants) showing the line-ends: "An aged man is but a paltry thing,/A tattered coat. . . ." Put periods and commas *inside* quotation marks; put semicolons and colons *outside:*

Now we understand the full meaning of "give me liberty, or give me death."	Period
"This strange disease of modern life," in Arnold's words, remains uncured.	Comma
In Greece, it was "know thyself"; in America, it is "know thy neighbor."	Semicolon
He left after "Hail to the Chief": he could do nothing more.	Colon

Although logic often seems to demand the period or comma outside the quotation marks, convention has put them inside for the sake of appearance, even when the sentence ends in a single quoted word or letter:

Clara Bow was said to have "It."
Mark it with "T."

If you have seen the periods and commas outside, you were reading a British book or some of America's little magazines.

When you have dialogue, signal each change of speaker with a paragraph's indentation:

"What magazines in the natural sciences should I read regularly?" inquired the student.

"Though moderately difficult, *Scientific American* and *Science* are always worth your time, but you'll want to explore afield from these," responded his advisor.

If in a dialogue a single speaker carries on for several paragraphs, place quotation marks before *each* paragraph, but after only the *last* paragraph.

Omit quotation marks entirely in *indirect* quotations:

She asked me if I would help her.
The insurance agent told Mr. Jones that his company would pay all valid claims within thirty days.
In his review of the play, J. K. Beaumont praised the plot as strong and incisive, but faulted the dialogue as listless and contrived in a few scenes. [Here, you are summarizing the reviewer's comments.]

If you are quoting a phrase that already contains quotation marks, reduce the original double marks (“) to single ones (‘):

Single Quotation Marks (on the Right)

ORIGINAL	YOUR QUOTATION
Hamlet’s “are you honest?” is easily explained.	**He writes that “Hamlet’s ‘are you honest?’ is easily explained.”**

Notice what happens when the quotation within your quotation falls at the end:

ORIGINAL	YOUR QUOTATION
A majority of the informants thought *infer* meant “imply.”	**Kirk reports that “a majority of the informants thought *infer* meant ‘imply.’ ”**

And notice that a question mark or exclamation point falls between the single and the double quotation marks at the end of a quotation containing a quotation:

“Why do they call it ‘the Hippocratic oath’?” she asked.
“Everything can’t be ‘cool’!” he said.

But heed the following exception:

“I heard someone say, ‘Is anyone home?’ ” she declared.

Do not use *single* quotation marks for your own stylistic flourishes; use *double* quotation marks or, preferably, none:

It was indeed an “affair,” but the passion was hardly “grand.”
It was indeed an affair, but the passion was hardly grand.
Some “cool” pianists use the twelve-tone scale.

Once you have thus established this slang meaning of *cool,* you may repeat the word without quotation marks. In general, of course, you should favor that slang your style can absorb without quotation marks.

Do not use quotation marks for calling attention to words as words. Use italics (an underscore when typing) for the words, quotation marks for their meanings.

This is taking *tergiversation* too literally.
The word *struthious* means "like an ostrich."

Italics

Similarly, use italics for numbers as numbers and letters as letters:

He writes a *5* like an *s*.
Dot your *i*'s and cross your *t*'s.

But common sayings like "Watch your p's and q's" and "from A to Z" require no italics.

Use quotation marks for titles *within* books and magazines: titles of chapters, articles, short stories, songs, and poems, and for unpublished works, lectures, courses, TV episodes within a series. But use italics for titles or names of books, newspapers, magazines, plays, films, TV series, long poems, sculptures, paintings, ships, trains, and airplanes.

Poe's description of how he wrote "The Raven" was attacked in the *Atlantic Monthly* [or: the *Atlantic.*]
We saw Michelangelo's *Pietà,* a remarkable statue in white marble.
We took the Sante Fe *Chief* from Chicago to Los Angeles.
He read all of Frazer's *The Golden Bough.*
His great-grandfather went down with the *Titanic.*
She read it in the *New York Times.*
They loved *Saturday Night Fever* [film].

Titles and Names

Handle titles within titles as follows:

"Tintern Alley" and Nature in Wordsworth **[book]**
" 'Tintern Abbey' and Natural Imagery" [articlc]
"The Art of *Tom Jones*" [article]
The Art of **Tom Jones [book]**

In the last example, notice that what is ordinarily italicized, like the title of a book *(Tom Jones),* is set in roman when the larger setting is in italics.

Italicize foreign words and phrases, unless they have been

assimilated into English through usage (your dictionary should have a method for noting the distinction; if not, consult one that has):

> **The statement contained two clichés and one *non sequitur*.**
> **The author of this naïve exposé suffers from an *idée fixe*.**

Other foreign expressions *not* italicized are: etc., e.g., et al., genre, hubris, laissez faire, leitmotif, roman à clef, raison d'être, tête-à-tête.

Use neither quotation marks nor italics for the Bible, for its books or parts (Genesis, Old Testament), for other sacred books (Koran, Talmud, Upanishad), nor for famous documents like the Magna Carta, the Declaration of Independence, the Communist Manifesto, and the Gettysburg Address, nor for instrumental music known by its form, number, and key:

> **Beethoven's C-minor Quartet**
> **Brahms's Symphony No. 4, Opus 98**

When a reference in parentheses falls at the end of a quotation, the quotation marks *precede* the parentheses:

> **As Ecclesiastes tells us, "there is no new thing under the sun" (1.9).**

ELLIPSIS

1. Use three spaced periods . . . (the ellipsis mark) when you omit something from a quotation. Do *not* use them in your own text in place of a dash, or in mere insouciance.
2. If you omit the end of a sentence, put in a period (no space) and add the three spaced dots. . . .
3. If your omission falls after a completed sentence, just add the three spaced dots to the period already there. . . . The spacing is the same as for case 2.

Here is an uncut passage, followed by a shortened version illustrating the three kinds of ellipsis:

To learn a language, learn as thoroughly as possible a few everyday sentences. This will educate your ear for all future pronunciations. It will give you a fundamental grasp of structure. And start soon.

(1)
To learn a language, learn . . . a few everyday sentences.
(2)
This will educate your ear. . . . It will give you a
(3)
fundamental grasp of structure. . . .

You can omit beginning and ending ellipses when you use a quotation within a sentence:

Lincoln was determined that the Union, "cemented with the blood of . . . the purest patriots," would not fail.

APOSTROPHE

It's may be overwhelmingly our most frequent misspelling as in "The dog scratched *it's* ear." No, no! *It's* means *it is. Who's* means *who is. They're* means *they are.* NO pronoun spells *its* possessive with an apostrophe: *hers, its, ours, theirs, yours, whose, oneself.*

For nouns, add apostrophe *-s* to form the singular possessive: *dog's life, hour's work, Marx's ideas.* Add apostrophe *-s* even to singular words already ending in *s: Yeats's poems, Charles's crown. Sis' plans* and *the boss' daughter* are not what we say. We say *Sissuz* and *bossuz* and *Keatsuz,* and should say the same in our writing: *sis's, boss's, Keats's.* Plurals *not* ending in *s* also form the possessive by adding *'s: children's hour, women's rights.* But most plurals take the apostrophe after the *s* already there: *witches' sabbath, ten cents' worth, three days' time, the Joneses' possessions.*

I repeat, the rule for making singulars possessive is to add *'s* regardless of length and previous ending. French names ending in silent *s*-sounds also add *'s: Camus's works, Marivaux's life, Berlioz's Requiem.* If your page grows too thick with double *s*'s, substitute a few pronouns for the proper names, or rephrase: *the death of Themistocles, the Dickens character Pip.*

The apostrophe can help to clarify clusters of nouns. These

I have actually seen: *Alistair Jones Renown Combo, the church barbecue chicken sale, the uniform policeman training program, the members charter plane.* And of course, *teachers meeting* and *veterans insurance* are so common as to seem almost normal. But an apostrophe chips one more noun out of the block. It makes your meaning one word clearer, marking *teachers'* as a modifier, and distinguishing *teacher* from *teachers.* Inflections are helpful, and the written word needs all the help it can get: *Jones's Renowned, church's barbecued, uniformed policeman's, members' chartered.* Distinguish your modifiers, and keep your possessions.

Compound words take the *'s* on the last word only: *mother-in-law's hat, the brothers-in-law's attitude* (all the brothers-in-law have the same attitude), *somebody else's problem.* Joint ownerships may similarly take the *'s* only on the last word *(Bill and Mary's house),* but *Bill's and Mary's* house is more precise, and preferable.

Again, possessive pronouns have no apostrophe: *hers, its, theirs, yours, whose, oneself.* Remember that *it's* means *it is,* and that *who's* means *who is;* for possession, use *its* and *whose.*

The double possessive uses both an *of* and an *'s: a friend of my mother's, a book of the teacher's, a son of the Joneses', an old hat of Mary's.* Note that the double possessive indicates one possession among several of the same kind: mother has several friends; the teacher, several books.

Use the apostrophe to indicate omissions: *the Spirit of '76, the Class of '02, can't, won't, don't.* Finally, use the apostrophe when adding a grammatical ending to a number, letter, sign, or abbreviation: *1920's;* his *3's* look like *8's; p's* and *q's;* he got four *A's;* too many *of's* and *and's;* she *X'd* each box; *K.O.'d* in the first round. (Some of these are also italics, or underlined when typed. See 417.) Contemporary usage omits the apostrophe in some of these: 1920s, *8*s, two *t*s.

HYPHEN

For clarity, hyphenate groups of words acting as one adjective or one adverb: *eighteenth-century attitude, early-blooming southern crocus, of-and-which disease.* Distinguish between a *high school,* and a *high-school teacher.* Similarly, hyphenate compound nouns when you need to distinguish, for example, *five sentence-exercises* from *five-sentence exercises.*

Hyphenate prefixes to proper names: *ex-Catholic, pro-Napoleon,* and all relatively new combinations like *anti-marriage.* Consult your dictionary.

Hyphenate after prefixes that demand emphasis or clarity: *ex-husband, re-collect* ("to collect again," as against *recollect,* "to remember"), *re-create, re-emphasize, pre-existent.*

When you must break a word at the end of a line, hyphenate where your dictionary marks the syllables with a dot; *syl·lables, syl-lables.* If you must break a hyphenated word, break it after the hyphen: *self-/sufficient.* Don't hyphenate an already hyphenated word: *self-suf-/ficient.* It's hard on the eyes and the printer. When you write for print, underline those line-end hyphens you mean to keep as hyphens, making a little equals sign: self=/sufficient.

Hyphenate suffixes to single capital letters *(T-shirt, I-beam, X-ray).* Hyphenate *ex-champions* and *self-reliances.* Hyphenate to avoid double *i*'s and triple consonants: *anti-intellectual, bell-like.* Hyphenate two-word numbers: *twenty-one, three-fourths.* Use the "suspensive" hyphen for hyphenated words in series: "We have ten-, twenty-five-, and fifty-pound sizes."

VIRGULE (SLANT, SLASH)

Spare this "little rod" (/), and don't spoil your work with the legalistic *and/or.* Don't write "bacon and/or eggs"; write "bacon or eggs, or both." Likewise, don't use it for a hyphen: not "male/female conflict" but "male-female conflict." Use the virgule when quoting poetry in your running text: "That time of year thou mayst in me behold / When yellow leaves, . . ."

SPELLING

The dictionary is your best friend as you face the inevitable anxieties of spelling, but three underlying principles and some tricks of the trade can help immeasurably:

Principle I. Letters represent sounds: proNUNciation can help you spell. No one proNOUNcing his words correctly would make the familiar errors of "similiar" and "enviorment." Simply sound out the letters: *envIRONment* and *goverNment* and *FebRUary* and *intRAmural.* Of course, you will need to be wary of some words *not* pronounced as spelled: *Wednesday* pronounced "Wenzday," for instance. But sounding the letters can help your spellings. You can even say "convert*i*ble" and "indel*i*ble" and "plaus*i*ble" without sounding like a fool, and you can silently stress the *able* in words like "prob*able*" and "immov*able*" to remember the difficult distinction between words ending in *-ible,* and *-able.*

Consonants reliably represent their sounds. Remember that *c* and often *g* go soft before *i* and *e.* Consequently, you must add a *k* when extending words like *picnic* and *mimic—picnicKing, mimicKing*—to keep them from rhyming with *slicing* or *dicing.* Conversely, you just keep the *e* (where you would normally drop it) when making *peace* into *peacEable* and *change* into *changEable,* to keep the *c* and *g* soft.

Single *s* is pronounced *zh* in words like *vision, occasion, pleasure.* Knowing that *ss* hushes ("sh-h-h") will keep you from errors like *occassion,* which would sound like *passion.*

Vowels sound short and light before single consonants: *hat, pet, kit, hop, cup.* When you add any vowel (including *y*), the first vowel will say its name: *hate, Pete, kite, hoping, cupid.* Notice how the *a* in *-able* keeps the main vowel saying its name in words like *unmistakable, likable,* and *notable.* Therefore, to keep a vowel short protect it with double consonant: *petting, hopping.* This explains the troublesome *rr* in *occuRRence:* a single *r* would make it say *cure* in the middle. *Putting* a golf ball and *putting* something on paper must both use *tt* to keep from being pronounced *pewting.* Compare *stony* with *sonny* and *bony* with *bonny.* The *y* is replacing the *e* in *stone* and *bone,* and the rule is working perfectly. It works in any syllable that is accented: compare *forgeTTable* as against *markeTing, begiNNing* as against *buttoNing,* and *compeLLing* as against *traveLing.*

Likewise, when *full* combines and loses its stress, it also loses an *l.* Note the single and double *l* in *fulFILLment.* Similarly, *SOULful, GRATEful, AWful*—even *SPOONful.*

Principle II. This is the old rule of *i* before *e,* and its famous exceptions:

_I_ before _e_
Except after _c_,
Or when sounded like _a_
As in _neighbor_ and _weigh._

It works like a charm: *achieve, believe, receive, conceive.* Note that *c* needs an *e* to make it sound like *s.* Remember also that *leisure* was once pronounced "lay-sure," and *foreign,* "forayn," and *heifer,* "hayfer." Memorize these important exceptions: *seize, weird, either, sheik, forfeit, counterfeit, protein.* Note that all are pronounced "ee" (with a little crowding) and that the *e* comes first. Then note that another small group goes the opposite way, having a long *i* sound as in German "Heil": *height, sleight, seismograph, kaleidoscope. Science* is a notable exception. *Financier,* another exception, follows its French origin and its original sound. *Deity* sounds both vowels as spelled.

Principle III. Most big words, following the Latin or French from which they came, spell their sounds letter for letter. Look up the derivations of the words you misspell (note that double *s,* and explain it). You will never again have trouble with *desperate* and *separate* once you discover that the first comes from *de-spero,* "without hope," and that SePARate divides equals, the PAR values in stocks or golf. Nor with *definite* or *definitive,* once you see the kinship of both with *finite* and *finish.* Derivations can also help you a little with the devilment of *-able* and *-ible,* since, except for a few ringers, the *i* remains from Latin, and the *-ables* are either French *(ami-able)* or Anglo-Saxon copies *(workable).* Knowing origins can help at crucial points: *resemblAnce* comes from Latin *simulAre,*" "to copy"; *existEnce* comes from Latin *existEre;* "to stand forth."

The biggest help comes from learning the common Latin prefixes, which, by a process of assimilation (*ad-similis,* "like to like"), account for the double consonants at the first syLLabic joint of so many of our words:

AD- (toward, to): _abbreviate_ (shorten down), _accept_ (grasp to).
CON- (with): _collapse_ (fall with), _commit_ (send with).
DIS- (apart): _dissect_ (cut apart), _dissolve_ (loosen apart).
IN- (into): _illuminate_ (shine into), _illusion_ (playing into).
IN- (not): _illegal_ (not lawful), _immature_ (not ripe).

INTER- (between): ***interrupt*** **(break between),** ***interrogate*** **(ask between).**
OB- (toward, to): ***occupy*** **(take in),** ***oppose*** **(put to),** ***offer*** **(carry to).**
SUB- (under): ***suffer*** **(bear under),** ***suppose*** **(put down).**
SYN- ("together"—this one is Greek): ***symmetry*** **(measuring together),** ***syllogism*** **(logic together).**

Spelling takes a will, an eye, and an ear. And a dictionary. Keep a list of your favorite enemies. Memorize one or two a day. Write them in the air in longhand. Visualize them. Imagine a blinking neon sign, with the wicked letters red and tall—defInIte—defInIte. Then print them once, write them twice, and blink them a few times more as you go to sleep. But best of all, make up whatever devices you can—the crazier the better—to remember their tricky parts:

DANCE attenDANCE.	**LOSE loses an O.**
EXISTENCE is TENSE.	**ALLOT isn't A LOT.**
There's IRON in this enviRONment.	**Already isn't ALL RIGHT.**
The resisTANCE took its STANCE.	**I for gaIety.**
There's an ANT on the defendANT.	**The LL in paraLLel gives me *el.***
LOOSE as a goose.	**PURr in PURsuit.**

When an unaccented syllable leads to misspelling, you can also get some help by trying to remember a version of the word that accents the troublesome syllable: acad*e*my—acaDEMic; defin*i*tely—defiNItion; irrit*a*ble—irriTATE; prep*a*ration—prePARE.

Many foreign words, though established in English, retain their native diacritical marks, which aid in pronunciation; *naïveté, résumé, séance, tête-à-tête, façade, Fräulein, mañana, vicuña.* Many names are similarly treated: *Müller, Gödel, Göttingen, Poincaré, Brontë, Noël Coward, García Lorca, Havlíček.* As always, your dictionary is your best guide, as it is, indeed, to all words transliterated to English from different alphabets and systems of writing (Russian, Arabic, Chinese, Japanese, and so on).

Here are more of the perpetual headaches:

accept—except
accommodate
acknowledgment—judgment
advice—advise
affect—effect*
all right*—a lot*
allusion—illusion—disillusion*
analysis—analyzing
argue—argument
arrangement
businessman
capital (city)—capitol (building)*
censor—censure*
committee
complement—compliment*
continual—continuous*
controversy
council—counsel—consul*
criticize—criticism
curriculum*—career—occurrence
decide—divide—devices
desert—dessert
dilemma—condemn
disastrous
discreet—discrete*
embarrassment—harassment
eminent—imminent—immanent*
exaggerate
explain—explanation
familiar—similar
forward—foreword
genius—ingenious*—ingenous*
height—eighth
hypocrisy—democracy
irritable
its—it's*
lonely—loneliness
marriage—marital—martial
misspell—misspelling
Negroes—heroes—tomatoes
obstacle
possession
primitive
principal—principle*
proceed—precede—procedure
rhythm
questionnaire
stationary—stationery
succeed—successful
suppressed
their—they're
truly
until—till
unnoticed
weather—whether
who's—whose*

CAPITALIZATION

You know about sentences and names, certainly; but the following points are troublesome. Capitalize:

---

*In the Glossary of Usage.

1. Names of races, languages, and religions—Negro, Caucasian, Mongolian, Protestant, Jewish, Christian, Roman Catholic, Indian, French, English, Black (as in Black English). But "blacks and whites in this neighborhood," "black entrepreneurs," "white storekeepers,"—especially in phrases that contrast blacks and whites, since *white* is never capitalized.
2. North, South, East, and West *only when they are regions*—the mysterious East, the new Southwest—or parts of proper nouns: the West Side, East Lansing.
3. The *complete* names of churches, rivers, hotels, and the like—the First Baptist Church, the Mark Hopkins Hotel, the Suwannee River (not First Baptist church, Mark Hopkins hotel, Suwannee river).
4. All words in titles, except prepositions, articles, conjunctions, and the "to" of infinitives. But capitalize even these if they come first or last, or if they are longer than four letters—"I'm Through with Love," *Gone with the Wind*, "I'll Stand By," *In Darkest Africa, How to Gain Friends and Influence People, To Catch a Thief.* Capitalize nouns, adjectives, and prefixes in hyphenated compounds—*The Eighteenth-Century Background, The Anti-Idealist* (but *The Antislavery Movement*). But hyphenated single words, the names of numbered streets, and the written-out numbers on your checks are *not* capitalized after the hyphen: *Self-fulfillment, Re-examination. Forty-second Street, Fifty-four . . . Dollars.*

   When referring to magazines, newspapers, and reference works in sentences, footnotes, and bibliographies, you may drop the *The* as part of the title; the *Atlantic Monthly*, the *Kansas City Star*, the *Encyclopaedia Britannica.* (Euphony and sense preserve *The* for a few: *The New Yorker, The Spectator.*)
5. References to a specific section of a work—the Index, his Preface, Chapter 1, Volume IV, Act II, but "scene iii" is usually not capitalized because its numerals are also in lower case.
6. Abstract nouns, when you want emphasis, serious or humorous—". . . the truths contradict, so what is Truth?"; Very Important Person; the Ideal.

Do not capitalize the seasons—spring, winter, midsummer.

Do not capitalize after a colon, unless what follows is normally capitalized:

> **Again we may say with Churchill: "Never have so many owed so much to so few."**
>
> ***Culture, People, Nature: An Introduction to General Anthropology* [title of book]**
>
> **Many lost everything in the earthquake: their homes had vanished along with their supplies, their crops, their livestock.**

Do not capitalize proper nouns serving as common nouns: *china, cognac, napoleon* (a pastry), *chauvinist, watt* (electricity). Usage divides on some proper adjectives: *French* [*french*] *pastry, Cheddar* [*cheddar*] *cheese, German* [*german*] measles, Venetian [*venetian*] *blinds.* Also somewhat uncertain are names with lower-case articles or prepositions like [Charles] de Gaulle, [John] von Neumann; in such cases, follow the lower-case form within sentences—*de Gaulle, von Neumann*—but always capitalize in full at the beginning of a sentence: *De Gaulle, Von Neumann.* (Many names, however, drop the article or preposition when the surname appears alone: [Ludwig van] *Beethoven,* [Guy de] *Maupassant.*) Breeds of animals, as in *Welsh terrier,* and products of a definite origin, as in *Scotch whiskey,* are less uncertain. When in doubt, your best guides are your dictionary and, for proper names, a biographical dictionary or an encyclopedia.

EXERCISES

1. *Correct these omissions of the comma, and, in your margin, label the ones you insert as* INTRODUCER, COORDINATOR, INSERTER, *or* LINKER:

1. We find however that the greatest expense in renovation will be for labor not for materials.
2. They took chemistry fine arts history and English.
3. We met June 1 1982 to discuss the problem which continued to plague us.
4. A faithful sincere friend he remained loyal to his roommate even after the unexpected turn of events.

5. Though she was a junior-college instructor teaching advanced calculus given at night during the winter did not intimidate her.
6. C. Wright Mills's *The Power Elite* which even after two decades is still one of the finest examples of sociological analysis available ought to be required reading in any elementary sociology course.
7. My father, who is a good gardener keeps things well trimmed.

2. *Correct these fragments, comma splices, and run-ons, adding commas and other marks as necessary:*

1. His lectures are not only hard to follow they are boring.
2. Stephano and Trinculo are the comics of the play never presented as complete characters they are not taken seriously.
3. The book deals with the folly of war its stupidity, its cruelty however in doing this the author brings in too many characters repeats episodes over and over and spoils his comedy by pressing too hard.
4. He left his second novel unfinished. Perhaps because of his basic uncertainty, which he never overcame.
5. She seems to play a careless game. But actually knows exactly what she is doing, and intends to put her opponent off guard.
6. His idea of democracy was incomplete, he himself had slaves.
7. She knows her cards that is she never overbids.
8. The problem facing modern architects is tremendous, it involves saving energy on a grand scale with untested devices and still achieving beautiful buildings.
9. The solution was elegant, besides being inexpensive, it was a wholly new approach.
10. Don't underestimate the future, it is always there.

3. *Add or subtract commas and semicolons as necessary in these sentences:*

1. Their travels are tireless, their budget however needs a rest.
2. They abhor economizing, that is, they are really spendthrifts.
3. Muller wants efficiency, Smithers beauty.
4. Abramson won the first set with a consistent backhand; some beautiful forehand volleys also helping at crucial moments.
5. The downtown parking problem remains unsolved; the new structures, the new meters, and the new traffic patterns having come into play about three years too late.

4. *Adjust the following sentences concerning the colon:*

1. Many things seem unimportant, even distasteful, money, clothes, popularity, even security and friends.

2. People faced with inflation, of which we have growing reminders daily, seem to take one of two courses; either economizing severely in hopes of receding prices, or buying far beyond their immediate needs in fear of still higher prices.
3. Depressed, refusing to face the reality of his situation, he killed himself, it was as simple as that.
4. To let him go was unthinkable: to punish him was unbearable.

5. *Add quotation marks and italics to these:*

1. Like the farmer in Frost's Mending Wall, some people believe that Good fences make good neighbors.
2. Here see means understand, and audience stands for all current readers.
3. For him, the most important letter between A and Z is I.
4. Why does the raven keep crying Nevermore? he asked.
5. In America, said the Chinese lecturer, people sing Home, Sweet Home; in China, they stay there.
6. The boys' favorite books were Huckleberry Finn, the Bible, especially Ecclesiastes, and Walden.
7. Germaine Greer's The Female Eunuch is memorable for phrases like I'm sick of peering at the world through false eyelashes and I'm a woman, not a castrate.

6. *Make a list of your ten most frequent misspellings. Then keep it handy and active, removing your conquests and adding your new troubles.*

7. *Capitalize the following, where necessary:*

go west, young man.
the south left the union.
the east side of town
the introduction to *re-establishing toryism*
east side, west side
the tall black spoke french.
she loved the spring.
health within seconds [book]
clear through life in time [book]
a doberman pinscher
the methodist episcopal church
the missouri river
my christian name begins with c.
the new york public library
the neo-positivistic approach [book]
the st. louis post-dispatch [add italics]
twenty-five dollars [on a check]
33 thirty-third street
the tundra occupies a large portion of northern canada.

13 The Written Examination

GRASPING THE ANSWER

We began with the thesis, that seminal organizer of knowledge and thought. We end with the same Big Idea now applied to written examinations. Here is my parting gift, guaranteed from experience. It will improve your results on any question, in any subject, asking for a discursive answer.

This is the secret: MAKE YOURSELF ANSWER THE QUESTION IN ONE SENTENCE. However well or poorly you are prepared, this forces all you know on the subject to its widest dimension. If you start your answer with this sentence, even desperately throwing in any old detail as it comes (as I used to do until I hit on the one-sentence idea), every detail will seem to illustrate your opening declaration, and your instructor will say, "Now *this* one is organized—a real grasp of the subject." So, start your answer with your seminal sentence, and your answer will sound like an essay. It will sound even more so if you have jotted down the points you want to cover, quickly saving best for last—the one you know best and can cover most fully. It will indeed *be* an essential essay. Your instructor, after all, needs no introduction.

Next point: incorporate the language of the question in your one-sentence opener. This works even with the broadest kind of question—those barn doors opened so wide you can drive in any kind of load:

1. **Discuss the fall of the Roman Empire.**
2. **What is the most valuable thing you have learned in this course?**
3. **Demonstrate your knowledge of the materials of this course.**

Your one-sentence openers might go like this:

1. **The Roman Empire fell because of decay from within and attack from without.**
2. **The most valuable thing I have learned this semester is that people usually conceal their true motivations from themselves.**
3. **The materials of this course illustrate biological evolution, particularly the role of mutation in the survival of the fittest.**

Jot down your points, quickly arranging for ascending order, and you are off and running. Finally, try to paragraph, with a topic sentence if you can, about once a page.

AN HISTORICAL QUESTION

1. Summarize Gibbon's reasons for the fall of the Roman Empire.

One-Sentence Answer

The Roman Empire fell because of decay from within and attack from without.

Jotted Outline

1. **Augustus**
2. **Tiberius-Caligula-Nero**
3. **Nerva, Trajan, Hadrian, the Antonines**
4. **Commodus**
5. **Mercenaries**
6. **Overextension**
7. **Rome and Byzantium**
8. **Goths**

Answer

Thesis

The Roman Empire fell because of decay from within and attack from without. After the five good emperors who extended the Pax Romana to the end of the second century A.D.—Nerva, Trajan, Hadrian, and the two Antonines—Gib-

First Half: Inner Decay

bon unfolds a long account of folly, luxuriance, insanity, and bloodshed. But he sees the seeds of decay already sown by the wily Augustus, as he calls him, who dissolved the remaining republican powers of the Senate under a fiction of senatorial authority that disguised a military dictatorship. This dictatorship of the emperor, now the "Caesar," expanded the borders but weakened the old Roman spirit of freedom and patriotic commitment.

Topic Sentence

Moral decay was also evident from the first years of empire. Augustus had tried to reform the profligacy of the upper classes, banishing both his wife and daughter for flagrant lewdness, as well as the poet Ovid, who was somehow implicated in the daughter's scandalous behavior, as the lecturer pointed out. That Rome could survive the inner decay displayed in the murderous orgies of Tiberius (A.D. 14–37), or in the insane Caligula (37–41), who made his horse a senator, or in the almost equally mad and more bloody Nero (54–68), is a wonder.

Topic Sentence

But Commodus (180–192), the adolescent wastrel who thought he was Hercules and fought men and beasts in the arena in Herculean costume—the son of good Marcus Aurelius Antoninus—begins Rome's long decline, in Gibbon's eyes. The few good emperors along the line could not sustain the overextended empire, defended by mercenaries rather than patriots, the leading citizens who were now luxuriating at home and keeping the populace happy with bread and circuses. The empire broke in two, with two loosely cooperating caesars, one in Rome, one in Byzantium. The tail began to wag the dog, as Byzantium gained ascendancy, and at one time as many as six caesars divided the power and luxuriated on the taxes.

Topic Sentence: Second Half, Outer Attack

The pressure of attack from without was sustained from the first on all the empire's borders—Scotland, Gaul, the Danube, the East. But how outer attack conspired with inner decay is nowhere better illustrated than in the account of the Goths, whose future king Alaric conquered Italy and sacked Rome in 410. Driven to the north banks of the Danube by the Huns, the Goths begged Valens, the caesar of the East, for admittance into the empire in 376. Gibbon estimates a population of nearly a million men, women, and children from the 200,000 Gothic warriors reported by the contemporary historian. When agreement was reached that they would settle in Thrace and defend the empire, the Romans began to ferry this multitude across the badly swollen river in canoes and boats of all sizes for many days and nights, losing many in the rapid current. Valens and his

counselors, whom Gibbon calls slaves decorated with the titles of prefects and generals, looked on the settlement as a rich bargain, since they could now keep and spend the gold the provinces sent in as taxes to hire mercenaries.

Topic Sentence: Inner and Outer Combine

But this was only the beginning of Roman greed and moral decay in the Gothic story. Valens had decreed that the warriors must surrender their arms before crossing the river and that they must give up their children to be sent to distant cities where they would be civilized and would serve as hostages to keep the Goths in line. But the Goths, whose weapons were their hereditary honor, bribed the Roman officials with their wives, daughters, sons, carpets, and linen, and entered the boats with weapons in hand.

Topic Sentence

Then Roman greed went farther. Instead of feeding the Goths as Valens had ordered, the officials sold them bread, dog meat, and meat from cattle killed by disease at outrageous prices—a slave for a loaf of bread, ten pounds of gold for a little bad meat. The Goths finally rebelled, devastated the country, fought Valens to a standstill, and settled independently in Thrace, where, though they became Christians, their hatred for the Romans smoldered until Alaric led them westward to conquer Italy and sack the ancient capital in A.D. 410. Aside from other forays into Italy, Alaric's victory illustrates clearly how moral decay combines with outer attack to contribute a major plunge in the long continuing fall of the Roman Empire.

Clincher

A LITERARY QUESTION

2. Discuss the role of the senses in Wordsworth's philosophy, identifying and analyzing the following passage:

Therefore I am still
A lover of the meadows and the woods,
And mountains; and of all that we behold
From this green earth; of all the mighty world
Of eye, and ear,—both what they half create,
And what perceive; well pleased to recognize
In nature and the language of the sense
The anchor of my purest thoughts, the nurse,
The guide, the guardian of my heart, and soul
Of all my moral being.

One-Sentence Answer

In this important passage from "Tintern Abbey," Wordsworth makes his clearest statement about the role of the senses in perceiving the natural world and establishing —or "nursing"—the inner being.

Jotted Outline—on another sheet, or in margin

1. **Outer nature—wild, cultivated (cottages)**
2. **Inner nature—world of eye and ear**
3. **Reality**
4. **Senses as creators**
5. **Senses as perceivers**
6. **Nature plus senses—soul and being**
7. **Perceived and created reality**
8. **Poetry—iambic pent—sincerity**

Answer

Thesis

In this important passage from "Tintern Abbey," Wordsworth makes his clearest statement about the role of the senses in perceiving the natural world and establishing —or "nursing"—the inner being. Background Knowledge **He has previously in this poem acknowledged the point with which he opens his "Immortality" ode that the unconscious and joyful impressions of boyhood, when he ran and jumped through these hills, have faded to the calmer impressions of maturity, which have mixed a sense of humanity (a "sad music") with the youthful joys in wild non-human nature.** Thesis Clinched

Topic Sentence

He has visited this same scene five years before, as he says at the beginning, and the impressions from that visit have nourished him as they recurred to his mind—actual pictures popping into his thoughts—in the frenzy of the city and times of depression (his own depressed feelings). These recollections have brought to him the same tranquil mood that now fills his soul and gives the impression of harmony with nature and a feeling that he "sees into the life of things." He says that his present recapturing of the scene and mood is made even better because he knows that this present visit, a kind of recharging of batteries, will similarly sustain him in the future.

Topic Sentence

In this quoted passage, he tries to analyze the psychological process and the nature of reality—a very important

statement. Here the uninhabited wilds of youthful joy have become "meadows and the woods and mountains." This is the more inhabited part of the view already mentioned in the cottages here and there among the woods, with smoke rising, still suggesting calm solitude, and the pastures divided by wild rows of heath. He refers to "this green earth," which again suggests cultivated fields and pastures rather than the surrounding wild woods.

Topic Sentence

All of this "mighty world," which is all of external reality, is perceived by eye and ear—the senses. But in fact, he says, these same senses "half-create" reality too. From this psychological exchange between external physical nature and the "language of the sense," which seems to half-perceive and half-create in a kind of dialogue, he nourishes his soul and moral being. He even seems to say, at the end, that this sensory experience *is* the soul of his moral being.

Thesis Amplified

But he also speaks of this interchange with nature, through the senses, as an anchor, a nurse, a guide, and a guardian, implying that his soul and being are something separate that the sensory experience works on. He seems uncertain what this entity "nature and the language of the sense" really is—an anchor, a nurse, a guide (a leader), or a guardian (a protector). These lines, I think, show Wordsworth working very hard to explain something he feels deeply, but which is hard to explain. These lines, which seem almost like prose statements, yet scan as iambic pentameter, convey the deep sincerity typical of Wordsworth's poetry and his ideas.

Clincher

A QUESTION IN THE SOCIAL SCIENCES

3. Brewer and Brewer contrast Freudian and Jungian ideas as the essential poles of psychological theory. Describe the basic similarities and contrasts.

One-Sentence Answer

Both Freud and Jung agree in the primacy of subconscious ideas, but Freud finds this realm of dreams and lost remembrances sexual and socially destructive, a negative pole, whereas Jung finds it archetypical and positive.

Jotted Outline

1. Freud-hypnosis-dualistic psychology
2. Jung's buried treasure
3. Archetypes
4. Schubert
5. Dementia praecox (schizophrenia)
6. Superego-Ego-Id
7. Freud negative—Jung positive

Answer

Thesis

Both Freud and Jung agree in the validity of unconscious or subconscious ideas, but Freud sets dreams and lost remembrances as a negative pole to social life whereas Jung finds them archetypal and positive. Freud, starting with hypnosis to get at the suppressed traumas of hysteria, became convinced that evidence from dreams was crucially informative. Jung, Adler, and others joined him. But Jung, analyzing his own dreams, as Freud had done, found joy, as if discovering buried secrets, rather than the fear and aversion in Freud's interpretations. Consequently, their polar split was between Freud's negative and Jung's positive views.

Thesis Amplified

Topic Sentence: First Half

Freud had actually built on the predominating psychology of G. H. Schubert, which saw, as in Stevenson's *Dr. Jekyll and Mr. Hyde,* a good daytime personality suppressing a nocturnal and savage one. Freud adopted this as he described infantile sexuality as the seat of evil, or antisocial impulses, to be repressed in maturity—sexual love of one's mother, murderous hatred of one's father, the famous Oedipus complex. Freud converted the, to him, traditional two-level psychology into three. Instead of a good surface and a destructive subsurface, he described a *superego,* the socially acceptable good set of values, and the *id,* the hidden sexual and violent side of personality, with the *ego,* or personal identity, negotiating and defining itself between the two.

Topic Sentence: Second Half

Jung, beginning with work on dementia praecox, or schizophrenia, evidently a deeper psychic trouble than hysteria, was attracted to Freud's work, joined him in editing a new journal, and in a new international psychoanalytic society. But Jung broke with Freud on the interpretation of dreams. Where Freud saw suppressed and unacceptable sexual drives, Jung saw archetypal patterns, built into the brain's caverns by evolution, up from savagery.

Jung sees two psychic levels in the unconscious where Freud sees only the libido (the *id*) containing rebellious infantile sexuality. Jung, like Freud, sees the unconscious retaining repressed drives, as expressed in dreams. But he sees these repressions as more broadly personal than explicitly sexual. This is the first level of Jung's unconscious, the somewhat negative and Freudian one. Beneath this is the collective unconscious, the positive reservoir of human experience built into the brain by evolution, which all people share, beyond or beneath the personal.

Topic Sentence

In short, Freud sees the unconscious as a threat, shared by all but built from personal traumas. Jung sees it more positively, containing personal and threatening suppressions, but supported by a positive and archetypical human consciousness built into human awareness by evolution, not so much suppressed as forgotten, a positive, universal, and archetypal source of energy that can be tapped through dreams and psychoanalysis.

Thesis Restated as Clincher

14
A Glossary of Usage

Speech keeps a daily pressure on writing, and writing returns the compliment, exacting sense from new twists in the spoken language and keeping old senses straight. Usage, generally, is "the way they say it." Usage is the current in the living stream of language; it keeps us afloat, it keeps us fresh—as it sweeps us along. But to distinguish yourself as a writer, you must always swim upstream. You may say, *hoojaeatwith?;* but you will write: *With whom did they compare themselves? With the best, with whoever seemed admirable.* Usage is, primarily, talk; and talk year by year gives words differing social approval, and differing meanings. Words move from the gutter to the penthouse, and back down the elevator shaft. *Bull,* a four-letter Anglo-Saxon word, was unmentionable in Victorian circles. One had to say *he-cow,* if at all. Phrases and syntactical patterns also have their fashions, mostly bad. *Like unto me* changes to *like me* to *like I do; this type of thing* becomes *this type thing; -wise,* after centuries of dormancy in only a few words *(likewise, clockwise, otherwise),* suddenly sprouts out the end of everything: *budgetwise, personalitywise, beautywise, prestigewise. Persuade them to vote* becomes *convince them to vote.* Suddenly, everyone is saying *hopefully.* As usual, the marketplace changes more than your money.

But the written language has always refined the language of the marketplace. The Attic Greek of Plato and Aristotle (as Aristotle's remarks about local usages show) was distilled from commercial exchange. Cicero and Catullus and Horace polished their currency against the archaic and the Greek. Mallarmé claimed that Poe had given *un sens plus pur aux mots de la tribu*—which Eliot rephrases for himself: "to purify the dialect of the tribe." It is the very nature of writing so to do; it is the writer's illusion that he has done so:

> **I have laboured to refine our language to grammatical purity, and to clear it from colloquial barbarisms, licentious idioms, and irregular combinations. Something, perhaps, I have added to the elegance of its construction, and something to the harmony of its cadence.**

—wrote Samuel Johnson in 1752 as he closed his *Rambler* papers. And he had almost done what he hoped. He was to shape English writing and speech for the next hundred and fifty years, until it was ready for another dip in the stream and another purification. His work, moreover, lasts. We would not imitate it now; but we can read it with pleasure, and imitate its enduring drive for excellence and meaning—making words mean what they say.

Johnson goes on to say that he has "rarely admitted any word not authorized by former writers." Writers provide the second level of usage, the paper money. But even this usage requires principle. If we accept "what the best writers use," we still cannot tell whether it is valid: we may be aping their bad habits. Usage is only a court of first appeal, where we can say little more than "He said it." Beyond that helpless litigation, we can test our writing by asking what the words mean, and by simple principles: clarity is good, economy is good, ease is good, gracefulness is good, fullness is good, forcefulness is good. As with all predicaments on earth, we judge by appeal to meanings and principles, and we often find both in conflict. Do *near* and *nearly* mean the same thing? Do *convince* and *persuade? Lie* and *lay?* Is our writing economical but unclear? Is it full but cumbersome? Is it clear but too colloquial for grace? Careful judgment will give the ruling.

THE GLOSSARY

A, an. *A* goes before consonants and *an* before vowels. But use *a* before *h* sounded in a first syllable: *a hospital, a hamburger.* Use *an* before a silent *h*: *an honor, an heir, an hour.* With *h*-words accented on the second syllable, most ears prefer *an: an hypothesis, an historical feat.* But *a hypothesis* is fully acceptable. Use *a* before vowels pronounced as consonants: *a use, a euphemism.*

Abbreviations. Use only those conventional abbreviations your reader can easily recognize: *Dr., Mr., Mrs., Ms., Messrs.* (for two or more men, pronounced "messers," as in *Messrs. Adams, Pruitt, and Williams*), *Jr., St., Esq.* (Esquire, following a British gentleman's name, or, occasionally, a U.S. attorney's, between commas and with *Mr.* omitted), *S.J.* (Society of Jesus, also following a name). All take periods. College degrees are usually recognizable: *A.B., M.A., Ph.D., D.Litt., M.D., LL.D.* Similarly, dates and times: B.C., A.D., A.M., P.M. Though these are conventionally printed as small capitals, regular capitals in your classroom papers are perfectly acceptable as are "lowercase" letters for a.m. and p.m. *A.D.* precedes its year *(A.D. 1066); B.C.* follows its year. Write them without commas: *2000 B.C. was Smith's estimate.* A number of familiar abbreviations go without periods: *TV, FBI, USSR, USA, YMCA,* though periods are perfectly OK or O.K. Certain scientific phrases also go without periods, especially when combined with figures: *55 mph, 300 rpm, 4000 kwh.* But *U.N.* and *U.S. delegation* are customary. Note that in formal usage *U.S.* serves only as an adjective; write out *the United States* serving as a noun.

Abbreviations conventional in running prose, unitalicized, are "e.g." (*exempli gratia,* "for example"), "i.e." (*id est,* "that is"), "etc." (*et cetera,* better written out "and so forth"), and "viz." (*videlicet,* pronounced "vi-DEL-uh-sit," meaning "that is," "namely"). These are followed by either commas or colons after the period:

The commission discovered three frequent errors in management, i.e., failure to take appropriate inventories, erroneous accounting, and inattention to costs.

The semester included some outstanding extracurricular programs, e.g.: a series of lectures on civil rights, three concerts, and a superb performance of *Oedipus Rex.*

The abbreviation *vs.,* usually italicized, is best spelled out, unitalicized, in your text: "The antagonism of Capulet versus Montague runs throughout the play." The abbreviation c. or ca., standing for *circa* ("around") and used with approximate dates in parentheses, is not italicized: "Higden wrote *Polychronicon* (c. 1350)." See also 358–60.

Above. For naturalness and effectiveness, avoid such references as "The above statistics are . . . ," and "The above speaks for itself." Simply use "These" or "This."

Action. A horribly overused catchall. Be specific: *invasion, rape, murder, intransigence, boycott.*

Adapt, adopt. To *adapt* is to modify something to fit a new purpose. To *adopt* is to take it over as it is.

Advice, advise. Frequently confused. *Advice* is what you get when advisers *advise* you.

Affect, effect. *Affect* means "to produce an *effect.*" Avoid *affect* as a noun; just say *feeling* or *emotion. Affective* is a technical term for *emotional* or *emotive,* which are clearer.

Aggravate. Means to add gravity to something already bad enough. Avoid using it to mean "irritate."

WRONG	RIGHT
He aggravated his mother.	**The rum aggravated his mother's fever.**

All, all of. Use *all* without the *of* wherever you can to economize: *all this, all that, all those, all the people, all her lunch.* But some constructions need *of: all of them, all of Faulkner.*

All ready, already. Two different meanings. *All ready* means that everything is ready; *already* means "by this time."

All right, alright. *Alright* is not *all right;* you are confusing it with the spelling of *already.*

Allusion, illusion, disillusion. The first two are frequently confused, and *disillusion* is frequently misspelled *disallusion.* An *allusion* is a reference to something; an *illusion* is a mistaken conception. You disillusion someone by bringing him back to hard reality from his illusions.

Alot. You mean *a lot,* not *allot.*

Among. See *Between.*

Amount of, number of. Use *amount* with general heaps of things; use *number* with amounts that might be counted: *a small amount of interest, a large number of votes.* Use *number* with living creatures: *a number of applicants,* a *number of squirrels.*

And/or. An ungainly thought stopper. See *Virgule,* 421.

Anxious. Use to indicate *Angst,* agony, and anxiety. Does not mean cheerful expectation: "He was *anxious* to get started." Use *eager* instead.

Any. Do not overuse as a modifier.

POOR	GOOD
She was the best of any senior in the class.	**She was the best senior in the class.**
If any people know the answer, they aren't talking.	**If anyone knows the answer, he's not talking.**

Add *other* when comparing likes: "She was better than *any other* senior in the class." But "This junior was better than any senior."

Any more. Written as two words, except when an adverb in negatives and questions:

She never wins *anymore*.
Does she play *anymore?*

Anyplace, someplace. Use *anywhere* and *somewhere* (adverbs), unless you mean "any *place*" and "some *place.*"

Appear. Badly overworked for *seem.*

Appreciate. Means "recognize the worth of." Do not use to mean simply "understand."

LOOSE	CAREFUL
I *appreciate* your position.	**I *understand* your position.**
I *appreciate* that your position is grotesque.	**I *realize* your position is grotesque.**

Area. Drop it. *In the area of finance* means *in finance,* and *conclusive in all areas* means simply *conclusive,* or *conclusive in all departments (subjects, topics).* Be specific.

Around. Do not use for *about:* it will seem to mean "surrounding."

POOR	GOOD
***Around* thirty people came.**	***About* thirty people came.**
He sang at *around* ten o'clock.	**He sang at *about* ten o'clock.**

As. Use where the cigarette people have *like:* "It tastes good, *as* a goody should," or "it tastes good the way a goody should." (See also *Like.*)

Do not use for *such as:* "Many things, *as* nails, hats, toothpicks. . . ." Write "Many things, *such as* nails. . . ."

Do not use *as* for *because* or *since;* it is ambiguous:

AMBIGUOUS	PRECISE
As I was walking, I had time to think.	**Because I was walking, I had time to think.**

As if. Takes the subjunctive: ". . . as if he *were* cold."

As of, as of now. Avoid, except for humor. Use *at,* or *now,* or delete entirely.

POOR	IMPROVED
He left, as of ten'o'clock.	**He left at ten o'clock.**
As of now, I've sworn off.	**I've just sworn off.**

As to. Use only at the beginning of a sentence: "As to his first allegation, I can only say. . . ." Change it to *about,* or omit it, within a sentence: "He knows nothing *about* the details"; "He is not sure [whether] they are right."

As well as. You may mean only *and.* Check it out. Avoid such ambiguities as *The Commons voted as well as the Lords.*

Aspect. Overused. Try *side, part, portion.* See *Jargon.*

At. Do not use after *where.* "Where is it at?" means "Where is it?"

Awhile, a while. You usually want the adverb: *linger awhile, the custom endured awhile longer.* If you want the noun, emphasizing a period of time, make it clear: *the custom lasted for a while.*

Bad, badly. *Bad* is an adjective: *a bad trip. Badly* is an adverb: *he wrote badly.* Linking verbs take *bad: he smells bad; I feel bad; it looks bad.*

Balance, bulk. Make them mean business, as in "He deposited the balance of his allowance" and "The bulk of the crop was ruined." Do not use them for people:

POOR	IMPROVED
The *balance* of the class went home.	**The *rest* of the class went home.**
The *bulk* of the crowd was indifferent.	***Most* of the crowd was indifferent.**

Basis. Drop it: *on a daily basis* means *daily.*

Be sure and. Write *be sure to.*

Because of, due to. See *Due to.*
Besides. Means "in addition to," not "other than."

POOR	IMPROVED
Something *besides* smog was the cause [unless smog was also a cause].	**Something *other than* smog was the cause.**

Better than. Unless you really mean *better than,* use *more than.*

POOR	IMPROVED
The lake was *better than* two miles across.	**The lake was *more than* two miles across.**

Between, among. *Between* ("by twain") has *two* in mind; *among* has more than two. *Between,* a preposition, takes an object; *between us, between you and me.* ("Between you and I" is sheer embarrassment; see *Me,* below.) *Between* also indicates geographical placing: "It is midway between Chicago, Detroit, and Toledo." "The grenade fell between Jones and me and the gatepost"; but "The grenade fell among the fruit stands." "Between every building was a plot of petunias" (or "In between each building. . . .") conveys the idea, however nonsensical "between a building" is. "Between all the buildings were plots of petunias" would be better, though still a compromise.

Bimonthly, biweekly. Careless usage has damaged these almost beyond recognition, confusing them with *semimonthly* and *semiweekly.* For clarity, better say "every two months" and "every two weeks."

But, cannot but. "He can but fail" is old but usable. After a negative, however, the natural turn in *but* causes confusion:

POOR	IMPROVED
He cannot but fail.	**He can only fail.**
He could not doubt but that it. . . .	**He could not doubt that it. . . .**
He could not help but take. . . .	**He could not help taking. . . .**

When *but* means "except," it is a preposition. "Everybody laughed but me."

But that, but what. Colloquial redundancies.

POOR	IMPROVED
There is no doubt but that John's is the best steer.	**There is no doubt that John's is the best steer.**
	John's is clearly the best steer.
There is no one but what would enjoy it.	**Anyone would enjoy it.**

Can, may (could, might). *Can* means ability; *may* asks permission, and expresses possibility. *Can I go?* means, strictly, "Have I the physical capability to go?" In speech, *can* usually serves for both ability and permission, though the clerk will probably say, properly, "May I help you?" In assertions, the distinction is clear: "He can do it." "He may do it." "If he can, he may." Keep these distinctions clear in your writing.

Could and *might* are the past tenses, but when used in the present time they are subjunctive, with shades of possibility, and hence politeness: "*Could* you come next Tuesday?" *Might* I inquire about your plans?" *Could* may mean ability almost as strongly as *can:* "I'm sure he could do it." But *could* and *might* are usually subjunctives, expressing doubt:

Perhaps he could make it, if he tries.
I might be able to go, but I doubt it.

Cannot, can not. Use either, depending on the rhythm and emphasis you want. *Can not* emphasizes the *not* slightly.

Can't hardly, couldn't hardly. Use *can hardly, could hardly,* since *hardly* carries the negative sense.

Can't help but. A marginal mixture in speech of two clearer and more formal ideas, *I can but regret* and *I can't help regretting.* Avoid it in writing.

Capital, capitol. Frequently confused. You mean *capital,* the head thing, unless describing the Capitol Building and Hill in Washington, D.C., the *capital* of the United States, or the *capitols* (buildings) where state legislators sit.

Case. Chop out this deadwood:

POOR	IMPROVED
In many cases, ants survive. . . .	**Ants often. . . .**
In such a case, surgery is recommended.	**Then surgery is recommended.**
In case he goes. . . .	**If he goes. . . .**
Everyone enjoyed himself, except in a few scattered cases.	**Almost everyone enjoyed himself.**

Cause, result. Since *all* events are both causes and results, suspect yourself of wordiness if you write either word.

WORDY	ECONOMICAL
The invasions caused depopulation of the country.	**The invasions depopulated the country.**
He lost as a result of poor campaigning.	**He lost because his campaign was poor.**

Cause-and-effect relationship. Verbal adhesive tape. Recast the sentence, with some verb other than the wordy *cause:*

POOR	IMPROVED
Othello's jealousy rises in a cause-and-effect relationship when he sees the handkerchief.	**Seeing the handkerchief arouses Othello's jealousy.**

Censor, censure. Frequently confused. A *censor* cuts out objectionable passages. *To censor* is to cut or prohibit. *To censure* is to condemn: "The *censor censored* some parts of the play, and *censured* the author as an irresponsible drunkard."

Center around. A physical impossibility. Make it *centers on,* or *revolves around,* or *concerns,* or *is about.*

Clichés. Don't use unwittingly. But they can be effective. There are two kinds: (1) the rhetorical—*tried and true, the not too distant future, sadder but wiser, in the style to which she had become accustomed;* (2) the proverbial—*apple of his eye, skin of your teeth, sharp as a tack, quick as a flash, twinkling of an eye.* The rhetorical ones are clinched by sound alone; the proverbial are metaphors caught in the popular fancy. Proverbial clichés can lighten a dull passage. You may even revitalize them, since they are frequently dead metaphors (see 302–03). Avoid the rhetorical clichés unless you turn them to your advantage; *tried and untrue, gladder and wiser, a future not too distant.*

Compare to, compare with. To compare *to* is to show similarities (and differences) between different kinds; to compare *with* is to show differences (and similarities) between like kinds.

Composition has been compared *to* architecture.
He compares favorably *with* Mickey Spillane.
Compare Shakespeare *with* Ben Johnson.

Complement, compliment. Frequently confused. *Complement* is a completion; *compliment* is a flattery: "When the regiment reached its full *complement* of recruits, the general gave it a flowery *compliment.*"

Concept. Often jargonish and wordy.

POOR	IMPROVED
The concept of multiprogramming allows. . . .	**Multiprogramming allows. . . .**

Connotation, denotation. Words denote things, acts, moods, whatever: *tree, house, running, anger.* They usually also *connote* an attitude toward these things. *Tree* is a purely neutral denotation, but *oak* connotes sturdiness and *willow* sadness in addition to denoting different trees. *A House Is Not a Home,* wrote a certain lady, playing on connotations and a specific denotation: a house of prostitution. *Woman* and *lady* both denote the human female, but carry connotations awakened in differing contexts:

A *woman* usually outlives a man. (Denotation)
She is a very able *woman.* (Connotation positive)
She is his *woman.* (Connotation negative)
She acts more like a *lady* than a *lady* of pleasure. (Connotations plus and minus)

Usage changes denotations: *a gay party* changes from a festive to a homosexual gathering. Usage also changes connotations. *Negro,* once polite, is now taboo for the once impolite *black. Chairman,* once a neutral denoter, now has acquired enough negative connotations to change a number of letterheads and signatures.

Beware of unwanted, or exaggerated, or offensive connotations: your reader may find you prejudiced.

Contact. Don't *contact* anyone: call, write, find, tell him.

Continual, continuous. You can improve your writing by *continual* practice, but the effort cannot be *continuous.* The first means "frequently repeated"; the second, "without interruption."

It requires *continual* practice.
There was a *continuous* line of clouds.

Contractions. We use them constantly in conversation: *don't, won't, can't, shouldn't, isn't.* Avoid them in writing, or your prose will seem too chummy. But use one now and then when you want some colloquial emphasis: *You can't go home again.*

Convince, persuade. *Convince* THAT and *persuade* TO are the standard idioms. *Convince* OF is also standard. *Convince* is wrongly creeping in before infinitives with *to.*

WRONG	RIGHT
They *convinced* him to run.	**They *persuaded* him *to* run.**
	They *convinced* him *that* he should run.
	They *convinced* him *of* their support.

Could, might. See *Can, may.*

Could care less. You mean *couldn't care less.* Speech has worn off the *n't,* making the words say the opposite of what you mean. A person who cares a great deal could care a great deal less; one who does not care "*couldn't* care less": he's already at rock bottom.

Could of, would of. Phonetic misspellings of *could've* ("could have"), and *would've* ("would have"). In writing, spell them all the way out: *could have* and *would have.*

Couldn't hardly. Use *could hardly.*

Council, counsel, consul. *Council* is probably the noun you mean: a group of deliberators. *Counsel* is usually the verb "to advise." But *counsel* is also a noun: an adviser, an attorney, and their advice. Check your dictionary to see that you are writing what you mean. A *counselor* gives you his *counsel* about your courses, which may be submitted to an academic *council.* A *consul* is an official representing your government in a foreign country.

Curriculum. The plural is *curricula,* though *curriculums* will get by in informal prose. The adjective is *curricular.*

Definitely. A high-school favorite, badly overused.

Denotation, Connotation. See *Connotation.*

Different from, different than. Avoid *different than,* which confuses the idea of differing. Things differ *from* each other. Only in comparing several differences does *than* make clear sense: "All three of his copies differ from the original, but his last one is *more* different *than* the others." But here *than* is controlled by *more,* not by *different.*

WRONG	RIGHT
It is different *than* I expected.	**It is different *from* what I expected.**
	It is not what I expected.
He is different *than* the others.	**He is different *from* the others.**

Discreet, discrete. Frequently confused. *Discreet* means someone tactful and judicious; *discrete* means something separate and distinct: "He was *discreet* in examining each *discrete* part of the evidence."

Disinterested. Does not mean "uninterested" nor "indifferent." *Disinterested* means impartial, without private interests in the issue.

WRONG	RIGHT
You seem disinterested in the case.	**You seem uninterested in the case.**
	The judge was disinterested and perfectly fair.
He was disinterested in it.	**He was indifferent to it.**

Double negative. A negation that cancels another negation, making it accidentally positive: "He couldn't hardly" indicates that "He could easily," the opposite of its intended meaning. "They can't win nothing" really says that they *must* win something.

But some doubled negations carry an indirect emphasis —a mild irony, really—in such tentative assertions as "One cannot be certain that she will not prove to be the century's greatest poet," or "a not unattractive offer."

Due to. Never begin a sentence with "*Due* to circumstances beyond his control, he. . . ." *Due* is an adjective and must always relate to a noun or pronoun: "The catastrophe *due* to circumstances beyond his control was unavoidable," or "The catastrophe was *due* to circumstances beyond his control" (predicate adjective). But you are still better off with *because of, through, by,* or *owing to. Due to* is usually a symptom of wordiness, especially when it leads to *due to the fact that,* a venerable piece of plumbing meaning *because.*

WRONG	RIGHT
He resigned *due to* sickness.	**He resigned *because of* sickness.**
He succeeded *due to* hard work.	**He succeeded *through* hard work.**
He lost his shirt *due to* leaving it in the locker room.	**He lost his shirt *by* leaving it in the locker room.**
The Far East will continue to worry the West, *due to* a general social upheaval.	**The Far East will continue to worry the West, *owing to* a general social upheaval.**
The program failed *due to the fact that* a recession had set in.	**The program failed *because* a recession had set in.**

Effect. See *Affect.*

Either, neither. One of two, taking a singular verb: *Either is a good candidate, but neither speaks well. Either . . . or (neither . . . nor)* are paralleling conjunctions. See 258.

Eminent, imminent, immanent. Often confused. *Eminent* is something that stands out; *imminent* is something about to happen. *Immanent,* much less common, is a philosophical term for something spiritual "remaining within, indwelling." You usually mean *eminent.*

Enormity. Means "atrociousness"; does not mean "enormousness."

the *enormity* of the crime
the *enormousness* of the mountain

Enthuse. Don't use it; it coos and gushes.

WRONG	RIGHT
She *enthused* over her new dress.	**She gushed on and on about her new dress.**
He was *enthused.*	**He was *enthusiastic.***

Environment. Frequently misspelled *enviorment* or *envirnment.* It is business jargon, unless you mean the world around us.

WORDY	IMPROVED
in an MVT environment	**in MVT; with MVT; under MVT**
He works in an environment of cost analysis.	**He analyzes cost.**

Equally as good. A redundant mixture of two choices, *as good as* and *equally good.* Use only one of these at a time.

Etc. Substitute something specific for it, or drop it, or write "and so forth."

Euphemism. Substituting positive for negative connotations: *passed away* for *died; put to sleep* for *killed; imbibed occasionally* for *drank constantly.*

Everyday, every day. You wear your *everyday* clothes *every day.*

Everyone, everybody. Avoid the common mismatching *their:*

"Everyone does *his* [or *her* but not *their*] own thing."

Exists. Another symptom of wordiness.

POOR	IMPROVED
a system like that which exists at the university	**a system like that at the university**

The fact that. Deadly with *due to,* and usually wordy by itself.

POOR	IMPROVED
The fact that Rome fell *due to* moral decay is clear.	*That* Rome fell *through* moral decay is clear.
This disparity is in part *a result of the fact that* some of the best indicators make their best showings in an expanding market.	This disparity arises in part *because* some of the best indictors. . . .
In view of the fact that more core is used. . . .	Because more core. . . .

Factor. Avoid it. We've used it to death. Try *element* when you mean "element." Look for an accurate verb when you mean "cause."

POOR	IMPROVED
The increase in female employment is a factor in juvenile delinquency.	The increase in female employment has contributed to juvenile delinquency.
Puritan self-sufficiency was an important factor in the rise of capitalism.	Puritan self-sufficiency favored the rise of capitalism.

Farther, further. The first means distance, actual or figurative; the second means more in time or degree. You look *farther* and consider *further,* before you go *farther* into debt.

Feasible. See *Viable.*

Fewer, less. See *Less, few.*

The field of. Try to omit it—you usually can—or bring the metaphor to life. It is trite and wordy.

POOR	IMPROVED
He is studying in the field of geology.	He is studying geology.

Firstly. Archaic. Trim all such terms to *first, second,* and so on.

Flaunt, flout. *Flaunt* means to parade, to wave impudently; *flout* means to scoff at. The first is metaphorical; the second, not: "She *flaunted* her wickedness and *flouted* the police."

Flounder, founder. Frequently confused. *Flounder* means to wobble clumsily, to flop around; *founder,* to sink *(The ship foundered),* or, figuratively, to collapse, or go lame (said of horses).

For. See 401.

Former, latter. Passable, but they often make the reader look back. Repeating the antecedents is clearer:

POOR	IMPROVED
The Athenians and Spartans were always in conflict. ***The former*** **had a better civilization;** ***the latter*** **had a better army.**	**The Athenians and Spartans were always in conflict. Athens had the better culture; Sparta, the better army.**

Fun. A noun. Avoid it as an adjective: *a fun party* ("The party was fun").

Further. See *Farther.*

Good, well. *Good* is the adjective: *good time. Well* is the adverb: *well done.* In verbs of feeling, we are caught in the ambiguities of health. *I feel good* is more accurate than *I feel well,* because *well* may mean that your feelers are in working order. But *I feel well* is also an honest statement: "I feel that I am well." Ask yourself what your readers might misunderstand from your statements, and you will use these two confused terms clearly.

Got, gotten. Both acceptable. Your rhythm and emphasis will decide. America prefers the older *gotten* in many phrases; Britain goes mainly for *got.*

Hanged, hung. *Hanged* is the past of *hang* only for the death penalty.

They hung the rope and hanged the man.

Hardly. Watch the negative here. "I can't *hardly*" means "I *can* easily." Write: "One can hardly conceive the vastness."

Healthy, healthful. Swimming is *healthful;* swimmers are *healthy.*

His/her, his (her). Shift to the neutral plural ("Students should sign their papers on the first page."), employ an *occasional* "his or her," or otherwise rephrase: *s/he* is cumbersome. *His* is still respectable when standing for both sexes so long as your reader can reasonably infer both. Something like "Men and women in science" near your beginning will help. You should, however, avoid these traps: "Any *man* who has endured privation in service . . . ," or "The secretary trying to please *her* boss . . . ," unless you are clearly writing *only* about men or women.

Historically. A favorite windy throat-clearer. Badly overused.

History. The *narrative,* written or oral, of events, not the events themselves. Therefore, avoid the redundancy "*recorded* history," likewise "*annals* of history," "*chronicles* of history." *History* alone can suffice or even itself disappear. "Archaeologists have uncovered evidence of events previously unknown to history" would be better without the misleading *to history.*

Hopefully. An inaccurate dangler, a cliché. "Hopefully, they are at work" does not mean that they are working hopefully. Simply use "I hope" or "one hopes" (but *not* "it is hoped"); not "They are a symbol of idealism, and, hopefully, are representative," but "They are a symbol of idealism and are, one hopes, representative."

However. Initial *however* should be an adverb: "However long the task takes, it will be done." For the "floating" *however,* and *however* versus *but,* see 404.

Hung. See *Hanged.*

The idea that. Like *the fact that*—and the cure is the same. Cut it.

If, whether. *If* is for uncertainties; *whether,* for alternatives. Usually the distinction is unimportant: *I don't know if it will rain; I don't know whether it will rain* [*or not*].

Imminent, immanent. See *Eminent.*

Imply, infer. The author *implies;* you *infer* ("carry in") what you think he means.

> **He *implied* that all women are hypocrites.**
> **From the ending, we *infer* that tragedy ennobles as it kills.**

Importantly. Often an inaccurate (and popular) adverb, like *hopefully.*

INACCURATE	IMPROVED
More importantly, **he walked home.**	*More important,* **he walked home.**

In connection with. Always wordy. Say *about.*

POOR	IMPROVED
They liked everything *in connection with* the university.	**They liked everything *about* the university.**

Includes. Jargonish, as a general verb for specific actions.

POOR	IMPROVED
The report includes rural and urban marketing.	**The report analyzes rural and urban marketing.**

Individual. Write *person* unless you really mean someone separate and unique.

Infer. See *Imply, infer.*

Ingenious, ingenuous. Sometimes confused. *Ingenious* means clever; *ingenuous,* naïve. *Ingenius* is a common misspelling for both.

Instances. Redundant. *In many instances* means *often, frequently.*

Interesting. Make what you say interesting, but never tell the reader *it is interesting:* he may not believe you. *It is interesting* is merely a lazy preamble.

POOR	IMPROVED
It is interesting to note that nicotine is named for Jean Nicot, who introduced tobacco into France in 1560.	**Nicotine is named for Jean Nicot, who introduced tobacco into France in 1560.**

Irregardless. A faulty word. The *ir-* (meaning *not*) is doing what the *-less* already does. You are thinking of *irrespective,* and trying to say *regardless.*

Irregular verbs. Here are some to watch; learn to control their past and past-participial forms. (See, also, *Hanged, hung; Lay; Rise, raise; Set, sit.*) Alternate forms are in parentheses.

arise, arose, arisen
awake, awoke, awaked (*but* was awakened)
bear, bore, borne
beat, beat, beaten
begin, began, begun
bid ("order"), bade, bidden

bid ("offer"), bid, bid
burst, burst, burst
drag, dragged (not drug), dragged
fit, fitted (fit, *especially intransitively*), fitted (*but* a fit person)
fling, flung, flung
get, got, got (gotten)
lay, laid, laid
lie, lay, lain
light, lit (lighted), lit (lighted)
prove, proved, proven (proved)
ride, rode, ridden
sew, sewed, sewn (sewed)
shine ("glow"), shone, shone
shine ("polish"), shined, shined
show, showed, shown (showed)
shrink, shrank (shrunk), shrunk (shrunken)
sow, sowed, sown (sowed)
spring, sprang, sprung
swim, swam, swum
swing, swung, swung
wake, woke (waked) waked
waken, wakened, wakened

Is when, is where. Avoid these loose attempts:

LOOSE	SPECIFIC
Combustion is when [where] oxidation bursts into flame.	**Combustion is oxidation bursting into flame.**

It. Give it a specific reference, as a pronoun. See 286–87, 390–91.

Its, it's. Don't confuse *its,* the possessive pronoun, with *it's,* the contraction of *it is.*

-ize. A handy way to make verbs from nouns and adjectives *(patron-ize, civil-ize).* But handle with care. Manufacture new *-izes* only with a sense of humor and daring ("they Harvardized the party"). Business overdoes the trick: *finalize,* a relative newcomer, has provoked strong disapproval from writers who are not commercially familiarized.

Jargon. A technical, wordy phraseology that becomes characteristic of any particular trade, or branch of learning, frequently with nouns modifying nouns, and in the passive voice. Break out of it by making words mean what they say.

JARGON	CLEAR MEANING
The *plot structure* of the play provides no *objective correlative.*	**The play fails to act out and exhibit the hero's inner conflicts.**

	The plot is incoherent. **The structure is lopsided.**
The *character development* of the heroine is excellent.	**The author sketches and deepens the heroine's personality skillfully.** **The heroine matures convincingly.**
Three *motivation profile studies* were developed *in the area of production management.*	**The company studied its production managers, and discovered three kinds of motivation.**
He *structured* the meeting.	**He organized (planned, arranged) the meeting.**

Kind of, sort of. Colloquialisms for *somewhat, rather, something,* and the like. Usable, but don't overuse.

Lay. Don't use *lay* to mean *lie. To lay* means "to put" and needs an object; *to lie* means "to recline." Memorize both their present and past tenses, frequently confused:

> **I *lie* down when I can; I *lay* down yesterday; I have *lain* down often. [Intransitive, no object.]**
> **The hen *lays* an egg; she *laid* one yesterday; she has *laid* four this week. [Transitive, *lays* an object.]**
> **Now I *lay* the book on the table; I *laid* it there yesterday; I have *laid* it there many times.**

Lead, led. Because *lead* (being in front) is spelled like the *lead* in *lead pencil,* people frequently misspell the past tense, which is *led.*

Lend, loan. Don't use *loan* for *lend. Lend* is the verb; *loan,* the noun: "Please *lend* me a five; I need a *loan* badly." Remember the line: "I'll *send* you to a *friend* who'll be willing to *lend.*"

Less, few. Don't use one for the other. *Less* answers "How much?" *Few* answers "How many?"

WRONG	RIGHT
We had *less* people than last time.	**We had *fewer* people this time than last.**

Level. Usually redundant jargon. *High level management* is *top management* and *college level courses* are *college courses.* What is a *level management,* or a *level course* anyway?

Lie, lay. See *Lay.*

Lighted, lit. Equally good past tenses for *light* (both "to ignite" and "to descend upon"), with *lit* perhaps more frequent. Rhythm usually determines the choice. *Lighted* seems preferred for adverbs and combinations: *a clean well-lighted place; it could have been lighted better.*

Like, as, as if. Usage blurs them, but the writer should distinguish them before he decides to go colloquial. Otherwise, he may throw his readers off.

> **He looks *like* me.**
> **He dresses *as* [the way] I do.**
> **He acts *as if* he were high.**

Note that *like* takes the objective case, and that *as,* being a conjunction, is followed by the nominative:

> **She looks like *her.***
> **He is as tall as *I* [am].**
> **He is tall, like *me.***

Like sometimes replaces *as* where no verb follows in phrases other than comparisons *(as . . . as):*

> **It works *like* a charm. (. . . *as* a charm *works.*)**
> **It went over *like* a lead balloon. (. . . *as* a lead balloon *does.*)**
> **They worked *like* beavers. (. . . *as* beavers *do.*)**

Literally. Often misused, and overused, as a general emphasizer: "We *literally* wiped them off the field."

Loan. See *Lend.*

Loose, lose. You will *lose* the game if your defense is *loose.*

Lots, lots of, a lot of. Conversational for *many, much, great, considerable.* Try something else. See *Alot.*

Majority. Misused for *most: "The majority* of the play is comic" [wrong].

Maximum (minimum) amount. Drop *amount.* The minimum and the maximum *are* amounts. Don't write *a minimum of* and *as a minimum:* write *at least.*

May. See *Can, may.*

Maybe. Conversational for *perhaps.* Sometimes misused for *may be.* Unless you want an unmistakable colloquial touch, avoid it altogether.

Manner. A sign of amateur standing. Use *way,* or *like this,* not *in this manner.*

Me. Use *me* boldly. It is the proper object of verbs and prepositions. Nothing is sadder than faulty propriety: "between you and *I,*" or "They gave it to John and *I,*" or "They invited my wife and *I.*" Test yourself by dropping the first member "between I" *(no),* "gave it to I" *(no),* "invited I" *(no).* And do NOT substitute *myself.*

Medium, media. The singular and the plural. Avoid *medias,* and you will distinguish yourself from the masses.

Might. See *Can, may.*

Most. Does not mean *almost.*

WRONG	RIGHT
Most **everyone knows.**	***Almost*** **everyone knows.**

Must, a must. A *must* is popular jargon. Try something else:

JARGON	IMPROVED
Beatup **is really a** ***must*** **for every viewer.**	**Everyone interested in film should see** ***Beatup.***
This is a ***must*** **course.**	**Everyone should take this course.**

Myself. Use it only reflexively ("I hurt *myself*"), or intensively ("I *myself* often have trouble"). Fear of *me* leads to the incorrect "They gave it to John and *myself.*" Do not use *myself, himself, herself, themselves* for *me, him, her, them.*

Nature. Avoid this padding. Do not write *moderate in nature, moderate by nature, of a moderate nature;* simply write *moderate.*

Near. Avoid using it for degree.

POOR	IMPROVED
a ***near*** **perfect orbit**	**a** ***nearly*** **perfect orbit** **an** ***almost*** **perfect orbit**
It was ***a near*** **disaster.**	**It was** ***nearly a*** **disaster [*or* nearly disastrous].**

Neither. See *Either.*

No one. Two words in America, not *noone,* or *no-one* (British).

None. This pronoun means "no one" and takes a singular verb, as do *each, every, everyone, nobody,* and other distributives. See 383.

Nowhere near. Use *not nearly,* or *far from,* unless you really mean *near:* "He was nowhere, near the end." See *Near.*

Number of. Usually correct. See *Amount of.*

Numbers. Spell out those that take no more than two words *(twelve, twelfth, twenty-four, two hundred);* use numerals for the rest *(101, 203, 4,510).* Spell out *all* numbers beginning a sentence. But use numerals to make contrasts and statistics clearer: *20 as compared to 49; only 1 out of 40; 200 or 300 times as great.* Change a two-word number to numerals when it matches a numeral: *with 400* [not *four hundred*] *students and 527 parents.* Numbers are customary with streets: *42nd Street, 5th Avenue,* which may also be spelled out for aesthetic reasons: *Fifth Avenue.* Use numbers also with dates, times, measurements, and money: *1 April 1986; 6:30* A.M. (but *half-past six*); *3 × 5 cards; 240 by 100 feet; 6'3"* (but *six feet tall*); *$4.99; $2 a ticket* (but *16 cents a bunch*).

You may use Roman numerals (see your dictionary) with Arabic to designate parts of plays and books: "Romeo's mistake (II. iii. 69)"; "in *Tom Jones* (XII. iv. 483)." But the new style is all Arabic: (2.3.69), (12.4.483). See 360. Also see *Per cent, percent, percentage.*

Off of. Write *from:* "He jumped *from* his horse."

On the part of. Wordy.

POOR	IMPROVED
There was a great deal of discontent *on the part of* those students who could not enroll.	**The students who could not enroll were deeply discontented.**

One. As a pronoun—"*One* usually flunks the first time"—see 8–9. Avoid the redundant numeral:

POOR	IMPROVED
One of the most effective ways of writing is rewriting.	**The best writing is rewriting.**

***The Ambassadors* is one of the most interesting of James's books.**	***The Ambassadors* is James at his best.**
The meeting was obviously a poor one.	**The meeting was obviously poor.**

In constructions such as "one of the best that . . ." and "one of the worst who . . . ," the relative pronouns often are mistakenly considered singular. The plural noun of the prepositional phrase *(the best, worst),* not the *one,* is the antecedent, and the verb must be plural too:

WRONG	RIGHT
one of the best [*players*] who *has* ever swung a bat	**one of the best [*players*] who *have* ever swung a bat**

Only. Don't put it in too soon; you will say what you do not mean.

WRONG	RIGHT
He *only liked* mystery stories.	**He liked *only* mystery stories.**

Overall. Jargonish. Use *general,* or rephrase.

DULL	IMPROVED
The overall quality was good.	**The lectures were generally good.**

Oversight. An unintentional omission: "Leaving you off the list was an *oversight.*" Unfortunately, officialdom has started to use it for *overview* or *supervisory.* Congress now has an Oversight Committee (perhaps several)—which sounds like a committee set up to catch omissions. Avoid this ambiguity. Keep your *oversights* meaning *oversights.*

Parent. One of those nouns aping a verb: *to rear, bring up, supervise, raise, love.*

Per. Use *a:* "He worked ten hours *a* day." *Per* is jargonish, except in conventional Latin phrases: *per diem, per capita* (not italicized in your running prose).

POOR	IMPROVED
This will cost us a manhour *per* machine *per* month a year from now.	**A year from now, this will cost us a manhour a machine a month.**
As *per* your instructions.	**According to your instructions.**

Per cent, percent, percentage. *Percent* (one word) seems preferred, though *percentage,* without numbers, still carries polish: "A large *percentage of* nonvoters attended." Use both the % sign and numerals only when comparing percentages as in technical reports; elsewhere, use numerals with *percent* when your figures cannot be spelled out in one or two words (2½ percent, 150 percent, 48.5 percent). Otherwise, spell out the numbers as well: *twenty-three percent, ten percent, a hundred percent.* See *Numbers.*

Perfect. Not "more perfect," but "more nearly perfect."

Personally. Almost always superfluous.

POOR	IMPROVED
I want to welcome them *personally.*	**I want to welcome them [myself].**
***Personally,* I like it.**	**I like it.**

Phase. Do not use when *part* is wanted; "*a phase* of the organization" is better put as "a *part* of the organization." A phase is a stage in a cycle, as of the moon, of business, of the financial markets.

Phenomena. Frequently misused for the singular *phenomenon:* "This is a striking *phenomenon*" (not *phenomena*).

Phenomenal. Misused for a general intensive: "His popularity was *phenomenal.*" A phenomenon is a fact of nature, in the ordinary nature of things. Find another word for the extraordinary: "His success was *extraordinary*" *(unusual, astounding, stupendous).*

Plan on. Use *plan to.* "He planned on going" should be "He planned to go."

Prejudice. When you write "He was *prejudice,*" your readers may be *puzzle.* Give it a *d:* "He was *prejudiced*"; then they won't be *puzzled.*

Presently. Drop it. Or use *now.* Many readers will take it to mean *soon:* "He will go *presently.*" It is characteristic of official jargon:

POOR	IMPROVED
The committee is meeting *presently*.	**The committee is meeting.** **The committee is meeting *soon*.**
He is *presently* studying Greek.	**He is studying Greek.**

Principle, principal. Often confused. *Principle* is a noun only, meaning an essential truth, or rule: "It works on the *principle* that hot air rises." Princi*pal* is the *a*djective: The high-school *principal* acts as a noun because usage has dropped the *person* the adjective once modified. Likewise, *principal* is the principal amount of your money, which draws interest.

Process. Often verbal fat. For example, the following can reduce more often than not: *production process,* to *production; legislative* (or *legislation*) *process,* to *legislation; educational* (or *education*) *process,* to *education; societal process* to *social forces.*

Proof, evidence. *Proof* results from enough *evidence* to establish a point beyond doubt. Be modest about claiming proof:

POOR	IMPROVED
This *proves* that Fielding was in Bath at the time.	**Evidently, Fielding was in Bath at the time.**

Provide. If you *absolutely cannot* use the meaningful verb directly, you may say *provide,* provided you absolutely cannot *give, furnish, allow, supply, enable, authorize, permit, facilitate, force, do, make, effect, help, be, direct, encourage. . . .*

Providing that. Use *provided,* and drop the *that. Providing,* with or without *that,* tends to make a misleading modification.

POOR	IMPROVED
I will drop, *providing that* I get an incomplete.	**I will drop, *provided* I get an incomplete.**

In "I will drop, *providing that* I get an incomplete," *you* seem to be providing, contrary to what you mean.

Put across. Try something else: *convinced, persuaded, explained, made clear. Put across* is badly overused.

Quality. Keep it as a noun. Too many *professional quality writers* are already producing *poor quality prose,* and *poor in quality* means *poor.*

Quite. An acceptable but overused emphatic: *quite good, quite expressive, quite a while, quite a person.* Try rephrasing it now and then: *good, very good, for some time, an able person.*

Quote, quotation. Quote your quotations, and put them in quotation marks. Distinguish the verb from the noun. The best solution is to use *quote* only as a verb and to find synonyms for the noun: *passage, remark, assertion.*

WRONG	RIGHT
As the following *quote* from Milton shows: . . .	**As the following *passage* [*or* quotation] from Milton shows: . . .**

Raise. See *Rise, raise.*

Rarely ever. Drop the *ever:* "Shakespeare *rarely* misses a chance for comedy."

Real. Do not use for *very. Real* is an adjective meaning "actual":

WRONG	RIGHT
It was *real* good.	**It was *very* good.** **It was *really* good.**

Reason . . . is because. Knock out *the reason . . . is,* and *the reason why . . . is,* and you will have a good sentence.

[The reason] they have difficulty with languages [is] because they have no interest in them.

Regarding, in regard to. Redundant or inaccurate.

POOR	IMPROVED
***Regarding* the banknote, Jones was perplexed. [Was he *looking* at it?]**	**Jones was perplexed by the banknote.**
He knew nothing *regarding* money.	**He knew nothing about money.**
She was careful *in regard to* the facts.	**She respected the facts.**

Regardless. This is correct. See *Irregardless* for the confusion.

Respective, respectively. Usually redundant.

POOR	IMPROVED
The armies retreated to their *respective* trenches.	**The armies retreated to their trenches.**
Smith and Jones won the first and second prize *respectively*.	**Smith won the first prize; Jones, the second.**

Reverend, Honorable. Titles of clergymen and congressmen. The fully proper forms, as in the heading of a letter (*the* would not be capitalized in your running prose), are *The Reverend Mr. Claude C. Smith; The Honorable Adam A. Jones.* In running prose, *Rev. Claude Smith* and *Hon. Adam Jones* will get by, but the best procedure is to give the title and name its full form for first mention, then continue with *Mr. Smith* and *Mr. Jones.* Do not use "Reverend" or "Honorable" with the last name alone.

Rise, raise. Frequently confused. *Rise, rose, risen* means to get up. *Raise, raised, raised* means to lift up. "He *rose* early and *raised* a commotion."

Sanction. Beatifically ambiguous, now meaning both "to approve" and "to penalize." Stick to the root; use it only "to bless," "to sanctify," "to approve," "to permit." Use *penalize* or *prohibit* when you mean just that. Instead of "They exacted *sanctions,*" say "They exacted *penalties*" or "enacted *restrictions.*"

Sarcasm. A cutting remark. Wrongly used for any irony.

Seldom ever. Redundant. Cut the *ever.* (But *seldom if ever* has its uses.)

Set, sit. Frequently confused. You *set* something down; you yourself *sit* down. Confine *sitting* mostly to people *(sit, sat, sat),* and keep it intransitive, taking no object. *Set* is the same in all tenses *(set, set, set).*

CONFUSED	CLARIFIED
The house *sets* too near the street.	**The house *stands* [*sits*] too near the street.**
The package *set* where he left it.	**The package *lay* [*sat*] where he left it.**
He *has set* there all day.	**He *has sat* there all day.**

Shall, will; should, would. The older distinctions—*shall* and *should* reserved for *I* and *we*—have faded; *will* and *would* are usual: "I will go"; "I would if I could"; "he will try"; "they all would." But *shall* remains in first-person questions: *Shall I call you tomorrow? Shall* in the third person expresses determination: "They shall not pass." *Should,* in formal usage, is actually ambiguous: *We should be happy to comply,* intended to mean "would be happy," seems to say "ought to be happy."

Should of. See *Could of, would of.*

Similar to. Use *like:*

POOR	IMPROVED
This is *similar* to that.	**This is *like* that.**

Sit. See *Set, sit.*

Situate. Usually wordy and inaccurate. Avoid it unless you mean, literally or figuratively, the act of determining a site, or placing a building: "Do not *situate* heavy buildings on loose soil."

FAULTY	IMPROVED
He is well *situated.*	**He is rich.**
Ann Arbor is a town *situated* on the Huron River.	**Ann Arbor is a town on the Huron River.**
The control panel is *situated* on the right.	**The control panel is on the right.**
The company is well *situated* to meet the competition.	**The company is well prepared to meet the competition.**

Situation. Usually jargon. Avoid it. Say what you mean: *state, market, mess, quandary, conflict, predicament.*

Size. Often redundant. A *small-sized country* is *a small country. Large in size* is *large.*

Slow. Go SLOW is what the street signs and the people on the street all say, but write "Go slowly."

So. Should be followed by *that* in describing extent: "It was *so* foggy *that* traffic almost stopped." Avoid its incomplete form, the gushy intensive—*so nice, so wonderful, so pretty*—though occasionally this is effective.

Someplace, somewhere. See *Anyplace.*

Sort of. See *Kind of, sort of.*

Split infinitives. Improve them. They are cliché traps: *to really know, to really like, to better understand.* They are one of the signs of a wordy writer, and usually produce redundancies: *to really understand* is *to understand.* The quickest cure for split infinitives is to drop the adverb. See 212–13, 394.

For a gain in grace, and often for a saving of words, you can sometimes change the adverb to an adjective.

POOR	IMPROVED
***to* adequately *think* out solutions**	***to think* out adequate solutions**
to enable us *to* effectively *plan* our advertising	**to enable us *to plan* effective advertising**

Structure. See *Jargon.*

Sure. Too colloquial for writing: "It is *sure* a good plan." Use *surely* or *certainly,* or rephrase.

Tautology. Several words serving where fewer—usually one—are needed, or wanted: useless repetition. Some examples:

attach [together]
[basic] essentials
consecutive days [in a row]
[early] beginnings
[final] completion
[final] upshot
[first] beginnings
[just] merely
mix [together]
[pair of] twins
(but, two *sets* of twins)
[past] history
refer [back]
repeat [again]
sufficient [enough]
whether [or not]

That, which, who. *That* defines and restricts; *which* is explanatory and nonrestrictive; *who* stands for people, and may be restrictive or nonrestrictive. See *Who,* and 253, 288, 402–03.

There is, there are, it is. However natural and convenient—it is WORDY. Notice that *it* here refers to something specific, differing distinctly from the *it* in "It is easy to write badly." (Better: "Writing badly is easy.") This indefinite subject, like *there is* and *there are,* gives the trouble. Of course, you will occasionally need an *it* or a *there* to assert existences:

There are ants in the cupboard.
There is only one Kenneth.
There are craters on the moon.
It is too bad.

They. Often a loose indefinite pronoun; tighten it. See 390, 391.

Till, until. Both are respectable. Note the spelling. Do not use *'til.*

Too. Awful as a conjunctive adverb: "Too, it was unjust." Also poor as an intensive: "They did not do too well" (note the difference in Shakespeare's "not wisely but too well"—he really means it). Use *very,* or (better) nothing: "They did not do well" (notice the nice understated irony).

Tool. Overused for "means." Try *instrument, means.*

Toward, towards. *Toward* is the better (towards in Britain), though both are acceptable.

Trite. From Latin *tritus:* "worn out." Many words get temporarily worn out and unusable: *emasculated, viable, situation,* to name a few. And many phrases are permanently frayed; see *Clichés.*

Type. Banish it, abolish it. If you must use it, insert *of:* not *that type person* but *that type OF person,* though even this is really jargon for *that kind of person, a person like that.* See 291.

Unique. Something *unique* has nothing in the world like it.

WRONG	RIGHT
The *more unique* the organization. . . .	**The *more nearly unique.* . . .**
the *most unique* man I know	**the *most unusual* man I know**
a *very unique* personality	**a *unique* personality**

Use, use of. A dangerously wordy word. See 288–89.

Use to. A mistake for *used to.*

Utilize, utilization. Like *use,* wordy. See 289.

POOR	IMPROVED
He *utilizes* frequent dialogue to enliven his stories.	**Frequent dialogue enlivens his stories.**
The *utilization* of a scapegoat eases their guilt.	**A scapegoat eases their guilt.**

Very. Spare the *very* and the *quite, rather, pretty,* and *little.* I would hate to admit (and don't care to know) how many of these qualifiers I have cut from this text. You can do without them entirely, but they do ease a phrase now and then.

Viable. With *feasible,* overworked. Try *practicable, workable, possible.*

Ways. Avoid it for distance. Means *way:* "He went a short *way* into the woods."

Well. See *Good.*

Whether. See *If.*

Which. See *Who, which, that.*

While. Reserve for time only, as in "*While* I was talking, she smoked constantly." Do not use for *although.*

WRONG	RIGHT
***While* I like her, I don't admire her.**	***Although* I like her, I don't admire her.**

Who, which, that. *Who* may be either restrictive or nonrestrictive: "The ones *who win* are lucky"; "The players, *who are all outstanding,* win often." *Who* refers only to persons. Use *that* for all other restrictives; *which* for all other nonrestrictives. Cut every *who, that,* and *which* not needed. See 283, 287, "the *of-and-which* disease" (287–88), and, on restrictives, and nonrestrictives, 288.

Avoid *which* in loose references to the whole idea preceding, rather than to a specific word, since you may be unclear:

FAULTY	IMPROVED
He never wore the hat, which his wife hated.	**His wife hated his going bareheaded.** **He never wore the hat his wife hated.**

Whom, whomever. The objective forms, after verbs and prepositions; but each is often wrongly put as the subject of a clause (388).

WRONG	RIGHT
Give the ticket to *whomever* wants it.	**Give the ticket to *whoever wants it.* [The whole clause is the object of**

	to; whoever is the subject of *wants.*]
The president, *whom* he said would be late. . . .	The president, *who* he said *would be late.* . . . [Commas around *he said* would clear the confusion.]
Whom shall I say called?	*Who* shall I say called?

BUT:

They did not know *whom* to elect. [The infinitive takes the objective case.]

Who's, whose. Sometimes confused in writing. *Who's* means "who is?" in conversational questions: "*Who's* going?" Never use it in writing (except in dialogue), and you can't miss. *Whose* is the regular possessive of *who:* "The committee, *whose* work was finished, adjourned."

Will. See *Shall.*

-wise. Avoid all confections like *marketwise, customerwise, pricewise, gradewise, confectionwise*—except for humor.

Would. For habitual acts, the simple past is more economical:

POOR	IMPROVED
The parliament *would meet* only when called by the king.	The parliament *met* only when called by the king.
Every hour, the watchman *would make* his round.	Every hour, the watchman *made* his round.

Would sometimes seeps into the premise of a supposition. Rule: Don't use *would* in an *if* clause.

WRONG	RIGHT
If he *would have* gone, he would have succeeded.	If he *had* gone, he would have succeeded.
	Had he gone, he would have succeeded [more economical].

Would of. See *Could of, would of.*

You (I, we, one). See 8–9.

Index